Contexts in Literature

World and Time: Teaching Literature in Context

Adrian Barlow

CAMBRIDGE
UNIVERSITY PRESS

CAMBRIDGE
UNIVERSITY PRESS

University Printing House, Cambridge CB2 8BS, United Kingdom

One Liberty Plaza, 20th Floor, New York, NY 10006, USA

477 Williamstown Road, Port Melbourne, VIC 3207, Australia

314-321, 3rd Floor, Plot 3, Splendor Forum, Jasola District Centre, New Delhi - 110025, India

79 Anson Road, #06-04/06, Singapore 079906

Cambridge University Press is part of the University of Cambridge.

It furthers the University's mission by disseminating knowledge in the pursuit of education, learning and research at the highest international levels of excellence.

www.cambridge.org
Information on this title: www.cambridge.org/9780521712477

© Cambridge University Press 2009

First published 2009

A catalogue record for this publication is available from the British Library

ISBN 978-0-521-71247-7 Paperback

Editorial management: Gill Stacey

Cover illustration: The Millennium Bridge and St. Paul's Cathedral in London.
© Peter Adams/Corbis.

To
Anne and Peter Stileman
for their friendship and encouragement
ever since I started teaching

Contents

Part 2: Teaching to the text: contextual close reading

Preface

This book is a companion to the *Cambridge Contexts in Literature* series. It has been written particularly for those who may be beginning their careers as teachers of English and, specifically, of English Literature. I hope it will also be helpful to those who have been teaching for some time and have recently felt the ground shifting under their feet. In some respects the subject as taught and examined today is very different from the English of twenty years ago; in others, however, it seems to some people not to have moved fast enough. I have set out to explore these differences and continuities, to see how they can be reconciled.

As the book's sub-title – *Teaching Literature in Context* – suggests, *World and Time* is both about attitudes to teaching literature today and about questions that can provoke real anxiety. How should one teach context in literature – and why? And what contexts should one teach anyway? I have written the book from a post-Curriculum 2000 perspective: it was in the 'Subject Criteria for English Literature', published by the Qualifications and Curriculum Authority (QCA) in 1999, that the new emphasis on context was first articulated. But whether one is teaching A levels in England, Auckland or Singapore, Highers in Scotland, the OIB in France, Advanced Placement in San Francisco, or the IB anywhere else, I hope the book's arguments and its approaches to teaching literature in context will be thought-provoking and of use.

During much of my career, I have been both a teacher and an examiner, closely involved in developing new A level syllabuses and specifications, in creating the Advanced Extension Award in English and launching the English Literature Admissions Test (ELAT). In *World and Time* I have tried to focus on both the teaching and the assessment of literature, so I should state at the outset my belief that the curriculum (what needs to be taught) should always determine the shape and scope of assessment, not the other way around. All teachers teach to the test, but anyone who *only* teaches to the test should not be teaching. Indeed, the whole point of contextual study is to make English a more open-ended subject than ever, one in which going beyond the set texts is essential. Giving students time and guidance to explore the literary landscape for themselves; encouraging them to take risks with what they read and showing them how to find connections between texts – these are what make for good A level teaching and hence for good students.

Much of this book is concerned with issues of transition from studying English Literature in the sixth form (that outdated but still useful shorthand for anyone taking an advanced pre-university course to the age of eighteen) to English Studies at university. Everyone preparing students for possible admission to an English degree should compare the Benchmark Statement for English, published by the Quality Assurance Agency for Higher Education (QAA) with the QCA Subject Criteria. Sometimes this emphasis on transition is explicit. For example, in Part 1 of this book I discuss the anxiety felt in Higher Education at the apparent loss of close reading skills from the sixth-form curriculum, and the way that university English departments sell themselves to prospective applicants.

Elsewhere it is implicit, particularly in Part 2 where I illustrate and discuss different types of context and explore ways of integrating close reading and contextual study. Here my aim is to show how at A level it is possible – necessary, in fact – to take students well beyond the point of thinking that plot, theme and character lie at the heart of textual analysis or that unseen practical criticism is a technique for unlocking the 'hidden meaning' of a poem or passage. Contextual study enlarges the frame of reference in which texts can be studied. I hope to show that it adds to the rewards of teaching literature. Above all, I want to argue that all good teaching should lead to greater enjoyment of literature and literary study – for both the teacher and the student.

Some of the material in this book has previously appeared, in earlier versions, in magazines and journals. I am grateful to the editors of *e-magazine*, *The Use of English* and *The International Journal of Youth and Adolescence* for allowing articles to be reproduced here. I am also grateful to many of my own adult students for their views and criticisms of some of the chapters. In particular Joy Dauncey, Lucy Barratt, Paul Crossley and Anil Malhotra have probably taught me more than I have taught them. To colleagues and friends in the English Association, the English and Media Centre and in Cambridge Assessment – Helen Lucas and Julia Hughes, Barbara Bleiman, Paul Norgate, Mike Smith, Sue Fiander and Mark Shannon – I also owe much. All have helped, one way and another, with the writing of this book. At Cambridge University Press I have been fortunate to have had such a supportive and patient editor as Matthew Winson. Gary Snapper's reading of the whole text in typescript has been invaluable. Gill Stacey, too, has played a large part in the making of this book and indeed of the whole *Cambridge Contexts in Literature* series. However, it is no exaggeration to say that, but for my wife Christine, *World and Time* would probably never have been started. And without her as my best critic it would certainly never have been finished.

Madingley Hall   29th February 2008
University of Cambridge

Introduction: What are we doing here?

This book deals with questions of context. It is concerned with the contexts – educational, academic and political – in which the subject 'English Literature' exists today; beyond that, it is concerned with the question of context in the teaching of literature: whether and how context should be taught; whether and how it is possible to reconcile close reading and context.

World and Time is thus about teaching Literature, that central part of the work of being an English teacher. It is concerned particularly with English at advanced level – whether A levels as such, Pre-U, the International Baccalaureate, or any other qualification marking the end of the secondary phase of education. This phase will for some students be the height of their encounter with English Literature; for others it will be the basis for their transition to literary studies at university. Teaching all these students side-by-side is a big challenge, creating sizeable challenges, too, for those who have to devise the sixth-form curriculum and the examinations that students will confront during or at the end of their courses.

I would be naive to pretend every teacher of English will agree that teaching Literature is indeed the central part of their job; naive also not to admit that 'Literature' itself is a contested term. What literature? Whose literature? Should the word have a capital letter? And should I not be talking anyway of 'literatures', of discourses or literacies? These questions will run implicitly, and sometimes explicitly, through this book; but running through it too is the certainty that teaching students how to engage with the written word is a fundamental responsibility, and that writing as practised by those who claim to be writers is both an individual creative art and a shared cultural process.

By 'engage' I mean something more than enjoy, though I am certain that it is the job of English teachers to help students discover how to enjoy the practice of reading, and that reading with enjoyment is a valuable life-skill worth spending time to acquire. Part of this job is thus to introduce students to literature, to *types of reading*, they might not otherwise have encountered on their own. But the other part of the job is to teach *ways of reading*, and it is with this side of 'engagement' that I am primarily concerned. Students must learn on the one hand how to appreciate – respond to, describe, analyse, evaluate – literary texts. Close reading is the fundamental critical skill. It is also, to be pragmatic, the fundamental transferable skill that students of English develop for, as Stefan Collini has argued, 'Close reading is inseparable from hard thinking.'[1]

At the same time, students need to be aware – and today more aware than ever – that texts can be described in different ways according to the contexts in which they were originally written, the contexts in which they have been read at different times in the past and in which they are being read today. It is with this relationship between close reading and context that much of this book is concerned.

Throughout *World and Time* I want to argue that we need to explore with students why Literature (*capital L this time to denote the subject rather than the body of written texts that form the basis of the subject*) matters enough to be a subject for academic study, standing alongside History, Mathematics or Science. To suggest that there just is not enough time in the timetable for the luxury of such discussion is simply to evade, Prufrock-like, the overwhelming question 'What are we doing here?' Part 1 of this book addresses the question in terms of principles, politics and pedagogy; Part 2 applies these principles to the discussion of a wide range of genres, texts and topics. Each discussion is accompanied by suggestions for developing new, reflective approaches to studying and teaching those books and authors that – let's admit it – make our subject so rewarding in the first place.

Part 1

Teaching Literature in context and context in literature

1 | Writers and readers: context and creativity

'English should be kept up.' *(John Keats)*

Who writes and why? Who reads and why? Would the world be any the poorer without novels, poetry or drama? Why do books matter? Why do they matter so much that the German poet Heinrich Heine was able to write, in 1820:

> Dort, wo man Bücher verbrennt, verbrennt man am Ende auch Menschen.
> *Wherever they burn books, eventually they will burn people too.*

In different contexts Heine's words have had different resonances. Historically, they looked back to the Inquisition and the fear that unorthodox ideas might undermine the authority of those in power, whether in Church or State. Prophetically they looked forward to the 20th century: to the burning of books by the Nazis, followed within a decade by the burning of millions of bodies. Symbolically they paid tribute to the power of books and to the ideas they could contain. When Marlowe's Dr Faustus realised his time was up and he was about to be tossed by the devils into the flames of Hell, his final despairing scream, 'I'll burn my books!' was a recognition of the power those books had had to determine the disastrous course of his life.

It's very easy to take for granted that students know why it's worth studying Literature. The trouble is, they take it for granted because we take it for granted. Do they (do we?) recognise the distinction between teaching 'Literature' and teaching 'Literary Studies'? It's simple to smile at Roland Barthes' axiom that 'literature is what gets taught' without thinking about its implications. Like it or not, we both transmit an idea of a cultural heritage and help to define it in the minds of our students by the books we choose for them to read. One of the assumptions underlying all the discussions in this book of individual texts, and of Literature teaching as a whole, is that looking at texts in different contexts is a constantly challenging exercise. If we – in teaching an author, a book or a single poem – do not find new things in the text and new ways of looking at the text then our teaching will be simply second-hand repetition of what was once fresh. When that happens, it is much harder to help our students gain an idea of how much the text has to offer. Students who are taught with a sense of the excitement of the subject will soon come to recognise the truth of Italo Calvino's definitions of a classic:

- A classic is a book which with each re-reading offers as much of a sense of discovery as the first reading.
- A classic is a book which even when we read it for the first time gives the sense of re-reading something we have read before.
- A classic is a book which has never exhausted all it has to say to its readers.[1]

Calvino is a distinguished novelist, and one way we can introduce the question 'Why study Literature?' is to focus on what writers themselves have to say about writing. This is an important strategy, for at a time when creativity is once more valued as a central focus of literary study it is right to attend again to the act of writing, and not only to the act of reading. This change of focus has been remarkably quick and very recent. Within Higher Education it has been identified as happening during the first decade of the present century. The 2007 QAA *Benchmark Statement for English* (a revision of the original 2000 document describing the characteristics of English as taught in Higher Education) has this to say in its Foreword:

> The striking increase in the number of programmes involving elements of creative, imaginative and transformative writing requires acknowledgement. The subject benchmark statement in 2000 made minor references to this domain, but ... this draft revision seeks to recognise and build on the vigour of the reconfigured subject.[2]

During this same period, revised A level Subject Criteria published by QCA have recognised a similar shift and now require students to 'articulate creative, informed and relevant responses to literary texts' (AO1: *GCE AS and A level subject criteria for English Literature*, QCA, September 2006). The word 'creative' had been notably missing from the original Curriculum 2000 Subject Criteria. This amendment has enabled nearly all the Awarding Bodies (the Exam Boards) in their latest specifications to include optional or even mandatory exercises in creative or re-creative writing as part of coursework: Literature students therefore will now be assessed as writers as well as readers. This is a fundamental shift, and its consequences will take a while to register.

Writers on writing

So what do writers themselves say about what they do, and why? Philip Larkin first:

> Poetry, like all art, is inextricably bound up with giving pleasure, and if a poet loses his pleasure-seeking audience, he has lost the only audience worth having, for which the dutiful mob that signs on every September is no substitute.[3]

This sounds a useful warning note – how can we, through our teaching, turn the 'dutiful mob' into a 'pleasure-seeking audience'? Should this be our job? I have already suggested that we have a responsibility to help students learn to enjoy the act and the art of reading – just as they should enjoy learning to become an IT specialist, an historian or a biologist. Learning to identify with the subject, in fact. Beyond that, however, Literature deals with challenging ideas as well as simply enjoyable experiences. The novelist Pat Barker puts it like this:

> Fiction should be about moral dilemmas that are so bloody difficult that the author doesn't know the answer. What I hate in fiction is when the author knows better than the characters what they should do.[4]

This can be as true of drama as of fiction – and of poetry: Miller's *All My Sons*, or Friel's *Translations*; Yeats' 'Easter 1916', Auden's 'September 1st 1939', Plath's 'Daddy', Heaney's 'Casualty' – all of these confront such dilemmas and can place the reader who responds to the play or poem in a moral dilemma too. 'Whose side am I on?' is a question students of whatever age find themselves asking all the time. One of the most difficult and sensitive parts of being a teacher of Literature is to help students accept that it is all right to be confused: how does Shakespeare enable us to admire Othello and be appalled by him at the same time?

Here is Susan Sontag:

> I think of the writer of novels and stories and plays as a moral agent ... A fiction writer whose adherence is to literature is, necessarily, someone who thinks about moral problems: about what is just and unjust, what is better or worse, what is repulsive and admirable, what is lamentable and what inspires joy and approbation.[5]

It can come as a surprise, in a post-structuralist era when so much discussion of literature focuses on its existence as part of a cultural process, to hear a writer speak so passionately about the moral dimension of her work. Here, by way of context, is a contrary view to Sontag's: it comes from an essay entitled 'The cultural politics of English Teaching' by the educationist Nick Peim.

> In deconstructing our familiar habits of thought, post-structuralism reveals more clearly the operations of institutionalised power in the curriculum, in the classroom, and in the ideas and practices of English teaching and teachers. The social dimension of education cannot be kept separate from our dealings with individuals. English cannot be thought of as the free space of open creativity that we may have wanted it to be ... Post-structuralist theory opens new vistas, giving a new handle on the subject's relations with the realm of the social. If the textual field becomes dynamic and unbounded – and if

literature must be seen as only a small portion of that field – textually focused work in English may range into entirely new territories. These areas may include a significant emphasis on the everyday world of textual encounters: media texts, popular fictions and non-fiction texts of all varieties.[6]

World and Time will certainly engage with some of these ideas: indeed, 'textually focused work' lies by definition at the heart of literary studies. It is surely, though, a false antithesis to imply that English teachers have kept the social dimension of education separate from their dealings with individuals. No one who has studied English would attempt to deny that language and literature exist within a social context; and in later chapters of this book I shall illustrate ways in which a variety of non-literary media texts of different kinds can provide fruitful and challenging contexts for a close reading of literary texts, canonical and otherwise. And in a fundamental respect all literature is a social activity: first, it involves one person (an author) talking to others (his or her readers); second, though the reader's first encounter with a text is likely to be a solitary one, all subsequent discussion of the book, whether in the context of an English lesson or elsewhere, is socially located and conditioned. I accept that. But I also relate to what Sontag has to say about the way writers work:

> Serious fiction writers think about moral problems practically. They tell stories. They narrate. They evoke our common humanity in narratives with which we can identify, even though the lives lived may be remote from our own. They stimulate our imagination. The stories they tell enlarge and complicate – and, therefore, improve – our sympathies. They educate our capacity for moral judgement.[7]

Susan Sontag writes as one of the most respected and admired American critics and novelists of her generation (she died in 2007), and her argument that writers, storytellers, are in an ethical sense educators – 'they educate our capacity for moral judgement' – puts a considerable onus on anyone teaching literature to students of any age, from sixteen to eighty-six. One of the most remarkable features of the literary scene in the past decade has been the growth of reading groups, made up equally of those who want to get more out of reading than they can do by reading on their own, those whose enjoyment of literature was stimulated by the teaching they received at school or university and those who know they missed out on such stimulation and want to find it now. Members of book groups today are those we taught yesterday or will teach tomorrow: they are people who, to borrow Larkin's phrase from 'Church Going', have discovered 'a hunger in themselves to be more serious'. Without wishing to sound pious, I am sure that helping students to discover such a hunger through the study of literature is part of the job of teaching Literature.

Such a position as I have just outlined sounds as if I am arguing that teachers and students should be more concerned with *what* texts have to say than with *how* they say them. But the way writers use words and the way readers read them or listen to them is equally a part of the study of literature: it is what makes each text distinctive; and learning how to explore both the uniqueness of texts and their relationships with each other is what Literature teachers teach. The novelist Hilary Mantel (see Chapter 9, pages 175–183) has this to say about the texture of texts:

> Fiction isn't made by scraping the bones of topicality for the last shreds and sinews, to be processed into mechanically recovered prose. Like journalism, it deals in ideas as well as facts, but also in metaphors, symbols and myths. It multiplies ambiguity. It's about the particular, which suggests the general: about inner meaning, seen with the inner eye, always glimpsed, always vanishing, always more or less baffling, and scuffled onto the page hesitantly, furtively, transgressively, by night and with the wrong hand.[8]

It would not be a bad way of beginning a Literature course to compare Mantel's ideas about what fiction is, and how novelists write, with 'The Thought Fox' by Ted Hughes, that defining poem about what poetry is and how poets write. Of course, to compare one text with another is a basic critical procedure, and it is useful to demonstrate to students the value of contextual and intertextual study as early as possible.

Contextual and intertextual study

How do writers talk to each other, and to us? Several of the texts discussed in Chapters 7 to 11 of this book make direct or indirect reference to other texts – and as soon as the connection is made by the reader, that person's understanding of the original text is enlarged.

A good illustration of this to discuss with students is Thomas Hardy's choice of title for one of his most famous poems, 'The Darkling Thrush'. Originally he called it 'By the Century's Deathbed', but his change of title introduced a striking word ('darkling') not present in the poem itself. In doing so he alerted readers to a famous stanza in Keats' 'Ode to a Nightingale':

> Darkling I listen; and, for many a time
>   I have been half in love with easeful Death …

'Darkling' here means in the dark (Keats' speaker has just mentioned that he is lying in 'embalmed darkness') and the speaker in Hardy's poem too is both literally and metaphorically in the dark, since it is evening and the world seems on the verge of a new dark age: Hardy is looking forward with scant optimism to the dawn of the 20th century. The thrush likewise is *in* the dark, but *out of* the darkness he sings his message of 'some blessed hope' which the speaker cannot grasp – just as the nightingale in Keats' poem sings 'in full-throated ease'.

Thus, by a change of title, Hardy has considerably extended the scope of the poem. The poet compares himself with Keats' speaker, who longed to escape 'the weariness, the fever and the fret' of life, and links the two birds who have the power, through their singing, to suggest the possibility of a different, better world to come. But the word 'darkling' is so distinctive – its meaning 'in the dark' rather than 'growing dark' described by both the OED and Webster's American Dictionary as 'poetic' – that its use in Hardy's title must set off other echoes. Indeed, a few minutes' Internet search will enable students to discover that Matthew Arnold, in 'Dover Beach' – his famous poem about the loss of faith in the modern world (Hardy's world too) – refers to the 'darkling plain':

> The world, which seems to lie before us like a land of dreams,
> So various, so beautiful and so new
> Hath really neither joy, nor love, nor light,
> Nor certitude, nor peace, nor help for pain;
> And we are here as on a darkling plain
> Swept with confused alarms of struggle and flight
> Where ignorant armies clash by night.

In that first line, setting up the prospect of a future that turns out to be a bitter disillusionment, Arnold directly echoes and inverts the expulsion of Adam and Eve from the Garden of Eden in Milton's *Paradise Lost*: 'The world lay all before them'. And it is actually Milton who anticipates both Keats and Hardy in linking the word 'darkling' with a bird, when in Book III of *Paradise Lost* he notes how the 'wakeful bird / Sings darkling' (ll.38–9). But behind Milton stands, inevitably, Shakespeare. In *King Lear*, the Fool reminds Lear that:

> The hedge-sparrow fed the cuckoo so long
> That it had its head bit off by its young.
> So, out went the candle, and we were left darkling.   (I.iv.214–6)

One of the most valuable uses of the Internet is its function as a giant concordance of literature in English. This is a resource that was simply unavailable to students a generation ago. Indeed, the sheer availability of information today has been in part responsible for the growing focus on context in literary study. As this brief pursuit of the word 'darkling' has shown, such information is no longer the preserve of scholars who have time and access to trawl through libraries in search of such connections. Students do not need to rely on notes in textbooks, telling them what connections to make: they can discover them for themselves. In doing so they discover how one text illuminates, and is illuminated by, other texts. Not surprising, perhaps, that a recent addition to the English papers sat by students at Oxford was entitled 'Text, Context, Intertext'.

'The community of literature'

Students, then, can quickly learn how writers as well as readers make such connections all the time:

> A writer is first of all a reader. It is from reading that I derive the standards by which I measure my own work and according to which I fall lamentably short. It is from reading, even before writing, that I become part of a community – the community of literature – which includes more dead than living writers.[9]

This is Susan Sontag again, and her idea of literature as a community provides another good starting point for a discussion of what Literature as a subject is, and what it has to offer. As students and as teachers, as readers, we can become part of that community. Before her, W.H. Auden had expressed the idea slightly differently when he said that 'Art is our chief means of breaking bread with the dead', adding, 'Without communion with the dead, a fully human life is impossible.'[10] This claim is one which the wayward English teacher, Hector, in Alan Bennett's play *The History Boys* has passed on to his students. When Irwin, the young History teacher recently arrived to take over the teaching of the Oxbridge candidates from Hector, asks the boys what goes on in his lessons, the replies he gets are puzzling:

> BOYS: Ask him, sir. We don't know sir.
> AKTHAR: It's just the knowledge, sir.
> TIMMS: The pursuit of it for its own sake, sir.
> POSNER: Not useful, sir. Not like your lessons.
> AKTHAR: Breaking bread with the dead, sir. That's what we do.
> IRWIN: What it used to be called is 'wider reading'.
> LOCKWOOD: Oh no, sir. It can be narrower reading. Mr Hector says if we know one book off by heart, it doesn't matter if it's really crap. The Prayer Book, sir. The Mikado, the Pigeon Fancier's Gazette … so long as it's words, sir. Words and worlds.[11]

Irwin, the utilitarian, fails to spot the Auden quotation in Akthar's reply, or to register the sacramental significance of 'breaking bread' (later in the play, the Headmaster says that Hector has 'an old-fashioned faith in the redemptive power of words'). He also fails to respond to the intertextual idea that, through literature, the present can share with, and learn from, the past. He simply labels this 'wider reading'. It is the student, Lockwood, who corrects him, by calling it 'narrower reading': the closest possible engagement with a book (knowing it 'off by heart') centred on its 'words, sir. Words and worlds.'

Hector's own teaching of poetry combines words and worlds, close reading and context, in a way which provides a useful case study, for teachers, of the dangers of jumping to the wrong contextual conclusions. Discussing Hardy's poem 'Drummer Hodge', he makes much of the fact that the soldier is given a name:

> The important thing is that he has a name … thrown into a common grave though he may be, he is still Hodge the drummer. Lost boy though he is on the other side of the world, he still has a name.[12]

What Hector misses is the fact that, for Hardy, 'Hodge' (the very word a conflation of hedge-hog) was an unacceptable 'nickname that affects to portray a class … the farm-labouring community'. In an essay published in 1883, 'The Dorsetshire Labourer', Hardy had attacked in withering terms the way Londoners labelled the agricultural workers they never met in real life:

> This supposed real but highly conventional Hodge is a degraded being of uncouth manner and aspect, stolid understanding and snail-like movement.[13]

So Hector is both right and wrong to stress that Hardy's drummer has a name: at the same moment he is apparently given by the poet a unique identity he is simultaneously de-individualised by being given a derisive generic nickname. Read in the context, therefore, of Hardy's own comments about the name Hodge, Hector's explanation seems a misreading of the poem.

'The intention of the text'

This is one of the problems that teaching literature in context poses. Was Hector wrong to draw the conclusion he did? Was he at fault for not apparently knowing how Hardy himself viewed the name 'Hodge'? Surely no one critic or reader can be expected to know every possible historical or biographical detail that might be relevant? And if not, does our interpretation of a text then depend simply on which contexts we happen to know, or choose or ignore, with each interpretation being equally valid? Surely this would imply that any text can mean anything, depending in which context it is read?

Umberto Eco, the Italian novelist and critic, roundly rejects this idea of an interpretative free-for-all. In his book *On Literature* he notes:

There is a dangerous critical heresy, typical of our time, according to which we can do anything we like with a work of literature, reading into it whatever our most uncontrolled impulses dictate to us. This is not true. Literary works encourage freedom of interpretation, because they offer us a discourse that has many layers of reading and place before us the ambiguities of language and of real life. But in order to play this game, which allows every generation to read literary works in a different way, we must be moved by a profound respect for the intention of the text.[14]

Eco's argument is that there are some things in texts that can never be disputed while others are open to interpretation or revision. Lady Macbeth may or may not have had children but Hamlet never married Ophelia. Some things, it can be said, are 'true' within the context of the text in which they exist. Other things may or may not be true: Lady Russell, in Jane Austen's *Persuasion*, may or may not have had Anne Elliot's best interests at heart when persuading her not to marry Frederick Wentworth. It is true, however, that she is willing at the end of the book to admit she had been wrong to do so. Does this make her more realistic, more human and therefore true to life as a character? The question of truth in a text is something that students need to confront quite early on, especially so that they recognise the limitations (in terms of textual analysis) of saying that something is 'true to life'. If truth in a text is reduced to a single truth, so that it means one thing and one thing only, then context would only be relevant or admissible if it served to reinforce that single meaning.

These are questions and issues that I discuss in Chapters 7 to 11 of this book. In teaching Shakespeare, for instance, I ask whether a student is justified in describing Othello as a 'black, Muslim mercenary' either in the context of 16th or of 21st century understanding of these terms. I ask whether it is true that the Holocaust has made *The Merchant of Venice* a more difficult play for us than it was for an earlier Elizabethan audience. It is important for students to gain an historical perspective and, at the same time, to see how far their own times can provide a context for discussion of texts old and new. So current or recent events – the Asian Tsunami, the execution of Saddam Hussein, to name but two – can frame discussions of texts ranging from the Bible to *A History of the World in 10½ Chapters*. An illustrated magazine article about Kate Winslet may provide a helpful context for re-reading Jane Austen, but an alleged discovery about the setting of a poem by T.S. Eliot may turn out to offer a false context.

I am concerned (always, I hope) with the contexts in which words themselves are used. So there are some detailed investigations – again, helped by Internet access – of the shifting meaning of words: 'watch' in Shakespeare, 'handsome' in Jane Austen. Genre, too, is always an important context, so there are several discussions of the sonnet in different guises and by different writers, and of non-fictional as well as fictional prose. Chapter 9 includes discussion of very recent fiction, by both famous and unknown writers; Chapter 10 looks specifically at essays, blogs and travel writing. In what sort of contexts can we place a book about which nothing (or very little) has so far been said? Can film adaptations of novels act as an illuminating context for the discussion of the novels themselves, or do they merely diminish the original texts? Historical and cultural genres, too, are essential contexts, so there are extended discussions in Chapters 7 and 11 of poems in the context of the Romantic period and of ways of teaching the literature of the Great War, and the Great War in British Literature. Questions of cultural identity – contested ideas of Englishness, for instance – provide a context for discussing William Blake, Rupert Brooke, E.M. Forster and Julian Barnes.

Ways of seeing

A book which has influenced me since the beginning of my teaching career is John Berger's *Ways of Seeing* (1972), and three times in *World and Time* I specifically use the detailed study of paintings or sculptures as a context for the discussion of literary texts: I discuss Wordsworth's sonnet 'Composed Upon Westminster Bridge' in the context of Stanley Spencer's painting of the Thames, *Swan Upping*. I also use war memorials as a context for analysing ways in which writers memorialise the Great War. As a context for studying a novel by Dickens I take as a starting point one of the key illustrations in the original edition of *A Tale of Two Cities*. I hope Berger would approve of my methods. I have also drawn heavily on his arguments in discussing the idea of the male gaze as a central idea in literature as well as in other media: my discussion of ways of seeing and ways of reading range from Jane Austen to Zadie Smith, with a particular focus on two contemporary novels, Hilary Mantel's *A Change of Climate* and Joe Treasure's *The Male Gaze*.

Recent developments in assessment at advanced level have put a much greater emphasis on comparative study, and I have already drawn attention above to the value of reading one text in the context of another. This is again the focus in Chapter 5, when I discuss the possibilities of context in unseen examinations of the sort increasingly used for university admission, the Advanced Extension Award (AEA) and the English Literature Admissions Test (ELAT) for instance. Throughout all these discussions I try to argue for the importance of seeing close reading and context as complementary, not contradictory, approaches to the teaching of Literature and literary studies, and my test of the validity of a context is always (I hope) the same: does it help me – and will it help my students – to see the text in a clearer light, a different light or a distorting light?

But, in the end, how can you tell? One example from my experience as an examiner as well as a teacher may give at least a clue and will demonstrate the increasing ingenuity and sophistication of students and their teachers today. In a 2002 Literature examination students were asked to discuss Herrick's poem 'Upon Julia's Clothes':

When as in silks my Julia goes,
Then, then, methinks, how sweetly flows
The liquefaction of her clothes!

Next, when I cast mine eyes and see
That brave vibration each way free,
– O how that glittering taketh me!

Some examiners were disconcerted to read answers which strayed well beyond the conventional analysis of the language and imagery. Should a script that drew a comparison between 'the liquefaction of her clothes' and the then infamous Monica Lewinsky's dress be rewarded or penalised? Candidates who took this comparison one stage further and linked the poem with the title of Philip Roth's novel *The Human Stain* (only just published at that time and also alerting the reader, through its title, directly to the same dress) baffled still further examiners who had not yet had time to read the book. And when other candidates anatomised the language by drawing on scathing feminist critiques of Herrick or skilfully invoking the concept of the male gaze to explode any idea of the poem's 'charm', it was clear that the assessment of critical appreciation could never be quite the same again. 'After such knowledge, what forgiveness?' Yet these students, and their teachers, had shown how contextual close reading could shine a revealing new light on a well-known text. It is this, I suggest, which makes teaching literature in context so important and so worthwhile.

2 | Assessing literature in context

'How will it seem to you, forty years on?' *(Harrow School Song)*

To get an impression of where English Literature stands now as a subject taught and examined, and a sense of how far it has travelled, it may help to look back at some A level questions of forty years ago.

Some of the questions bear little resemblance to the types of question asked today. Here, for instance, is a commentary task on *Othello*:

> OTHELLO: Never, Iago. Like to the Pontic sea
> Whose icy current and compulsive course
> Never retiring ebbs, but keeps due on
> To the Propontic, and the Hellespont;
> Even so my bloody thoughts, with violent pace,
> Shall ne'er look back, ne'er ebb to humble love,
> Till that a capable and wide revenge
> Swallow them up. Now by yond marble heaven,
> In the due reverence of a sacred vow,
> I here engage my words.
> IAGO: Do not rise yet.
> Witness you ever-burning lights above,
> You elements that clip us round about,
> Witness that here Iago doth give up
> The execution of his wit, hands, heart,
> To wronged Othello's service. Let him command,
> And to obey shall be in me remorse,
> What bloody business ever.

> i) Re-write the passage in MODERN ENGLISH. Your object is to make the meaning as clear as possible.
> ii) Indicate the **exact** context in **not more than two or three sentences**.
> iii) Comment briefly on those aspects of the passage which contribute most towards its particular effects.
>
> (UCLES, English A level Paper 2, Shakespeare, June 1967)

Candidates had twenty-five minutes to answer all three of these questions; they were then expected to repeat the exercise with another commentary on a second play, before writing two essays. Many teachers today would blench at the prospect of having to paraphrase Othello's speech; they might also reasonably argue that paraphrasing Shakespeare is a reductive and impossible task: to ask a candidate to put into 'MODERN ENGLISH' a phrase such as 'a capable and wide revenge' in its context in an eight-line sentence seems utterly to deny the poetic variousness of the language. Whether or not such questions were easier to mark reliably than today's questions is another matter.

Even the fact that this exercise had to be repeated with a second play (the choice was *The Winter's Tale*, *Antony and Cleopatra*, *Love's Labour's Lost* and *Henry IV, Pt I*) points up a significant difference from today's approach. So-called 'context questions' like this one were designed primarily to reveal how well the candidate knew the text. Exactly where does this scene come? Exactly what does this sentence mean? Today, A level commentary questions are more often designed to show how well candidates can use their knowledge of the text *as a whole* to discuss and contextualise the given passage. Open book examinations and coursework have also made 'context questions' of the 1967 kind increasingly redundant.

The essay questions from this Shakespeare paper are also revealing. Here are the two essay questions on *Othello*:

> **Either** (*a*) 'Shakespeare in *Othello* presents tragedy at the level of domestic life.' How far do you agree, and in what ways does Shakespeare exploit this quality?
>
> **Or**   (*b*) '... an extravagant and wheeling stranger
>   Of here and everywhere.'
> What use does Shakespeare make of Othello's race and background?

The formula 'How far ... and in what ways?' is still adopted today, designed of course to encourage candidates to consider possible alternatives to the proposition in the question. It is likely, however, that a modern question might offer more of a prompt – perhaps along the following lines:

> 'Shakespeare presents *Othello* as a domestic rather than a public tragedy.'
> Does this seem to you an adequate way of describing the play and its dramatic impact?

The alternative 1967 question, on Othello's race and background, is one that could still appear, and it is a good illustration of the fact that questions of context have not been invented only in the last few years. The quotation from the play forms a good preface to the question: Roderigo's colourful but prejudiced description of Othello provides candidates with a springboard for their answer and highlights questions of context that go to the heart of the play. (See Chapter 8, pages 144–152 for a discussion of Venice as a context for *Othello* and *The Merchant of Venice*.)

Other questions from this old Shakespeare paper are more problematic:

> It has been argued that the gap of sixteen years in the action of *The Winter's Tale* is fatal to the dramatic unity of the play, but that it serves a more important purpose. What is this purpose?

Such a question should not be set. It requires candidates to describe a specific but unidentified purpose: if they cannot read the examiner's mind, their essay is bound to fail. The question as couched, 'What is this purpose?', is closed: it is not open for debate or analysis. Candidates cannot argue with the proposition; neither can they discuss a much more interesting one already embedded in the question – that the sixteen-year gap in the action between Acts 3 and 4 'is fatal to the dramatic unity of the play'. As it stands the question revealingly implies that a thematic issue (redeeming of the sins of the parents by the reconciling love of the children of the next generation) is more important – *i.e. more interesting* – than the structure of the play and its impact as drama on the audience. This is a question which, by privileging the concept of the play as literary text, inhibits students from discussing the play's most significant context, the stage.

Another question from this paper is even worse:

> 'In writing *Love's Labour's Lost* Shakespeare was merely having fun.' What evidence is there in the play that Shakespeare was writing for his own amusement?

The only answer to this question is 'None'.

Asking questions of context

Turning to the other A level English papers set by Cambridge in 1967, it is striking how often E.M. Forster features. *A Passage to India* was a set text in the paper 'Chaucer and Other Major Authors', and a choice of three questions was offered, at least one of which presented an interesting contextual challenge:

> In what way does *A Passage to India* readily lend itself to dramatic adaptation? What, in your opinion, are the qualities of the book which would be most readily lost or seriously affected in any adaptation, however good?

There is still a problem with the wording of the question: 'In what way [singular]?' implies that there is only one, which candidates must identify. There would have been no difficulty had the questions asked 'In what ways [plural]?' In fact, the second sentence of the question – with its reference to 'qualities' – implicitly contradicts the first.

However, it is interesting to see students being invited to consider a novel in the context of its adaptation (though notice the underlying implication that no adaptation can be quite as good as the original novel). Although the David Lean film version of the novel did not appear until 1984, *A Passage to India* had been adapted first for the stage and then for television in 1965, with Sybil Thorndyke as Mrs Moore and Virginia McKenna as Adela Quested. Although 1965 was long before the era of video or DVD recordings, it was a reasonable assumption that many A level students would have seen this BBC 'Play of the Month': the question would have pleased as many candidates and their teachers as it must have annoyed purists for whom discussion of adaptation to a medium as ephemeral as TV was not a legitimate literary topic. (For a discussion of film adaptation as a context for analysis of *Atonement*, see Chapter 9, pages 205–214.)

Forster also featured in Paper 7 ('Literature Since 1900') where his collection of essays, *Abinger Harvest*, was a set text. It is many years since any exam board or awarding body chose a collection of essays as a set text. He appeared for a third time in the Special Paper, where the questions showed a strong Leavisite concern with 'life' and 'values':

> 'Forster's novels are always centred on a contrast between a false form of life and a true form.' How far do you find this applicable?

> From your reading of Forster how far would you say that there is a pattern of values to be perceived?

Forty years on: the evolution of English Studies

E.M. Forster in fact provides a good index of the way in which English Literature has evolved as a subject. In the 1960s he and D.H. Lawrence represented still the high points of literary modernism, although neither of them had published a novel since the 1920s, Lawrence having died in 1930 and Forster's posthumous novel, *Maurice*, not having yet appeared. When a 'Casebook' of critical essays on *A Passage to India* was published by Macmillan in 1970, its editor was Malcolm Bradbury – at that time one of the leading academic critics of modernism and the modern novel. Bradbury summed up the case for Forster's novel in these terms:

> I have tried, in these introductory comments, not to suggest a conclusion about the book; rather to indicate what complicated problems the book has set for those who have tried to read it closely. Is it primarily a novel of 'rhythm' – or a novel of society and politics and human relationships? Is it an optimistic novel, pointing to the unity hidden behind all things, or a pessimistic one? But whatever we decide about such questions, we will, I think, be likely to

grant that *A Passage to India* is a remarkable modern novel. To put it like
that is to raise questions not just about what the book is in itself – but how
it compares with the other great English novels of the century. It does, I had
better say, seem to me among the greatest: along with *Women in Love* or *Lord
Jim* or *Ulysses*. It has their fullness of imaginative force. It assimilates many
of the technical aspects of twentieth-century modernism in art – the sense
that art, faced by social confusion, can produce coherence chiefly through
the exploration of its own symbolic ordering powers – and also many of its
intellectual aspects – its sense of progressive despair or failed hope through
history, its search for a new historiography for an ominous century. But of
course that quality of moral balance, which … is one essential aspect of
Forster's liberalism, informs this book too. If it abounds in contradictions,
it withdraws from extremities. The qualities of living intelligence and
questioning control, which in the liberal notion should shine through works of
art, remain vivid and strong. The book touches us not only through its fullness,
and its artistry; it also touches us through its decency. And that, too, seems a
very important thing for us to say about it.[1]

Bradbury writes here with a sense of diffident personal engagement ('I have tried
… I think … I had better say') that is itself Forsterian. Bradbury once memorably
described Forster as looking in photographs 'as though he had been taking lessons
in unassertiveness training'. Phrases such as 'fullness of imaginative force' or
'its own symbolic ordering powers' and 'the qualities of living intelligence and
questioning control' again show the continuing influence of F.R. Leavis and
Scrutiny on the generation of teachers who had learned from him and his circle
how to treat English (i.e. English Literature) as a serious moral discipline. Now
it was Bradbury and his generation who were training the next generation of
English teachers. But during this same period a strong reaction was setting in,
and Bradbury's view of literary criticism and the value of literary study was being
radically challenged. When in 1995 Macmillan published a volume of essays on
E.M. Forster in their 'New Casebooks' series, the editor Jeremy Tambling wrote in
terms savagely critical of Forster and, by implication, of Bradbury:

But the triangular relationship of Forster to modernism, homosexuality and
empire is problematic, and I have tried to show that it is one central issue.
His interest in 'friendship' – with its complex relationship to homosexuality –
made him unable to move out of nostalgia, or sexual diffidence about himself
and about gender-issues, or to become incisive about the enormity of British
rule in India … For me, English modernism itself failed to revalue gender
issues and collapsed back into a conservatism that did not spur Forster to
anything new after *A Passage to India*. Forster failed to make anything of his
own homosexuality, which in some ways is understandable, given this English

conservative agenda, and though he justified his failure to himself on the grounds that his novels were to speak for all, not merely for a homosexual grouping, his liberalism prevented the emergence of anything more interesting and transgressive, kept him from a socialist vision and kept him from seeing fully the structures of oppression – class, race and gender-based – that he was part of. Though his liberalism permitted him to see much of what was involved in imperialism, his homosociality made for a foreclosure on the implications of that, too. Yet criticism needs to engage with Forster, not just to pick up on the positive aspects of his work which are easily elided in discussion, but also to read that institutional dominant discourse which belonged to the national ideology, to understand which liberalism was so inadequate a paradigm (as well as complicit with it). It was this discourse which prevented the emergence of modernism and radical thinking. Looking back from the standpoint of the 1990s, with the Forster films in place, it might almost seem that nothing has altered since the failure of modernism to change anything in England in the first decades of the century, when Forster was writing.[2]

To compare these two approaches to Forster, to modernism and to literary criticism, is to see how far the 'Theory Wars' of the last quarter of the 20th century shifted the ground on which English as a subject was standing. Phrases such as 'the structures of oppression – class, race and gender-based' and 'that institutional dominant discourse which belonged to the national ideology' presented a severe challenge to those teaching and examining students of literature still at the stage of making their first acquaintance with complex texts. But it is interesting to see that towards the end of the first decade of the 21st century Tambling's Marxist rhetoric seems at least as old-fashioned as Bradbury's liberal humanism. Peter Barry, in *English in Practice* (2003), echoes this idea and notes that the 'post-theory' era

is characterised by (among other things) an apparent return to the view that every degree-level teacher of literature is primarily a period specialist (a medievalist, an early modernist, a Romanticist, and so on), rather than primarily a post-structuralist or deconstructionist, or a Marxist, or a feminist – a very significant shift.[3]

He goes on to suggest that today's 'default approach' to literary study is broadly 'historicist … and committed to the endeavour of reconstructing the cultural and historical moment of a work's first appearance'.[4]

It's worth remarking here, in passing, that whereas university teachers may be period specialists, teachers of Literature in school or college English departments have to be generalists, able to teach across the broad range of English Literature at least from Shakespeare onwards, and preferably back to Chaucer. Yet fewer and fewer graduates are emerging with degrees that give them this breadth of knowledge in sufficient depth. This is one reason why the returning tendency towards contextuality – 'reconstructing the cultural and historical moment of a work's first appearance' (Peter Barry's words again) – is still resisted by some younger teachers, as well as by their elder colleagues, brought up by teachers who in their time were taught that literature was literature precisely because it transcended its historical moment.

Canon vs critical literacy

On the other hand, there are those who consider that context itself is not enough, unless it adopts an explicitly political agenda. In 2004 the National Association of Teachers of English (NATE) published a report, *text : message*, which argued for an entirely different focus for English Studies:

> Critical literacy is becoming universally acknowledged as a principal objective of our work (Luke, 2000). In Higher Education, this activity is often identified with discourse analysis: the process of identifying patterns of linguistic and social practices.[5]

The report is consequently highly critical of A level English Literature's failure to

> position itself explicitly in relation to the aesthetic, cultural and linguistic pluralism of a society in which students – and teachers – have to negotiate a cultural landscape more complex than that suggested by the course as it stands …. Nor does the course provide even a basic grounding in essential modern literary notions such as linguistics, cultural studies and post-colonialism.[6]

The first thrust of this criticism is in part an attack on A level English Literature for sticking to the conventional canon – a complaint both exemplified and undermined by the fact that Shakespeare is the only compulsory author. In the 2007 versions of the A level Subject Criteria for English Literature, students and their teachers have far greater licence than in the past to choose their own texts and, in the substantial coursework offering, to assert their own critical and cultural priorities.

Two further defences against NATE's criticisms can be offered: first, it is universities themselves who now lament new undergraduates' lack of knowledge of the basic canon (the 'landmarks of literature') and specifically deplore students' lack of awareness of literary chronology. The increased emphasis on 'wider reading' demanded by the QCA Subject Criteria is an attempt to redress this lack. Second, NATE's own assertion that linguistics, cultural studies and post-colonialism are 'modern literary notions' itself needs deconstructing: are these things no more than fashions, and is it anyway the job of English Literature at A level to provide a grounding in linguistics, or in cultural studies? The writers of the NATE Report are themselves aware of the limits of what can be achieved in the time available to teach English at A level, suggesting ways to lighten 'the independent reading load' by

> ensuring that poetry, drama and short stories – genres that can be read and taught simultaneously in class – form a substantial proportion of the syllabus, so that there are not too many long novels for students to cover independently.[7]

Such an approach may be pragmatic; it is surely reductive. No wonder universities complain about students' unwillingness or inability to read substantial texts. Equally reductive is the idea that English Literature as a subject is essentially an interdisciplinary seedbed, where texts are read not to illuminate the discipline of English but to nurture an interest in other 'literary notions' – the very phrase suggesting that these things are insubstantial, subject to the latest whim.

'What is at the heart of English Studies?'

Peter Barry, once more, writing this time as Reviews Editor of the journal *English*, has put this very forcefully:

> What is at the heart of English Studies? I can tell you. It is precise criticism and scholarship, close observation, exact description, the making of specific connections, and the construction of logical arguments closely based upon those specifics. I can also tell you what the heart of English is not. It is not broad-sweep speculative generalisations about 'identities' or 'discourses' or other abstract nouns.[8]

Precise criticism and scholarship, close observation, exact description and the making of specific connections: it would be hard to find a better list of the ingredients of close reading and contextual study – of the skills that A level teachers should be teaching and that students need to learn. Every lesson should include opportunities for teachers to teach and for students to practise these skills; and when Heads of Department choose the right syllabus/specification for their staff and students to follow, their chief criterion for selection should be, how much scope for such an approach is allowed by the programme of study embedded in the syllabus?

The second criterion should be, how much flexibility in choice and range of texts and topics does the specification allow? It is as true today as ever in the past that teachers will base their choice of syllabus on the range of set texts – indeed, for many teachers and students the set texts (the subject content) still define the syllabus far more explicitly than the skills students must bring to the study of these texts. Knowledge of the texts, rather than knowledge of how to read the texts, comes first and many English teachers still only pay lip-service to the proposition underlying all the theoretical debates of the past thirty years: that how we read matters as much as what we read.

Surprisingly, however, there are several underlying questions to be asked about the actual concept of a set text – questions which rarely surface, but which teachers should ask themselves and, from the start of any course, discuss with their students. If they don't, students are all too likely to assume that there is no need to waste time on any text that is not 'set'.

Setting set texts

But, set for what? Set for study, obviously; which almost certainly means, set to be studied by students under the guidance of their teacher. It is rare for a student to study a set text independently without discussion in class or teacher intervention. Should this be as rare as it is?

Probably, but not always, set texts are also set to be examined. This will inevitably affect the way they are taught, whether a teacher is thinking of how to introduce *Much Ado About Nothing* at Key Stage 3, *Macbeth* at GCSE or *Hamlet* at A level.

Shakespeare is the only author specified by name for examining at these three levels between ages 14–19. He provides a good illustration of the pressure examinations place on the way texts may be set, selected by teachers and studied by students. For A level English Literature – though not English Language and Literature – Shakespeare is compulsory: depending on which specification is being studied, the play may be set and assessed internally (by coursework) or externally.

- First, a teacher's selection of play will be limited by the range prescribed in the specification. The awarding body will have tried to avoid setting plays students may already have encountered at GCSE; and at GCSE it will have tried to avoid repeating Key Stage 3 texts.
- Second, teachers will want a play that suits their students. Choosing between *Othello* and *Henry IV pt. 2* may be easy with some classes, and more difficult with others.
- Third, they will hope to find a play they themselves will enjoy teaching: it is hard on the students to be taught by teachers who cannot share their enjoyment of the text.
- Fourth, they will have to judge whether the play can be taught in the time available (which may rule out *Hamlet*, but not *The Tempest*).

- Fifth, they have to ask basic questions: Do we have copies of the play in stock, or shall we (or the students) have to buy new copies? What resources have we got – teaching notes, lesson plans, video or DVD?

Add to this the possibility of the play's being taught by a young teacher. How much time and support can a Head of Department afford to give to an NQT who has never taught *The Tempest* before and who may not have studied Shakespeare at university? How much time can the NQT give to the proper preparation of the text? All set texts need preparation, even those the teacher has taught before.

By the time all these factors have been weighed the choice of play will have narrowed considerably, perhaps down to one. And these factors apply to the choosing of set texts for all papers at all levels. Even texts chosen for coursework have to meet the requirements of the specification and the assessment objectives: prose, poetry or drama? Pre- or post-1800? 1945? Post-1990? For comparative or for contextual study? To be studied on its own or as part of a cluster of texts to illustrate the student's grasp of a genre or theme?

Most teachers welcome, at least up to a point, the framework of a syllabus: they can balance their choice of individual texts with the need to construct a worthwhile and coherent course. On the other hand, set texts can come to seem a tyranny, preventing teachers from doing what most of them regard as their most important tasks as teachers of English: to share with their students their own enjoyment of reading and, in doing so, to encourage them to develop as enthusiastic, skilful and critical readers of texts of all kinds.

Who sets set texts? In England, the Qualifications and Curriculum Authority (QCA) determines the choice of Shakespeare texts at Key Stage 3. At GCSE and AS/A level, the Awarding Bodies (still referred to by most teachers as the Exam Boards) work from the Subject Criteria to ensure that the texts they set for each unit will enable students to cover the full course requirements. They themselves may chafe at the constraints and inconsistencies of the criteria, but they try to select texts that teachers will want to teach, both staple texts from the canon of English and American Literature – though a glance at set texts lists of twenty-five and fifty years ago shows just how well set texts lists have reflected the fluidity of the canon – and recent books that may or may not in due course become established. Their choice combines idealism, realism and an eye on the market. They try to provide as wide a range as possible. They test the limits of what is regarded as acceptable: *White Teeth*, which has already appeared on at least one A level list, would have been regarded as too risky at one time. When Ian McEwan's acclaimed novel *Atonement* was first set, the *Daily Telegraph* ran a prominent article denouncing it as an unsuitable book for A level students to have to study or for (women) teachers to have to teach. The QCA Code of Practice governing all public examinations 14–19, explicitly forbids the use of material 'liable to cause offence' in setting question papers.

There are serious problems here, however. Some teachers today are reluctant to teach set texts for which there isn't already a body of published support or critical material: the poetry of Sylvia Plath will always be a more popular choice than the poetry of Anne Stevenson, the plays of Harold Pinter safer than those of Pam Gems. This leads inevitably to a shrinking list of set texts. At its most extreme, at GCSE, there is a danger that students year after year may never experience any novel other than *Of Mice and Men* nor any post-Shakespeare play other than *An Inspector Calls*. Departmental budgets, too, may well prevent some teachers being as innovative as they would like in experimenting with a new text that may or may not go down well with their students. In any case, with the pressure of performance targets, league tables and every other pressure to maximise results, experimenting with texts carries real risks. Although some awarding bodies have been offering teachers the option of teaching non-fiction prose texts – biography and travel writing, for example – for many years, the take-up remains small. And not everyone wants to study *Fever Pitch*.

Nor does everyone agree that contemporary literature should be on the curriculum at all. Helen Gardner, in her 1982 book *In Defence of the Imagination*, put the argument for concentrating on the literature of the past in the following terms:

> The present tendency to stress the literature of the twentieth century at the expense of the literature of earlier times, and the attempt to remake the literature of the past in the image of the present, is to give young people a mess of pottage for their birthright. Their years at school and at the university are the years when they should be filling up their camel's hump, taking in nourishment that will sustain them through years when practical necessities and the duties of their daily lives may leave them little time for concentrated reading. All good teachers want to have students who read widely for themselves, and are happy to talk with them about their reading and to learn from them; but it is the responsibility of teachers to choose what works are to be studied, as being of primary importance and of value both in themselves and in their influence on succeeding generations. The heart of any good curriculum in literature must be what has proved through the ages its wearability, and its power to liberate, illuminate, and support. The young can be trusted to find its true relevance for themselves.[9]

Many teachers might still tacitly agree with Helen Gardner that texts which have proved their ability to 'liberate, illuminate, and support' should be at the heart of the curriculum. These are good old-fashioned Arnoldian adjectives: 'Who prop, thou ask'st, in these bad days my mind?' wrote Arnold in his famous sonnet 'To a Friend', praising the Greek dramatist Sophocles who 'saw life steadily and saw it whole'. Many teachers, though, (including perhaps some of the above) will also feel uncomfortable at the idea of identifying for study books which are of 'primary importance and of value both in themselves and in their influence on succeeding generations'. Literature as a subject providing ethical guidance (a genuinely 'humane', humanising discipline) rather than cultural analysis (tending towards a branch of social science) remained a widely held view among teachers until the 1980s; then it became unfashionable, elitist, authoritarian. Now perhaps it is returning, but it's doubtful whether even those who held fast to the Arnoldian faith throughout what they saw as the 'dark days' of post-modernism would argue against setting 20th and now 21st-century texts for study.

It must be part of the job of English teachers to teach students to be aware of, and respond to, developments in contemporary writing. Indeed, identifying and celebrating good modern writing is one way in which the students of today can help to ensure the health of literature for the future. Waiting until a text has demonstrated what Gardner called its 'wearability' risks burdening it with the weight of 'heritage'. It is important and valuable for students to be exposed to challenging writers and challenging new writing. Learning how to make their own judgements about books and writers is one of the key skills they should take with them when their last formal lesson in English is over.

A further problem is that the size of set text lists may soon start to shrink: increasingly, examiners now have neither the time nor the experience to prepare to examine papers that may have up to thirty-two questions on sixteen different texts. It is a depressing fact that the most reliable of all question papers would have only one question on only one text. Increasingly, too, A level English Literature specifications are focusing on wider areas as well as individual set texts. Discussion of topics such as the gothic tradition or post-colonial literature, where specified texts may be set alongside a wider range of reading chosen by the candidate, places great demands on examiners and leads to understandable anxiety on the part of teachers.

The end of set texts?

Hasn't the idea of set texts therefore had its day? The whole notion of set texts for English carries certain assumptions: for a start, that Literature is best studied and examined through individual whole texts, or small clusters of related texts, or individual texts supported by wider reading. It also assumes that there are such things as literary texts ('English Language and Literature' A level distinguishes between 'literary and non-literary texts'), which will 'merit serious study at this level'. For some, entitlement in English still implies being entitled to discover the scope of English Literature as well as the scope of literary study. From such a perspective, set texts fulfil a clear and important function.

For others, however, the whole idea of privileging Literature within the context of a subject called 'English' needs to be challenged. 'Set' texts and set text lists are themselves seen as evidence of an authoritarian imposition of cultural norms that are ideologically driven. Literature from this perspective should not be seen to have any special claim to creativity; it should be seen as one among various spoken, written or visual-media discourses. The teacher's role is to teach critical literacy rather than literary appreciation (see the comments in Chapter 1, page 7, by Nick Peim of the School of Education, Birmingham University). In this context, students study texts not to find out what makes them unique but what makes them symptomatic. Set texts as currently understood – whole texts that proclaim themselves as in some sense 'literature' – hardly belong here. They would certainly occupy a much smaller and less prominent space.

This debate is an important one for all English teachers. However, it is not a new debate; indeed, for many critics and teachers, it now has a curiously old-fashioned ring. The feminist critic, Elaine Showalter (in *Teaching Literature*, 2003), puts it well:

> The message of the eighties was that literature itself was political, and that external crises could be countered by pointing to the racist or sexist or post-colonial subtexts of the syllabus. Missing in both these responses was a reflection on teaching itself as a humane, humanistic, value-laden art.[10]

Since the advent of *Curriculum 2000* – and in fact for some time before that – English teaching has moved steadily towards the middle ground between these two positions. And for those teachers who continue to see themselves as practising a humane, humanistic, value-laden art and teaching a humane, humanistic, value-laden subject there will still be a central place for set texts in the future. They will continue to define for students the context of the subject English Literature.

3 | The case for close reading

'So if we look closely (and looking closely is what English Studies is about) ...'

(Peter Barry **English in Practice**, *2003)*

The number of applicants to read English Studies at UK universities has been increasing dramatically, says UCAS[1]: 55,581 applications in 2007 (a rise of 7.6% on 2006). In terms of demand, English Studies come fifth, behind Law, Psychology, Pre-clinical Medicine and Management Studies. Given that in 2006 (according to provisional figures published by the Joint Council for Qualifications[2]) the number of students taking English subjects at A level was 86,640, these numbers indicate how high a proportion of A level candidates intend to continue their English studies. Of course, there will be a significant group of the UCAS applicants who have not taken A level English at all: IB candidates, for instance; mature students; overseas candidates – all of whom will have had very different experiences of studying English from those who have followed the *Curriculum 2000* specifications in English Language, English Language and Literature or English Literature.

Will they all have been equally well prepared for the study of English at university? Who will have taught them? What will they have learned? Will they have the knowledge and the skills that university teachers expect at level 1? Current views, as expressed by academic spokesmen, tend to be downbeat or downright despairing. Gary Day, from De Montfort, says bleakly:

> Literature is disappearing from the curriculum in schools. And it's on the way out in universities. During the 1980s and 1990s there were plenty of people only too happy to say there was no such thing. Usually professors of English. But now the bureaucrats have picked up the baton and are saying that skills are more important than subject matter. Such statements undermine our professionalism. They diminish the very thing that defines us as academics, our knowledge and understanding of our discipline.[3]

Less journalistically, but in the same vein, Terry Eagleton begins his chapter on 'The Functions of Criticism' in *How to Read a Poem* (2007):

> I first thought of writing this book when I realised that hardly any of the students of literature I encountered these days practised what I myself had been trained to regard as literary criticism. Like thatching or clog dancing, literary criticism seems to be something of a dying art. Since many of these students are bright and capable enough, the fault would seem to lie largely with their teachers. The truth is that quite a few teachers of literature nowadays do not practise literary criticism either, since they, in turn, were never taught to do so.[4]

It's not clear from this whether Eagleton is referring to new graduates who have just completed a first degree or to new undergraduates fresh from school. If the latter, it is worth noting that, according to recent research by the DfES, 49% of English teachers in secondary schools do not have a degree in the subject, and 20% have no post-A level qualification in the subject at all.[5] If those UK teachers, therefore, who do have degrees in English but were not taught literary criticism are added to those who have no degree in the subject but teach English in secondary school, it is open to question whether many school teachers today could teach an art which Eagleton (albeit ironically) nostalgically depicts as a quaint survival of Merrie England.

Is English out of touch?

According to some commentators, the gap between English as a subject at school and English as a discipline at university has become such a chasm that there is no longer any useful sense in which A level English can be described as a preparation for degree level English Studies. The 2004 NATE report, *text : message*, on the future of A level English condemns the *Curriculum 2000* English Literature specifications offered by the awarding bodies in these terms:

> A level English Literature has still made only modest moves towards the linguistic, historical and cultural positions which underlie university English Studies, and which pose vital questions regarding the nature of culture, language and texts in society. As currently constituted, the course allows only a narrow conception of what literature is and has been, and does not adequately deal with wider questions concerning the nature of reading and the relationship between literature, the media and society.[6]

Such criticisms are not new: Robert Eaglestone's *Doing English* (1999), for instance, had argued that the concept of English Studies embodied by A level English (as English Literature was called prior to *Curriculum 2000*) had not changed since the introduction of A levels in 1951 and had failed to keep pace with the way English was evolving in Higher Education. What Eaglestone did not ask was *why* this had happened. This is revealing because, before the 1990s, the A level curriculum had been under the control of the examination boards which – with the exception of the Associated Examining Board (AEB) – had all been more or less closely linked to the universities. The names of the boards – University of London School Examinations Board, Northern Universities' Joint Matriculation Board, etc. – showed as much. If the universities, then, had wanted A level English course content to keep pace with change in Higher Education English teaching, it could be argued that they were in a position to engineer this. From the time, however, that the remit of SCAA (the Schools Curriculum and Assessment Authority, subsequently the Qualifications and Curriculum Authority, QCA[7]) was extended in the 1993 and 1998 Education Acts to embrace post-compulsory education – 'Key Stage 5' – as well as the National Curriculum, the input of universities into A Level syllabus development was reduced almost to nil. The exam boards were rebranded 'awarding bodies' and were no longer answerable to the universities but to their Regulator, QCA – which, though nominally independent, was in turn answerable to Whitehall.

QCA's *Curriculum 2000* was central to the Government's modernisation agenda for education. As Ann Hodgson and Ken Spours of the London University Institute of Education have pointed out, 'Modernisation meant making A levels more accessible and this was the major discourse carried out with the education profession'.[8] But the education profession, in these terms, excluded Higher Education; as Hodgson and Spours conclude:

> The view of universities largely mirrors that of the teachers and lecturers involved in the delivery of *Curriculum 2000*. Universities are supportive of its principles, but critical of the new qualifications – for example, the perception of a rushed and superficial AS ... Moreover, universities do not see *Curriculum 2000* as 'their' reform and, as a consequence, they do not believe it is their role to drive through breadth of study at advanced level.[9]

It was particularly the emphasis on 'breadth of study' that had led to the introduction of AS, encouraging schools to insist that students should take four or even five subjects in the first year of the sixth-form. These subjects were to be taught in a modular structure and examined (at a new standard, between GCSE and A level) either in January and/or June of Year 12; consequently both teaching time and time for independent study in all subjects were squeezed. That this has had a profound effect on how students of English develop as potential recruits to English Studies at university is unarguable, for what Hodgson and Spours say of the AS experience generally has applied specifically to English:

> The new AS, with its high-stakes assessment in the first year, led to teacher didacticism and learner instrumentalism, as both focused on maximising grade attainment. One unfortunate side effect of this process was the lack of time and energy devoted to encouraging advanced level learners to develop the skills of independent study required at this level.[10]

Curriculum 2000 has itself gone rapidly out of date: from 2008 onwards, English Literature students have to be examined on no fewer than six texts for AS and a further six at A level. (Originally students were assessed on a minimum of eight texts.) This gesture in the direction of widening students' experience of reading may be welcomed in principle; but it will in practice lead to still further didacticism and instrumentalism, with still less opportunity for students and their teachers to engage meaningfully in the literary criticism whose loss Terry Eagleton laments.

The habit of close reading

For Eagleton, literary criticism is based on 'the habit of close reading';[11] but, having defended literary theorists against the charge that they killed off literary criticism ('almost all major literary theorists engage in scrupulously close reading'), he continues:

> ... it is not as though many students today do not read poems and novels fairly closely. Close reading is not the issue. The question is not how tenaciously you cling to the text, but what you are in search of when you do so.[12]

But as far as transition from A level English Literature to degree level English Studies is concerned, close reading *is* the issue. Two influential reports from the HEA English Subject Centre have highlighted close reading as not only the most important skill that students need to bring with them to their university studies but also as the least effectively acquired. First, the 2004 report, *Four Perspectives on Transition: English Teaching from Sixth Form to University*, found that close reading was identified as 'useful' or 'very useful' by more sixth-form and first-year undergraduate students, and by more A level and undergraduate teachers than any other skill. On the other hand, university teachers highlighted students' 'generally poor abilities in this area and unwillingness to involve themselves in the discussion of textual detail, preferring to maintain argument on the level of the general'.[13]

The second report, *Teaching Shakespeare: A Survey of the Undergraduate Level in Higher Education* (2006), revealed that 89% of university teachers regarded students as 'at best "adequately" and in many cases "poorly" prepared for their studies':

> Most respondents felt that the main problems concerned students' lack of linguistic, historical and cultural knowledge. Respondents were also clear that this was not a problem unique to studying Shakespeare:
> – They are no worse prepared to study Shakespeare than they are to study any historically remote author.
> – Students lack confidence in handling close reading and analysis of Shakespeare's language, but also in how to read play texts more generally.[14]

When the same respondents were asked to comment on what steps they took to remedy this poor preparation, they commented that 'Much of our teaching goes into unpicking bad habits, in particular naïve character-based criticism or flat-footed A2 "context"', and went on to emphasise 'the importance of exercises in close reading carefully selected extracts as a way of building students' knowledge and confidence'.[15]

These comments are revealing. First, they suggest that the respondents were unaware that in the *Curriculum 2000* specifications (introduced in 2000 and replaced by a revised curriculum phased in from September 2008), the study of Shakespeare is only required at AS (and not even then if students are studying English Language and Literature); a small minority of students study a second Shakespeare text at A2 – and if they do, this possibly means that they study no other play text for A level at all. Furthermore, only one of the awarding bodies currently sets a written paper on Shakespeare at AS with a compulsory question based on close study of a passage from a prepared play; in all the others, Shakespeare is examined by coursework where close study of passages (the type of remedial work envisaged by the HE respondents) is unlikely to feature.

This lack of emphasis at A level on close reading does indeed spread more widely than Shakespeare. When QCA introduced Subject Criteria for A level English Literature, these included five weighted Assessment Objectives, of which only one – with a maximum weighting of 20% of all the marks available – addressed students' ability to analyse and respond to language, form and structure at all. By contrast, assessment of various forms of contextual knowledge and awareness (historical, biographical, literary, cultural and critical) could be weighted as heavily as 80%. When these Criteria appeared in 1999, they sent out a clear signal that the scope for setting papers which consisted solely or mainly of critical comment and analysis had almost disappeared. And so it proved: opportunities in examinations for close study of passages from set texts were usually reduced, and for the majority of A level students the only opportunity for analysis of an unseen poem or passage occurred within the final, synoptic paper, where the text set for discussion would usually be linked thematically to a pre-prepared topic. Thus, for instance, candidates taking AQA(a) English Literature – overwhelmingly the most popular of all A level specifications – would know that the unseen passage(s) they would be asked to discuss would be linked to the literature of war.

In defence of the awarding bodies, it should be said that this approach was not only pragmatic (with a specified minimum number of texts to be studied, there could no longer be the luxury of a whole paper devoted to unseen comment and analysis) but also a genuine attempt to integrate contextual study and close reading in a coherent way. But it is worth pointing out that A level English Literature specifications based on the QCA Subject Criteria are now out of step with other post-16 assessment models: the widely praised International Baccalaureate (IB) has an unseen critical appreciation paper; unseen comment and appreciation forms one third of the written assessment in the US Advanced Placement (AP) examination in English; the *Option Internationale* of the French Baccalauréat has compulsory unseen critical appreciation; the UCLES International A level, taken worldwide, has a popular Practical Criticism paper; and the new Cambridge Pre-U qualification in English has a compulsory Critical Appreciation paper worth 25% of the total marks. The lack of an equivalent method of assessment in the UK A level has been thrown into even starker relief by the decision of Oxford University English faculty to set an English Literature Admissions Test (ELAT) to be sat by every one of its applicants from 2007 onwards. This test is straightforwardly a test of comparative practical criticism. (See Chapter 5, pages 71–72.)

Close reading in the post-theory era

It appears that, after a period of strong reaction against a pedagogy and a methodology that could be dismissed as 'formalist' or 'Leavisite', in the post-theory era the tendency for teachers both at A level and in Higher Education is once again to speak unashamedly of close reading as a primary skill. In his book *On Literature* (2002) J. Hillis Miller has argued that:

> Slow reading, critical reading, means being suspicious at every turn, interrogating every detail of the work, trying to figure out by just what means the magic is wrought. This means attending not to the new world that is opened up by the work, but to the means by which that opening is brought about.[16]

He goes on to distinguish between the two forms of 'critical reading' that have characterised what he calls 'this demystification': 'rhetorical reading' and 'cultural criticism'. He argues that while 'cultural criticism is interrogation of the way a literary work inculcates beliefs about class, race or gender relations,' it is essential for the 'rhetorical reader to be adept in all the habits of 'close reading'.[17]

Elaine Showalter, too, argues the case for close reading. In *Teaching Literature* (2003) she takes issue with Terry Eagleton who

> jokes that close reading 'seemed to imply that every previous school of criticism had read only an average of three words per line', and that 'it encouraged the illusion that any piece of language ... can be adequately studied or even understood in isolation'.[18]

Her own view of the value of close reading is more positive:

> The close reading process, or *explication de texte*, that we use in analysing
> literary texts does not have to come with the ponderous baggage of the New
> Criticism, or with political labels. Before or along with attention to factors
> outside the text, students have to understand something about the verbal,
> formal, and structural elements of the words themselves. Close reading can
> be a neutral first step in understanding literature. But this sort of reading is
> far from intuitive, and if we want students to learn how to do it, we need to
> give them both models and practice.[19]

At this point we return to the statistics with which this discussion began. Showalter
is here addressing teachers of students in Higher Education. If close reading skills
are to be learned by students, then teachers must teach them. Unless sixth-form
students are given the opportunity to devote time to developing the 'habit of close
reading' (it is significant that both Eagleton and Hillis Miller use this phrase),
and unless teachers themselves have already developed this habit, then Higher
Education will continue to lament the absence of close reading skills in each
year's new intake. And since, as we have seen, almost half of English teachers in
secondary education do not have a degree in English, it is important to find and
promote new ways in which the habit can be shared.

One good example of a new way can be found on the website of the University
of Cambridge English Faculty, which maintains a virtual classroom, accessible to
students, and teachers (and anyone else). It has a section entitled 'Introduction to
Practical Criticism' and explains:

> The classes which follow this introduction are designed to introduce you to
> some of the methods and vocabulary of practical criticism, and to give some
> practical advice about how you can move from formal analysis of a poem and
> of its meaning to a full critical reading of it … Above all, however, the classes
> are intended to raise questions about how practical criticism can be used. Do
> poems look different if they are presented in isolation from the circumstances
> in which they were written or circulated? Do our critical responses to them
> change if we add in some contextual information after we have closely analysed
> them? Do our views of a poem change if we hear it read, if we see the original
> manuscript, or if instead of simply seeing the words on a page, as I.A. Richards
> would have wished, we see words on a screen?[20]

This kind of pedagogical approach, exemplifying Showalter's position ('a neutral
first step'), suggests perhaps one way of ensuring that in the future close reading
may no longer simply be what gets lost in transition.

4 | 'Context' in context

HEADMASTER: After all, it's not how much literature they know. What matters is how much they know about literature.

*(Alan Bennett **The History Boys**, 2004)*

What are we really talking about when we talk about context?

In the middle of Zadie Smith's *White Teeth* (2000) an English lesson is in progress. Miss Roody is struggling to get her class to discuss Shakespeare's Sonnet 127 (the first of the Dark Lady sonnets). She has asked them to comment on the line *Thy black is fairest in my judgement's place*. Irie, a fifteen-year-old London girl whose mother is second-generation West Indian and whose father is English, asks:

> 'Is she black?'
>   'Is who black?'
>   'The dark lady.'
>   'No, dear, she's *dark*. She's not black in the modern sense. There weren't any ... well, Afro-Carri-bee-yans in England at that time, dear. That's a more modern phenomenon, as I'm sure you know. But this was the 1600s. I mean I can't be sure, but it does seem terribly unlikely, unless she was a slave of some kind, and he's unlikely to have written a series of sonnets to a lord and then to a slave, is he?'[1]

Irie, puzzled by this put-down, replies:

> 'I just thought ... like when he says, here: *Then will I swear, beauty herself is black* ... And the curly hair thing, black wires – '
>   Irie gave up in the face of giggling and shrugged.
>   'No, dear. You're reading with a modern ear. Never read what is old with a modern ear. In fact that will serve as today's principle – can you all write that down please.'[2]

The teacher is asking Irie to read the sonnet in the context of Shakespeare's own time: to suppose, as Irie does, that the dark lady might look like her, is to take the poem out of context. This seems obvious but at the same time obviously wrong: Shakespeare is always being read with a modern ear, so why is not it a legitimate critical practice to place a text in a modern context?

In Shakespeare's own day, Queen Elizabeth I herself did this, when she objected to a performance of *Richard II* being staged at the time of the rebellion of the Earl of Essex: 'Know you not that I am Richard?' she demanded. The Laurence Olivier film version of *Henry V*, made in 1943 and released shortly before the Allied invasion of France, was designed to speak to the modern moment, Henry's successful campaign on Norman soil offering a good omen for the imminent Normandy landings. No audience today can watch *The Merchant of Venice* without having the memory of the Holocaust in the back of its mind. At the same time, though, it must remember that Shakespeare's earliest audiences might have had a very different perspective on the treatment of Shylock (see Chapter 8, pages 144–152). How important then is it, teaching Shakespeare or any other author, to put the text into context? And what context?

Contexts vs sources

The historical contextualising of Shakespeare has gathered momentum during the past forty years, partly as a reaction to the success of a book published in Britain in the 1960s, Jan Kott's *Shakespeare Our Contemporary*. The critic and playwright Tony Howard has summed up Kott's importance like this:

> *Shakespeare Our Contemporary* became amazingly controversial, really divisive. There were those who dismissed Kott as some obscure East European who was distorting Shakespeare (he stressed, for instance, that there is a great deal of cruelty, nightmarish elements, in *A Midsummer Night's Dream*). But on the other hand, led by theatre people like [Peter] Brook, many believed Kott was crystallising what has always been true – the fact that we don't just come to Shakespeare because he is great, eternal, and takes us back into the past, but because he is always reflecting the present. This found its way into the best work of the RSC and the National, and it's continued ever since. Certainly all the teaching or talking about Shakespeare that I've ever done has always been based on the assumption that *while we read Shakespeare to find out about the past, the true reason for using him is because, uniquely, he reflects the present and tells us about ourselves* [italics added].[3]

As teachers it is important to ask ourselves where we stand, before we try to teach students about context. Much of the emphasis on Shakespeare in context has come precisely from those who believe (as Tony Howard explains) that Kott's approach to Shakespeare distorts the plays. Since the 1980s the proponents of New Historicism and Cultural Materialism have argued that:

> Cultural contexts are often as important as specific sources in the attempt to understand a particular work. They place the literary text – as closely as a late-twentieth-century reader can – within the cultural milieu of its production.[4]

This explanation, by an American scholar and critic, Virginia Mason Vaughan, is important for two reasons. First, it acknowledges that contextualising has its limitations: different ages will have different, and always imperfect, ways of looking at the past. Second, it emphasises that texts do not spring fresh from the mind of individual writers who have not been conditioned in any way by the society in which they live: they are 'produced', ready for consumption, and they emerge from a 'cultural milieu' which is more significant than the single author whose name appears on the title page. Later in the Introduction to her book *Othello, A Contextual History*, Vaughan spells this out more fully:

> I also believe that historicising provides ways in and out of the text, bridging the gap between Shakespeare's age and our own ... Historical contexts can serve as a means to the end of understanding. They remind us that no truth is absolute, that our own readings and hearings take place within a discrete historical epoch and are therefore subject to qualification and even dismissal by future generations.[5]

If this is true for Shakespeare it must be true for all authors. In 2005 Cambridge University Press published a lengthy book of essays entitled *Jane Austen in Context*. It was an addition to the 'Cambridge Edition of the Works of Jane Austen', scholarly editions of all the novels, plus volumes of *Juvenilia* and *Later Manuscripts*. In the Preface to *Jane Austen in Context* the editor Janet Todd – also the editor of the whole series – writes:

> This volume of entries on aspects of Jane Austen's life, works and historical context necessarily speaks to the interests of the twenty-first century: it treats nationalism and empire as well as transport and the professions, print culture along with dress and manners, the agricultural background of her life as well as the literary.[6]

'This volume,' Janet Todd continues, 'simply aims to suggest ways of looking at the novels through this moment's version of late 18th- and early 19th-century history and culture.' There have of course been many books published about the background to Jane Austen's novels, most of them (like this one), identifying the author herself as the point of focus: *Jane Austen and Her World* or *Jane Austen's Bath*, etc. However, Janet Todd's remarks signal an important point about context and contextual study, that much of it is concerned with the way the present looks at the past ('this moment's version' of it) and the way the past speaks to the present. If we are teaching students to understand what is involved in working with context, we must make clear that it is always a two-way process. Our discussions about Jane Austen are in a sense a dialogue: we interrogate the novels and the novels speak to us, but students need to distinguish between the Austen who speaks from her time (the early 19th century) and the Austen whose voice could equally well belong to the 21st century.

Sometimes this is straightforward enough, but even so students will need help: if Mansfield Park is described as a 'modern-built' house, what exactly does modern mean here? Built within the last hundred, fifty or ten years? In what style – Palladian, Gothick? Does it imply (because it is not stated) that Sir Thomas Bertram built it himself with money made from his plantations in Antigua? We need to help students understand why (indeed, whether) these questions matter. When Jane Austen describes the Musgroves, in *Persuasion*, as being 'like their house', in undergoing a process of 'modernisation, perhaps of improvement', her irony has to be explained: 'modernisation' may be clear enough, but does 'improvement' carry the same undertones today that it did for Jane Austen?

Two further examples: the opening sentence of *Pride and Prejudice* ('It is a truth universally acknowledged …') articulates a view of money and marriage that may have belonged to the early 19th century but is not one widely shared today. By comparison, the key authorial comment in *Emma* – 'Seldom, very seldom does complete truth belong to any human disclosure; seldom can it happen that something is not a little disguised, or a little mistaken' – should still be recognised (even if not admitted) as a universal truth.

Background and foreground

There are, of course, dangers in contextual study. Simply turning background information into foreground is no help to students, and it is a frequent lament of university teachers that undergraduates arrive assuming that the downloading (in its most literal sense) of historical and biographical material is all that is needed for a good essay. That the more they can tell the reader about the life of an author, the closer they will get to understanding the texts written by that author, is one delusion students need to be warned about early on.

Equally dangerous, if texts become simply a source of historical information – documents of a period stripped of their literary significance – then students risk moving away from literary studies altogether and into historical or cultural studies. War poetry is a good example here. If the poems by Wilfred Owen or Siegfried Sassoon are treated primarily as sources of evidence for life in the trenches or of the terrors of No Man's Land, then are they not in a sense being devalued as literary texts? Why teach them in English classes if they are studied in History?

This is not to deny, of course, that such poems can make a contribution to students' understanding of the First World War, though some historians are now loudly challenging the picture of war presented by the poets – as if it were actually the job of poets to present objective accounts in the manner of a news reporter. Niall Ferguson for instance, in *The Pity of War* (the title taken, ironically, from Wilfred Owen) argues that:

> The persistence of the idea that the war was 'a bad thing' owes much to the genre known as 'war poetry' (usually meaning 'anti-war'), which became firmly established in British school curriculums [*sic*] in the 1970s ...[7]

Ferguson also blames recent writers such as Pat Barker (*Regeneration*) and Sebastian Faulks (*Birdsong*) as well as some historians – who, he implies, ought to have known better – for perpetuating what he almost calls the myth of the Great War; but he breaks off to conclude that

> it is important to recognise that these remain minority views. In fact, a remarkably large number of historians have insisted, and continue to insist, that the First World War was not 'senseless'. If it had its evil side then it was a necessary evil.[8]

In the ten years since his book was published it has become increasingly important to ask, as English teachers, how far we should contextualise any discussion of the poetry of the Great War in Ferguson's terms. We now have to redefine this poetry in the context of such historical revisionism, and the discussions of war poetry in Chapter 11 (pages 246–254) are an attempt to do just this.

It is interesting that Ferguson's approach – challenging the conventional wisdom and putting forward a strongly contrary argument – bears a clear resemblance to the approach advocated by the young History teacher, Irwin, in *The History Boys* (2004). During a lesson taught jointly by Irwin and their charismatic English teacher, Hector, the students discuss ways of writing about the Holocaust for their Oxbridge exams. When Hector asks, 'Why can you not simply condemn the camps outright as an unprecedented horror?' the boys, trained by Irwin, are first of all embarrassed by what they see as Hector's naïve question, then they challenge him:

> LOCKWOOD: No point, sir. Everybody will do that. That's the stock answer, sir ... the camps an event unlike any other, the evil unprecedented, etc., etc.[9]

Hector is outraged by this: 'Etcetera is what the Nazis would have said, the dead reduced to a mere verbal abbreviation.' Trying to get the students to focus on words not abstractions he asks, 'What have we learned about language?' But Lockwood is not to be deflected by his former mentor's attack, and his friends soon join in:

LOCKWOOD: All right, not etcetera. But given that the death camps are generally thought of as unique, wouldn't another approach be to show what precedents there were and put them ... well ... in proportion?
SCRIPPS: Proportion!
DAKIN: Not proportion then, but putting them in context.
POSNER: But to put something in context is a step towards saying it can be understood and that it can be explained. And if it can be explained it can be explained away.[10]

When Irwin chips in to congratulate Posner on making a good debating point, the boy replies, 'It isn't "good". I mean it, sir.' And what he means is that context and contextualising threaten the uniqueness of an event – or of a text.

Putting the claims of context into context

This neatly contextualises the danger of context; and it is the basis for Peter Barry's caution, in his book *English in Practice*, about allowing the emphasis on context to go too far:

Context, then, has its claims; but if we allow its unlimited expansion, without ever formulating criteria which put its claims in context, then we may find there is little left which can properly be called literary studies.[11]

Barry is concerned that the study of texts has now become secondary to the study of the historical circumstances and social conditions in which the texts were or are produced:

Context tends to overwhelm text, so that we begin to find that historical work progressively replaces textual work. The text is disenfranchised (we refuse to be figured by its bounds), and our standards and procedures become those of history. This is fine if we believe that History is the new English, but not otherwise.[12]

It is important to recognise that English Literature teachers have become caught in the middle of this debate. A contrary view to Barry's is expressed by Richard Jacobs, in *A Beginner's Guide to Critical Reading* (2001), who argues that 'texts and contexts are always in dynamic and volatile relations with each other and that the contexts of a text are multiple, changing over time and from reader to reader'. He continues:

We need to think of the making of meaning as a process that happens between the text and the reader, and that such meaning is socially and culturally produced, changing and various and multiple. We need to think of the writer as a product as well as a producer, and of texts as interventions in social process. And we need to think of contexts as a network of pressures and debates in which all readers are entangled. Readers too are products, subject to contexts. Contexts are the changing conditions of possibility for the production and consumption of the text. Contexts are the process whereby the text finds and makes a place in the world, the ways in which it is enabled to speak and the ways in which it makes a difference.[13]

If the theoretical position underpinning these comments is a combination of reader response and cultural materialism, the tone and terms of Jacobs' argument – 'product', 'producer', 'social process' – need to be highlighted and debated with students. It is worth asking the question, what difference would it make to an understanding of literary study if the words and phrases above were replaced by 'work of art', 'author' and 'creative process'? Nevertheless, Jacobs' image of contexts as 'a network of pressures and debates in which all readers are entangled' is a valuable one. Even better is his later description of the act of contextualising as 'an opening of doors on to other contexts, an opening out that returns us to the text in an adventure that never finishes'.[14]

This view of context and of the possibilities of contextualising as a critical practice is one that the discussions of individual texts, and of groups of texts, in Part 2 of this book seeks to exemplify. In addition, though, Part 2 seeks to demonstrate that context is only part of the story and that the real value of contextual study is to inform the close reading of texts. Even more important, if context can expand our view of a text and its meaning, close reading can (or should) keep the act of contextualising itself in context. If it doesn't, then the contexts may be false or falsely applied.

Again, *The History Boys* provides an instructive example: the discussion of Thomas Hardy's poem 'Drummer Hodge'. Hector encourages the boys to learn poems by heart. This process is viewed with scepticism by his colleague, the old-fashioned History teacher, Mrs Lintott, who asks 'What's all this learning by heart for, except as some sort of insurance against the boys' ultimate failure?'[15] It's a prophetic question since most of the boys do fail to live up to Hector's hopes for them. None more so than Posner, the least confident but most anxious to please of all the pupils, who has come to Hector one day having learned 'Drummer Hodge' by heart:

HECTOR: Good. Very good. Any thoughts?

Posner sits next to him.

POSNER: I wondered, sir, if this 'Portion of that unknown plain / Will Hodge for ever be' is like Rupert Brooke, sir. 'There's some corner of a foreign field ...' 'In that rich earth a richer dust concealed ...'

HECTOR: It is. It is. It's the same thought ... though Hardy's is better, I think ... more ... more, well down to earth. Quite literally, yes, down to earth. Anything about his name?

POSNER: Hodge?

HECTOR: Mmm – the important thing is that he has a name. Say Hardy is writing about the Zulu Wars or later the Boer War possibly, these were the first campaigns when soldiers ... or common soldiers ... were commemorated, the names of the dead recorded and inscribed on war memorials.[16]

We have already noticed how Hector misses the significance of the name Hodge (see Chapter 1, page 12) but here the memorialising context is valuable, throwing light on the title and making the reader aware of something that might otherwise have been overlooked. Here too, though, the naming significance is missed in the other contextualising that takes place here, when Posner reads back into Hardy an idea from Rupert Brooke. Reading one text in the context of another is one of the central skills that students have to learn, but it does Posner here no service to endorse (as Hector does) his misreading of the intertextual relationship between the two poems. Contrary to what Posner and Hector think, Hardy's thought is actually the precise opposite of Brooke's; and if Hector had paid as much attention to the title of Brooke's poem as he did to 'Drummer Hodge', he would not have said that 'It's the same thought'.

Brooke's sonnet is called 'The Soldier' – the individual's name being explicitly withheld: his identity, once he is buried in a foreign field, is to be subsumed in that of England's. By his own assertion he is to become a patriotic metonym, a part representing the whole. Drummer Hodge's destiny, by contrast, is far from metonymic: the 'mound' beneath which he lies 'uncoffined' will never be 'forever England': indeed, Hodge himself 'never knew' what he had died for and England does not value him: he is thrown into 'a common grave' and becomes for ever 'a portion of that unknown plain' where his forgotten, decomposing corpse will eventually nourish 'some Southern tree'– African, rather than English. Hardy's poem – and Hardy's conception of the English soldier – is certainly worth comparing with Brooke's, but Hector has missed the essential point of contrast by giving more weight to the context than to the text. Hector may be a charismatic English teacher but Bennett is careful to show that he is also a flawed one.

'Enlarging the frame of attention'

Hector's misreadings of Hardy serve as a cautionary tale, but the tale is not meant to undermine the value of context and contextual study: it serves, rather, to demonstrate how close reading and context should be part of the same critical approach to texts, not opposites always in tension. His reading of 'Drummer Hodge' is not close enough to allow him to interpret the poem adequately in the context of Brooke's sonnet. Reconciling what have often been taken as opposites in literary studies is at the heart of the practice of contextual close reading, a point made forcefully by Rick Rylance and Judy Simons in one of the most influential books to have been published since the advent of Curriculum 2000, *Literature in Context*:

> Should critical attention be primarily aimed at the appreciation – in the widest sense – of textual detail, focused on the particular words to be found in particular works? Or should it enlarge the frame of attention by placing literary works in wider contextual relationships? The answer is, of course, that it should do neither exclusively. A criticism which is not in confident possession of a text's detail is unlikely to be convincing when it moves to assessing its relationship to context. By the same token, a commentary which is ill-informed about the contexts in which works are written and received seems wilfully to deny those important parts of literary works which make strong connections with the world that surrounds them.[17]

The word appreciation 'in its widest sense' implies defining the key features and evaluating the impact of a text. In terms of contextual close reading, it implies trying to 'spotlight' (Rylance and Simons again) 'the relationship between textual detail and the surrounding range of factors which bear upon the creation and understanding of its significance.'[18] Demonstrating this relationship to students, and teaching them how to explore and apply it themselves is a central task in teaching Literature. It is also the central focus of Chapter 6 of this book, which attempts to demonstrate the principle Rylance and Simons prescribe by an extended discussion of Wordsworth's sonnet 'Composed Upon Westminster Bridge, September 3rd 1803'.

5 | Moving on: from 'English Literature' to 'English Studies'

'Definition of an academic subject: nothing with "Studies" in its name.'
*(John Clare, quondam **Daily Telegraph** Education correspondent)*

It's not so long ago that 'English' as an A level subject title meant 'the study of Literature': for some Awarding Bodies it was used like this until the advent of Curriculum 2000. At university it can still mean this; just as at one time a degree called 'English Language and Literature' meant Literature plus Anglo-Saxon, or Literature with a token paper on the study of language. Now, it is necessary for puzzled Admissions Tutors to distinguish between A level 'English Language', 'English Language and Literature' and 'English Literature' – three separate subjects with three separate sets of Subject Criteria and methodologies. Even 'English Literature', which has been the focus of this book, can be broken down into three: Literature itself, 'literary study' and 'literary studies'. It may be helpful to distinguish between them like this:

Literature: the subject as defined by the body of knowledge to which it refers – English Literature, the canonical and extra-canonical texts and authors who form the object of study.

Literary study: study involving texts which define themselves as 'literary' rather than non-literary.

Literary studies: the study of literature, and the study of what studying literature involves (how we read, as well as what we read).

The QCA Subject Criteria for English Literature (revised 2006) use the term 'literary studies' without defining it, though making clear that the subject is solidly based on the study of literary texts:

> AS and A level studies in English literature should build on the knowledge, understanding and skills established at GCSE introducing students to the discipline of advanced literary studies and should require reading of the major literary genres of poetry, prose and drama.[1]

In university English departments, it is more likely that the subject will still be referred to simply as English: indeed, the QAA Benchmark Statement defines 'English' as

> a versatile academic discipline characterised by the rigorous and critical study of literature and language. It is concerned with the production, reception and interpretation of written texts, both literary and non-literary; and with the nature, history and potential of the English language.[2]

Notice how each step of this definition prioritises literature before language, writing before speaking. Indeed, the investigation of spoken English quickly shades off into Linguistics, taught in different departments by people who speak a different academic language.

'Read the prospectus': what universities want

How then should teachers help their A level students navigate their way through the university and departmental prospectuses in search of the right English course on the right university campus? The basic answer is, by not leaving the students to do it all themselves. Hard pressed enough as they are, teachers should put themselves in the shoes of their own sixth-form students beginning to explore the university and English Faculty websites. To do so is to realise what a bewildering variety of courses and approaches to literary study are on offer. And since students applying to UK universities usually prepare their applications during the fourth term of a two-year course, this exploration needs to begin earlier, perhaps as early as the second term of the AS year. This is the time when students need most help and support from their teachers, for the undergraduate pages of an online prospectus for English can look frankly intimidating:

> The course aims to revisit big methodological questions that your previous training at school or college may have circumscribed, and to revitalise your work as you approach it at undergraduate level.[3]

This was Oxford's website in 2008, hinting – in language opaque to most students and perhaps startling to some teachers – that schools should have spent more time making explicit the 'big methodological questions' that underpin literary studies. There is also the hint that students will need to have their work and their enthusiasm for the subject brought back to life – after the deadening way it was taught at school or as a result of the hurdles of AS and A level assessment? Oxford doesn't say, but at least this is a wake-up call to A level teachers: their students, this is suggesting, should have had the chance to ask what, why and how literature should be studied. When the QCA Subject Criteria confront this question, under the heading 'Knowledge and Understanding', they produce this formula:

> Specifications should require students to use their detailed knowledge and understanding of individual works of literature to explore relationships between texts and to appreciate the significance of cultural and contextual influences on readers and writers.

It is context, even more than close reading, which now provides the link between literary studies at A level and at university. The prospectuses spell this out emphatically, if not elegantly. Here are a few examples:

> The course aims to … enable study of text in historical/cultural contexts and develop appreciation of significance of such contexts on the representation of allegedly 'universal' concepts; to appreciate how our own historical/cultural location affects our understanding of literature.[4]

Again the sub-text here (from the Manchester online prospectus) is that new undergraduates are likely to arrive assuming that texts contain a 'universal', essentialist meaning, a false idea they need to unlearn as quickly as possible. Exeter's prospectus defines the 'discipline-specific skills' students will be able to demonstrate, after completing the introductory module 'Past and Present 1':

> a basic ability to analyse the literature of an earlier era and to relate its concerns and its modes of expression to its historical context

> a basic ability to interrelate texts and discourses specific to their own discipline with issues in the wider context of cultural and intellectual history.[5]

Once more, the terms here need to be unpacked for the benefit of students. We can see from these examples how universities expect that new undergraduates will already have some understanding of what the discipline of literary studies involves. But how many students, just embarking on the second year of a two-year advanced course, could fully grasp what is meant by interrelating 'texts and discourses with issues in the wider context of cultural and intellectual history'? Will they understand – will they have been invited to think about? – the significance of 'discourses' (plural)? This is why they need more help – often, a great deal more help – in interpreting university English course descriptions when they go online.

Perhaps they order these things better abroad. Here is a description of a first-year course (English 111: 'Literature from Sonnets to Comics') offered by the University of Auckland, New Zealand:

We enjoy a wide range of texts – poetry, drama, novel, novella, satire, live-action film, animated film, comic, children's story – as we work back gradually from the 21st century to Shakespeare. We explore texts, terms, contexts, theory and approaches. We consider new findings about human minds and human nature relevant to literature and life. We stress creative and critical thinking and reading and writing, in our authors and in our responses to them.[6]

This sounds more accessible, and simply more fun. Even here, though, students need some guidance and perhaps some caution: the reading list is formidable and the course is either cramming in a great deal into a single semester, or it is going to offer only a cursory glance at each author (including Shakespeare and Tolstoy) while expecting students to do most of the work themselves. In fact, of course, this is one of the key difficulties many students encounter when they first make the transition to reading English at university: they will have a great deal to read and they will not spend nearly so much time analysing individual texts or even groups of texts as they did at school.

Face-to-face teaching and independent study

The annual university lament that new students arrive expecting to be spoonfed is both justified and unjustified. The way AS and A level teaching has been structured since the advent of Curriculum 2000 has allowed much less time for students to learn the arts of independent study. To pre-empt complaints from students – and increasingly from their parents – some university prospectuses now spell out how much face-to-face teaching a student should expect to receive for each module: Durham's English Department estimates that each of its modules will demand 200 hours of study, of which only 25.5 hours will involve face-to-face teaching – and the bulk of that (21 hours) will be in lectures, the rest in tutorials and essay handing-back sessions. By contrast students should expect to spend 174.5 hours reading in detail the texts to be discussed during the course and the recommended background, critical and theoretical texts to accompany them.

York also spells out the implications of workload and contact hours:

Studying for a degree is a full-time job, and undergraduates are expected to devote around 40 hours a week to their university studies. Formal contact hours vary from term to term … however, you will be expected to spend much of your time as an independent scholar, not only engaging with primary texts and critical responses to them but also researching the cultural and historical contexts out of which literature springs.[7]

'The cultural and historical contexts out of which literature springs': phrases like this occur in prospectus after prospectus, but it is significant to find it here linked explicitly to the idea of independent research. York, acknowledging that most students 'are on a steep learning curve regarding independent study', offers *Historical Approaches to Literature*, a second-term course aimed at 'developing skills in historical and contextual interpretation and research'.

It is therefore worth spending time discussing how such courses might actually be taught, what students should expect to have to do for themselves and what their tutors will expect of them. With short and pressurised university terms (not forgetting the probability that many students will also need to find part-time jobs), anticipating how they'll need to work on their own from the start of term one is really important. In spite of all the other pressures of teaching an advanced syllabus to students who are studying at least two – and possibly a lot more than two – other A level subjects, preparing students for transition to university literary study is essential. How, for instance, should a teacher help a student understand what will be involved in a module such as this, from Stanford University?

> *Masterpieces of Contemporary Literature* – Prose, poetic and dramatic works from the late 19th century to the present; focus is on British literature. Social, cultural and historic contexts of writers such as Woolf, Eliot, Forster and Joyce; how their experimentations with form and narrative voice reflected major technological, political, and aesthetic concerns such as WWI, suffrage debates, and empire. Questions of legacy: how writers in today's post-colonial Britain, such as Zadie Smith and Ian McEwan, are inheritors of literary movements as well as innovators.[8]

It's clear from this description that, despite its title, *Masterpieces of Contemporary Literature* is not going to cover only literature that students would regard as contemporary: a more accurate title might be 'Modernism and its inheritors'. The idea of legacy is an interesting one, which ensures that the discussion does not get exclusively bound up in the discourse of post-colonial theory. It's interesting, too, how the title of this course announces that the focus is to be on texts as works of art ('Masterpieces') while the emphasis in the course description is actually on placing authors, rather than their individual works, in context.

The QAA Benchmark Statement for English

Once again, for A level students who will be fully occupied completing their first year or starting their second year courses, thinking in these much broader terms will be a challenge. It is good that the revised Subject Criteria for English Literature put much more emphasis on studying texts comparatively, in clusters and in the context of themes, genres, etc. Even so, prospective university applicants still need encouragement to start thinking in these broader terms when making their applications or if going for interview. A valuable starting point, as a teacher, would be to spend some time comparing the QAA Benchmark Statement of English with the QCA Subject Criteria, to see where they converge and where the Benchmark Statement places its main emphasis. The points of continuity and difference can then be highlighted with students, as part of the help given to them as they start to think about the transition from A level to degree level English.

It is worth, however, remembering that the Subject Criteria are mandatory and prescriptive: they set out the minimum that must be taught and must be covered in examinations. They specify how the examinations must be structured, and they tie teaching and assessment explicitly to the Assessment Objectives. It is this, more than anything else, which has caused English to be so heavily circumscribed since the introduction of Curriculum 2000. In effect, it makes 'teaching to the test' inevitable. By contrast, the QAA Benchmark Statement is essentially descriptive rather than prescriptive, synthesising the various strands of course provision from English Faculties throughout Britain. It is in no sense a statutory document, though individual English departments are now increasingly going out of their way to show how their courses are consistent with the Benchmark Statement.

Aims, Objectives, Learning Outcomes

Perhaps the most helpful way in which these QCA and QAA documents are aligned is that each highlights the Aims, Objectives and Learning Outcomes for A level and for degree level courses. The QAA Learning Outcomes are defined under the following headings: subject-specific knowledge, subject-specific skills, and key (transferable) skills. Where individual departments also use these headings (or variations of them) it is possible to tell quite quickly what the main characteristics of the English teaching in that department will be. For example, the Aims for English Literature (course code Q300) as taught at Durham, whose English Department was judged the leading department in the UK in 2007, are as follows:

Aims
- to recruit students of the highest calibre and potential who hold a strong interest in English literature
- to provide, facilitate and monitor high-quality teaching and learning in a flourishing and productive research environment
- in line with modular principles of flexibility and student choice, to offer a syllabus and approaches which maintain the canon of English literature and allow students to explore non-canonical areas

- to develop students' conceptual and analytical skills by exposing them to a variety of literary critical approaches
- to promote and develop, to a high degree of competence, a range of skills which are at once subject specific and transferable, will fit them for a wide variety of professions and employment, and encourage a lifelong engagement with literature.[9]

At first glance this list offers a rather conservative set of aims: the emphasis is explicitly on the study of literature, and on maintaining the canon of English Literature (while allowing students 'to explore non-canonical areas': some English Departments have tended to put the emphasis the other way round – one famously offering a paper called 'Firing the Canon'). On the other hand, teachers and students will be heartened to see that the course aims to 'encourage a lifelong engagement with literature': here school and university aims for English Literature coincide.

They might similarly be encouraged by one of the Aims and Objectives announced by York, for its introductory module, Approaches to Literature: 'By the end of this course you will be expected to demonstrate *an appreciation of the power of imagination in literary creation*' [italics added][10]. And this is not just a pious statement at the start of the Prospectus: it is threaded into the later descriptions of individual modules:

> A major focus of this module is the exploration of relationships between literary texts and the historical, social and political contexts, which shaped their imaginative creation. Lectures and seminars will therefore pay particular attention to cross-cutting themes such as class, industrialisation, religion, travel, imperialism and science. Key movements such as realism and decadence also prompt us to consider the connections between literature and other art forms (music, painting, etc.).[11]

Appreciation, imagination, creation: teachers should ensure that students look out for these words when trawling the English department websites and prospectuses. And if all this seems suddenly daunting to students thinking of English as the subject for them, some English Departments have advice and reassurance on hand. Here is Cambridge:

> **How can I prepare for an application?** There is no easy answer to this, except possibly the words of John Milton: 'read any books whatever come to thy hands, for thou art sufficient both to judge aright, and to examine each matter'. To read widely, and to read works outside your A level syllabus, is the best preparation for applying for any English course.[12]

It is significant that for the Milton quartercentenary (2008) Cambridge students of English from Milton's old college, Christ's, produced a special *Paradise Lost* website: www.christs.cam.ac.uk/darknessvisible. Exceptionally well presented, full of insight, close reading and good contextual material, this website – perhaps more than anything else anxious sixth-formers will find in their searches – shows how much pleasure and reward students can get from reading English Literature at university.

> *Non minima pars eruditionis est bonos nosse libros* ('Not the least part of erudition is to know good books' – inscription over the door of Bishop Cosin's Library, University of Durham)

Preparing students (i): poetry and translation

For students wondering whether to read English at university, poetry often remains the greatest barrier. Many find it simply less interesting than working on fiction and drama. Their teachers, too, may find it less appealing to teach. The range of poetry being taught at A level continues to narrow, fewer students encountering Chaucer, Milton or the metaphysical poets even when these are offered as set texts.

In turn, Admissions Tutors and those teaching first-year undergraduates often lament this lack of interest in poetry. Those few who still expect a student to arrive having at least a brief acquaintance with *Paradise Lost* sigh about falling standards in sixth-forms, and ask whether the new students have been taught anything at all.

Such comments do less than justice to the subject and to its teachers. Teaching poetry is a demanding art, but one worth using from the start of a course to challenge bright students and to encourage them to think more widely and deeply about the nature of literary study. Getting students to work together on a difficult poem, using such a poem as the starting point for research and exploration of the text, or of other texts to which it may be linked, is always worthwhile. Indeed it is a necessary step in the process of transition.

The following discussion takes as its starting point ways of teaching two recent and difficult poems by Seamus Heaney. From there it moves on to raise issues of translation with which students can also engage. The point is to help both students and teachers broaden their horizons by working on texts that might at first seem 'too difficult' or 'too remote' from their main AS or A level courses. If Admissions Tutors are looking for students who are willing to go beyond the limits of the syllabus and explore English Literature for themselves, teachers must encourage every stage of this exploration.

Bann Valley Eclogue*

(*Sicelides Musae, paulo maiora canamus*. Virgil, Eclogue IV)

1 POET:
Bann Valley Muses, give us a song worth singing.
Something that rises like the curtain in
Those words *And it came to pass* or *In the beginning*.
Help me to please my hedge-schoolmaster Virgil
And the child that's due. Maybe, heavens, sing
Better times for her and her generation.

2 VIRGIL:
Here are my words you'll have to find room for:
Carmen, ordo, nascitur, saeculum, gens,
Ferrea, aurea, scelus, Lucina.
Their gist in your tongue and province should be clear
Even at this stage. Poetry, order, the times,
The nation, wrong and renewal, iron and gold.

3 POET:
Lucina. Rhyming with Sheena. Vocative, First
Declension. Feminine gender. The Roman
St. Anne. Who is *casta Lucina*, chaste
Star of the birth-bed. And secular star,
Meaning star of the *saeculum*, brightness gathering
Head great month by month now, waiting to fall.

4
You were raised on the land they drove your father off.
You had his country accent and little to learn
Of the facts of life when you read your first poems out
To Octavian, feeling the length of the line
As if you were dressing husks off a hank of tow
Or measuring wheal for thatch. Holding your own

5
In your own way. *Pietas* and stealth. If ex-servicemen
Were cocks of the walk at home, hexameters
Would rule the roost in Rome. You would understand us
Latter-day scholarship boys and girls, on the cusp
Between elocution and *duchas*. Faces that were japped
With cowdung once now barefaced to camera, live.

6 VIRGIL:
Whatever stains you, you rubbed it into yourselves,
Earth mark, birth mark, mould like the bloodied mould
On Romulus's ditch-back. When the waters break
Bann's stream will overflow, the old markings
Will avail no more to keep east bank from west.
The valley will be washed like the new baby.

7 POET:
Pacatum orbem: your words are too much nearly.
Even 'orb' by itself. What on earth could match it?
And then last month, mid morning, the wind dropped.
An Avernus chill, birdless and dark, prepared.
A firstness steadied, a lastness, a born awareness
As name dawned into knowledge: I saw the orb.

8 VIRGIL:
Eclipses won't be for this child. The cool she'll know
Will be the pram hood over her vestal head.
Big dog daisies will get fanked up in the spokes.
She'll lie on summer evenings listening to
A chug and slug going on in the milking parlour.
Let her never hear close gunfire or explosions.

9 POET:
Why do I remember St Patrick's mornings,
Being sent by my mother to the railway line
For the little trefoil, untouchable almost, the shamrock
With its twining, binding, creepery, tough, thin roots
All over the place, in the stones between the sleepers.
Dew-scales shook off the leaves. Tear-ducts asperging.

10
Child on the way, it won't be long until
You land among us. Your mother's showing signs,
Out for her sunset walk among big round bales.
Planet earth like a teething ring suspended
Hangs by its world-chain. Your pram waits in the corner.
Cows are let out. They're sluicing the milk-house floor.

11
We know, little one, you have to start with a cry
But smile soon too, a big one for your mother.
Unsmiling life has had it in for people
For far too long. But now you have it in you
Not to be wrong-footed but to first-foot us
And, muse of the valley, give us a song worth singing.

* All eleven stanzas were originally published in 1999; when the poem was re-published in *Electric Light* (2001) only stanzas 1, 2 and 6 to 10 were retained, and two of the stanzas had been significantly altered.[13]

Getting started

A poem like Seamus Heaney's 'Bann Valley Eclogue' challenges any reader, no matter what their age and experience of reading poetry. For any student whose previous experience of Heaney has been limited to a few of his earliest poems, it may appear off-putting with its obscure references, its Latin, its form – 'What is an eclogue, anyway?' Yet reading difficult poetry, and beginning to see ways of exploring it, is valuable experience for any students and, beyond that, raises some very interesting questions:

- Where is the Bann Valley? Why is it an important place for Heaney?
- What is a Muse? Why does the poem begin with 'Bann Valley Muses'?
- What is an eclogue? What is special about Virgil's Fourth Eclogue?
- Why is the Fourth Eclogue important as a way of understanding this poem?
- What similarities does Heaney find between himself and the Roman poet?
- What is the significance for this poem of a) Hesiod and the Golden Age?
  b) Lucina (and why is she 'the Roman St Anne'?) c) Avernus?
- How does this poem relate to a particular historical moment?
- What is a hedge-school and why does the speaker in the poem call Virgil his 'hedge-schoolmaster'?
- What links this poem with others, such as Wordsworth's 'Ode on Intimations of Immortality', W.B. Yeats' 'The Second Coming' and 'Prayer for My Daughter', Louis MacNeice's 'Prayer before Birth'?
- Which other poems by Heaney help to make this poem clearer, or are themselves clarified for you by 'Bann Valley Eclogue'? (Try, for instance, Heaney's poem 'Making Strange'.)

These in turn lead on to other questions, focusing on the poem itself as poetry and on a reader's response to it:

- How much work should a reader have to do in tracking down and understanding the references in a poem?
- How important are the changes made to the poem by Heaney himself between its first appearance in print (*Times Literary Supplement*, 4th October, 1999) and its later appearance in *Electric Light* (2001)?
- How does 'Bann Valley Eclogue' relate to Heaney's other, earlier poetry, and to other poems in the collection in which it appears?

As with all good English teaching, the teacher's first job here is to ask questions about the poem that will prompt students to start asking other questions of their own; then to act as chairman or facilitator, enabling the group to try reaching a consensus about their answers, to establish a collective appreciation of the poem and an assessment of what they have learned from asking these questions and looking for the answers. It may of course be impossible to reach unanimity. This does not matter; students need to learn that, concerning literary judgment, it is in the common pursuit, rather than in the common conclusion, that the value of the exercise lies. In the meantime, they need help to get going, and 'Bann Valley Eclogue' provides an excellent starting point for Internet research that has nothing to do with looking for a pre-written essay to download.

It is interesting and humbling to work at a difficult poem like this first with a group of other teachers: trying it for ourselves makes us more patient with our students when they attempt to find answers to the same questions. 'Bann Valley Eclogue' also offers a valuable insight into the way poets wrestle with poetry in the making, and raises the question, 'When is a poem complete?' (Paul Valéry was admired by W.H. Auden for saying that a poem is never finished; it is only abandoned.)

The poem and its publishing history

Heaney's poem was commissioned by the Poet Laureate, Andrew Motion, who had invited a number of poets to write a poem to be broadcast on National Poetry Day (October 1st) 1999. Since this poem describes a specific event – a total eclipse of the sun – which happened on August 11th that year it was probably drafted in no more than six weeks. Heaney duly read extracts on the BBC on October 1st and three days later published 'Bann Valley Eclogue' as an eleven-stanza poem in the *Times Literary Supplement*. It was a shock, therefore, to find that when it appeared in his next collection, *Electric Light* (2001), it had been significantly shortened (see page 55, above).

Which, now, is the 'whole' poem? What, if anything, is gained or lost by publishing a final shorter version? Why does Heaney omit the stanzas that deal specifically with the correspondence between his family's history and Virgil's? What are the effects of omitting the last stanza? Working together on questions such as these enables students to see at first hand what is involved in asking questions about a poem's publishing history, about the stability of texts and the validity of contexts: In what ways does Virgil's *Fourth Eclogue* (whose importance is signalled by Heaney's epigraph) provide a way into this poem both from a contextual, and from an intertextual, perspective?

Between 1999 and 2001, Heaney also revised two of the individual stanzas. Stanza 2 was re-published like this:

> Here are my words you'll have to find room for:
> *Carmen, ordo, nascitur, saeculum, gens,*
> Their gist in your tongue and province should be clear
> Even at this stage. Poetry, order, the times,
> The nation, wrong and renewal, then an infant birth
> And a flooding away of all the old miasma.

Stanza 7 also had changes: lines three and four had originally read:

> And then, last month, mid-morning, the wind dropped.
> An Avernus chill, birdless and dark, prepared.

Now, revised, it appeared like this:

> And then, last month, at noon-eclipse, wind dropped.
> A millennial chill, birdless and dark, prepared.

Are there gains and losses here, or just losses? Are the changes made on the basis of accuracy ('mid-morning' corrected to 'noon-eclipse') or of accessibility for future readers who won't remember the specific eclipse to which Heaney refers? When the poem first appeared it was only a month since the eclipse had been front-page news worldwide. Which versions work better in terms of their impact on the reader or listener: imagery, rhythm, sound? Reading later versions of the poem in the context of earlier versions – indeed reading late poems by Heaney in the context of his earlier and (for most people) better-known poetry – opens up a poem such as 'Bann Valley Eclogue' in new and unexpected ways. And this is doubly so when the poem is also read in the context of other writing to which it is intertextually related, explicitly or implicitly. Above all, it focuses on the way in which poetry is an ongoing dialogue between the poets of the present and the poets of the past: students need to reflect on T.S. Eliot's comments from his essay 'Tradition and the Individual Talent' (1920):

The difference between the present and the past is that the conscious present is an awareness of the past in a way and to an extent which the past's awareness of itself cannot show.

Someone said: 'The dead writers are remote from us because we *know* so much more than they did.' Precisely, and they are that which we know.[14]

Heaney's poetry exemplifies this almost better than Eliot's own. Nearly every poem in his next collection, *District and Circle* (2006) can show this. Let students try to apply the questions asked of 'Bann Valley Eclogue' to one of its key poems, 'To George Seferis in the Underworld'.

To George Seferis in the Underworld

The men began arguing about the spiky bushes that were in brilliant yellow bloom on the slopes: were they caltrop or gorse? ... 'That reminds me of something,' said George. 'I don't know ...'

That greeny stuff about your feet
is asphodel and rightly so
but why do I think *seggans?*

And of a spring day
in your days of '71: Poseidon
making waves in sea and air
around Cape Sounion, its very name
all ozone-breeze and cavern-boom,
too utterly this-worldly, George, for you
intent upon an otherworldly scene
somewhere just beyond
the summit ridge, the cutting edge
of not remembering.

The bloody light. To hell with it.
Close eyes and concentrate.
Not crown of thorns, not sceptre reed
or Herod's court, but ha!
you had it! A harrowing, yes, in hell:
the hackle-spikes
that Plato told of, the tyrant's fate
in a passage you would quote:
'They bound him hand and foot,
they flung him down and flayed him,
gashing his flesh on thorny *aspalathoi*
and threw him into Tartarus, torn to shreds.'

As was only right
for a tyrant. But maybe,
dare I say it, George, for you
too much i' the right,
if still your chance to strike
against his ilk,
a last word meant to break
your elected silence.

And for me a chance to test the edge
of a word like *seggans,* smuggle it back in
like a dialect blade, hoar and harder
than what it has turned into
these latter days:
sedge, marshmallow, rubber-dagger stuff.

This poem first appeared in the *Times Literary Supplement* in 2004, and was
later reprinted, with revisions to the last two stanzas, in *District and Circle*.[15] The
epigraph (unattributed by the poet, and left hanging as a kind of clue) comes from
Roderick Beaton's biography of the Greek Nobel prize-winning poet, George Seferis,
who died in 1971:

> After lunch, they climbed the hill opposite the ancient temple. This was an
> ordeal for George, but he was full of enthusiasm. The men began arguing
> about the spiky bushes that were in brilliant yellow bloom on the slopes: were
> they caltrop or gorse? Pavlopoulos recalled the popular name, in Greek, from
> an old folk song. That reminds me of something,' said George. 'I don't know
> …'. And he would say nothing more, all the way back to Athens. That night, as
> George explained afterwards to Pavlopoulos, he had found the word he was
> looking for: it was *aspalathoi*.[16]

After this discovery, Seferis wrote what was to be his last poem, *'Epi Aspalathoi'*
('On Gorse'), an attack on the military junta in Greece against whom he had been
a powerful critic:

'On Aspalathoi …'
Sounion was lovely that spring day –
The Feast of the Annunciation.
Sparse green leaves around rust-coloured stone,
Red earth, and aspalathoi
With their huge thorns and their yellow flowers
Already out.
In the distance the ancient columns, strings of a harp still vibrating …

Peace.
What could have made me think of Aridaios?
Possibly a word in Plato, buried in the mind's furrows:
The name of the yellow bush
Hasn't changed since his time.
That evening I found the passage:
    'They bound him hand and foot,' it says,
    'they flung him down and flayed him,
    they dragged him along
    gashing his flesh on thorny aspalathoi,
    and they went and threw him into Tartarus, torn to shreds.'

In this way Aridaios, the terrible Pamphylian tyrant,
Paid for his crimes in the nether world.[17]

Vision and revision

The questions students need to research here include:

- Why should the politics and poetry of George Seferis have appealed to Seamus Heaney?
- How does Heaney make use in his own poem of Seferis's poem 'Aspalathoi'?
- What does the phrase 'elected silence' in Heaney's poem refer to with reference to Seferis?
- What do you think of the changes Heaney made to the last two stanzas when the poem was published in *District and Circle* in 2006?

As was only right
for a tyrant. But still, for you, maybe
too much i' the right, too black and white,
if still your chance to strike
against his ilk,
a last word meant to break
your much contested silence.

And for me a chance to test the edge
of *seggans*, dialect blade
hoar and harder and more hand-to-hand
than what is common usage nowadays:
sedge marshmallow, rubber-dagger stuff.

Both 'Bann Valley Eclogue' and 'To George Seferis in the Underworld' have been praised and attacked by critics (reviews of the poems, from both angles, can easily be found on the Internet). Getting students to work in groups to research, discuss and appreciate poems as demanding as these can unlock some of the doors barring access to modern poetry. This kind of work could well provide matter for AS or A2 coursework: it not only gives students confidence to approach a poem through its difficulties rather than through the easier passages, it also encourages them to debate and to argue about poetry, knowing that there is no single right answer.

Issues of translation

It's significant, too, that in both these poems, Heaney is preoccupied with issues of translation. In 'Bann Valley Eclogue' he is told to find room in his language for words from Virgil's Fourth Eclogue. But which is his language – Irish (Gaelic) or English? In 'To George Seferis' he is as puzzled by the Gaelic word *seggans*, a word which has, he feels, lost a power that he wants to recover. His conclusion is that language (specifically the English language) is no longer serious enough for the political realities about which he tries to write. Using it has become – even for a poet – a child's game: 'rubber-dagger stuff'.

Translation in fact is another valuable avenue to explore when helping students to respond to poetry. Here is a second translation of '*Aspalathoi*' – this time by the poet and biographer, Peter Levi. Few will be able to translate from modern Greek, but putting two translations side by side gives students a chance to analyse and evaluate different effects achieved by two English-language versions of the same poem:

It was beautiful, Sounion, that day of the Annunciation
again in the spring season.
A handful of green leaves among the rusty rocks
the red earth and the gorse
with big needles ready and yellow bloom.
Far off the ancient columns, strings of a harp still echoing ...
Tranquillity.

What could have reminded me of Aridaios?
I think one word in Plato, lost in the channels of the mind;
the name of the yellow bush
has not altered since those times.
In the evening I found the passage;
'They bound him hand and foot', he tells us,
'they threw him down and flayed him,
dragged him to pieces, tore him apart
on the thorny gorse-bushes
and went and flung him into hell in rags.'
So in the world below he payed his crimes,
Pamphylian Aridaios, most miserable tyrant.[18]

- Where do the translations vary most sharply?
- Which of these two translations, as a poem, makes the bigger impact?
- These English versions of the Seferis poem contain a further translation – of a passage quoted in 'Aspalathoi' by Seferis (originally from Plato's *Republic* 'They bound him … hell in rags' / 'torn to shreds'). Which seems the more plausible, and which the more vivid, translation?

The politics of translation

Any discussion of what is gained and lost in translation, both literally and politically, can benefit from taking place in the context of Brian Friel's play *Translations* (1981). When a troop of English soldiers arrives in a remote Irish village to re-map the area and to anglicise all the local Irish place names, the officers are astonished to find that the local peasant people can talk fluently in Latin and Greek but know hardly a word of English. Lieutenant Yolland is the officer responsible for changing all the names on the new map of Ireland. He senses that his Englishness, epitomised by his inability to speak another language, means that he will never be accepted:

> Even if I did speak Irish I'd always be an outsider here, wouldn't I? I may learn the password but the language of the tribe will always elude me, won't it?[19]

And when one of the locals, Hugh, quotes at him a poem he has written in Latin, 'after the style of Ovid' which he then has to translate into English, Yolland silently agrees with him that 'English succeeds in making it sound … plebeian.' The paradox of the play is that the Irish peasants are, in their language and literature, much more sophisticated than their English colonisers, but they have to admit that they too are trapped by language. As Hugh says to Yolland:

> I understand your sense of exclusion, of being cut off from a life here […] but remember that words are signals, counters. They are not immortal. And it can happen that a civilisation can be imprisoned in a linguistic contour that no longer matches the contour of … fact.[20]

Translation then can free those who are trapped in and by a language; it can also express powerfully a sense of exclusion and loss. Indeed, if Robert Frost is right that 'poetry is what gets lost in translation' let students test this out for themselves. Here, for instance, is a well-known poem by Yeats followed by a translation by the leading French poet Yves Bonnefoy:

Down by the Salley Gardens

Down by the Salley Gardens my love and I did meet;
She passed the Salley Gardens with little snow-white feet.
She bid me take love easy, as the leaves grow on the tree;
But I, being young and foolish, with her would not agree.

In a field by the river my love and I did stand,
And on my leaning shoulder she laid her snow-white hand.
She bid me take life easy, as the grass grows on the weirs;
But I was young and foolish, and now am full of tears.

Au Bas des Jardins de Saules

Au bas des jardins de saules je t'ai rencontrée, mon amour.
Tu passais les jardins de saules d'un pied qui est comme neige.
Tu me dis de prendre l'amour simplement, ainsi que poussent les feuilles,
Mais moi j'étais jeune et fou et n'ai pas voulu te comprendre.

Dans un champ près de la rivière nous nous sommes tenus, mon amour,
Et sur mon épaule penchée tu posas ta main qui est comme neige.
Tu me dis de prendre la vie simplement, comme l'herbe pousse sur la levée,
Mais moi j'étais jeune et fou et depuis lors je te pleure.[21]

- What immediate differences are apparent?
- Does it matter that 'little snow-white feet' become '*un pied qui est comme neige*' or that 'now am full of tears' is translated as '*depuis lors je te pleure*'?
- What happens when the woman is no longer spoken of in the third person ('she' in Yeats) but addressed in the second person ('*tu*') throughout the French translation?

These questions and others that arise from comparing any translated poem with its original, or any two translations of the same text, can take students a long way into the study of language and the nature of poetry.

Sometimes, too, translation opens up ideas that were not even in the original text but which add a new level of meaning or significance. In W.G. Sebald's remarkable novel *Austerlitz* (published in Germany 2001, in England 2003) the middle-aged narrator, describing weekends at the boarding school to which as a young boy he had been sent, recalls in the original text how the pupils were left by the teachers to their own devices:

Ohne jede Aufsicht spazierten dann einige von uns herum ...[22]
(Some of us wandered about without any supervision ...)

But in the published translation (Penguin 2003) this sentence becomes

Then some of us would wander about at our own sweet will …[23]

echoing directly the description of the Thames in Wordsworth's sonnet (see Chapter 6, page 87): 'The river glideth at his own sweet will'.

- Is this a legitimate translation?
- Does its sense depend upon a reader's identifying its original source?
- Does it help the reader better to understand the feeling of freedom that the boys experienced?
- Has the translator in fact enriched (or over-enriched) the original, rather blander, account of the weekends?

Heaney, translation and politics

Many A level students will have had some experience, no matter how limited, of translating literary texts from one language into another, and it is perhaps a shame that such an exercise is usually treated as a linguistic matter, rather than an intertextual or intercultural one. But they should have the chance to see how seriously poets today take translation: Ted Hughes' *Tales from Ovid* (1998) for instance, Simon Armitage's version of *Sir Gawain and the Green Knight* (2006) or Seamus Heaney's *Beowulf* (2000). Indeed, in a revealing preface to his translation, Heaney highlights a number of key issues for translators – and for poets. First, he concedes that he had generally tried to be faithful to the Old English love of compounds:

> Usually … I try to match the poet's analogy-seeking habit at its most original; and I use all the common coinages for the lord of the nation, variously referred to as 'ring-giver', 'treasure-giver', 'his people's shield' or 'shepherd' or 'helmet'. I have been less faithful, however, to the way the poet rings the changes when it comes to compounds meaning a sword or a spear, or a battle or any bloody encounter with foes. Old English abounds in vigorous, evocative and specifically poetic words for these things, but I have tended to follow modern usage and in the main have called a sword a sword.[24]

However, he goes on to explain certain circumstances where he deliberately chose contemporary words of Ulster dialect rather than mainstream English in order to give the poem a contemporary political resonance:

> There was one area, however, where certain strangeness in the diction came naturally. In those instances where a local Ulster word seemed either poetically or historically right, I felt free to use it. For example, at lines 324

and 2988 I use the word 'graith' for 'harness', and at 3026 'hoked' for 'rooted about', because the local term seemed in each case to have special body and force. Then, for reasons of historical suggestiveness, I have in several instances used the word 'bawn' to refer to Hrothgar's hall. In Elizabethan English, bawn (from the Irish bó-dhún, a fort for cattle) referred specifically to the fortified dwellings that the English planters built in Ireland to keep the dispossessed natives at bay, so it seemed the proper term to apply to the embattled keep where Hrothgar waits and watches. Indeed, every time I read the lovely interlude that tells of the minstrel singing in Heorot just before the first attacks of Grendel, I cannot help thinking of Edmund Spenser in Kilcolman Castle, reading the early cantos of *The Faerie Queene* to Sir Walter Raleigh, just before the Irish would burn the castle and drive Spenser out of Munster back to the Elizabethan court. Putting a bawn into *Beowulf* seems one way for an Irish poet to come to terms with that complex history of conquest and colony, absorption and resistance, integrity and antagonism, a history that has to be clearly acknowledged by all concerned in order to render it ever more 'willable forward / again and again and again'.[25]

'Hoked' is a word Heaney has used before in his poetry – for instance in the poem 'Terminus' (1987): 'When I hoked there, I would find / An acorn and a rusted bolt' – so to use it in his *Beowulf* is not so much to place his translation in the context of his mainstream poetry, but to remind us how often his mainstream poetry is an act of translation, designed to 'test the edge of a word' (his phrase from the poem 'To George Seferis in the Underworld'). Then to choose a word ('bawn') for its 'historical suggestiveness', specifically to make a connection between Hrothgar's castle in *Beowulf* and the fortified dwellings of the English planters in 16th-century Ireland, is to take this strategy a decisive stage further: by a carefully willed choice of translated word, Heaney places the Old English epic into an entirely new context, that of the vexed history of Anglo-Irish ascendancy and resistance.

When, almost as a personal aside, Heaney recalls the English Elizabethan poet Edmund Spenser being driven out of Ireland back to London, he adds yet another context, the relationship between poets across time. What he omits to add – though it would have made a precise connection with his own writing at this time – is that Spenser's response to his experiences in Ireland was to turn to Virgil and write *The Shepherd's Calendar*, his sequence of eclogues written as the Elizabethan age and the 16th century were both coming to an end. In these pastoral poems Spenser interprets his own sense of dispossession and anxiety by adapting Virgil's themes and voices. Heaney would do just the same, four hundred years later, in 'Bann Valley Eclogue'.

Using material of this kind lifts discussion of translation away from being primarily a matter of linguistic faithfulness. It gives students the opportunity to explore for themselves the political as well as the poetical potential of literary language. It also puts such questions about the nature and significance of poetry and poetic language into a much broader context – one which will be invaluable for every student making the transition from A level to undergraduate study of literature. And it is through this kind of enquiry and exploration that students learn to listen to poets listening to each other.

'Stretch and challenge': from S level to A*

During nearly sixty years of existence, A levels have changed out of recognition: they began as an examination for a small academic elite of students, mainly aiming for what was then the exception rather than the rule – a university degree that would be a passport into almost any profession. It was the examination that allowed grammar school boys (and some girls) to join that elite and find their way to Oxford and Cambridge, to Durham, London or St Andrew's; or, perhaps more often, to the big civic universities with campuses in the suburbs of cities such as Birmingham, Cardiff or Glasgow. Ironically, there was far less pressure on students taking A levels than there is today: the idea that you might need three A grades to read English at any university would have seemed laughable. 'Two Bs and a C' became a standard target offer. Alongside A levels, there was originally an S (for scholarship) level paper. This, in an era before grants or loans, was taken by students who would need financial assistance if they were to go to university: it was a high stakes, competitive examination designed to test two things: skill in close reading of unseen passages, and breadth of reading – how widely had the student read beyond the demands of his or her syllabus? For example:

> 'Books without the knowledge of life are useless; for what should books teach but the art of living?' Discuss this question from Dr Johnson.
>
> (Cambridge 'S' Paper, 1967)

A question such as this, besides assuming that all candidates have heard of Dr Johnson, is a kind of game played by academics, teachers and pupils who all know the rules. It assumes both a breadth of reading and a philosophical way of thinking about the value of literature that would exclude most people from this particular game. It lobs phrases such as 'knowledge of life' and 'the art of living' cheerfully at the candidate, confident that he (assumed to be generically male in those days) will lob them back at the examiner, giving them the appropriate spin.

The introduction of student grants, coinciding with the first big expansion of universities in the 1960s, made the Scholarship Paper redundant, but it survived as the S (Special) Paper, to be taken by students as a way of catching the eye of Admissions Tutors to signal that they could perform at a standard above A level.

It had two classes only: 1 and 2; other than these, a candidate was Unclassified. During the 1970s and 1980s, the number of candidates taking the S Paper dwindled and by the 1990s it had become almost exclusively the preserve of students from the independent sector: Admissions Tutors stopped demanding a result in the S Paper, so teachers stopped entering students for it. If you only needed a B to get a place to read English, why risk a U in the Special Paper?

Once the expansion of university provision got under way in the 1960s, and again in the 1990s, the picture changed: candidate numbers soared, universities started demanding higher grades, syllabuses started to proliferate. A level examination results were (and are) used to measure the performance not only of students but of their teachers and their schools. 'English' became three subjects – English Language, English Language & Literature and English Literature – and was joined by overlapping subject areas such as Theatre Studies and Media Studies. Other new(er) subjects like Psychology and Information Technology offered stiff competition. As more and more universities began to demand higher grades for English (which by 2008 had become the fourth most popular subject for prospective undergraduates applying to British universities) teachers and students applied themselves ever more strictly to the challenge of getting A grades – and duly achieved them. Curriculum 2000, with its modular structure and ample opportunities for re-takes, encouraged the widespread view that A levels were being dumbed down: it was becoming the exam it was impossible to fail, and getting A grades was something students were starting to expect as a right not as a major achievement. This at least is how it was (and is) annually presented in the press and by some politicians.

Has A level English Literature got easier?

The truth is less simple. The standard of the examination, in terms of the questions asked and the level of knowledge and understanding demanded, has not necessarily been lowered. But with the introduction of rigid mark schemes, tied to specific assessment objective weightings, it has become easier for teachers to teach to the test and for students to refine their answers by re-sitting individual modules (the notorious 'bite-size chunks') and 'banking' higher marks towards their final total. This has been especially true if they have re-taken AS modules, which are set and marked at a standard between GCSE and full A level, but which count for 50% of the final A level total.

Here is an example of how this paradoxical situation works. Before Curriculum 2000 an A level student who had studied Philip Larkin's 1974 collection of poems *High Windows* could get a question along these lines:

> Write a critical appreciation of 'High Windows', paying particular attention to
> the development of thought and feeling in the poem. [The poem would then
> be printed on the question paper.]

Such a question certainly calls on skills of critical analysis and appreciation, but requires no contextualising. It could as well be answered by a student who had never read any other poem by Larkin as by one who had studied *High Windows* for two terms.

By contrast, the Curriculum 2000 AS equivalent of such a question might have looked like this:

> Write a critical appreciation of 'High Windows'. In your answer
> * pay particular attention to the language and imagery of the poem
> * discuss Larkin's choice of this poem as the title poem for the collection
>   you have studied.

Here the bullet points were specifically tied to two Assessment Objectives: AO3 ('show detailed understanding of the ways in which writers' choices of form, structure and language shape meaning') and AO5i ('show understanding of the contexts in which literary texts are written and understood'). Teachers preparing candidates for this particular paper knew that the focus of the question would be on these two assessment objectives; they knew the format of the questions, for they would have been to training sessions run by the Awarding Bodies themselves or by other providers of in-service training. In all these respects the examination might be thought easier than in the past. Yet the question itself asked a good deal more of the student, especially of the AS student. No longer could it be answered as an unseen: students needed to be able to place the poem in the context of the other poems in *High Windows*; they also needed to understand how it related to Larkin's own themes and to the concerns and view of life (and death) running through his poetry as a whole.

It was in this way that, with the introduction of Curriculum 2000, it could be said A levels in English Literature were becoming both easier and harder. At the same time, some teachers argued that, in a question such as this one, the opportunity for students to demonstrate real in-depth skills of close reading were being sacrificed on the altar of context. Others took the view that the introduction of the contextual element provided an overdue corrective to the so-called 'Leavisite' decontextualised approach to practical criticism.

This latter view is summed up (or travestied, depending on your perspective) by Janet Maybin:

Leavisite 'close reading' and 'practical criticism' treats literary texts as independent, self-contained objects, with a fixed meaning and literary essence waiting to be discovered by the skilful reader. The Leavisite critic's approach to analysing language and style, in order to extract explicit and implicit meanings … leads to the promotion of those who conform to a particular ideal of the writer and can most easily be studied in a decontextualised way.[26]

It is certainly true that the introduction of Curriculum 2000 saw the end of free-standing, unseen critical appreciation papers. The growing demand for questions placing texts of different kinds and periods in context meant that at most a single critical appreciation question featured in specifications (as syllabuses were now called) and this question was usually asked in the context of a paper focusing on a particular theme, genre or period. Typically, such a question usually appeared in the synoptic paper, the final paper of the six units and the one designed to test the range of skills and the depth of understanding acquired by the student across the whole course. These synoptic units were, almost without exception, genuinely demanding and pitched at a level above that of previous A level papers.

Synoptic assessment and the Advanced Extension Award (AEA)

Unfortunately, the synoptic unit mark did not determine the final award, and a student could achieve a high overall mark (and hence a top grade) while still not performing well on the synoptic unit. Not surprisingly, therefore, university Admissions Tutors paid little attention to the synoptic unit – even if they knew what it was: one of the major criticisms of Curriculum 2000 was that Higher Education had been largely excluded by QCA from the design and development of Subject Criteria or the new specifications. Nor were they much more interested (at first, at least) in the other new qualification that appeared at the same time as Curriculum 2000, the Advanced Extension Award (AEA).

This was a pity. Launched by the then Minister responsible for Higher Education (Baroness Blackstone) as a 'world class test', the AEA was unloved mainly because it was misunderstood. It was assumed that the exam would be like the former S Paper in its dying days, taken only by students from independent schools who could be intensively coached. In fact, English AEA confounded all these expectations: it was taken up by students from the state maintained sector, the FE and Sixth-form College sector and the independent sector in almost equal proportions. When a UCAS Subject Expert Panel reviewed the standard of the examination in 2004, it was agreed that the performance of students achieving a Distinction for the English AEA was equivalent to that of an undergraduate who, after a year of study, showed signs of being on track to achieve a first-class degree.

There were three key features of the AEA which made it so popular that in each year from 2002 onwards its candidature increased by 10%, despite persistent (premature) reports that AEA was about to be phased out.

- It was designed to be accessible to students whichever English A level they were taking: English Language, English Language & Literature or English Literature: the material presented in the paper ranged from classic literary texts to non-literary media passages and phonetic transcripts of speech or conversation.
- It was designed to assess the depth of students' understanding of English rather than the breadth of their knowledge.
- It had only a single Assessment Objective, so that holistic responses could be marked holistically: *The AEA in English will assess candidates' abilities to apply and communicate effectively their knowledge and understanding of English, some of its methodologies and texts, using the skills of critical analysis, evaluation and synthesis.*[27]

The examination consisted of two sections. Candidates were presented with a selection of unseen material linked by a theme or topic: the material was divided into two parts – primary texts and critical, theoretical or biographical material. In Section A of the paper students selected two or more of the passages and compared them in any way they chose. But first, they had to explain what it was they intended to explore or illustrate by their comparison, and at the end of the essay they had to assess how far they thought they had succeeded in what they set out to do. In Section B students had a choice of five questions, usually based on propositions contained in one or more of the secondary passages. In answering their chosen question, they were expected to refer not to their wider reading but to the primary reading material supplied for the examination.

In this way the examination itself provided the contextual material for the questions that candidates must answer. Close reading and context were explicitly linked. Every question invited the student to show his or her responsiveness to literary and/or non-literary texts; and in being able to frame their own tasks in Section A, candidates could focus on issues that interested them and demonstrate the skills they had learned in whichever English subject they had studied, no matter which specification they had followed.

The response to AEA English

Since its launch in 2002, AEA English has been granted increasing respect. The NATE report *text: message* (2004) identified 'its strengths as a possible model of A level English study':

Firstly, the anthologised nature of the assessment provides breadth, a quality currently associated with Language study rather than with Literature. The challenging nature of the texts, however, also necessitates depth, in that successful students will have encountered and digested similar forms through wider reading. Secondly, this is a paper that demands greater cultural awareness from students. Were it taught to all students, rather than to a relatively aware elite, it would require teachers to address cultural movements and critical contexts – and not merely as 'literary' contexts. Indeed, knowledge of language development, function and usage would be as requisite as a canonical overview of literature ... Thirdly, the AEA provides an independent approach to text that prepares students for the challenges of English study in Higher Education.[28]

This is a striking endorsement of the belief that an unseen paper can provide a framework for contextual study, and that it can validly assess the depth as well as the breadth of students' knowledge and understanding. The view of students, too, has been revealing, for many of them have found it a liberating experience to tackle a paper that makes no prior demands in terms of Assessment Objectives or set texts. Unseen, of course, does not mean unprepared: all the work done in their main A level or other English courses is preparation for an examination such as this.[29]

The English Literature Admissions Test (ELAT)

It is in fact one of the problems of Curriculum 2000 that it has all but removed the opportunity for students to demonstrate their response to unseen material, and good classroom practice needs to find room to reinstate this. Without any experience of such work, students are likely to find the transition to studying English at university still more challenging. It is significant, for instance, that Oxford has reacted to the difficult business of selecting students for English by introducing a pre-admissions test, ELAT (the English Literature Admissions Test), based entirely on unseen critical appreciation.

This test, taken half way through the fourth term of a two-year sixth-form course, is designed to enable students to show their response to the 'stretch and challenge' of a demanding examination. The Government and QCA are confident that the revised English A levels, with synoptic assessment spread across two A2 units (one of which will be coursework) and a new A* grade , will contain 'stretch and challenge' enough, but politicians' educational catchphrases tend to have a hollow ring.

The ELAT[30] is currently taken by all students, worldwide, who apply to read English at Oxford University. Like the AEA, it requires students to compare two or three texts – this time from a sequence of six linked poems or passages. It is a single-question paper, and again like the AEA, students must explain at the outset what they plan to explore or illustrate through their comparison of the passages selected from the unseen material provided.

Preparing students (ii): comparing texts and taking risks

Behind all such tasks lie two implicit questions:

- How does my reading of one text in the context of another enhance my response to either or both texts?
- What new questions does the second text prompt me to ask about the first (and vice versa)?

Making these questions explicit to students is a valuable introduction to comparative unseen work of this kind. Here is an example:

> Sir Walter, Elizabeth and Mrs. Clay returned one morning from Laura-place, with a sudden invitation from Lady Dalrymple for the same evening, and Anne was already engaged, to spend that evening in Westgate-buildings. She was not sorry for the excuse. They were only asked, she was sure, because Lady Dalrymple being kept at home by a bad cold, was glad to make use of the relationship which had been so pressed on her, – and she declined on her own account with great alacrity – 'She was engaged to spend the evening with an old school-fellow.' They were not much interested in any thing relative to Anne, but still there were questions enough asked, to make it understood what this old schoolfellow was; and Elizabeth was disdainful, and Sir Walter severe.
>
> 'Westgate-buildings!' said he; 'and who is Miss Anne Elliot to be visiting in Westgate-buildings? – A Mrs. Smith. A widow Mrs. Smith, – and who was her husband? One of the five thousand Mr. Smiths whose names are to be met with every where. And what is her attraction? That she is old and sickly. – Upon my word, Miss Anne Elliot, you have the most extraordinary taste! Every thing that revolts other people, low company, paltry rooms, foul air, disgusting associations are inviting to you. But surely, you may put off this old lady till to-morrow. She is not so near her end, I presume, but that she may hope to see another day. What is her age? Forty?'
>
> 'No, Sir, she is not one and thirty; but I do not think I can put off my engagement, because it is the only evening for some time which will at once suit her and myself. – She goes into the warm bath to-morrow, and for the rest of the week you know we are engaged.' 'But what does Lady Russell think of this acquaintance?' asked Elizabeth.

'She sees nothing to blame in it,' replied Anne; 'on the contrary, she approves it; and has generally taken me, when I have called on Mrs. Smith.'

'Westgate-buildings must have been rather surprised by the appearance of a carriage drawn up near its pavement!' observed Sir Walter. – 'Sir Henry Russell's widow, indeed, has no honours to distinguish her arms; but still, it is a handsome equipage, and no doubt is well known to convey a Miss Elliot. – A widow Mrs. Smith, lodging in Westgate-buildings! – A poor widow, barely able to live, between thirty and forty – a mere Mrs. Smith, an every day Mrs. Smith, of all people and all names in the world, to be the chosen friend of Miss Anne Elliot, and to be preferred by her, to her own family connections among the nobility of England and Ireland! Mrs. Smith, such a name!'

(Jane Austen *Persuasion*, 1818)

On its own, this passage provides plenty of scope for discussing Jane Austen's representation of family tensions or of the monumental egotism of Sir Walter Elliot. Her use, too, of different registers and rhetorical effects highlights the contrast between the speakers in this conversation. The fact that Sir Walter and Elizabeth ask Anne 'what this schoolfellow was' rather than 'who' both depersonalises and desexualises Anne's friend. It anticipates the way Sir Walter's sneering repetition of 'Mrs Smith' ('A widow … a mere … an every day Mrs Smith') will also desocialise her.

These are the kinds of details and interpretations that students need to learn to look for themselves, but such responses are complicated if the passage is then read in the context of the following:

There are three parts of Bath which we have thought of as likely to have Houses in them. – Westgate Buildings, Charles Street, & some of the short streets leading from Laura Place or Pulteney St: – Westgate Buildings, tho' quite in the lower part of the Town are not badly situated themselves; the street is broad, & has rather a good appearance. Charles Street however I think is preferable; The Buildings are new, & its nearness to Kingsmead fields would be a pleasant circumstance. – Perhaps you may remember, or perhaps you may forget that Charles Street leads from the Queen Square Chapel to the two Green park-Streets. – The Houses in the Streets near Laura Place I should expect to be above our price. – Gay Street would be too high, except only the lower house on the left hand side as you ascend; towards *that* my Mother has no disinclination; – it used to be lower rented than any other house in the row, from some inferiority in the apartments.

(Jane Austen, letter to her sister Cassandra, 1801)

This extract from one of Jane Austen's letters immediately raises questions about the extract from *Persuasion*:

- How does Jane Austen's own view of Westgate Buildings differ from that of Sir Walter?
- In what ways do the tone and style of the letter resemble or differ from the tone and style of the novel?
- Is the difference in date of the two passages at all significant? (Jane Austen died in 1817 and *Persuasion* was published posthumously.)
- Do the two passages together give a clearer or more complicated idea of Jane Austen's attitude towards Bath?

Jane Austen is always thought of as the novelist who defined Bath in fiction. But she was not the first to write of the city in a novel. Here for instance is a passage from Tobias Smollett's *Humphrey Clinker* (1771):

> Every upstart of fortune, harnessed in the trappings of the mode, presents himself at Bath, as in the very focus of observation – Clerks and factors from the East Indies, loaded with the spoil of plundered provinces; planters, negro-drivers, and hucksters from our American plantations, enriched they know not how; agents, commissaries, and contractors, who have fattened, in two successive wars, on the blood of the nation; usurers, brokers, and jobbers of every kind; men of low birth, and no breeding, have found themselves suddenly translated into a state of affluence, unknown to former ages; and no wonder that their brains should be intoxicated with pride, vanity, and presumption. Knowing no other criterion of greatness, but the ostentation of wealth, they discharge their affluence without taste or conduct, through every channel of the most absurd extravagance; and all of them hurry to Bath, because here, without any further qualification, they can mingle with the princes and nobles of the land. Even the wives and daughters of low tradesmen, who, like shovel-nosed sharks, prey upon the blubber of those uncouth whales of fortune, are infected with the same rage of displaying their importance; and the slightest indisposition serves them for a pretext to insist upon being conveyed to Bath, where they may hobble country-dances and cotillons among lordlings, squires, counsellors, and clergy ... Such is the composition of what is called the fashionable company at Bath.

A passage such as this provides a striking context within which to re-read the two Austen passages. How does the snobbery of the speaker here compare or contrast with that of Sir Walter Elliot? Where on the social scale delineated by Smollett's speaker would Jane Austen and her mother stand? What clues are there, if any, to suggest that this passage is taken from a work of fiction rather than an essay or piece of journalism? At what audience is each of the three main speakers or narrators in these passages aiming, directly or indirectly? Which of the Austen passages would you choose to compare with the Smollett, and why?

Putting together such linked passages quickly provokes students into asking questions like these for themselves; and having looked for the questions, they will as soon start looking for the answers. If you were to add an extract from the essay on Bath by Angela Carter discussed in Chapter 10 (pages 227–231), you would be well on your way to creating your own ELAT-style paper. In essence, all close reading is comparative, for we always bring our experience of reading other texts to bear on the text under scrutiny, and students need to be encouraged to do this consciously, and from an early stage.

Teaching to the test?

'Teaching to the test' has become a synonym for bad teaching, or for teaching under bad conditions, i.e. where teacher and student feel they cannot afford to risk anything or any time not directly related to the narrow demands of a syllabus and the still narrower demands of an individual paper or unit. It is what happens when the assessment determines the curriculum, rather than the other way around. But it does not have to be like this. Good English teaching always involves taking risks, and the habit of 'wider reading' is as important as the habit of close reading. Both are essential if a student is to be ready for the transition from A level's literary study to literary studies at university. And the one provides a context for the other, reading any text in the light of another being the necessary condition for developing a genuine literary judgment, for understanding what writers do and why writing matters.

Part 2

Teaching to the text: contextual close reading

6 | World and time: close reading and context

'Sweet Thames! Run softly, till I end my song.'

*(Edmund Spenser **Prothalamion**, 1596)*

Teaching the techniques of contextual close reading is a doubly demanding task. Neither close reading nor context can be learned by any kind of osmosis. From the start, students need to be aware of what contexts may be important or helpful, and in what circumstances; they need to learn too that contexts have their own limitations, and that they can all too easily become a substitute for looking closely at the text(s) under scrutiny. This chapter describes two linked teaching and learning approaches which can help to make students aware of the questions they need to ask of texts and of contexts. By looking closely at first a painting and then a poem; and afterwards by comparing the questions they need to ask in order to transform their first impressions into a deeper, more complex appreciation of what lies behind the images on the canvas or on the page – by such a process students can begin to understand what it means to be an active, questioning reader, and how, as readers, they are actively involved in the process of making meaning.

....

The painting is Stanley Spencer's *Swan Upping* (1915–1919) and the poem, Wordsworth's sonnet 'Composed Upon Westminster Bridge, September 3rd, 1803' (first published 1807). Both are famous; both are often taken to celebrate 'Englishness', though in different ways. Spencer's painting has appeared on the cover of anthologies of English Literature, especially outside the UK, e.g. the Norton Anthology, published in the United States. Wordsworth's poem, even more anthologised, has been described as '[one of] those sonnets which are among the most splendid pieces in our patriotic literature'.[1] Each takes the Thames as its immediate setting; both belong within a well-established tradition of depicting and writing about the Thames, a tradition stretching from Wenceslaus Hollar and Edmund Spenser to Stanley Spencer and T.S. Eliot.

Swan Upping is reproduced in monochrome on page 79 and can be accessed in colour at www.tate.org.uk/servlet/ViewWork?workid=13700&tabview=image For Wordsworth's sonnet, see page 87 below.

Figure 1: Stanley Spencer's painting, *Swan Upping*, was begun in 1915 and finished in 1919 after his return from the First World War.

Primary and secondary contexts

The previous paragraph contains a lot of primary and secondary contextual information about both the picture and the poem.

Primary contexts	Secondary contexts
Title of picture / poem *Date* of composition / publication *Identity* of painter / poet *Subject / setting*: the Thames *Tradition:* both fit within an established tradition	*Reception*: both are famous; (publication history: reproduced or reprinted in anthologies) *Interpretation*: both assumed to celebrate 'Englishness': used to establish national identity (Spencer) or to promote it (Wordsworth)

You could ask students to look at this list (better still, to draw up their own) and then define the term 'context' as used here. Each of these contexts offers a different perspective on the picture or the poem, a new way of the looking at the image or the words *in relation to something else*. It isn't necessary to have all these contexts in the frame, as it were, at the same time. One could discuss 'Upon Westminster Bridge' (the abbreviated title to be used from here on) in the context of other poems by Wordsworth, without referring at all to the wider context of other poems about the Thames. Or one could analyse *Swan Upping* in the context of Englishness, without knowing it was painted between 1915 and 1919: what does it have, if anything, in common with other paintings that are also held to celebrate 'Englishness' – Hogarth's *The Roast Beef of Old England*, for instance, or Frith's *Derby Day*? Would comparing it with these pictures add to one's understanding and appreciation of *Swan Upping*? The answer is that it might if one were trying to establish why this picture had become so much more famous than other paintings done by Spencer at the same time; it could help to explain the poem's reception over time. On the other hand, if one were trying to identify the distinctive features of Spencer's style of painting, then this context might be no help at all.

Two ways of thinking about context suggest themselves here: one is that (as the word suggests) it is something which, when woven into the fabric of the text or image itself, enriches the texture. Knowing that 'Upon Westminster Bridge' is by Wordsworth and is written in a particular verse form not only gives one more to say about the poem, it adds valuable points of reference and comparison one did not have before. The other is that a context can be a frame placed as it were around the picture or the poem. Different frames (with different colours, shapes or materials) will make one see the object differently: some will enhance the clarity of the image; others may detract from it. Often two frames will complement each other; at other times two contrasting frames may simply distract one from seeing the image – or reading the poem – clearly. This can be true particularly if one is a primary context and the other secondary. Knowing, for instance, that Spencer's painting has appeared on the cover of a Norton Anthology of English Literature adds nothing to one's understanding of how the picture was painted. On the other hand, knowing that the title is *Swan Upping*, which refers to a long-standing English social tradition, may well say something about the picture's appeal. Suppose Spencer had called it, in mock homage to Picasso, *The Blue Punt* instead?

These contexts, then, divide into matters of fact (primary) and questions of reception and interpretation (secondary). To assess how much a student who is just starting to develop confidence in close critical reading needs such information, it is only necessary to present the painting and the poem stripped of all context – simply paint on a canvas and words on a page.

The painting first: start with what may seem too obvious to need saying. This is a painting showing a river (or more specifically a riverside) scene. Someone on a bridge is watching people below in a boatyard. The boats are pleasure craft (punts, skiffs) but the people in the foreground are all working. It is the person on the bridge, the onlooker, who is not. At first glance the oddest thing is the man getting out of the rowing boat and carrying a swan over his shoulder: who is he, and why is he doing this? Apart from the name on the flag, just visible as the Ferry Hotel, there is nothing to identify the location, or the river, or even the country. So why does the scene nevertheless look English rather than French, say, or Italian? What are the clues?

Titles as contexts (i): *Swan Upping*

As with a poem, so with a picture: never underestimate the title. *Swan Upping* is both helpful and misleading. The painting shows Cookham Bridge over the Thames, and the forecourt of Turk's Boatyard, before the Great War a very popular place to hire punts and skiffs. The title refers to an old Thames ritual: each year in late July young swans are rounded up by watermen and their bills marked to identify them as belonging either to the Crown or to one of the City Livery companies, the Vintners or the Dyers. For several generations the Turk family, owners of the Boathouse at Cookham, Spencer's village, held the Royal Warrant to supervise the Swan Upping ceremony, which had become quite a lively social occasion.

This, however, is not what Spencer captures in his picture; instead, he shows the swans, unceremoniously trussed in carpenters' bags, being bundled ashore and looking decidedly miffed. Perhaps they had good cause. A generation before Spencer another artist, George Dunlop Leslie R.A., had described the Swan Upping ceremony in his memoir of the Thames, *Our River*. Leslie knew Cookham well, having spent as a young man several summers there and having kept a punt at Turk's Yard, the very scene of Spencer's painting. Leslie's sympathies were entirely with the swans:

> The swan hopping or upping, which takes place every year, is a cruel remnant of the customs of old times, and it would be well if it could be dispensed with; setting aside the pain inflicted on the tender bill of the bird, there is much cruelty practised in catching the swans, which is performed in a very clumsy fashion with long hooks, by men who have little or no feeling for the poor birds. I am astonished to see respectable members of the old City Companies, accompanied by ladies and children on pleasure barges, regarding the scene with perfect complacency; let them if they like by all means have a pleasant outing on the river, with all the pomp and ceremony that belongs of right to city dignitaries, but let them dispense with the boatmen and their swan-hooks, who dash about after the swans in every direction, the men encouraged to their work by frequent potations of beer. For days after an upping, the poor swans seem greatly depressed, and remain sulking in out-of-the-way corners.[2]

Years after painting *Swan Upping,* Spencer wrote that it was seeing the swans being trundled down Cookham High Street in a wheelbarrow that had first suggested the subject of the picture to him, as if he had been attracted by this strange juxtaposition of the mundane and the ritual. He shows no interest in the social or traditional aspects of Swan Upping. He simply observes it as one riverside activity among many; it goes on, almost unnoticed, not even interrupting the daily routine of preparing the punts for hire. But is that really what's going on?

The early morning light on the water downstream beyond the bridge clearly suggests that the day's work is only beginning, but the light in the foreground suggests that the sun is now firmly in the south – the shadows indicate that it is almost overhead, as if it were midday, and the light catches the top of the head and elbow of Mr Turk. Then again, the figures inspecting the blue punt are standing wholly in shadow in the nearest, darkest corner of the picture. Their limp arms and stooping bodies seem to suggest the tiredness of a day's work that began long ago. These apparent contradictions make *Swan Upping* a much more complex painting than at first appears, one that raises as many questions as it answers.

Close reading: composition and complexity

The bridge, although at the top of the picture, divides the composition into two. Behind it the water shimmers in the early morning light, calm and inviting. The sky, however, is less placid: arms of darkening cloud stretch out, and are echoed by the waving branches of the cedar tree in the right hand corner. The wind is beginning to get up, and the flag of the Ferry Hotel starts to billow. The figure on the bridge (a man or a woman? and wearing biblical garments?), has been leaning over the side but turns to stare at the woman in a brown hat who emerges from the shadows behind the boathouse roof. This enigmatic woman is a disconcerting presence: her sudden appearance has startled the other figure, whom Spencer has painted with left elbow raised both to show the action of abrupt turning and to point to the approaching stranger.

In the foreground of the picture there are other signs of trouble: the water is painted in a quite different way, suggesting a turbulence much greater than that simply caused by the waterman stepping out of his boat. Spencer himself thought this was a failure of the painting; he later admitted that he had not finished *Swan Upping* 'with the care and intensity with which I had begun it ... The nearest water could have been more water than I made it'.[3] Nevertheless, the agitated surface of the river, more waves than ripples, contrasts powerfully with the flat brown surface of the boatyard.

Then there is the tension between the figures. The waterman leans forward, knees bent, as he steps ashore with the swan on his back. Like the figure on the bridge his elbow is raised, so high in fact that his arm completely obscures his face. (Spencer here echoes the figure of the servant carrying a basket in Giotto's *Presentation of the Virgin in the Temple,* one of the frescos in the Scrovegni Chapel in Padua.) As he struggles out of the skiff, his forward-pointing elbow is balanced by the backward-stretching neck of the swan he carries. This swan gazes forlornly at its companions in the boat, trussed and waiting their turn. Its gangling neck exactly echoes the shapes of the clouds and of the cedar tree's branches behind the bridge. Similarly, it is echoed by the flap of the waterman's apron, and by the limply outstretched arms of the workmen holding up the punt. In this way, Spencer creates both a strong rhythm and a powerful tension of forward and backward movement in the composition.

The women with the punt cushions contribute their own tension, too. Spencer identified them as two village girls, the Bailey daughters, and if one seems to be bringing cushions down to the water's edge the other appears to be heaving hers (which looks more like a mattress than a cushion) out of the boat. The angle of the girl in the boat suggests that she, like the waterman behind her, might be about to step ashore. If so, then the relationship between the girls with the cushions is unresolved. The question remains: is this the beginning or the end of a day's work?

What is striking is the way Spencer celebrates the dignity, almost the reverence, of working on and by the river. Indeed, he explained that in painting the picture he had wanted to take the 'in-church feeling out of church': sitting during a service in his pew in the north aisle of Cookham church, he had been able to hear the punts being put on the river outside, and he wanted to convey the idea that what he could hear going on outside beyond the east wall of the church was as much a part of worship as what was happening inside. To achieve this, Spencer had prepared the picture in his mind, and had made the original studies (in pencil and in oils) from memory, only going down to the river afterwards to check that he had created the effect he wanted.

Perhaps this helps to give the picture its haunting intensity. Spencer knew the river and the boatyard intimately; as a boy he had spent hours and hours gazing over the side of Cookham bridge to watch the boats and the people come and go. From this store of childhood memories was later to come the inspiration for his final great unfinished sequence of paintings, *Cookham Regatta*. It is striking that in *Swan Upping* Spencer is again gazing down on the scene, but here he is as it were hovering above the river, looking towards the bridge and almost on a level with it. He is close enough to be able to see and paint in every rivet, but far enough away to paint the jetty at the river's edge zigzagging into the distance before it reaches the bridge.

At the start of his career as an artist (he left the Slade Art School in 1912) Spencer had thought of Cookham as 'a kind of earthly paradise', a place of infinite promise. To try to capture this vision, he had begun work on *Swan Upping* in March 1915, but only the upper portion was completed before he left Cookham to join the Royal Army Medical Corps. Throughout the rest of the war the canvas stood facing the wall of his bedroom; and the memory of it came to haunt him. In 1916 he was posted to Macedonia, and later volunteered to be an infantryman:

> As the war drew to an end it became increasingly agonising to me wondering if I should be snatched away. As an infantry man what would have been the use if I had said to the sergeants 'I have a picture at home and I just want to finish it before going into this attack'.[4]

In the artist's mind this picture absolutely represented Cookham. Until the painting could be finished, his vision of the place which meant everything to him would be incomplete:

> This made the sudden appearance of fresh supplies of ammunition arriving and orders for the beginning of a new offensive insupportable to the spirit. It can be imagined what I felt when I did at last walk into my bedroom at home and see this picture leaning with its face to the wall on the far side of the big bed ... There we were looking at each other; it seemed unbelievable that it was a fact.[5]

He set straight back to work, completing the picture in 1919.

Critics have been amazed at the apparent coherence of the picture despite the four-year gap between the painting of the upper and lower sections. Most viewers do not notice the apparent discontinuity for which Spencer reproached himself. Yet returning to the picture had been far from straightforward: 'It was,' Spencer said, 'a very difficult matter getting back to this painting.'[6]

Inevitably the war, and the trauma of fighting and surviving, affected the way he painted this apparent idyll of village and river life. But, as the composition and the execution of the painting shows, with all the in-built tensions already noted, Spencer had from the start foreseen how the war would threaten his earthly paradise. All this ambiguity is summed up in the single, central image of the picture, but it is an image that critics have all but failed to notice. For why, finally, is the punt in the foreground of the painting blue? Clearly Spencer needed to paint it a colour other than brown, otherwise it would have been lost in the brown of the boatyard forecourt. But he could have painted it green, for green is the other traditional colour for Thames punts, especially when used for fishing. In 1936 Spencer, who probably painted more punts than any other artist in the 20th century, was to paint the boatyard as seen from the bridge (standing exactly where the leaning figure stands in *Swan Upping*); in that picture he included a green punt. In fact, what Spencer has done here is to paint an impossible punt, one that immediately upsets all the assumptions of a typically English riverside idyll that the picture had seemed to present, and which embodies all the tensions of the composition.

Just as punts are not blue, neither in Spencer's day did they have boarded decks or tills at both ends. Only one end of a Thames punt should be boarded, the other sloping down to the bottom of the boat. What's more, punts are symmetrical, and Spencer has painted this punt with one end seven boards wide, and the other nine. This punt breaks all the rules, and the workmen are literally overshadowed by it; they crouch behind as if it is less a punt than a barricade; and with its sharp-ended, black-painted decks it seems almost menacing. Indeed, its nearer end even looks set to cut into the planking of the jetty like the sharpened blade of a chisel. Thus, just as the woman emerging out of the shadows onto the bridge suggests the unease with which Spencer must have watched the war approaching his beloved Cookham, so his blue punt – painted into the picture in 1919 as soon as he had returned to England at the end of the war – compels the onlooker to accept that, though life continues, it has been turned upside down. The ominous blue punt looks less like a pleasure boat to carry day-trippers down the Thames than a ferry boat to transport them across the Styx.

It would of course have been strange had Spencer taken up his paint brush again as if nothing had happened in the four years he had been away at the war. No wonder he admitted he had difficulty finishing the picture in the way he had begun it. No wonder *Swan Upping* is so full of disturbance, tension and dislocation. No wonder Spencer later recalled how, as a young artist, everything had seemed to him 'fresh and to belong to the morning. My ideas were beginning to unfold in fine order when along comes the war and smashes everything.' No wonder his final comment on this picture was, 'Oh no it is not proper or sensible to expect to paint after such experiences.'[7]

Reviewing the evidence: what difference does context make?

Looking closely at a picture like this can be a valuable way to introduce some of the techniques of contextual close reading. Spencer's *Swan Upping* presents a scene, but you have to look carefully at the picture to understand what the scene is actually about. And you need help: without the title, and without any idea what Swan Upping is about, it's hard to make sense of what is going on, other than to offer a very general comment such as 'It's a riverside scene' or 'It's a boatyard on a summer's day'. With careful study of the way the picture is arranged you can learn a lot about its composition: the balance, the tensions, etc. The palette of colours, the treatment of light, the atmosphere of the picture (which is surprisingly dark when seen on the wall in Tate Britain: most reproductions of the picture make it seem lighter) – all of these help to shape the viewer's response. But on their own, without any context, these features do no more than draw attention to themselves and to the picture as a visual object. Which is fine – as far as it goes – and students should always be encouraged to look closely, both at paint on canvas and words on a page: their initial, unmediated responses are to be valued. Discovering what we like; what interests, excites or moves us (and why) is an essential part of education. Art appreciation, like literary appreciation, is about deciding what we value and why we value it. 'Appreciation' in its original sense stems from the act of putting a price on something. But in developing these critical skills first impressions should never be last impressions; and it is important for students to discover both how much they can find from looking at a picture or a poem without any contextual support, and then to measure how far putting a picture or a poem in context changes their view, and develops their first impressions.

Titles as contexts (ii): 'Composed Upon Westminster Bridge, September 3rd, 1803'

Ask a group of students unfamiliar with the following poem (some may already have encountered it in an anthology) for their first impressions (without revealing the poet's name or the poem's title):

Earth has not anything to show more fair:
Dull would he be of soul who could pass by
A sight so touching in its majesty:
This city now doth like a garment wear
The beauty of the morning; silent, bare,
Ships, towers, domes, theatres, and temples lie
Open unto the fields, and to the sky;
All bright and glittering in the smokeless air.
Never did sun more beautifully steep
In his first splendour valley, rock, or hill;
Ne'er saw I, never felt, a calm so deep!
The river glideth at his own sweet will:
Dear God! The very houses seem asleep;
And all that mighty heart is lying still!

It is worthwhile, depending on their confidence in working together and their experience of responding to unfamiliar texts, to give students some prompts to focus these first reactions:

- What do you think the poem is about?
- Note anything that strikes you about the way it is written: form, structure, etc.
- Pick out any features of the language and imagery that appeal to you on first reading.
- What would help you to gain a fuller understanding of the poem?
- How much or how little impact does it make on you?

Answers to the first prompt are likely to highlight 'sunrise', 'the city' and/or 'early morning'; some students may suggest 'the difference between the city and the country' or 'the power of nature'. Occasionally a student will try to go further: 'Is it about death?', 'Is the poet talking about the power of nature and the power of man?' All of these responses are valuable and can lead to a probing discussion of what a first encounter with the poem actually reveals; but at this stage it is important to resist giving away the poet's name or the poem's title.

The second prompt, like the first, is best treated as an invitation to be as objective as possible. Depending on how much prior knowledge they have, some students will at once identify the poem as a sonnet; others may identify iambic lines. If they do not recognise the poem as a sonnet, they may try to unravel the rhyme scheme, although this will be a challenge to those who have so far only been used to identifying rhyme schemes with clearly identified stanza forms. Some editors – from F.T. Palgrave in his 1861 anthology, *The Golden Treasury*, onwards – have misleadingly printed the poem as three separate quatrains and a couplet. This is not how Wordsworth set it out, but it can be worthwhile presenting both layouts to get students to discuss whether this makes any difference to their first impressions or to their understanding of the poem. Some students will spot the difference in focus and tone between the first eight lines and the following six; others may pick out the list of single words in lines five and six, this last point at once opening up a discussion of whether or not lists like this are inherently 'poetic' – indeed, what preconceptions (if any) about 'poetic language' do the students have? Very quickly, then, a brief first encounter with the poem can give rise to some wider ranging discussion about features of poetry, but at this stage it is often better simply to ask students to note the questions that arise and come back to them as part of their later, fuller investigation of the poem.

So far, the prompts have deliberately been objective; what follows begins to encourage a more subjective response based on the evidence already collected. Comments may range from the entirely personal ('I liked the way the river is described'; 'I didn't like the way the poet just lists the things he sees and doesn't describe them') to the more technical: 'Is the city being personified?' Some students are drawn to or put off by the exclamation marks: 'Why is he so excited? At this point it is worth getting them to identify some of their assumptions about the poem and the author. Why do they assume the poet is a man? When do they think the poem might have been written? Which city do they think the poem might be written about? These questions can quickly refocus a discussion that might be in danger of becoming too diffuse and will lead students both back into the poem, back to the language and on to the next prompt. Any discussion which highlights the importance of titles is worthwhile; and so, while 'Who wrote the poem?' 'When was it written?' 'Who was it written for?' will be important, at this stage it is better to spend time on 'What is the poem called?'

Wordsworth and Westminster Bridge

When first published in 1807, the poem was entitled, 'Composed Upon Westminster Bridge, September 3rd, 1803'. This title is curious, for several reasons: by the time it was reprinted in 1836, Wordsworth had re-dated it 1802, but that is only one issue: as it stands the title implies, literally, that the poet had been standing on the bridge, looking out at the city, when inspiration had struck him, and that he had done this in early September. None of which is true. Later editors have sometimes deleted the date altogether; others have reduced the title to 'Upon Westminster Bridge' or even simply to 'Westminster Bridge' – as if the bridge, and not what could be seen from it, were the subject of the poem. Does any of this matter?

Well for a start, but only for a start, at least the title says that the poem is about London, and the Thames. It is a worthwhile and revealing exercise, before revealing the real title, to ask students to choose a title themselves, or to give them a range of alternatives – including one or more of the actual titles – and ask them to select the one they like best and to explain what is gained and lost by choosing or discarding the others:

'City Sunrise'
'A View from a Bridge'
'Golden Gate'
'On the Rialto'
'The Sleeping Giant'

It is at once clear that, without Wordsworth's title, there is nothing explicitly identifying the scene as London: could it not as well be New York (as in Arthur Miller's play *A View from the Bridge*)? Or San Francisco ('Golden Gate') or Venice? Confident students might point out that the language of the poem suggests it was written before either the Brooklyn Bridge or the Golden Gate Bridge had been built; but Venice would fit: it has no shortage of 'ships, towers, domes, theatres and temples' – and Wordsworth did write a sonnet about the city ('On the Extinction of the Venetian Republic'). The reference to 'fields' would be problematic, however. Indeed, 'fields' present problems at a first reading of the poem, even if London is identified straightaway as the location. Which fields? Can they be seen from Westminster Bridge? Could they have been, in Wordsworth's day? The church of St Martin in the Fields (now on the corner of Trafalgar Square) was certainly not out in the country by the turn of the 18th century. Where therefore would the poet have had to be standing, in order to see the fields, anyway? Certainly not on the bridge.

'Composed upon Westminster Bridge' is a phrase which itself needs unpacking. Some students may immediately spot the ambiguity: does it mean that this is to be a poem composed on the subject of Westminster Bridge itself (as in the formal titles of 17th-century lyrics, e.g. Robert Herrick's poem 'Upon Julia's Clothes')? The trouble is that the poem is conspicuously not about the bridge itself – any more than Wordsworth's 'Tintern Abbey' (expanded title: 'Composed a Few Miles Above Tintern Abbey') is actually about the ruined monastery situated in the Wye Valley. Logically, then, the title should suggest that Wordsworth was standing on Westminster Bridge in the early morning and admiring the view eastwards, looking towards the city. He must have been looking eastwards because there were no domes to be seen west of the bridge (though 'dome' need not be limited to the dome of St Paul's Cathedral: it could more generally refer to any impressive building, as in Kubla Khan's 'stately pleasure dome'). The direction in which the poet was facing can be deduced from internal evidence – what the poem describes is to be seen to the east: 'the City' lies east of Westminster Bridge. However, at this point some external evidence may provide a context that will help students understand the title, and the poem, more clearly:

> It was a beautiful morning. The city, St Paul's, with the river and a multitude of little boats, made a most beautiful sight as we crossed Westminster Bridge ... there was even something like the purity of one of Nature's own grand spectacles.

This is an extract from the Journal of Wordsworth's sister Dorothy, evidently describing the same scene, and recorded on the same occasion, as her brother's poem. Her phrase 'one of Nature's own grand spectacles' exactly sums up the central idea of the sonnet as embodied in the first line of the octave – 'This is the most beautiful sight to be seen anywhere in the world' – and in the sestet – 'There has never been a more beautiful sunrise than this one, even in a natural landscape' ('valley, rock, or hill').

How much does the poet really see?

Here we have already started to link Wordsworth's argument to the structure of a sonnet; at this point, then, it can be worth getting students to focus again on the poem, rather than the title: what is the poet talking about? How does he shape his argument? How does he exploit the form of the sonnet? Does he attempt to shape our response as reader or is he only concerned with his own response as observer (no suggestion in the poem, incidentally, that he had been sharing the view with his sister)?

To begin with the last point: although Wordsworth uses the first person 'I' in the poem, he does so only once, and quite late on ('Ne'er saw I, never felt ...'). Before this, the poem proceeds by a series of confident generalisations, which suggest or state explicitly that the way the speaker reacts to the scene in front of him is the way any normal person would react: 'Dull would he be of soul who could pass by / A sight so touching in its majesty ...'. In fact, Wordsworth is less concerned in the poem with describing precisely what he sees than with recording its uniqueness: there is 'not anything' more beautiful than this to be seen on earth – which could imply that the only place you might find a better view is in heaven; and, indeed, the line

> All bright and glittering in the smokeless air

suggests that the view he has of London – or at least of those images which catch his eye as he surveys the city: the ships, towers, domes, theatres and temples – is less a view of a real urban location than a vision of a celestial city. London was not in Wordsworth's day, any more than in ours, naturally bright, glittering and smokeless. The insistent negatives in the sonnet (the sestet's emphatic opening 'Never did sun more beautifully shine' anticipating and echoing the other negatives just noted) all suggest that the speaker is seeing something no one else has ever seen. There is a contradiction here, or at least a tension, which students are often quick to spot. On the one hand the view / vision is unique; on the other, any normal person would be struck by it. It's worth asking at this point whether Wordsworth is implying that he expects other people to be like him, or whether actually he is drawing a distinction between the majority who are 'dull of soul' (like the crowd that 'flowed over London Bridge' in *The Waste Land* – another defining 'view from the bridge'?) and those like him who are so attuned to Nature that they can immediately respond to the 'majesty' of 'Nature's own grand spectacle'. Taking him literally is to undermine his argument: how can he *know* that there has never been a more beautiful sunrise than the one he is seeing? How can he be certain this is the most beautiful sight to be seen anywhere on earth? Not all readers have been prepared to accept Wordsworth at his own estimation here: for example, the American writer Ivor Winters, one of the leading exponents of the New Criticism, complained:

> The opening line is an example of one of the worst formulae of amateur writing:
> 'Earth has not anything to show more fair ...'
> The line says nothing about the scene. 'She is the most beautiful woman I have ever seen.' 'What a glorious day!' This is the ultimate in stylistic indolence.[8]

Wordsworth himself, however, has trouble with what he sees. Ask any group of readers how Wordsworth presents London in the poem. The answer will come back, quite correctly, that London is personified. But as what – a man or a woman? 'Mighty heart' in the last line surely suggests a man; and the river Thames, metonymic as always of London itself, 'glideth at his own sweet will' so there might seem to be no argument. But 'majesty' is ambiguous, not quite gender-neutral. Though normally one might associate majesty with kingship (and Wordsworth, when he wrote this poem, had no experience of being ruled by a queen, Victoria not coming to the throne for another thirty years) the vision of London as seen from Westminster Bridge is 'touching in *its* majesty'. 'Touching' suggests intimacy; it suggests appealing to one's sympathetic emotions, which is not what you expect majesty to do. So the phrase 'touching in its majesty' is actually almost an oxymoron if majesty implies grandeur and aloofness, whereas touching suggests vulnerability, laying oneself open to an emotional response. Indeed, this idea of laying oneself open is explicitly developed in a remarkable image of feminine vulnerability when Wordsworth writes that:

> silent, bare,
> Ships, towers, domes, theatres and temples lie
> Open unto the fields and to the sky …

It is almost as if, in a sexual sense, the city, personified as a naked woman, offers herself to Nature. And Nature in this poem is unambiguously masculine, the sunrise ('his first splendour') on this occasion more spectacular than ever. It's certainly curious that Wordsworth is so impressed by majesty in the first place: less than ten years before the writing of this poem he had been an ardent republican, caught up in the French Revolution in Paris. His strongest image of female majesty (and vulnerability) would have been the guillotining of Marie-Antoinette. His later disillusionment with the Revolution was accelerated by the spectacular manner in which Napoleon rose to become Emperor – as the iconic images painted by Ingres, showing Napoleon enthroned and assuming the mantle of majesty, all too clearly show. It is surely revealing that, with such ambivalent feelings towards monarchy, Wordsworth translated this ambivalence into his poem about London.

Wordsworth's text: visions and revisions

A further problem, compounding this ambivalence, is embodied in the word 'bare'. Students can be easily confused by the apparent inconsistency of the city's buildings being 'bare' when only a line earlier they had read that:

> This city now doth like a garment wear
> The beauty of the morning.

Today's students are not alone in their confusion. Early readers of the poem complained to Wordsworth about the ambiguity; and as late as 1836, when he was revising the poem for re-publication, he proposed the following amendment:

> The city now doth on her forehead wear
> The glorious crown of morning;

Comparing drafts of texts is always a valuable way to help students understand the process by which poems are produced and then presented to the public. It also gives them practice and confidence in identifying what works and what does not work for a poem, for the poet and for the reader. What would have been gained and lost by this revision? Does the replacement of 'This city' by 'The city' not signal a loss of focus? And isn't this loss of focus further emphasised by the rather cumbersome personification that follows. At least it is now clear that the city is to be conceived as female – though that still leaves unresolved the problem of the 'mighty [*sc.* masculine] heart' in the last line. Presumably, too, Wordsworth conceived that the body of the city could still be 'bare' even if she is wearing a crown – that is, the early morning sun – tilted forward onto her forehead. The image comes perilously close to bathos, and it is as well that Wordsworth stuck to the earlier version. He was of course a compulsive reviser/rewriter of his poetry, as the various versions of *The Prelude* attest, and some of his revisions do represent a real improvement.

When 'Westminster Bridge' was going to press for the first time in 1807, Wordsworth made a last-minute revision to line 2 (the handwritten and amended version given to the printer has survived), changing 'Dull would he be of heart' to 'Dull would he be of soul'. Ask students why they think the poet might have made such a change: someone might say, with real insight, 'To avoid anticipating the use of 'heart' as the climax of line fourteen.' Understanding (as such a student would have done) the importance of every word, phrase or rhyme in the context of the poem as a whole, not just of a line or stanza, is an important lesson; and it is one which helps explain another reason for substituting 'soul' for 'heart'. Clearly, the new word sets up an alliteration with 'sight' in the following line, which itself echoes the sibilance in 'pass' and maj-*es*-ty. It also glances back at the *sh*- sound of 'show' in line 1. Is this important? If so, why?

For a start, in the fourteen lines of the poem there are no fewer than sixteen words beginning with the sound *sh* or *s,* including *c*ity (l.4). This in itself helps to generate a strong forward momentum to the poem, at the same time allowing the poet to signal key words and sentences which begin and/or end with the sound *s*. At the physical centre of the poem (ll.5b to 8) is the description of what Wordsworth claims actually to see; and the three key words in this sentence all begin with s: 'Silent … sky … smokeless'. None of these three words is usually associated with descriptions of a city: it is literally unnatural for a city to be silent; urban buildings block out the sky, and the air is rarely unpolluted. What these words indicate is that Wordsworth is actually investing the city with the qualities and characteristics of the countryside, and he draws attention to them by linking them to the poem's dominant *s* chain.

Wordsworth's London Eye

Stand on Westminster Bridge today and, looking east, you will see first the London Eye and the buildings of the South Bank complex (the Royal Festival Hall, etc.). Immediately down river you'll see Hungerford Bridge, taking trains from Charing Cross Station across the Thames. Only in the distance will you glimpse the skyline of the city and, just, St Paul's Cathedral. What you get is a general, wide-angle view of London. What you don't get is any sense of the relationship of the city to the countryside beyond it. You can, though, from the top of the London Eye – and this is the irony: Wordsworth in his poem was celebrating a view that did not yet exist, for even in his day, from almost ground level on London Bridge, he would not have been able to see what he claims in the poem to have seen. In other words, he both sees and imagines at the same time. This sense of a dual perspective applies both to place (what he sees) and time (when he sees it) in exactly the same way that the sonnet's octave exclaims at 'the most beautiful view in the world' and the sestet exclaims at 'the most beautiful view there has ever been'.

Comparing viewpoints: Spencer and Wordsworth

There is a parallel here with Stanley Spencer's painting, *Swan Upping*. As we saw, that is a picture of both a timeless scene and a scene disturbed by being located in a very specific time, the First World War. It shows both the view *from* the bridge (what the person leaning over the bridge actually sees) and the view *of* the bridge – and the painter's own viewpoint is well above ground level, able to look both beneath and above Cookham Bridge: he is in fact at the same level as the bridge. As with Spencer, then so with Wordsworth: both of them imagine, remember and describe a view that does not literally exist. Spencer envisioned the scene of the River Thames on a July day in this way – and Wordsworth did the same in his poem. How do we know? Because Dorothy's journal entry, cited above, is dated July 31st 1802; yet the poem is dated, with the same precision as if it were itself a journal entry, September 3rd.

Contexts as perspectives

Before asking why there should be this discrepancy in dates – which will take us into territory we have not yet entered, the historical and biographical contexts in which the poem was written – it is worth pausing to take stock of where this discussion of a famous poem has so far been focused: what would students encountering this sonnet for the first time have started to discover? Following the initial 'blind reading', when they had no context for discussion other than the words on the page and their own prior experience of poetry, supplying the title will have provided them with the following primary contexts in which to place the poem:

- it is a poem about London
- it is a sonnet
- it is a poem belonging to the Romantic period
- it is a poem by Wordsworth.

Each of these provides a perspective from which to view the poem; and contextual close reading always involves choosing and examining a perspective and, usually, comparing perspectives to see how they alter the way in which the poem appears to us, the way we read it. Our discussion of this poem so far has centred on what the poem claims to be about (the subject matter), how it is described (the language) and how it is organised (the structure). All three of these came together in the identifying of the chain of *s* sounds and of its significance. The process of deconstruction – problematising the image of majesty, querying the gender of the personified city, challenging the clothing/naked contradiction – helped to identify points in the poem where the representation of the city came under strain: the *aporia* or cracks in the apparently unified surface of the picture created by Wordsworth in this sonnet.

A comparison can usefully be made here with the way in which, in *Swan Upping*, the apparent calm and unity of the picture is undermined by the tensions in the composition, the instability of the angle of the sun and the changes in the manner of painting the water. Such a comparison helps students to tackle difficult and important questions: does identifying these *aporia* undermine the picture or the poem in the eyes of the viewer or reader? Or does it, on the contrary, draw attention to a previously unsuspected complexity and subtlety in the composition? Close critical reading demands that students should not shy away from such questions.

References outside the mere one hundred and nine words of the poem itself – the same number of words as in the paragraph above – have been sparse. There was the speculative query about Wordsworth's attitude to 'majesty' in the light of his political views and the French Revolution; there was a glancing connection with *The Waste Land*, a brief critical comment (unchallenged) by Ivor Winters and there was a short, undeveloped discussion of the history of composition and revision of the poem. There were repeated references to the fact that the poem is a sonnet, and to the differences and similarities between the octave and the sestet; so far, however, there has been no mention of the technical organisation or effects of the sonnet and, in particular, no discussion of the ending of the poem.

Asking students occasionally to pause and reflect (as here) on where they have got to in the discussion of any text is a valuable way of refocusing a discussion and of identifying the strands of their discussion that need to be taken further. It is also the moment at which one can discuss possible new directions, getting them to ask the questions that the text itself prompts them to ask. Thus, in what ways can the four contexts listed above enhance a student's reading of 'Upon Westminster Bridge'?

Comparing 'Upon Westminster Bridge' with Wordsworth's other London poems

How much prior experience of poetry students possess will determine which poems could be used to compare with Wordsworth's vision of the city. Not many will, perhaps, have been introduced to *The Waste Land* but more will have come across Blake's 'London'; and the stark contrast between these two near-contemporary poems – in terms of form, tone, perspective and language – immediately highlights some central issues.

> I wander thro' each charter'd street,
> Near where the charter'd Thames does flow,
> And mark in every face I meet
> Marks of weakness, marks of woe.
>
> In every cry of every man,
> In every Infant's cry of fear,
> In every voice, in every ban,
> The mind-forg'd manacles I hear.
>
> How the Chimney-sweeper's cry
> Every black'ning Church appals;
> And the hapless Soldier's sigh
> Runs in blood down Palace walls.
>
> But most thro' midnight streets I hear
> How the youthful Harlot's curse
> Blasts the new-born infant's tear,
> And blights with plagues the Marriage hearse.

Although both poems claim to offer personal impressions of the city, Blake's begins with 'I', while Wordsworth does not introduce the personal pronoun until line 11. The repetition of 'charter'd' and the identifying of different individuals (the infant, the harlot, the soldier, etc.) in Blake's poem remind us that the sense of excited freedom Wordsworth seems to experience derives from a city which is silent and where people are conspicuously absent. Not that 'Upon Westminster Bridge' represents his sole or even his dominant view of London, of course. Offering students Wordsworth's 'London 1802' for comparison can be a shock:

> Milton! Thou shouldst be living at this hour:
> England hath need of thee: she is a fen
> Of stagnant waters: altar, sword, and pen,
> Fireside, the heroic wealth of hall and bower,
> Have forfeited their ancient English dower

Of inward happiness. We are selfish men;
O! raise us up, return to us again;
And give us manners, virtue, freedom, power.
Thy soul was like a Star, and dwelt apart;
Thou hadst a voice whose sound was like the sea:
Pure as the naked heavens, majestic, free,
So didst thou travel on life's common way,
In cheerful godliness; and yet thy heart
The lowliest duties on herself did lay.

Once again, the title is problematic: is this a poem about London in 1802? Or a poem about England, written in London? Is it a poem that takes London to be a synecdoche of England in the same way that 'altar, sword and pen' are synecdoches perhaps for religion, defence and freedom of speech? Is it a poem not about London at all but about Milton? Here, too, Wordsworth's use of the sonnet form (where, incidentally, he follows Milton rather than Shakespeare) is worth comparing: the contrasting focus of octave and sestet, and the low-key ending (almost a dying fall) – as if the poem ends in silent meditation of the character of the man, rather than of the achievement of the poet.

A further instructive parallel can be drawn with Wordsworth's 1808 description of St Paul's Cathedral:

A visionary scene: a length of street
Laid open in its morning quietness,
Deep, hollow, unobstructed, vacant, smooth,
And white with winter's purest white – as fair,
And fresh and spotless as he ever sheds
On field or mountain. Moving form was none,
Save here and there a shadowy passenger –
Slow, shadowy, silent, dusky, and beyond
And high above this winding length of street,
This noiseless and unpeopled avenue,
Pure, silent, solemn, beautiful, was seen
The huge majestic temple of St. Paul
In awful sequestration, through a veil,
Through its own sacred veil of falling snow.

There are some revealing comparisons and contrasts to be drawn between this evocation of the city in the snow and Wordsworth's earlier depiction of the city at sunrise. Just how visionary is the 'visionary scene' Wordsworth offers here? How apt would that phrase be to describe the way he presents what he sees (or at least says he sees) from Westminster Bridge?

Similarities with 'Upon Westminster Bridge' include:

Early morning – almost nobody around: 'moving form was none', 'unpeopled'
Lack of noise: 'morning quietness', 'silent' (twice), 'noiseless'
Lists: lines 3, 8, 11
Beauty of city equalling nature: 'fresh and spotless as he [winter] ever sheds / On field or mountain'
Majesty: St Paul's a 'huge majestic temple'
Exposure / vulnerability: the street 'laid open'
Structure: fourteen lines, iambic pentameter.

Differences from 'Upon Westminster Bridge' include:

Setting: winter not summer
Focus and perspective: emphasis on close-up description of street from ground level, not a panoramic bird's-eye overview; culmination of description a single building, not all the houses of London
Figurative language: no use of metonymy or synecdoche
Length: ten words shorter, and more repetition
Tone: quieter; lack of exclamations or exaggerated language
Structure: not a sonnet; written in blank verse.

Identifying these or other similarities and differences leads students to pay renewed attention to the language, form and techniques of 'Upon Westminster Bridge'. In particular, the discovery that the description of St Paul's is not a sonnet (it is in fact a fourteen-line extract from a longer, unpublished poem that Wordsworth wrote in 1808) is critical: it will help students to define for themselves exactly what a sonnet is or isn't, and what it can and cannot do. A three-way comparison, including the sonnet 'London 1802', will make the point even more clearly. 'London 1802' also supplies references to 'majesty' and nakedness, which start to suggest a recurring pattern of imagery that students can follow up for themselves – for instance by researching the other London sonnet that dates from this period: 'The world is too much with us'.

The context of 1802

But when exactly is this period? And isn't it strange that Wordsworth should have been writing, almost simultaneously, sonnets that paint such different pictures of London? Answering these questions introduces questions of context that lead into the history of Wordsworth's times and into the history of Wordsworth's own life, before leading back to the poem which has prompted all these questions in the first place.

As one approaches the village of Burley in the New Forest, there is an old milestone by the roadside, showing the miles to Ringwood and Bournemouth.

On most milestones this is the only kind of information that is usually presented, but on the side of this one is an unusual inscription, 'Treaty of Amiens 1802 Peace Restored'. Today the Treaty of Amiens is all but forgotten but, as this milestone suggests, it was thought important in its time, and it was certainly important for Wordsworth. In fact, the Treaty of Amiens was greeted in England generally with the same enthusiasm that VE Day (Victory in Europe) was greeted in 1945 – and for the same reason: it seemed to herald the end of a European War. Specifically, it was intended to bring a halt to the first phase of the Napoleonic Wars, in which Europe as a whole had been struggling to resist the empire-building ambitions of Napoleon. One consequence of these ambitions had been to make it as unthinkable for ordinary British citizens to travel to France as it was for them to travel to Germany during the Second World War. Wordsworth had been a particular victim of this enforced isolation: when he had been forced to leave Paris in a hurry during the latter stages of the Revolution, he had left behind a pregnant girlfriend, Annette Vallon, who subsequently gave birth to his daughter, Caroline. In the eight years that had passed he had never been able to see Annette again, nor to meet his daughter. The Peace of Amiens gave him his first opportunity.

Wordsworth's biographers have always struggled with this particular period of his life (July, August and September, 1802) because by July 1802 Wordsworth was either engaged or on the point of becoming formally engaged to the woman he later married, Mary Hutchinson. Indeed, he and his sister Dorothy drove almost directly from Mary's home in Yorkshire to London to catch the stage coach to Dover for the crossing to France. This is how he and Dorothy came to be on Westminster Bridge in the early hours of 31st July 1802. Far from lingering on the Bridge to admire the view, he was sitting on a coach being driven rapidly across the river: presumably he could not have spent more than a minute on the bridge itself.

Wordsworth in France, August 1802

What was his mood as he crossed the bridge? Some biographers have concluded that he must already have known that Annette was not going to stand in the way of his marrying Mary, since the sonnet he wrote is so ecstatic in tone. Others have suspected he was going to France precisely to ask Annette whether or not she now expected him to do his duty – marry her and become the legal and visible father of Caroline. In other words, his engagement to Mary Hutchinson would depend on the outcome of his visit to France. No correspondence or other record survives to answer this critical question and, revealingly but maddeningly, Dorothy's diary is virtually blank for the whole month of August, the exact period that they spent in Calais with Annette and her daughter. Any conclusion, therefore, about what happened in France is speculative: Wordsworth wrote one rather ambiguous sonnet to his daughter during this period ('It is a beauteous evening'):

It is a beauteous evening, calm and free;
The holy time is quiet as a Nun
Breathless with adoration; the broad sun
Is sinking down in its tranquillity;
The gentleness of heaven broods o'er the Sea:
Listen! The mighty Being is awake,
And doth with his eternal motion make
A sound like thunder – everlastingly.
Dear child! Dear girl! that walkest with me here,
If thou appear untouch'd by solemn thought
Thy nature is not therefore less divine:
Thou liest in Abraham's bosom all the year
And worshipp'st at the Temple's inner shrine,
God being with thee when we know it not.

Two interesting contrasts with 'Upon Westminster Bridge' appear in this sonnet. First, it depicts sunset, not sunrise; second, unlike the 'mighty heart' which is 'lying still', here the 'mighty Being [God? Nature?] is awake', and not merely awake but ominously making a sound like everlasting thunder. (This poem is set on Calais beach, and it is worth asking students to compare it with Arnold's description of the sea's 'melancholy long withdrawing roar' in 'Dover Beach'.) Does the sestet suggest that Wordsworth found Caroline disappointingly frivolous – 'untouch'd by solemn thought'? What is his attitude to his daughter and her mother?

The final three lines of the poem may reveal more than he had intended, for the phrase lying in 'Abraham's bosom' is a well-known euphemism for being dead. Does this suggest that for most of the year he does not think about her (and Annette?) at all? Certainly, they parted at the end of August apparently without any plans to meet again: Wordsworth returned almost at once to Yorkshire and was married to Mary within a month.

Dorothy was too overcome to attend the wedding, and this reflects a further complicating factor. As Frances Wilson asks in her important biographical study, *The Ballad of Dorothy Wordsworth* (2008):

Did William feel more intensely towards his sister than he did towards Mary Hutchinson? As a young woman Dorothy fixed her libido on her brother and never moved on, but was the pain she experienced when he married Mary the agony of sexual jealousy or simply resistance to change – or was it something else altogether?

In Calais, once certain that Annette would make no claim upon him, Wordsworth had bought a wedding ring for Mary. But the night before his marriage he had given the ring to Dorothy who had slept with it on her finger, only returning it to him as he set off for the church.

This extraordinary entanglement of emotions and relationships (Wordsworth, his sister Dorothy, his daughter Caroline, his mistress Annette Vallon and his bride Mary Hutchinson) may shed some light on the puzzling date in the title, 'Composed Upon Westminster Bridge, September 3rd, 1803'. This was the original date given when the poem was first published in 1807, and Wordsworth did not change 1803 to 1802 until a revised edition of his poems appeared nineteen years later. The date in early September suggests at least that Wordsworth revised or completed the poem on that day. It could also suggest he wanted to separate the poem from the exact biographical circumstances which had led to its composition: not July 31st 1802, but September 3rd 1803. He had good reason to do this. Apart from Dorothy, very few of his family knew about Annette and Caroline, and it was important that this should remain the case in the future, as well as for the present. Presumably this helps explain the very unusual gap in Dorothy's journal. Certainly the story of Wordsworth's illegitimate child did not become public knowledge until nearly a century after his death.

Then, too, Wordsworth may have wanted to put a distance between 'Upon Westminster Bridge' and the other London sonnets he wrote in that year, 'London 1802' and 'Written in London, September, 1802', a poem expressing his disillusion with modern man's materialism and indifference to Nature:

> O friend! I know not which way I must look
> For comfort, being as I am, oppressed,
> To think that now our life is only dressed
> For show – mean handiwork of craftsman, cook,
> Or groom! We must run glittering like a brook
> In the open sunshine, or we are unblest;
> The wealthiest man among us is the best;
> No grandeur now in nature or in book
> Delights us. Rapine, avarice, expense:
> This is idolatory, and these we adore;
> Plain living and high thinking are no more;
> The homely beauty of the good old cause
> Is gone; our peace, our fearful innocence,
> And pure religion breathing household laws.

If this poem was also composed immediately after his return to London from Calais, it suggests a strong contrast with the way he describes the city in 'Upon Westminster Bridge'. Here the city has become the antithesis of nature: it is defined, and condemned, entirely by the worldliness of its inhabitants. This is a reminder that, in the other poem, people hardly intrude at all: they have not yet woken up and the poet has the vision of a transfigured London to himself:

> Ne'er saw I, never felt, a calm so deep:
> The river glideth at his own sweet will.
> Dear God! The very houses seem asleep,
> And all that mighty heart is lying still!

Given the extraordinary contrast between these two poems, both describing London, both dated September, both completed between the time he returned to England and the day of his marriage (4th October), it is perhaps not surprising that he changed – whether advertently or otherwise – the date of 'Upon Westminster Bridge' from 1802 to 1803 to hide such glaring inconsistencies. At the very least, these poems demonstrate the conflicting emotions that Wordsworth was experiencing at this time.

Assessing the value of different contexts

This discussion of what Wordsworth was doing in July, August and September 1802 may seem to have gone too far away from the text of 'Upon Westminster Bridge', and it is important always to ask students to evaluate for themselves the significance of different contexts: how much, if anything, does this biographical and historical information add to their understanding of the poem? It will certainly add to their understanding of the circumstances in which it came to be composed, and it will be a reminder of the need to take titles seriously – but not necessarily at face value. And how far does re-reading 'Upon Westminster Bridge' in the context of other sonnets written at the same time change their earlier view of the poem? How, for instance, did they first interpret the last line, and how do they now understand it? What exactly is 'that mighty heart'? Does the phrase refer to the people who live in London and who make it come alive – in a literal sense, the workers who pollute the 'smokeless air', but who make the city work? These same people are the 'selfish men' ('London 1802') who are 'unblest' ('Written in London, September, 1802')? Or is London itself 'that mighty heart' – and, if so, of what? Of England? Of that 'stagnant fen' that needs another Milton to bring it back to its senses? Such questions should prompt a discussion in which students have to think not just about the phrase 'mighty heart', but also about the words that conclude the poem, 'lying still'. It's a phrase that has given critics a lot of trouble.

Critical contexts

In his challenging guide for English Literature students, *Doing English* (2000), Robert Eaglestone offers a challenging reading of 'lying still':

The intrinsic attitude is often called 'formalism' because it is concerned, above all else, with *the form* of the text, its structure and language. It assumes that there is something special and uniquely 'literary' in the way literary texts use language. Because of this, the intrinsic attitude concentrates on the language of the text as its central object, considering things like the choice of metaphors, the use of symbols, structure, style, contrasts, images, and the development of the plot, to work out what a text means. Although these forms of criticism might sound rather dull and unrewarding, following the intricate paths taken in a text and looking closely at the twists and turns of its language can produce quite remarkable readings and effects. In fact, the very intense scrutiny of the 'words on the page' can result in the most unusual and challenging interpretations of texts, as the multiple and often unclear meanings of each word are weighed up and evaluated. As you concentrate on the words themselves, their meaning becomes not clearer, but more ambiguous (or *indeterminate*). This is most obvious when looking at poetry.

For example, there is a sonnet by the English poet William Wordsworth (1770–1850) called 'Composed Upon Westminster Bridge', which describes all of London, seen from the bridge at dawn, stretched out and radiant: 'Earth has not anything to show more fair' and the city 'like a garment' wears 'the beauty of the morning'. The poem finishes with these lines:

Dear God! The very houses seem asleep
And all that mighty heart is lying still!

The first meaning of 'lying still' is that the city is spread out, not moving, lying motionless asleep. But the word 'lying' has another meaning, of course: to lie is not to tell the truth. Perhaps the sonnet is implying that the city, *despite* all the beauty of the morning light, is still not telling the truth. The sunrise makes London look wonderful but really the city, 'that mighty heart', is still a den of deceit, corruption, falsehood and lies. By concentrating on the language – on the *form* of the text – two separate readings have emerged. On the one hand, London is beautiful, quiet and still in the dawn light. On the other, London seems beautiful, but underneath and despite all this beauty it is deceitful and corrupt. These readings are contradictory and mutually exclusive: either London is really deeply beautiful and peaceful or it's actively scheming, lying and dishonest. Which reading you choose depends on the way you interpret 'lying still'.[9]

Eaglestone's interpretation drew a stinging rebuke from a reviewer, Roger Knight, in a review of *Doing English* called 'Doing English In' (*Use of English*, 2000):

The alert 'A' level or first year university student (the target audience for *Doing English*), wondering how far to trust the intrinsic/extrinsic contrast, is bound to be disconcerted by the author's own critical practice. For his commentary on 'Westminster Bridge' is no more than a caricature of the 'intense scrutiny' it is intended to exemplify. Wordsworth is surely the least ironic of poets and in 'Westminster Bridge' there is no irony at all. How do we know? Obviously, in general usage 'lying' is a word with two meanings (so is 'fair' which, with no more and no less relevance the critic might have reminded us also means 'just'); but 'lying' could only be ironic, could only mean 'deceitful *and* corrupt', if all that preceded it could be construed as cynical and double-edged; if, somehow, we could convince ourselves that the 'majesty', the 'beauty' and the 'calm' are superficial or false; that Wordsworth had invoked those states in bitter observation of the corruption at the 'mighty heart' of the city. However, if we really are 'concentrating on the language – on the form of the text', such a reading becomes preposterous. We can only persuade ourselves that 'two separate readings' are possible by paying no attention to the form and (far from 'looking at the words on the page with great rigour') limiting our 'concentrating' to one word. Mr Eaglestone limits himself thus and, in so doing, defies the rest of 'Westminster Bridge' to have any influence over the 'reading'. It is only in defiance of the poet's art that one can say 'Which reading you choose depends on the way you interpret "lying still".' Mr Eaglestone believes that 'literature stimulates an unlimited proliferation of meanings'. Here, on the contrary, it is because Wordsworth controls (in a positive sense 'limits') the meaning that he is still able to tell upon his readers, that they are able to share his vision, enter into the tranced moment. We do not *choose* to be affected in this way. As speakers of the language with a degree of good will towards the author, we open ourselves to the 'form of the text', to the experiences in which it is grounded and which it articulates.[10]

Who is right, Eaglestone or Knight? Does Eaglestone deserve the critical contempt that Knight heaps upon him? If for no other reason than to demonstrate that they should never believe everything that critics say, or anything just because it appears in print, students could be invited to analyse the arguments put forward in these two passages, and to reach their own conclusions on the basis of their own close study of the texts discussed above.

Eaglestone's approach is, it must be admitted, problematic. Is there such a thing as an 'intrinsic attitude'? He is surely talking about the attitude of those critics who adopt the view that meaning is intrinsic to a text and that there can be such a thing as literary language; and while apparently setting out to disparage such a view ('These forms of criticism might sound rather dull and unrewarding') he ends up showing that the opposite is true. He implies that language and form are the same thing ('By concentrating on the language – on the *form* of the text – two separate readings have emerged') but actually does not mention the form of the sonnet or its contribution to the meaning and effects of the poem at all. He produces a striking list of epithets to condemn the city ('den of deceit, corruption', etc.) without demonstrating how he arrives at this list other than by his controversial reading of the poem's final phrase, 'lying still'.

Surely, then, Knight is justified in his lofty dismissal of Eaglestone's 'critical practice'? Knight's argument is that 'lying still' must mean 'lying quietly asleep' because the poem is a record of 'a tranced moment'; and because anyone who knows anything about Wordsworth knows him to be incapable of irony, and anyone who has 'a degree of goodwill towards the author' will accept that the poem means what it says unless 'somehow, we could convince ourselves that the 'majesty', the 'beauty' and the 'calm' are superficial or false'.

The problem with Knight's argument is that 'a tranced moment' is, precisely, a moment when one does *not* see things clearly, as they really are; and Wordsworth acknowledges this both implicitly and explicitly. He does it implicitly both by the way he confuses the gender of the city in the very act of personifying it (see page 91 above) and by his ambiguous attitude towards 'majesty'; he does it explicitly by his use of two key words. First, the line

All bright and glittering in the smokeless air

draws attention to itself by the second adjective: something which glitters reflects light back into the eye of the beholder: the effect is to be dazzled. It is as unusual for the city to glitter as it is for the air to be smokeless. Second, in line 13, he exclaims that 'the very houses seem asleep' as if to acknowledge that what he sees may not reflect reality. Students quickly learn, whether from Shakespeare or Jane Austen, that the word 'seems' always implies 'but may not actually be so'.

If we take 'Upon Westminster Bridge' entirely in isolation, bringing no fore-knowledge of Wordsworth or of his other writing to bear, then it is true that at first reading 'all that mighty heart is lying still' does not appear to carry any ironic undertone. It is, after all, an apparently very low-key way to end a sonnet; and Wordsworth, in following Milton's preferred sonnet structure, has denied himself a final rhyming couplet to draw attention to the last word of the poem. (Ask students to contrast this last line with, for instance, Shakespeare's bitter last-line attack on deceptive appearances: 'Lilies that fester smell far worse than weeds' [Sonnet 94].) And yet, 'still' does carry a force that draws attention to the word in a way that Knight does not acknowledge: structurally, it completes the chain of *s* sounds that, as shown above, runs through the sonnet from first line to last, highlighting for the reader so many of the key words in the poem. Furthermore, Knight's argument depends precisely on de-contextualising 'Upon Westminster Bridge', for as soon as it is read alongside its immediate 1802 contemporaries ('London 1802' and 'Written in London, September, 1802') it becomes harder to accept that Wordsworth neither intended, nor was aware of, the ironic implications of his thoroughly ambiguous vision of London at sunrise. It is a 'visionary sight' only glimpsed (and this is yet a further irony) by someone travelling at speed across the Thames and therefore condemning himself as 'dull … of soul' because he too has perforce to 'pass by' this 'sight so touching in its majesty'. He cannot tell the coachman to pause while he takes in the view, for he is in a hurry to catch a boat at Dover. The accomplishment of the poem lies precisely in its ability to suggest a comprehensive vision of London, contemplated by someone with time to stop and stare, whereas in fact the opposite is true. The poem as written is a carefully reconstructed and elaborated memory by someone who was on a coach picking up speed as it crossed the bridge, ensuring that the passengers had no option but to 'pass by'. It is no coincidence that, at the *volta* of the sonnet, in the transition from the octave to the sestet ('Never did sun …'), Wordsworth shifts from present to past tense as he records his own personal response to the view as memory, not as direct experience: 'Ne'er saw I, never felt, a calm so deep'.

Poetry in the context of examinations

There was a time when Wordsworth's 'Upon Westminster Bridge' was almost as well known as his 'Daffodils'; today it is probably much better known, in the UK frequently featuring in anthologies of poems set for GCSE and A level examinations. Do any children these days still learn by heart 'I wandered lonely as a cloud' – or any other poem? What makes some poems famous, while others fade from view? Students need to reflect on such questions; and encouraging them to do so is as much part of developing their critical awareness, as is training them in the techniques of close reading.

Part of the answer has just been given: examinations and anthologies. Both of these become contexts within which the poem is read, and they can help to shape readers' views of a poem, both of its value and of its function, in particular ways. Here are three ways in which examinations may shape students' views of 'Upon Westminster Bridge':

- The simple fact of being set for study in an examination (e.g. GCSE or AS level) gives it status: it must – as the QCA Subject Criteria put it – be good enough to 'merit serious consideration'.
- The type of question that students will eventually have to answer determines its relative importance: is it being studied so that the student can write an essay about Wordsworth's poetry? If so, then it might easily be seen as a less important poem than, for instance, 'Tintern Abbey' or 'Intimations of Immortality'. Has it already been studied simply as one poem in a GCSE anthology alongside a miscellaneous selection of poems by other authors?

If so, then not only may it have been studied without reference to any other poems by Wordsworth at all; instinctively, students may think it less important / less sophisticated or 'difficult' than a poem to be studied for A level.

- What type of question will students eventually answer that may involve 'Upon Westminster Bridge'? Are they preparing for a paper in which they will have to write a discursive essay requiring them to focus on at least three or four poems by Wordsworth to explore, say, his idea of nature? Or will they have to write a critical commentary – perhaps focusing on just one named poem – to demonstrate their skills of close reading as well as their understanding of key themes in Wordsworth's poetry? If the former, a teacher may only spend a relatively short time on a poem such as 'Upon Westminster Bridge'; if the latter, the poem's compact size and form make it ideal for detailed study and discussion. These two different approaches will inevitably help shape a student's valuation of the poem.

How much scope does any of these scenarios allow for contextual close reading under examination conditions? Isn't it safer just to concentrate on teaching close reading without context – traditional practical criticism, in fact? Here is an example of an AS level essay on the poem, written by a student half way through an A level course. Judge how far, within the limits of a timed examination, it meets the requirement to:

Demonstrate understanding of the significance and influence of the contexts in which literary texts are written and received.

(QCA Subject Criteria for English Literature, 2006: Assessment Objective 4)

Discuss Wordsworth's description of London in the sonnet 'Composed Upon Westminster Bridge'. In the course of your answer
- Look closely at the effects of language, imagery and form
- Comment on how the poem's methods and concerns relate to others by Wordsworth that you have studied.

The sonnet is not like most sonnets in that it does not propose or solve any problems but is simply a comment on the beauty of London, more specifically 'the beauty of the morning'. The narrator is keen to emphasise the beautiful sight of the city that he witnesses on the bridge – 'a sight so touching'. He is clearly affected by this moment and he suggests that you would have to be 'Dull ... of soul' if you did not stop to witness this amazing sight. However, the narrator is clear in emphasising that this sight is certainly a rare occasion for him; 'Never did sun more beautifully steep / In his first splendour' and also 'Ne'er saw I, never felt, a calm so deep.' With this in mind, it can be implied that the narrator is indirectly describing the city as usually an ugly place. He emphasises the general ugliness of the city by saying that that it is strange to see it in this light. There is plenty of evidence in the sonnet to support this idea.

London, with sewage being pumped into the Thames, and muck in the streets was certainly not a nice place to live at that time. It is important to realise that although densely populated, the fact that the narrator is on a bridge means that he doesn't witness this and everything seems serene — it is therefore only a personal view which hides the true grimness of the city.

The evidence that London is not usually as beautiful as the narrator says includes the use of subtle words. 'This city now does like a garment,' — the word now is specific and not generalised, which suggests the city's usual ugliness. Also supporting this is the narrator's reference to 'smokeless air' implying the fact that there is usually smoke. Finally, he describes that the 'very houses seem asleep' — 'seem' suggests a façade of tranquillity which in effect is what this poem is trying to describe.

Wordsworth is much more renown[ed] with describing the beauty of nature, celebrating its power and influence — this therefore makes this sight of London unexpected. There are though instances in the sonnet where he does not fail to mention the influence of nature. He describes the various buildings as lying 'open unto the fields, and to the sky' — this shows that he is in effect comparing and connecting the city and the countryside. The narrator also says that 'the river glideth at his own sweet will', this gives the image of the city being artificial and the river that runs through it (a part of nature) real. In effect, in the river he sees the beauty of his homeland and although talking about London, the poem is really detailing the ugliness of cities in general and the quality that nature possesses in comparison to them.

The sonnet relates in part to a view stated in 'Tintern Abbey' where the narrator declares that 'these forms of beauty' (nature's elements) 'in lonely rooms and mid the din / of towns and cities, I have owed them'. Here is another connection between city life and nature — the city is noisy ('din') and the narrator needs to return to the Wye to restore him to tranquillity of mind.

Also in 'Written in London, September, 1802', the narrator describes the fact that 'No grandeur now in nature or in book / Delights us'. Instead values are in wealth and 'The wealthiest man among us is the best'. Wealth and richness is associated with city life and therefore the narrator is keen to emphasise the problem that city life causes in comparison to the 'grandeur' of nature.

It is important to bear three things in mind about this essay: first, it is written under exam conditions (50 minutes) with no time for redrafting or second thoughts. Second, it is written by a student only half way through an A level course: she is still developing technical skills that in a year's time she will have refined a lot further. Nevertheless (and this is the third point) she has answered the question very carefully. The essay title, with its associated bullet points, does not ask for a straightforward critical appreciation of the whole poem: it asks candidates to 'Discuss Wordsworth's description of London in the sonnet' and to do so both by focusing on the effects of language, imagery and form, and by relating the poem's 'methods and concerns' to those in other poems by Wordsworth they have studied. In the course of an essay of just over 600 words she manages rather deftly to do the following:

- identify a way in which this poem differs from other sonnets
- place the poem in an historical context
- contrast the unexpected beauty of London in the morning light with 'the general ugliness of the city'
- comment on the significance of the speaker's viewpoint (paragraph 2)
- focus on the effect of 'subtle' words such as 'Never', 'now', 'smokeless' and 'seem'
- address the critical debate (cf the controversy between Eaglestone and Knight above, pages 102–106) about whether or not the city is 'lying', by referring to 'a facade of tranquillity' – a very good phrase
- relate the romantic view of nature expressed in this poem to two other poems, using appropriate quotation to link the discussion
- present a mainly well-argued, personal view of the poem.

An essay like this exemplifies the value of contextual close reading: it illustrates how a student's analysis of the poem *in the light of the question asked* is enhanced by her understanding of its literary, historical, biographical and textual contexts. Some of these are dealt with explicitly, some implicitly; all economically. To write with this degree of economy, however, is to demonstrate the range of teaching and the quality of learning that has led up to this exam performance. This is not an essay that could have been written by a student relying solely on his or her skill in practical criticism to respond to a question such as the one asked here. Here, indeed, her awareness of the significance and influence of the poem's contexts enriches the student's appreciation of the words on the page.

Why are some poems better known than others?

But is 'Upon Westminster Bridge' in the end a poem little more than a celebrity poem: one that is famous for being famous? Why is it so much better known than most of the other sonnets Wordsworth wrote? In his own lifetime his sonnets (and he wrote over a hundred of them, barely half-a-dozen of which are still read today) were not rated very highly, and he was even moved to write one complaining about the way critics dismissed them – and indeed the whole genre:

> Scorn not the sonnet; Critic, you have frown'd,
> Mindless of its just honours; with this key
> Shakespeare unlock'd his heart; the melody
> Of this small lute gave ease to Petrarch's wound ...

It was probably an anthology published after his death that brought 'Upon Westminster Bridge' to a new, worldwide, audience and gave the poem a significance that Wordsworth never dreamed of. In 1861, eleven years after his death, a radical new anthology appeared: *The Golden Treasury of the best songs and lyrical poems in the English language*, edited by Francis Turner Palgrave. Palgrave was a friend of Tennyson, to whom the anthology was dedicated. His *Golden Treasury* (still in print, and updated from time to time) was an attempt, first, to classify English (*sc.* British, plus Longfellow, Whitman and Emerson) poetry and, second, to bring this poetry to a new audience who had previously – he assumed – been denied access to the sort of poetry he valued:

> If this Collection proves a storehouse of delight to Labour and to Poverty, – if it teaches those indifferent to the Poets to love them, and those who love them to love them more, the aim and desire entertained in framing it will be fully accomplished.   (from the dedication 'To Alfred Tennyson, Poet Laureate')

Almost at once *Palgrave*, his name by now eponymous, became a standard school textbook, used as the set text for School Certificate examinations in English until well after the Second World War. For nearly a century, schoolchildren learned their poetry (and indeed, literally learned it by heart) from Palgrave. The taste he shaped established a taxonomy of English poetry that still persists today: he excluded, for instance, all long poems, and poems written in blank verse or heroic couplets – the Augustan poets are almost entirely absent. Thus, in representing Milton, or Wordsworth (Palgrave's favourite poet, with far more entries than anyone else, including Shakespeare) the editor added as many short poems as he could find, and included a significant number of Wordsworth's sonnets of which most of the Victorian poetry reading public had been previously unaware. Among these was 'Upon Westminster Bridge'.

It appears literally as the central poem in the entire anthology,[11] spanning pages 250–251: the Poems and Notes run from page 1–502. Before it comes Keats' 'Ode to a Nightingale'. After it is Shelley's 'Ozymandias'. It is as if these poems represent for Palgrave the heart of English poetry, just as, in 'Upon Westminster Bridge', London represents the 'mighty heart' of – what? of England? of the British Empire? of the world? This is certainly how the poem came to be read, and how Palgrave intended it should be read. In his Notes to Book 4 (which he calls the Book of Wordsworth) he wrote ecstatically of Wordsworth, Keats and Shelley that:

> They added a richness in language and a variety in metre, a force and fire in narrative, a tenderness and bloom in feeling, an insight into the finer passages of the Soul and the inner meanings of the landscape, a larger and wiser Humanity ... In a word, the nation which, after the Greeks in their glory, has been the most gifted of all nations for Poetry, expressed in these men the highest strength and prodigality of its nature.[12]

Ten years after the Great Exhibition of 1851 had celebrated the expansion of the British Empire and the achievements of British technology, Palgrave had no doubt that England's poets were equally worthy of celebration:

> Poetry gives treasures 'more golden than gold', leading us in higher and healthier ways than those of the world, and interpreting to us the lessons of Nature. But she speaks best for herself. Her true accents, if the plan has been executed with success, may be heard throughout the following pages: – wherever the Poets of England are honoured, wherever the dominant language of the world is spoken, it is hoped that they may find fit audience.[13]

English poetry was now the finest in the world (second only to 'the Greeks in their glory') and English 'the dominant language of the world'. Wordsworth was, for Palgrave, the finest poet of the age; and the poem that best interpreted the lessons of Nature and transformed London, the normally smoke-obscured city or the 'stagnant fen', into the most beautiful place that the world had ever seen was the poem to which he gave pride of place in his anthology, 'Upon Westminster Bridge'. The emotions that Wordsworth had felt as he crossed the Thames on his way to France on 31st July 1802 were no doubt complex, and the process of recollecting, ordering and translating them into the form and language of a sonnet took several years. But even he might have been surprised to see the poem transformed into an imperial anthem, taught, learned by heart and still today set for examinations.

But it isn't only school curricula that ensure the survival of this poem: 'Earth has not anything to show more fair' has become an all purpose rent-a-quote, much abused by journalists and estate agents. When the Queen Mother died in 2002, and crowds queued all day across Westminster Bridge in order to file past her coffin as it lay in state in Westminster Hall, the *Daily Telegraph* (April 9th) entitled its leading article 'That Mighty Heart' and quoted extensively from the poem. There was an appropriateness to this which the leader writer probably did not realise: citing the poem which, as we have seen, came to be a hymn to the empire of which London was the hub, was a fitting tribute to the woman who was – though most people had forgotten this – the last crowned Empress of India.

7 | Poetry in context

'I have just cause to make a pitiful defence of poor Poetry, which from almost the highest estimation of learning is fallen to be the laughing-stock of children.'

*(Sir Philip Sidney **An Apology for Poetry**, 1595)*

Of all literary genres, poetry may seem to be the one where the value of contextual study is most strongly contested. Phrases such as 'the words on the page' and 'the verbal icon' reinforce the idea of the poem as sufficient in itself. They seem to resist any idea that a poem's meaning and significance should need external mediation. However, in each of the four sections in this chapter the aim is to show that opposites such as intrinsic or extrinsic evidence are beside the point: the architecture of a poem (its structure, form, metre and diction, etc.), and the literary, cultural or historical landscape within which it belongs relate to each other in exactly the same way as the architecture of a building relates to its location.

The first two sections link directly with the extended discussion of Wordsworth's 'Upon Westminster Bridge' in Chapter 6. Poems by Shelley and Coleridge ('Ozymandias' and 'This Lime-Tree Bower My Prison') are analysed in terms of the circumstances of their composition and offer opportunities for discussing with students the relationship between the form of the poems and the subject matter with which they deal. In each case, close scrutiny of the language and imagery is an integral feature of the discussion.

In the third section, T.S. Eliot's short and almost forgotten poem 'Usk' is discussed both in the context of the poet's other, major poems and of a newspaper report claiming to have unlocked the 'secret' of the poem. There are suggestions too for introducing students, through this poem, to the concept of intertextuality and the ways in which it is exploited by Eliot and other poets.

In the final section, a discussion of the sonnet form as a context for analysing and evaluating a wide range of texts, by poets from Shakespeare to Seamus Heaney, insists that literary contexts – no less than historical, biographical or cultural contexts – have their place and, as should always happen, can draw the students back to focus in depth on the poems themselves.

'Ozymandias': Shelley and Smith

Students often worry about whether and how it is possible to say that one text is better than another. The ensuing discussion of two linked poems sets out to do the following things:

- It offers a comparative close reading of both poems, focusing on voice, structure, imagery and sound, as well as on the development of argument in each poem.
- It discusses the context in which the poems were written.
- It asks what has led to one of the poems being still famous after 200 years and the other almost completely forgotten.
- It challenges the assumption that one of the poems deserves its fame while the other does not and takes issue with the kind of Internet commentary on which some students rely too readily.

· ·

'Write a poem about an exhibit at your local museum.' Not necessarily an exciting prospect, but in 1817 two poets took part in a competition to write a sonnet about the latest sensation at the British Museum, a huge torso of Pharaoh Ramses II, recently 'acquired' from Egypt. The poets were Percy Bysshe Shelley and his friend Horace Smith. Both published their poems in 1818: Shelley's became one of the best known sonnets in the English language; Smith's soon sank almost without trace.

Why do some poems survive for centuries while others vanish? Is it to do with the fame of the author? True, Shelley remains a well-known name, though most of his poems are rarely read today. And who has heard of Horace Smith? Or is it a matter of packaging? 'Ozymandias' is a good title, as exotic in its way as Coleridge's 'Kubla Khan'. Smith by contrast called his poem, 'On A Stupendous Leg of Granite, Discovered Standing by Itself in the Deserts of Egypt, with the Inscription Inserted Below'. But was his poem as bad as the title? Even if Shelley's is the better sonnet, has Smith's been unfairly under-rated? Can we tell?

Here is Smith's poem:

In Egypt's sandy silence, all alone,
   Stands a gigantic Leg, which far off throws
   The only shadow that the Desert knows:
'I am great OZYMANDIAS,' saith the stone,
   'The King of Kings; this mighty City shows
'The wonders of my hand.' – The City's gone, –
   Nought but the Leg remaining to disclose
The site of this forgotten Babylon.
We wonder, – and some Hunter may express
Wonder like ours, when thro' the wilderness
   Where London stood, holding the Wolf in chace,
He meets some fragment huge, and stops to guess
   What powerful but unrecorded race
   Once dwelt in that annihilated place.

And here is Shelley's:

I met a traveller from an antique land
Who said:—Two vast and trunkless legs of stone
Stand in the desert. Near them on the sand,
Half sunk, a shatter'd visage lies, whose frown
And wrinkled lip and sneer of cold command
Tell that its sculptor well those passions read
Which yet survive, stamp'd on these lifeless things,
The hand that mock'd them and the heart that fed.
And on the pedestal these words appear:
'My name is Ozymandias, king of kings:
Look on my works, ye mighty, and despair!'
Nothing beside remains: round the decay
Of that colossal wreck, boundless and bare,
The lone and level sands stretch far away.

It is interesting to see at once how differently they treat the same subject. Perhaps Smith's single 'gigantic Leg' is less impressive than Shelley's 'Two vast and trunkless legs of stone'. Shelley also refers to the head and makes much of its 'shatter'd visage'; Smith says nothing about it. On the other hand, Shelley makes no reference to any city, while for Smith's Ozymandias, the city was to be his lasting memorial rather than the statue. These differences are interesting, but they do not on their own tell us which is the better poem or why Shelley's should be more famous than Smith's.

What about the narrator? Shelley's speaker reports what a traveller 'from an antique land' has told him. The effect of 'antique' here is to suggest both far off in time and remote in distance. It isn't clear whether the traveller has returned home after visiting the antique land or whether the antique land is where he originally comes from; but, rather like Coleridge's Ancient Mariner, he seems to have a need to tell his story: it pours straight out. Smith's speaker by contrast takes us himself to 'Egypt's sandy silence'. As readers, we are expected to share the poet's astonishment at this 'forgotten Babylon': 'We wonder ... wonder like ours'. Does Smith's rhetorical repetition of 'wonder' overstate his case? Shelley doesn't spell out how we should react: he lets the ruined statue dwarfed by the endless desert speak for itself.

How effectively does each poet use the sonnet form? Smith is at first glance the more conventional: his poem divides clearly into an octave and a sestet, and closes with a rhyming couplet; Shelley's does neither of these. Smith, though, has an ingenious rhyme scheme, which only uses four rhymes but does so with clever variation: the first quatrain rhymes *abba*, the second *abab* – allowing for the important half-rhyme *stone / gone*. Lines 9–11 rhyme *ccd* while 12–14 rhyme *cdd*. In this way, repetition does not create monotony: instead, it creates a sense of unease appropriate to the ideas expressed in the sestet. You could add that this sense of unease is heightened by the closeness in sound of *chace* and *guess*. The picture – like the rhyme scheme, like the half-rhymes – nearly fits together but not quite. 'That annihilated place' Smith's speaker refers to (and with which 'we' are familiar) is London – but not London as we know it: London almost wiped off the map.

While Shelley's rhyme scheme is more fractured (fragmented?) than Smith's, there is hardly any break between his octave and the sestet. Indeed, the word 'And' which begins line 9 implies that the speaker is simply continuing his description; and the way that lines 10 echoes line 7 (*kings* significantly rhymed with *things*) further destroys any sense of a break. If there is a *volta*, a turning point in the sonnet, it is surely between lines 11 and 12: after the powerfully emphatic climax –

> 'My name is Ozymandias, king of kings:
> Look on my works, ye mighty, and despair!'

– comes the crushingly ironic 'Nothing beside remains'. It is easy to overlook the skill with which Shelley builds up to this effect: from line 1 onwards, words such as *land*, *stand* and *sand* all anticipate the central syllable and sound of the tyrant's name, Ozy*man*dias. Other internal rhymes serve a similar function: *trunkless*, *sunk* and *wrinkled* announce the */k/* sound that will make 'king of kings' such a resounding phrase. Some phrases actually combine the two sounds – 'cold com*man*d' and 'ha*n*d that mo*ck*ed', for example.

Throughout the poem, too, Shelley achieves an effect that poets from Wordsworth and Coleridge onwards often aimed at: the sublime. For the Romantics, nature at its most powerful and overwhelming inspired sublime feelings of awe and fearfulness at man's insignificance in the face of nature. During the 18th century philosophers such as Immanuel Kant had distinguished between the Beautiful and the Sublime: the former had 'shape and form' while the latter was 'boundless'. Thus, when Shelley closes his sonnet with the 'colossal wreck' of Ozymandias lost in the 'lone and level sands' which are 'boundless and bare' he creates an immediately striking image of the sublime, to which readers have responded ever since.

Some readers object to Shelley's cumbersome syntax in lines 3–8. It is harder, they claim, to piece together the meaning of the relative clause beginning 'whose frown …' than it is to understand the general significance of the image. Whose hand? Whose heart? Other readers have condemned Smith's sonnet for lacking the subtlety and universality of Shelley's. The Wikipedia entry, for instance, used to claim:

> Shelley's poem refrains from stating a specific moral as such, and instead presents a vivid tableau, leaving readers to draw their own conclusions and ponder upon the themes ... Nor does it address an audience of a specific time or place ... the audience is whoever is reading the poem and not just a Londoner. The image of a destroyed London will have no more or less effect on someone not from London than Ozymandias' statue.

I disagree. Apart from the strange claim that only Smith's fellow Londoners will think his poem speaks to them or be affected by the image of a destroyed London – does Ground Zero mean nothing to anyone who is not a New Yorker? – Smith's poem has an ending quite different from, but no less sublime in the Romantic sense than, Shelley's. Shelley's image of decay, the 'shatter'd visage' of Ozymandias, remains safely over the horizon in 'an antique land (line 1) ... far away (line 14)': it represents no immediate threat to the laconic 'I' in the poem, nor to the European civilisation he embodies. Tyrants will come and go, his poem confidently implies, but civilisation outlasts them. (Shelley was writing only two years after the Battle of Waterloo and the defeat of Napoleon.)

By contrast, Smith's poem expresses no such confidence. Smith anticipates a time when the same fate that befell Ozymandias' city will befall modern civilisation. And he goes further: it's not, for him, just a question of the sands of time covering the traces of past glory – as it is for Shelley. For Smith, civilisation will ultimately go into reverse. Urban man will be replaced by the primitive hunter chasing, or being chased by, the wolves who have reclaimed the 'annihilated place' where the city used to be. You could not have a more vivid image of the insignificance of man or of the vanity of human wishes.

In this way, Smith's poem seems no less sublime than Shelley's. Far from being limited to 'an audience of a specific time or place' (19th-century London), it speaks to us in a way that even Shelley's poem cannot. For today, Smith's phrase 'forgotten Babylon' has acquired an unexpected resonance: in 1982 no less a modern Ozymandias than Saddam Hussein started to rebuild for himself the Babylonian palace of King Nebuchadnezzar in the middle of the desert. Iraqi workers laid millions of new bricks on top of the old palace ruins, each brick inscribed with the words, 'In the era of Saddam Hussein, protector of Iraq, who rebuilt civilisation and rebuilt Babylon.' But after only a few years these new bricks began to disintegrate and crumble back into sand.

....

Throughout, this discussion has stressed the points of similarity and difference between the two poems – sonnet form, narrative voice, description and location of the statue, etc. Getting students to look closely at these things for themselves, or to work in groups to study one sonnet each before coming together to identify key ways in which the two poems resemble or differ from each other; approaches such as these will give them a focus and a platform for a debate about which of the poems they find more effective – and why.

The discussion challenges a widely accessed critique of the two poems. Students need to develop the confidence to make such challenges for themselves. Using the Internet and library resources will easily lead them to other such debates, though first it may be better to select two or three such critical commentaries and invite the students to interrogate them in the same way as shown above – by asking how carefully the critics have actually read the poems.

The romantic image of a poet waiting for inspiration to strike still holds. So it may come as a shock to learn that one of the most famous of Romantic poems was written as a result of a pub competition. Students need to ask how particular poems came to be written, how they were first received, how and why they are still being received today – and then to ask how much difference, if any, this makes to the ways in which they respond to, and value, the poems themselves.

Using web-based and other electronic sources of information is an inescapable part of literary study today. It can be immensely valuable, provided that students learn how to be continually monitoring the usefulness and credibility of what they are discovering. The following websites offer some useful starting points for further work on the two 'Ozymandias' poems:

- For background on Shelley, Smith and Ozymandias, the Wikipedia article cited above is useful: (en.wikipedia.org/wiki/Ozymandias). Students should always check its reliability against other sites covering the same ground.
- For information about the Romantic idea of the Sublime, students can explore the excellent Victorian Web site: www.victorianweb.org/philosophy/sublime/sublimeov.html
- How did the statue of Ramses II get to be in the British Museum in the first place? www.thebritishmuseum.ac.uk/aes/aescoll3.html

Conversation with Coleridge: 'This Lime-Tree Bower My Prison'

This discussion of one of Coleridge's best known 'conversation' poems, 'This Lime-Tree Bower My Prison', begins with an examination of the circumstances in which the poem was written and ends with a glance at the way in which it was received by the person to whom it was addressed: Charles Lamb. These contexts are integrated into a detailed close reading, focusing both on a key intertextual phrase 'in the great city pent' and on the poet's treatment of light and sound. Coleridge himself insists on the context of writing by placing an author's note at the head of the poem. The idea of the poem as a conversation further contextualises it by linking it with other poems such as 'Frost at Midnight'. Questions for students to discuss could include:

- Is it important to know any more than Coleridge himself tells the reader?
- What is the value of calling this a 'conversation' poem? In what ways could the term be misleading?
- What are the most striking rhetorical or linguistic features of the poem?
- What do the intertextual references contribute to the reader's experience of the poem?
- Is the title really important? Would it have been a significantly different poem if called 'A Twilight Walk' or 'To Charles Lamb'?
- Does it matter what Charles Lamb thought of the poem?

. . . .

'This Lime-Tree Bower My Prison' is an odd title. How many other titles come from the second line of a poem, not the first? And how many include the word 'prison' – not counting Oscar Wilde's 'Ballad of Reading Gaol'?

> *In the June of 1797 some long-expected Friends paid a visit to the author's cottage; and on the morning of their arrival, he met with an accident, which disabled him from walking during the whole time of their stay. One evening, when they had left him for a few hours, he composed the following lines in the garden-bower.* (Note written by Coleridge to preface the poem)

This lime-tree bower, a shady spot with a seat, was actually in his neighbour's garden: Coleridge used to find it a good place to escape for a bit of peace and quiet. Exactly the opposite of a prison, in fact.

This is the point: imprisonment and escape are key ideas in 'This Lime-Tree Bower My Prison', and the title makes this clear. Coleridge felt trapped, for his injury kept him at home while William and Dorothy Wordsworth and his oldest friend, Charles Lamb, set off for their evening walk on the Quantock Hills. He'd been looking forward to it, partly no doubt as a perfect excuse for getting out of the house (he didn't get on with his wife). More importantly, he had wanted to share with the Wordsworths and Lamb their enjoyment of a dramatic landscape he had already described to them:

> that still roaring dell, of which I told:
> The roaring dell, o'erwooded, narrow, deep,
> And only speckled by the midday sun.

Watching them watching this would have been important: he had been sure that sharing the walk would give him:

> Beauties and feelings, such as would have been
> Most sweet to my remembrance even when age
> Had dimm'd mine eyes to blindness!

Like Wordsworth recalling the daffodils that 'flash upon that inward eye / Which is the bliss of solitude', Coleridge had wanted to replenish his store of happy memories. In fact, of course, he already had firmly in his mind's eye the view across the Bristol Channel and the sunset that Lamb and the Wordsworths were experiencing; it's what he describes in the first two sections of the poem:

> Now my friends emerge
> Beneath the wide wide Heaven – and view again
> The many-steepled tract magnificent
> Of hilly fields and meadows, and the sea,
> With some fair bark, perhaps, whose sails light up
> The slip of smooth clear blue betwixt two Isles
> Of purple shadow!

'This Lime-Tree Bower My Prison' is one of the poems that Coleridge labelled *'conversation poems'*, though he had some difficulty with the term. At first he tried *'conversational poem'*, and these lines show how he used the fluency of blank verse to create a relaxed conversational voice for the poem: the lack of rhyme and the absence of endstopping make you almost – but not quite – forget that Coleridge is writing in iambic pentameter. The carefully placed hesitation 'perhaps', offsetting the insistent use of alliteration (sea … some … sail … slip, etc.), also suggests the ebb and flow of casual speech, without being in any way casual writing.

As the poem develops, however, it resolves itself into a conversation with only one figure: Coleridge's oldest school-friend, Charles Lamb. 'This Lime-Tree Bower My Prison' actually carries the inscription

ADDRESSED TO CHARLES LAMB, OF THE INDIA HOUSE, LONDON

and the apparent formality of this is a deliberate contrast with the studied informality of the poem. Lamb, an essayist and critic, was at the centre of the London literary world of his day and a major figure in the story of English Romanticism. Unlike Coleridge and Wordsworth, however, Lamb always lived in, or on the edge of, London. This was partly from choice, because he loved London and city life; partly through necessity, because this was where he earned his living – as a clerk in the East India Company's offices. Mainly it was because of the 'strange calamity' Coleridge refers to: Lamb's sometimes mentally unstable sister, Mary, had killed their mother, and Lamb had committed himself to being her legal guardian for the rest of his life. This is why Coleridge refers to Lamb's 'sad yet patient soul' and calls him 'My gentle-hearted Charles', not once but three times during the poem.

In labelling Lamb 'OF THE INDIA HOUSE', Coleridge implies that he belongs to, is almost chained to, the London-based company for whom he worked. He describes his friend as longing to escape from London and get away to the country:

> Thou hast pined
> And hunger'd after Nature, many a year,
> In the great City pent.

'Pent' is important. It means imprisoned, also implying 'struggling to escape' – as in 'pent-up anger'. Coleridge presents Lamb as desperate to escape from the city; and the phrase 'In the great City pent' draws attention to itself by its inversion of the expected word order (a figure of speech called *hyperbaton*: syntactically, you'd expect to say Lamb had been 'imprisoned in the great city'). Surprisingly, it is a key intertextual phrase: Coleridge used it again in *Frost at Midnight*, referring to himself this time; Wordsworth used it at the end of Book 7 of *The Prelude* and Keats actually entitled one of his poems 'To One Who has Been Long in City Pent'. They all borrowed it from Milton, who coined the phrase in *Paradise Lost*, comparing Satan's excitement on entering the Garden of Eden with the joy of someone who, after being 'long in city pent / Where houses thick and Sewers annoy the Aire[1],' escapes to the country and feels free at last.

Which brings us back to Lamb, and to the poet in his lime-tree bower. To his surprise, Coleridge finds he has stopped worrying about what he is missing, and has been enjoying what he can see from under the branches:

> Pale beneath the blaze
> Hung the transparent foliage: and I watch'd
> Some broad and sunny leaf, and lov'd to see
> The shadow of the leaf and stem above
> Dappling its sunshine!

He does not have to use simile or metaphor here to evoke something he can only imagine: he simply records what he can see for himself. His lime-tree bower now turns out not to be a prison at all: the two negative experiences (being forced to stay at home and being unable to share his friends' company on the walk) are cancelled by the positive experience of realising he has escaped from a prison that was nothing but his own self-pity. In a remarkable sentence Coleridge expresses this by enclosing his prison within a double negative and turning it into a positive:

> Nor in this bower,
> This little lime-tree bower, have I not mark'd
> Much that has soothed me.

Now we can see why Coleridge chose his title: from this point in the poem, *all* negatives are turned to positives:

> Nature ne'er deserts the wise and pure;
> No plot so narrow, be but Nature there,
> No waste so vacant, but may well employ
> Each faculty of sense, and keep the heart
> Awake to Love and Beauty!

Negatives (no, not, nor, never) all begin with /n/. There are several in the last paragraph of the poem, often appearing powerfully at the beginning of a line or sentence. But here too, negatives are cancelled out, offset by a balancing group of six positive /n/ sounds: the equally powerful repetition of 'Nature' and 'now'. And just as imprisonment turns into escape, so images of darkness turn into light: the sun reflected on the elm trees' 'ancient ivy' makes 'their dark branches gleam a lighter hue'; the poet watches 'the black wing' of the last rook 'vanishing into light'.

Finally, when the sun has gone down, the same transformation from negative to positive is continued with sound. Even the sound of a bird in flight had (says Coleridge)

> a charm
> For thee, my gentle-hearted Charles, to whom
> No sound is dissonant which tells of Life.

The poem thus ends on a powerful note of affirmation: the last word is 'Life'. Whether the 'creeking' of a rook's wing really had a charm for Lamb, though, is doubtful: Coleridge was projecting his own feelings onto those of his friends – as he had done all through the poem. Certainly Lamb wasn't persuaded by the countryside: he suffered 'intolerable dullness' whenever he had to spend time out of London; to the end of his life he complained about poets who 'entice men from the cheerful haunts of streets'. And though he wrote to thank Coleridge for the poem, Lamb's final comment on 'This Lime-Tree Bower My Prison' must have startled its author:

> For God's sake (I never was more serious), don't make me ridiculous any more by terming me gentle-hearted in print ... Substitute drunken-dog, ragged-head, seld-shaven, odd-ey'd, stuttering, or any other epithet which truly and properly belongs to the gentleman in question.
>
> (Letter to Coleridge, August 1800)

'My seldom-shaven Charles'? Somehow it doesn't have quite the same ring.

• • • • • • • • • • • • • • • • • • • •

Much of this analysis has centred on the title of the poem, and the way Coleridge draws attention to the importance of 'this little lime-tree bower'. Working with students on titles is often a good strategy to get them to interrogate the poems themselves more closely. Just as the title of Wordsworth's sonnet 'Composed Upon Westminster Bridge' (see Chapter 6, pages 88–90) raised all sorts of textual and contextual issues, and just as the contrast between the titles of the Ozymandias sonnets may have had an impact on their relative popularity, so here the poem's title matters. It highlights the central issues of imprisonment and escape. Do other titles used by Coleridge have a similar function? Is Kubla Khan himself really the key to Coleridge's most famous poem? Would 'Frost at Midnight' have been a different poem if it had been entitled 'To Hartley'?

The poems by Wordsworth, Shelley and Coleridge so far discussed are among the most famous Romantic texts in the canon of English poetry. Taken together, how far do they help students to gain an understanding of what the term 'Romantic' can mean?

False context?: T.S. Eliot's 'Usk'

Sometimes a lesser known poem by a famous poet can throw an interesting light on his or her major work. Retrieving and discussing such poems can be a worthwhile way of demonstrating to students the greater range of a poet's writing. It can also, as with T.S. Eliot's 'Usk', be a good introduction to studying a difficult work such as *The Waste Land*, since this very short poem picks up some of the themes and techniques of Eliot's first masterpiece and looks forward to the writing of his second, *Four Quartets*. It provides, for example, an excellent starting point for discussing the importance of intertextuality in Eliot's writing.

Here again, the title of the poem provides an important but contested context. The starting point for the following discussion is a newspaper report claiming to have identified the poem's real location.

....

'Usk' is one of T.S. Eliot's least known poems. Written in 1935, hidden in his *Collected Poems* as one of five 'Landscapes', overlooked by readers and critics, its eleven lines have become almost invisible. In 2003, however, a flurry of headlines brought 'Usk' into the news. 'T.S. Eliot scholar finds answer to pub poet's riddle' announced the *Guardian*. Other papers followed the story. Professor Philip Edwards of Liverpool University had made a discovery: a village near the Monmouthshire town of Usk not only boasted an old once-whitewashed well but, nearby, an inn called the White Hart. The meaning of the poem, claimed the *Guardian* story, was now clear: 'Don't look for a deer or anything on four legs behind the white well; look instead for the White Hart Inn behind the well at Llangybi, Usk, and you'll know you're in the right place.'[3]

'Usk' a cryptic poem about the pleasures of going to the pub? Really?

Professor Edwards calls 'Usk' a 'short but baffling poem'. It is certainly short: sixty-five words, just ten of which are more than one syllable. None of the words is on its own obscure, although the verb 'spell' may be puzzling. But 'spell' provides a clue to the first half of the poem. Taken together with 'enchantments' and other words evoking medieval romance (the 'lance', for instance) or mystery (wells, often credited with magical or miraculous significance), 'do not spell' suggests a warning not to spend too much time pursuing the traditions and superstitions of the past. Yet the poem speaks to someone who is on a quest: the reader is invited to join the poet on a private pilgrimage to a chapel, not in a valley or a village but literally over the hills and far away. He is certainly not in search of a pub – as the first words of the poem make clear.

White Hart Inns still abound – a reminder of how widespread the white hart symbol once was. It was prominent in the Quest for the Holy Grail – and hence in Arthurian legend. The white hart came to represent in Christian art and literature the idea of the resurrected Jesus. In the Wilton Diptych, at the National Gallery in London, Richard II is shown wearing a white hart jewel, as are all the angels surrounding the Virgin Mary. Is this the authentic context in which, as readers of Eliot's poem, we should take the white hart? If so, then one way at least of reading 'Usk' is to see it as a poem about a search for faith – and anyone who reads Eliot knows that such a search occupies much of his later poetry, certainly the poetry following *The Waste Land* (1922).

The first part of 'Usk' concludes with a warning that legend and tradition are appealing but should be treated cautiously: 'Gently dip …'. Eliot put this line in quotation marks: a few minutes' Internet search reveals that it comes from a song by the Elizabethan dramatist George Peele, from his 1595 play *The Old Wives' Tale*, which is itself a play concerned with old superstitions and enchantments:

> Gently dip, but not too deep,
> for fear thou make the golden beard to weep.
> Fair maid, white and red,
> stroke me smooth, and comb my head,

In a recording he made of 'Usk', Eliot read this line in a sing-song voice as if it were part of a nursery rhyme – perhaps a line remembered from his childhood.

As a poet, he believed strongly in the value of such personal memories. He once wrote to a friend, when he was having difficulty composing *Little Gidding*: 'The defect of the whole poem, I feel, is the lack of some acute personal reminiscence (never to be explicated, of course, but to give power from well below the surface) …'.[4] He expected these reminiscences to remain buried. They were important for him but not for the reader. If Eliot, then, did indeed go to Llangybi and find the White Hart Inn behind an old well, he would have enjoyed the fact that the mystical animal in the poem is polysemic, that it has more than one connotation, but he would not have expected his readers to identify all these meanings. In one sense, therefore, the poem is a warning to readers not to dig too deeply, or they will overlook the real significance of the poem. Whatever else he was, Eliot was not a 'pub poet' as the *Guardian* labelled him.

All Eliot's poems are conversations, both with the reader (and, sometimes, with himself) and with other writers and other texts. It is often argued today that all texts borrow from other texts whether explicitly or implicitly, deliberately or unconsciously. Language is never new: words and ideas are constantly recycled and reinterpreted in the light of how they have been used in the past. This emphasis on intertextuality applies in particular to Eliot, and he was acutely aware of what he was doing by using direct and indirect allusion. In *The Waste Land*, for example, the accumulation of quotations and echoes ranging from the *Upanishads* to Ragtime literally represent 'these fragments I have shored against my ruins'.

In 'Usk' too Eliot uses a wide range of reference. Besides the quotation from George Peele, two other echoes are worth noticing. 'Glance aside', with its internal rhyme word 'lance' seems to be echoing Shakespeare's Sonnet 139, a poem in which the speaker says:

> Dear heart forbear to glance thine eye aside,
> What needs't thou wound with cunning when thy might
> Is more than my o'erpress'd defence can bide?

Unlike Shakespeare, however, Eliot uses the phrase 'glance aside' emphatically. In eleven lines there are no fewer than eight imperatives; and these injunctions, together with the dominance of single-syllable words, give 'Usk' an unexpected force. As you read, the poem as a whole sounds in fact like an incantation, itself a kind of spell. A further device, adding to this sense of a forceful spell, is the pairing of strong alliterating sounds (**br** / **br**; **d** / **d**; **p** / **p**) in the first, middle and last lines.

For Eliot, then, 'glance aside' is a powerful command: 'Don't keep looking back to the past' (represented by the knightly lance, a symbol of chivalry but also of war and hence of conflict). At the same time, the lure of the past is strong, and the final destination, a hidden chapel associated with a hermit, hardly seems to belong in the modern world. Significantly, Shakespeare again anticipates Eliot's past / present dilemma. In Sonnet 76 he asks:

> Why with the time do I not glance aside
> To new-found methods, and to compounds strange?

He answers his own question later in the poem: 'all my best is dressing old words new' – finding new ways of re-saying the same thing. Eliot's poem, too, finds new ways to express powerful old words. If in one sense 'Usk' is about a quest or pilgrimage, then the key command of the poem, 'Lift your eyes', echoes one of the most famous lines from Old Testament: 'I will lift up mine eyes unto the hills, from whence cometh my help' (Psalm 121). Eliot never uses the word 'hills' in 'Usk', but his description of the landscape in which his search is located suggests clearly the undulating Breconshire countryside of the Vale of Usk where the hills do indeed 'gently dip'. This echo from George Peele's play thus refers *backwards* to the well which embodies the superstitions of the past and *forwards* to the landscape where the quest, the pilgrimage, will end. It is the middle line, the pivot, of the poem.

The idea of the remote chapel is an important symbol in Eliot's poetry. In *The Waste Land* the 'decayed hole among the mountains' ('What the Thunder Said') is the Chapel Perilous of the Grail Quest, now empty ('only the wind's home') and derelict, a symbol of the death of faith:

> It has no windows, and the door swings,
> Dry bones can harm no one.   (lines 389–90)

In *Four Quartets*, Eliot describes the chapel of Little Gidding as 'the end of the journey … the world's end'. It is a place 'where prayer has been valid' and where 'History is now and England'. The chapel of the hermit in 'Usk', the destination of another quest to the world's end (where earth meets sky), thus links the two most important poems of Eliot's career in an unexpected way. Far from being just a 'short but baffling' landscape poem, 'Usk' reflects Eliot's continuing search for an answer to 'that overwhelming question' first asked in 'The Love Song of J. Alfred Prufrock'. It also suggests his growing confidence that an answer is to be found, not in the 'Unreal City' of *The Waste Land* nor in myths and legends, but in the quieter landscape whose contours are described in the second half of 'Usk'.

This change of mood is reflected in the way 'Usk' is written. The first half of the poem is restless and disjointed from the start, the lines disrupted by repeated breaks. The opening line begins with a warning ('Do not …', the first of four negatives in the poem – all in lines 1–6); it has no clear rhythm, it ends awkwardly and is the only line in the poem for which there is no rhyme. By contrast, in the rest of the poem there are no negatives and no punctuation pauses until the middle of the final line 11. The idea of the quest is emphasised in the three-times repeated 'Where', while the sense that the destination is in sight is reinforced by the final triple rhyme of the last three lines. These are not accidental effects. Eliot himself once said, 'No *vers* is *libre* for the man who wants to do a good job.'

'Usk' reveals much about Eliot's ways of thinking and writing. It also changes the way we think about his earlier poetry, and his later. In one of his most important essays, 'Tradition and the Individual Talent', Eliot himself acknowledged this:

> What happens when a new work of art is created is something that happens simultaneously to all the works of art which preceded it. The whole existing order must be, if ever so slightly, altered … The past is altered by the present as much as the present is directed by the past.[5]

The relationship of any text to other texts, and (in Eliot's case) to the texts to which it speaks directly through quotation, echo and allusion, provides a valuable contextual starting point. And each time we change the context in which 'Usk' is read – whether in relation to the group of poems called *Landscapes,* to its own geographical setting, or in relation to the author's life and other writing as a whole – we open up new ways of responding to a poem I have described as 'almost invisible', yet which rewards close reading. But while some contexts are illuminating, others are not. Eliot may or may not have stopped at the White Hart Inn for a glass of sherry while he puzzled over the *Times* crossword. If he did, does it make any difference to the poem or to how we can read it? Surely not.

In any case, in 1935 (the year of 'Usk's composition) Eliot went on a motoring holiday into Wales with John Morley, his friend and co-director of Faber and Faber. Together they visited the grave of the metaphysical poet Henry Vaughan in the churchyard of Llansantffraed beside the river Usk. Did they on the same journey perhaps make a brief diversion in search of the hermit memorably described by John Kilvert in his dairy for July 1872? Kilvert describes his own visit to 'the Revd. John Price, Master of Arts of Cambridge University and Vicar of Llanbedr Painscastle' as a pilgrimage and – using the same adjectives that Eliot later uses in 'Usk' – describes the hermit's chapel as 'his grey hut in the green cwm'.[6]

· · · · · · · · · · · · · · · · · · · ·

The Guardian article 'T.S. Eliot scholar finds answer to pub poet's riddle' can be found at books.guardian.co.uk/news/articles/0,6109,1013056,00.html.

HarperCollins AudioBooks publish a recording, *T.S. Eliot Reading The Waste Land and Four Quartets.* (ISBN 0-00-104687-x) This also contains several other poems from his *Selected Poems*, as well as *Landscapes*, including 'Usk'. It is significant that when, on this recording, Eliot comes to read 'Usk' he announces the poem thus: 'Usk, in Wales'. Llangybi (the location suggested by Professor Edwards) is in Monmouthshire, which was, until the county boundary revisions of the 1970s, an English county – not in Wales at all.

When is a sonnet not a sonnet?: form as context

In the previous discussions in this chapter, contexts have been mainly historical, biographical and intertextual, or they have dealt with the context of a poem's composition and reception. Now the focus changes to form as context. Students will be familiar (or will think they are) with the basic idea of a sonnet, but asking them to research and evaluate the differences between Petrarchan, Shakespearean and Miltonic sonnets will quickly take them into discussions about the relationship between form and content.

- How far can the definitions of a sonnet be stretched?
- Is the form of a sonnet governed by rules or conventions?
- What expectations does a reader bring to a poem which presents itself as a sonnet, even if it does not have fourteen lines?
- Why has the sonnet proved the most resilient of all closed verse forms used in English?

....

When is a sonnet not a sonnet? One meaning of the word is simply 'a short poem of a lyric character' (that's from the Oxford Dictionary) – in other words, something like a short song. John Donne's early love poems are contained in a collection he called *Songs and Sonnets*, but none of them would we call a sonnet today. Indeed, Donne (who wrote some of the most powerful religious sonnets in literature – 'Death be not proud', 'Batter my heart', etc.) was clearly in two minds about the value of sonnets: he wrote in a letter of 1609 (the year in which Shakespeare's Sonnets were first published as a collection), 'He is a fool which cannot make one Sonnet, and he is mad which makes two.' Other writers have been equally ambivalent. Wordsworth admitted in a letter to Walter Savage Landor (1802), 'I used to think the sonnet egregiously absurd', but he went on to write over a hundred sonnets of his own including one that began 'Scorn not the sonnet'. In another he wrote

> for me,
> In sundry moods, 'twas pastime to be bound
> Within the Sonnet's scanty plot of ground;
> Pleased if some Souls (for such there needs must be)
> Who have felt the weight of too much liberty,
> Should find brief solace there, as I have found.

It is clear from this that Wordsworth thought that the 'scanty plot of ground' was itself a welcome relief after the freedom ('too much liberty') to write in whatever form one chooses. He came to like the strict form of the fourteen-line poem with rules you had to obey. He particularly admired the sonnets that Milton had written, and tried to copy the style of poems such as 'On his blindness'. What would he have thought then of some of Shakespeare's sonnets which seem to break, flagrantly, all the rules?

If you think that all Shakespeare's sonnets have fourteen lines or that they are always written in iambic pentameter lines, or that they follow a set number of rhyme-schemes, prepare for a surprise. Sonnet 145 is written in tetrameter lines (eight syllables, rather than the usual ten); Sonnet 126 has only twelve lines, while Sonnet 99 has fifteen lines:

> The forward violet thus did I chide:
> Sweet thief, whence didst thou steal thy sweet that smells,
> If not from my love's breath? The purple pride
> Which on thy soft cheek for complexion dwells
> In my love's veins thou hast too grossly dy'd.   5
> The lily I condemned for thy hand,
> And buds of marjoram had stol'n thy hair;
> The roses fearfully on thorns did stand,
> One blushing shame, another white despair;
> A third, nor red nor white, had stol'n of both,   10
> And to his robbery had annexed thy breath;
> But, for his theft, in pride of all his growth
> A vengeful canker eat him up to death.
>   More flowers I noted, yet I none could see,
>   But sweet or colour it had stol'n from thee.   15

The extra line here is the first one, for the rhyming word 'chide' belongs with 'pride' (line 3) and 'dy'd' (line 5), and it cannot simply be edited out as a careless mistake – perhaps an alternative opening line which Shakespeare would have removed if he had been checking the printer's proofs more carefully. If the poem had begun with line 2 ('Sweet thief ...') it would have fitted the pattern of a conventional fourteen-line sonnet, but we, the readers, would not know that the poet is *apparently* addressing a particular flower, the violet. Nor would we realise, when we reached line 6, that the first line has been a piece of deliberate indirection: *actually* he is speaking to his lover, telling him what he had said to the violet, the lily, the marjoram and the roses. (It is significant that the phrase 'Sweet thief' has already been used by Shakespeare to refer to the lover, in Sonnet 35.) No, this sonnet was meant to break the fourteen-line rule. Does this matter? Was Shakespeare just experimenting, or was he trying to make a point by drawing special attention to the poem? Whatever the answer, we have here a sonnet which, in the strict sense, isn't a sonnet.

The sonnet is the great survivor of English poetry. First appearing in the early 16th century, as an experiment in translation, it has been popular in every century since, except perhaps for the 18th: from Sir Philip Sydney and Edmund Spenser in the Elizabethan era, to John Donne and George Herbert in the Jacobean age that followed; from Milton to Wordsworth and from Elizabeth Barrett Browning to Gerard Manley Hopkins; from Thomas Hardy to Tony Harrison and Seamus Heaney and Simon Armitage. But few of these always or only wrote conventional sonnets: Milton, for instance, usually ignored the division that traditionally comes between the octave (the first eight lines) and the sestet (the remaining six lines); Hopkins wrote what he called 'curtal sonnets' – carefully scaled down sonnets of 10 ½ lines, such as 'Pied Beauty' and 'Ash Boughs'. Tony Harrison has written many sonnets of sixteen lines, and Heaney continues to publish poems that he calls sonnets but which seem to break most of the rules of sonnet form. The first of his 'Sonnets from Hellas' (in *Electric Light*, 2001), for instance, though of fourteen lines, seems to pay scant attention to line length or rhyme:

> It was opulence and amen on the mountain road.
> Walnuts bought on a high pass from a farmer
> Who'd worked in Melbourne once and now trained water
> Through a system of pipes and runnels of split reed
> Known in Hellas, probably, since Hesiod –
> That was the least of it. When we crossed the border
> From Argos into Arcadia, and farther
> Into Arcadia, a lorry load
> Of apples had burst open on the road
> So that for yards our tyres raunched and scrunched them
> But we drove on, juiced up and fleshed and spattered,
> Revelling in it. And then it was the goatherd
> With his goats in the forecourt of the filling station,
> Subsisting beyond eclogue and translation.

This seems to break the following 'rules':

- only lines eight and nine have ten syllables *and* can be scanned as conventional iambic lines, stressing the second, fourth, sixth syllable, etc.
- most of the lines are eleven syllables or more
- the poem can't be subdivided into two units of eight and six lines each, nor into the Shakespearean form of three quatrains (four-line stanzas), plus a final couplet.

And yet, is the sonnet really as irregular as it seems? The last two lines clearly rhyme (*station / translation*). So – almost – do the previous two lines (*spattered / goatherd*) and, before that, lines eight and nine (*load / road*). In the earlier part of the poem there are no clear rhymes like these; there are, however, some near rhymes, such as *road / reed* and *farmer / father.* Doesn't this suggest that the poem is travelling (like the poet himself, driving into the region of Arcadia – in Ancient Greece the setting for pastoral poetry) towards some sort of resolution, the rhymes becoming more precise as the poem progresses towards its climax? But it is not the resolution or climax the poet is expecting: having got to Arcadia, almost intoxicated ('juiced up') by the 'raunched' apples, he is confronted by a sight so bizarre (the ancient goatherd with his goats cluttering up the forecourt of the modern filling station) that it defies his imagination as a poet. He cannot translate it or fit it into an appropriate pastoral form, such as the eclogue, and so he just has to describe what he sees. The poem records this extraordinary scene like a photograph, but one which achieves for the reader what Heaney has described as 'the otherness of an image with the power, in Yeats's words, "to engross the present and dominate memory".'[6]

Fourteen-line sonnets, even if 'of lyric character', are clearly not songs designed to be set to music. They are often written in the form of an argument, the speaker talking to himself, or asking questions and hardly waiting for an answer. It is rare for there to be more than one voice in a sonnet. And yet a sonnet can be very nearly a song, and a song can be very nearly a sonnet. Here is a lyric poem, written to be accompanied on the lute, by Thomas Campion (1567–1620):

> When thou must home to shades of underground,
> And there arrived, a new admired guest,
> The beauteous spirits do engirt thee round,
> White Iope, blithe Helen, and the rest,
> To hear the stories of thy finish'd love
> From that smooth tongue whose music hell can move;
>
> Then wilt thou speak of banqueting delights,
> Of masques and revels which sweet youth did make,
> Of tourneys and great challenges of knights,
> And all these triumphs for thy beauty's sake:
> When thou hast told these honours done to thee,
> Then tell, O tell, how thou didst murder me!

Like many sonnets this has a 'When … then' construction, and builds up to a stunning and unexpected climax – though line 6, one realises after reading line 12, sounded a warning note. It has a rhyming couplet that, recapitulating the 'when … then' of the poem as a whole, puts some of Shakespeare's in the shade. But of course, with its two regular six-line stanzas, each made up of quatrain + couplet, this poem clearly isn't a sonnet at all. The lute tune composed by Campion to accompany it can be repeated exactly in the second half of the poem – which could not happen with a sonnet. Actually, many of Shakespeare's sonnets really reach their climax in line 12, with the couplet simply summing up, or re-stating, the situation rather than adding anything new. See how often Shakespeare puts a full stop at the end of line 12, emphasising that he has completed three quatrains which *could* have been set to music. Sometimes, in fact, his couplets seem almost banal or trite, tagged on uncomfortably to what has gone before:

> Or else of thee this I prognosticate:
> Thy end is truth's and beauty's doom and date. (Sonnet 14)

> For as the sun is daily new and old,
> So is my love still telling what is told. (Sonnet 76)

> No want of conscience hold it that I call
> Her 'love' for whose dear love I rise and fall. (Sonnet 151)

This apparent awkwardness may be one reason why many sonnet writers have preferred to abandon the couplet, and some have actually hidden the fact that they are writing sonnets at all. Here are two of the most famous poems from the Great War: are they both sonnets?

The Soldier

If I should die, think only this of me:
That there's some corner of a foreign field
That is for ever England. There shall be
In that rich earth a richer dust concealed;
A dust whom England bore, shaped, made aware,
Gave, once, her flowers to love, her ways to roam,
A body of England's, breathing English air,
Washed by the rivers, blest by suns of home.
And think, this heart, all evil shed away,
A pulse in the eternal mind, no less
Gives somewhere back the thoughts by England given;
Her sights and sounds; dreams happy as her day;
And laughter, learnt of friends; and gentleness,
In hearts at peace, under an English heaven.

Futility

Move him into the sun –
Gently its touch awoke him once,
At home, whispering of fields unsown.
Always it woke him, even in France,

Until this morning and this snow.
If anything might rouse him now
The kind old sun will know.

Think how it wakes the seeds, –
Woke, once, the clays of a cold star.
Are limbs, so dear-achieved, are sides,
Full-nerved, – still warm, – too hard to stir?
Was it for this the clay grew tall?
– O what made fatuous sunbeams toil
To break earth's sleep at all?

Both poems are fourteen lines in length; both deal with the subject of death in war; both have the sun and earth as key images. Brooke's poem is a conventional Petrarchan sonnet, whose sestet rhymes *efgefg*. Owen's poem is not at first glance a sonnet at all, and a purist might say that with its short lines and its seven-line stanzas it could never be one. On the other hand it conforms to the two-part structure and builds to a powerful climax where the last two lines function as a couplet, but one reinforced by the linking rhyme words 'tall ... toil ... all'. Nor is Owen's poem afraid of rhetorical phrases and effects: lines 10 and 11, for example, and the crescendo of questions in the second stanza. In fact with these and the climactic 'fatuous sunbeams' it resists all the attempts at consolation that 'The Soldier' offers to the listener ('blest by suns of home'), as if Owen's poem is almost a direct riposte to Brooke's, replacing the too-comfortable assumptions of the earlier poem ('this heart, all evil shed away ...', etc.) with the sense, literally, of futility: 'Was it for this the clay grew tall?'

In the end, whether the poem is or is not strictly a sonnet is really less important than whether it has the power to 'engross the present and dominate memory' as Yeats (who rarely wrote sonnets) so memorably said.

....

There is a fuller discussion of Shakespeare's sonnets in 'The silent speaker in Shakespeare's sonnets' (Chapter 8, pages 152–157). For a different context in which to discuss Rupert Brooke's sonnet 'The Soldier', see Chapter 4 (page 43) and Chapter 10 (pages 236–244): 'Travel writing in a literary context: Brooke's *Letters from America*'.

A useful website where students can begin to investigate the sonnet in a world-literature context can be found at www.sonnets.org/java.htm.

8 | Shakespearean contexts

FABIAN: If this were played upon a stage now, I could condemn it as an improbable fiction.

*(Shakespeare **Twelfth Night**, c.1600, III.iv.121)*

It would of course be easy to devote a whole book – or several books – to the question of how to teach Shakespeare in context. Nor is this a recent question that has only just started to worry academics, teachers and examiners. The first section of this chapter reproduces an English Association pamphlet, *The Teaching of Shakespeare in Schools*, from 1908, a century ago, which shows how old (but still how modern) this debate is. The precise issue of how Shakespeare can be contextualised has already been touched on in Chapter 4: 'Context' in context (pages 36–38).

Since the rise of post-colonial theory – indeed, since the Second World War – questions of race, creed and identity have underscored much of the critical debate and most of the performances of plays such as *Othello* and *The Merchant of Venice*. Perhaps not surprisingly these have become two of the plays most frequently set for GCSE and A level – though it is worth pointing out that, more and more, students study Shakespeare for coursework, not for written exams, and therefore teachers themselves have the greatest say in which plays get studied.

Current approaches to the assessment of Shakespeare at A level are described in the commentary that frames *The Teaching of Shakespeare in Schools*, while the Venetian contexts of Shakespeare's two Venetian plays are the focus of the discussion that follows. At a time when Venice is one of the most visited cities in the world, does the city of today, as seen by tourists and TV audiences, provide a relevant context for the examination of plays first performed four hundred years ago?

Shakespeare's sonnets are mostly under-explored by students. The discussion centring on a particular, not-well-known, poem (Sonnet 140 'Be wise as thou art cruel, do not press') suggests ways in which a close reading and intense focus on the language of the poem can help students to identify unexpected contexts and to move outwards to make connections with other poems in the sequence.

Moving outwards and making connections is also the theme of the final discussion, 'A word and its contexts', which starts with a very minor character – the Priest in *Twelfth Night* – and asks why he should be the only character in the whole of Shakespeare to own a watch. Exploring this question leads on to a second question, what does the word 'watch' mean in Shakespeare? Pursuing both these questions offers a model of how to engage students in the detailed examination of Shakespearean text and how to illustrate for them the necessary relationship between text and dramatic action.

Teaching Shakespeare: 1908 seen from 2008

It is unusual for an English Association pamphlet to be quoted twice in one week in the national press; doubly so when the pamphlet dates from 1908. But this happened in 2006 when one of the EA's first publications, *The Teaching of Shakespeare in Schools*, was cited both in the *Times Educational Supplement* (29 September) and in *The Independent* (5 October).

These references were prompted by the Royal Shakespeare Company's launch of a campaign to improve the teaching of Shakespeare in schools. At the launch Maria Evans, Director of Learning at the RSC, had said, 'Shakespeare in schools is still influenced by the literary criticism which taught plays as if they were the same as novels and poetry. We don't yet put enough emphasis on performance.' The RSC pointed to *The Teaching of Shakespeare in Schools* as evidence that this concern has dated back at least a century: in the final paragraph the anonymous author had written, 'There is a danger in the classroom, with textbooks open before us, of our forgetting what drama really means.' The following discussion reproduces in full the 1908 pamphlet, which raises critical questions about how far the work on Shakespeare done with students has really progressed in the past hundred years.

· · · · · · · · · · · · · · · · · · ·

Does the doctrine L.C. Knights expounded back in 1933 in 'How Many Children Had Lady Macbeth?' ('The only profitable approach to Shakespeare is a consideration of his plays as dramatic poems, of his use of language to obtain a total complex emotional response') really still hold? If so, is this a problem confined to schools? Clearly not, for the new University of Warwick – RSC collaboration, The CAPITAL Centre, is dedicated to 'creativity and performance in teaching and learning'. Its press release says that by moving 'from the texts of literature to the texts of performance' the Centre aims to 'break down barriers between the theatre and the academy to pioneer and investigate non-traditional modes of teaching'.

Yet while few teachers in secondary or higher education would quarrel with these aims, anxiety about what should be the prime focus of Shakespeare study in schools remains. In 2006 the Higher Education Academy (HEA) English Subject Centre published a report by Neill Thew, *Teaching Shakespeare: a survey of the undergraduate level in higher education*, which found that 89% of those responding to its survey believed that students were 'at best "adequately" and at worst "poorly" prepared for their studies in Shakespeare':

> Most respondents felt that the main problems concerned students' lack of
> linguistic, historical and cultural knowledge … students lack confidence in
> handling close reading and analysis of Shakespeare's language, but also in
> how to read playtexts more generally …

Respondents variously stressed the importance of increasing students'
sensitivity to Shakespeare's language; to historical context; and to genre.

(Thew: 3.3, p.7)

These familiar criticisms, if justified, require a thoughtful and positive response.
How should Shakespeare be taught? How should Shakespeare be examined? How
far should the latter determine the former? How much prior study and knowledge
of Shakespeare should HE tutors of first-year undergraduates expect?

There are no easy answers to these questions, but some examples of current
practice will highlight the problems. Students taking the *Option Internationale
Britannique* of the French Baccalauréat, for instance, prepare a single play on
which they are examined orally by a pair of external examiners: half an hour before
their exam, they are given a passage of about thirty lines and allowed to prepare
a ten-minute commentary on the passage, which they then deliver and about
which they are questioned for a further five minutes. Is this a better or worse way
to prepare for the transition to studying Shakespeare at university than the latest
British options in the reformulated A levels of 2008?

Awarding Body	AS or A2, and Unit title	Assessment method
AQA(a)	A2: 'Extended Essay and Shakespeare Study'	*Coursework*: students include discussion of a Shakespeare play in their extended essay (alongside a comparative study of two other texts)
AQA (b)	AS: 'Dramatic Genres'	*Coursework*: one essay on a single play on 'an aspect of dramatic / tragic genre'
Edexcel	AS: 'Explorations in Drama'	*Coursework*: one essay on any Shakespeare play, to include comparison with another play and analysis of critical response
OCR	A2: 'Drama and Poetry pre-1800'	*Closed book examination*: one essay on a specified text, responding to a view of the play
WJEC	A2: 'Shakespeare and Poetry in Context'	*Closed book examination*: one essay comparing a Shakespeare play with another, non-Shakespeare text
Cambridge Pre-U	'Drama'	*Closed book examination:* one essay from a choice of two, one of which will be passage-based.

This table makes it clear that from 2008 onwards an English Literature student's experience of Shakespeare, post-16, will depend very much on which A level specification his or her teachers have chosen to follow. It also suggests that opportunities for close reading on the one hand or for contextual study, on the other, may be limited. Shakespeare remains a protected author (indeed, the only protected author) in the National Curriculum, and students studying Shakespeare for an advanced course will have had to encounter his plays at Key Stage 3 and at GCSE. But is this progression the best preparation, and how does it compare with progression routes in the past? The English Association's 1908 pamphlet remains one of the very few documents which attempts to trace a child's encounters with Shakespeare from the ages of twelve to eighteen, and continues to offer a challenge to everyone teaching Shakespeare today.

THE TEACHING OF SHAKESPEARE IN SCHOOLS

All proposals which affect higher study are rigidly conditioned by the exigencies of the timetable, and in most secondary schools it is difficult, as matters stand at present, to secure more than two periods a week for the teaching of English literature. These are, of course, utterly inadequate for the purpose, but in suggesting and criticising we are bound to take into account the limitations imposed upon the teacher. How, then, are we to cover the ground? Above all, how are we to secure the recognition due to Shakespeare as the supreme figure of our literature? To crowd out other writers is disastrous; contemporary poetry, for instance, has special claims upon us, and its educational value is very great. To be practical, a Shakespeare programme must be modest; only a limited number of plays can be read during a pupil's life at school. But the choice of suitable plays is all-important, and must vary with the age of the readers. Like the commentators on Shakespeare, we must map out 'periods'. At best the work, even in the higher classes, is by nature introductory; the essential thing is, from the first, to make the introduction interesting.

The first point to decide is how much time, in a school working under normal conditions, can be set apart for the study of Shakespeare. A practical plan adopted in some schools is to devote the literature periods in one term every year exclusively to it. This, or its equivalent in time, is needed to preserve the balance between Shakespeare and other writers. The work may be arranged on a graduated scale to suit the needs of the different classes. A beginning may be made in the lowest classes with a song from the plays, a few detached lines chosen for their poetic beauty, an occasional speech, and finally a complete scene, such as the Hubert and Arthur episode in *King John,* the tragical comedians in *A Midsummer Night's Dream,* King Henry at Agincourt, or the Forum scene of *Julius Caesar.*

It is important that the class should be introduced to this complete scene by hearing it read aloud, and that a sufficient explanation of verbal difficulties should at once follow the reading: the passage can be taken later as a prepared lesson.

At what age should the study of the plays as a regular part of the curriculum begin? There appears to be a difference of opinion among teachers on this question, and in the practice of the schools themselves there is a similar difference, the age varying from twelve to fourteen. Twelve is the downward limit in the four years' course which the Board of Education formulated a short time ago. The age of twelve may be accepted as a suitable starting-point, and, in order to make their suggestions both definite and practical, the Committee mark off three stages of Shakespearean study intended to cover a child's school-life – (1) between the ages of twelve and fourteen, (2) between the ages of fourteen and sixteen or seventeen, (3) from seventeen upwards. In actual practice there will, of course, be transition and overlapping, for which the teacher must provide.

I. BETWEEN THE AGES OF TWELVE AND FOURTEEN

The formidable difficulty which the language of Shakespeare offers to a beginner is the first thing to grapple with, and help must be given liberally. Probably the best play for a beginner is *Julius Caesar,* which is noble in theme and simple in style; and *Henry V* may be suggested as an alternative. It would be well to follow with a comedy, in order to show the diversity of Shakespeare's genius: the choice lies between *The Merchant of Venice* (probably the best introduction to the comedies), *Twelfth Night, A Midsummer Night's Dream,* and *As You Like It.* The teacher should take the play as completely as possible, selecting scenes which form the connecting links in the main plot and give the children a clear idea of the chief characters.

The primary task of the teacher at this stage will be to make the play intelligible as a whole. A few suggestions are offered as to method.

(1) *Reading.* It is desirable that all the Shakespeare chosen for study should be read aloud in class. The living voice will often give a clue to the meaning, and reading aloud is the only way of ensuring a knowledge of the metre. In a class of beginners the teacher must take a liberal share of the reading, but the

pupils should be brought into play. They can be cast for some of the parts; the Forum scene in *Julius Caesar* comes one step nearer the dramatic if the teacher is Antony and the other parts are distributed and the class is transformed into a Roman mob shouting for the will.

(2) *Repetition.* Obviously some of the finer passages taken in the reading should be committed to memory.

(3) *Study of Plot.* On a modest scale and within practicable limits this should be attempted from the first. The main outline of the story alone should be discussed; an underplot should, wherever possible, be sacrificed, in order to concentrate on the central features. In the case of *Julius Caesar* or *Henry V* a few well-chosen extracts from North or Holinshed will prove helpful – for instance, the paragraph of simple narrative which suggested Antony's funeral oration, or the speech of Henry at Agincourt.

(4) *Study of Characterisation.* Obviously this will be elementary, but a definite attempt should be made to realise the leading characters as far as young boys and girls are able to appreciate them. Such a point as the contrast between Brutus and Cassius is easy to indicate.

Where the pupils take a full play, it may be possible to call attention to a few special points based clearly and definitely on the speeches of the leading characters. To prevent misunderstanding, it may be well to quote an instance from the speeches of Brutus in *Julius Caesar.* In the soliloquy, 'It must be by his death' (II. i. 10–34) Brutus confesses that Caesar is above reproach, and has shown no inclination to abuse his power; but, if he is crowned, he may alter, and therefore he must be killed. Immediately afterwards Brutus denounces this just and moderate rule as ' high-sighted tyranny' under which no man's life is safe *(ib.* 118–9). Later, looking back on the murder, he speaks of having

> struck the foremost man of all this world
> But for supporting robbers.   (IV. iii. 22–3)

The class would see the inconsistency or could easily be made to see it; the problem for them would be 'Is Brutus sincere?' They should know enough of his character to answer 'Yes', and the teacher can then give the explanation. But subtle points of this nature must be few in number; in fact they are mainly an experiment to test the brighter wits of the class. And further, they must be based only on brief quotations: a phrase, a line, or at most a sentence, is long enough. The data must be such that a line or two on the blackboard will suffice. If an apology were needed for advising a resort to that unpoetic implement, it would be that these first steps in criticism must be made perfectly clear. It is not advisable, at this stage, to turn over the leaves of the text; beginners cannot be expected to keep firmly in mind even a short sequence such as this. The evidence must be marshalled.

(5) It is assumed, in the suggestions outlined here, that grammatical and linguistic instruction will be kept entirely in the background, and only such explanation given as is necessary for the clear understanding of the text.

II. BETWEEN THE AGES OF FOURTEEN AND SIXTEEN OR SEVENTEEN

The advance at this stage will be considerable, for the subject can be treated systematically and the range of choice will be far wider. The texts of the plays already named can be thoroughly studied, and further plays can be added to the curriculum, viz. *Richard III, Richard II,* both parts of *Henry IV* (of course in a school edition), *King John, The Tempest, Macbeth, Much Ado About Nothing, Henry VIII.*

Attention should be fixed on the following points:
(a) The general dramatic conduct of the plot: the sources of the story and their treatment by Shakespeare may be studied profitably in this connection. Holinshed, for instance, throws a flood of light on Shakespeare's dramatic method.
(b) The detailed delineation of character.
(c) Diction and metre.
(d) Verbal difficulties, references and allusions.

Pupils should also be made acquainted with the chief facts of Shakespeare's career and the conditions of stage-representation in his time. The form of the Elizabethan theatre actually influenced the dramatic writing: for instance, the platform-stage lent itself to sustained rhetoric to an extent not possible in the present day; and the popular 'jig' between the acts with the accompanying improvisation of the Fool not only explains historically the element of comic relief to be found in Elizabethan tragedy, but reveals the supreme art of Shakespeare in making the action of a mere intruder an integral part of the drama. The Porter's speech in *Macbeth* is an interesting illustration.

Reading and repetition should still be regarded as essential: by far the most satisfactory method of starting work upon a play is to read it through in class, dwelling on the broad outlines of plot and characterisation, and postponing the study of *minutiae*. The plan takes time, but it has the compensating merit of fixing attention on the essential points to begin with, and of rousing the interest of the class.

III. FROM THE AGE OF SEVENTEEN AND UPWARDS

The difficulties of adjusting the curriculum are felt acutely at the top of the school; hence it may not be possible in the Shakespeare lessons to study more than a single play, and in that case the preference should be given to tragedy. *Hamlet,* and *Coriolanus* (the style of which is exceptionally difficult for a young reader) should be reserved for the highest form, and there *King Lear* is also possible. But the ideal method would be to study two plays of contrasted types: (a) comedy and tragedy; (b) early work and late work; (c) a play of Shakespeare and a play of Marlowe: *Edward II,* for instance, and *Richard II,* in which Shakespeare has broken with the Marlowe tradition while still retaining traces of its influence; (d) a study in development, such as the advance from *A Midsummer Night's Dream* to *The Tempest,* or from the horseplay of *The Taming of the Shrew* to the wit and charm of *Much Ado About Nothing*; (e) a study in textual criticism, such as *Henry VIII* illustrated by typical instances of the verse of Fletcher. In any case, the pupils should be competent to make some comparison between any one play they are studying and Shakespeare's other plays; or between Shakespeare and other dramatists – Greek, French, or German – who come within their range of reading. Attention should be drawn to the special characteristics of Shakespeare's comedies, histories, and tragedies, to the change in his outlook and temper, in his style and versification; and some introduction may be given to Shakespearean criticism and bibliography. The teacher should make a judicious selection of readings from the leading critics, especially where those critics are poets: the best things of Coleridge and Swinburne, the *obiter dicta* of Goethe and Tennyson, form a golden treasury of Shakespearean criticism. Much depends upon the school library, which should be fully equipped with Shakespearean works of reference; the books recommended in Dr Sidney Lee's pamphlet may be regarded as the indispensable minimum.

At this stage the reading will be confined to passages specially chosen for their dramatic point or poetic beauty: they will gain a certain emphasis from the fact of their being singled out for such a purpose. They may also be committed to memory.

Sustained *viva voce* discussion by the class should be encouraged; it is essential that they should realise that criticism is not a mysterious thing manufactured by editors and commentators, but a living process of thought to which even they can contribute.

Lastly, paperwork, followed by the teacher's comments, will, with this type of pupil, be of the utmost importance.

Composition as a branch of Shakespearean study need not be reserved for the third period, though it is naturally there that it will be systematically employed and be most fruitful in results; good sixth-form work will reach the level of the critical essay. But in the earlier stages the choice of subject must be discriminating; the good old rule, the simple plan to tell a child to 'sketch the character of Brutus' is not by any means extinct and infallibly produces one result – the victim flies, quite rightly, to the school edition and 'conveys' a page of the introduction. The object of a composition should be to wake the imaginative faculty. A child who is told 'Suppose you were in the Forum when Caesar's funeral took place, and you heard Brutus and Antony speak; tell me all about it', will visualise the scene, and will even show some gleams of insight into character. Composition of this kind can be begun soon after the introductory stage, and should invariably be written in the first person. A very good composition might be read aloud in class by its author. It is surprising what good work of this kind will be done, and how original it sometimes may be. As an illustration, the case may be quoted of a boy who had to write from Macbeth's castle just after hearing the news that an avenging army was on its way from England: he impersonated the Porter, and wrote to a drawer at the 'Cheshire Cheese' in Fleet Street, an old comrade of his, wishing himself back at a London tavern where travellers slept secure. Indeed, in the hands of older pupils, work of this kind may even take a literary cast. A boy of seventeen, set to write a character of Cassius by Brutus corresponding to Cassius' speech ' Well, Brutus, thou art noble', wrote a copy of verses beginning

> Mistrust him not, for he is true as steel

and made Brutus debate with himself whether Cassius was acting from envy of Caesar, and whether his hands were clean in the matter of Lucius Pella; and finally let him stifle all doubt with the reflection that public troubles were preying on Cassius' mind and giving a false impression:

> For now his better nature's overcast.

That picture of self-delusion and the kindly touch at the close showed, for so young a writer, fine critical insight.

Teachers would do well not to undervalue the help afforded by the best kind of Shakespearean readings and still more by dramatic representation. Some schools act a play of Shakespeare yearly: this is to treat it as a work of art, and one would imagine the plan a keen incentive to appreciation. But the experiment is costly, and involves much time and labour. The suggestion is worth considering whether it would be feasible for pupils to act in class one or more scenes from every play they study. It might come as a climax to the 'trivial round' of lessons. In London and in large provincial centres it is possible to let schoolchildren see a performance at the theatre; this plan should be encouraged wherever it is practicable. There is a danger in the class-room, with text-books open before us, of our forgetting what drama really means, and burying the poet beneath a mass of comments, conundrums, and morals. The life and colour and movement of the acted play come as a revelation to those who have hitherto associated it inevitably with a sense of mental effort. There is a charming story of a girl, who had studied a number of the plays, exclaiming after a first visit to the theatre, 'It is wonderful how well Shakespeare goes on the stage!' Let us avail ourselves, as far as means admit, of the actor's art to touch the text with life and set before our pupils a vivid aspect of criticism, a new and delightful form of appreciation.

(*English Association Pamphlet* No. 4, 1908,
reproduced by permission of the Trustees)

It is remarkable, encountering this vision from a hundred years ago of how Shakespeare could be taught, to see how much emphasis is placed on context and close reading. From the age of twelve, pupils are to be made aware of Shakespeare's use of sources. By fourteen they should be discussing the plays in terms of the conditions and conventions of Elizabethan theatre. By seventeen they should be starting to compare Shakespeare's early and late work, with particular focus on (for instance) the development of his comic method; they should be starting to compare Shakespeare and Marlowe, and they should be aware of their own ability to contribute to critical debate about the plays. Particularly interesting, too, is the value placed upon empathetic, adaptive and transformative writing – approaches that we might have imagined being introduced much closer to our own time. From the second phase (fourteen upwards) there is a clear emphasis on reading closely, especially on understanding and evaluating the effects of diction and metre.

Although some of the underlying assumptions of this project are today rejected or at least questioned (that *Julius Caesar* makes a good starting point because it is 'noble in theme and simple in style' for instance; or that 'obviously' students should be expected to learn the 'finer' passages by heart), the writer's commitment to ensuring that students and teachers do not forget 'what drama really means' is one that should still underpin all teaching of Shakespeare today. His final plea – 'Let us avail ourselves, as far as means admit, of the actor's art to touch the text with life and set before our pupils a vivid aspect of criticism, a new and delightful form of appreciation' – is a plea to see performance itself as the best way of gaining a critical insight into Shakespeare. It is also the key reason why this forgotten document of 1908 has resurfaced, a hundred years later, at a time when there is perhaps less consensus than ever about how (and indeed whether) Shakespeare should still be taught.

Venetian contexts: *Othello* and *The Merchant of Venice*

This discussion of Shakespeare's two Venetian plays focuses on the following questions:

- Does Venice today provide a helpful context for a study of these two plays?
- How much did Shakespeare know about Venice?
- Does it matter (to our reading of *The Merchant of Venice* and *Othello*) how much Shakespeare knew about Venice?
- Is it true that after the Holocaust *The Merchant of Venice* has become a more difficult play for us than it was for Shakespeare's original audience?

....

Venice is one of the best known and least known cities in the world. If St Mark's Square is, as Napoleon thought it, Europe's finest drawing room, the narrow canals and narrower alleyways are a labyrinth of back passages in which even Venetians lose their way. We think we know the sights: but for everyone who has seen (or seen photos of) the Rialto Bridge, how many will realise that when Shylock talks of being persecuted by Antonio 'on the Rialto' he is not talking about the famous bridge but about the markets on the western side of the bridge? This may not matter, but does it matter that at the far end of the Rialto market there is a fine sculpture of a hunchback, known as Old Gobbo (*gobbo* being the Italian for hunchback), a well-loved Venetian character? Or could it make any difference to one's enjoyment of, or response to, *The Merchant of Venice* to have stood in the Ghetto (which Shakespeare never mentions and about which he apparently knew nothing) and looked at the memorial to the Jews of Venice who were rounded up here in 1942 and deported to the death camps? Knowing what we know, can we read or see the play as if the Holocaust had never happened?

As one of the great tourist destinations of the world (and perhaps of all time), Venice is an open city which appears to welcome foreigners. Visitors who come today buy into the myth of Venice as cheerfully as they buy into the myth of the Bard: on your right as you head up the Grand Canal you will see (according to your guide book) Desdemona's house – though it cannot be: it fronts right on to the water, so there would have been nowhere except on a boat for Roderigo and Iago to have stood to torment Brabantio at his bedroom window. On the other hand, this location makes some sense of what Roderigo says to Desdemona's father, when he tells him that she has been:

> Transported with no worse or better guard
> But with a knave of common hire, a gondolier,
> To the gross clasps of a lascivious Moor ... (I.i.122–4)

Shakespeare certainly knew enough about the reputation of gondoliers to know Brabantio would think them most unsuitable chaperones for Desdemona. He also knew enough about the way gondolas looked to describe the way they sat very low in the water (much more so in the 16th than in the 21st century: the bow and stern have been progressively raised in the past 150 years): in *As You Like It*, Rosalind mocks Jaques' claims that too much travelling has made him melancholy by saying that unless he dresses and behaves like someone who has travelled a lot, 'I will scarce think you have swam in a gondola' (IV.i.35). Jessica and Lorenzo make good their escape in a gondola: until the 19th century gondolas were fitted with discreet black cabins (*felze*), making them perfect for romantic assignations. The revival of the carnival, the proliferation of hawkers and tourist shops selling Venetian masks may bring to life for some students Shylock's cry of dismay when he hears from Launcelot Gobbo that there is to be a carnival procession through the streets:

> What are there masques? Hear you me, Jessica,
> Lock up my doors, and when you hear the drum
> And the vile squeaking of the wry-necked fife,
> Clamber not you up to the casements then
> Nor thrust your head into the public street
> To gaze on fools with varnished faces. (II.v.27–32)

It is rare for a tourist to see into a private house in Venice. The windows are usually dark, or curtained, or shuttered, as Shylock's were. If someone goes through a front door, the most you glimpse is usually just a stairwell, or a passage into a courtyard. What goes on inside these houses is very private, because so much of Venice life is lived out of doors or in bars, cafes, restaurants. This is an important aspect of both *Othello* and *The Merchant*: Desdemona and Jessica are both stolen (led away secretly) from the house where their fathers imagine they are kept safe and inviolable. Lorenzo admits openly that he is stealing Jessica, telling the impatient Gratiano and Salerio:

> When you shall please to play the thieves for wives,
> I'll watch as long for you then.   (II.vi.23–4)

For her part, by throwing the casket of valuables out of her window for Lorenzo to catch, Jessica is not only robbing her own father, she is in effect giving away her own virginity. Emma Smith, writing about *Othello* in the *Writers and their Work* series, stresses the point that in Shakespeare's Venetian world the house is the closed space of the female, that it is a metaphor for female virginity. Outside the house, in the streets and by the canals and the harbour, Venice is a place – like all big city ports – where sexual favours can be bought and sold. Having successfully stolen Desdemona from Brabantio's house ('O thou foul thief!' are the outraged father's first words to his new son-in-law), Othello carries her off to Cyprus where he talks cheerfully about their relationship in terms of a financial investment:

> Come my dear love,
> The purchase made, the fruits are to ensue.
> The profit's yet to come 'tween me and you.   (II.iii.8–10)

Shakespeare's characters speak the international language of Venice, spoken by merchants and traders from all over the world. In the Canareggio area of the city, just beyond the Ghetto, is a series of full-length statues showing merchants dressed in distinctly non-Venetian clothes and wearing outsize turbans on their heads. One of the most striking examples stands in a niche beside the door of Tintoretto's house on the Fondamenta dei Mori. Traditionally these statues have been identified as Moors – and indeed some of them stand in the Campo dei Mori. But were these the same kind of Moor that Othello was, or that the Prince of Morocco is ('Mislike me not for my complexion' are his first words to Portia – *Merchant of Venice*, II.i.1)? It is actually more likely that they were merchants from Morea in Greece or even that they were Sephardic Jews from the Levant who were prominent in Venetian Jewish life in the 16th century. Othello's reference to 'a malignant and a turbanned turk' (V.ii.351) needs to be treated cautiously in the light of these figures; not only Turks wore turbans.

The danger of reading Shakespeare's Venice only with modern eyes and without understanding the context in which the plays were written is highlighted by the following passage from an A-level student's coursework essay on *Othello*:

Othello, as a black, Muslim mercenary in a 'civilised', Christian society is in an inherently vulnerable situation. His human vulnerability is largely due to his allotted position in the Venetian social structure. Despite adopting Venetian custom and demeanour, he is constantly labelled 'Moor' in reminder of his difference. Stripped of the benefits of noble Venetian birth, Othello must rely on military prowess to survive in society, consequently striving to establish his 'reputation' as barometer of his acceptance. As a General he is tolerated in the execution of his function, but he can never be accepted as a member of the *polity*, as the outrage of Brabantio at Othello's marriage to Desdemona clearly indicates, Othello earning the epithet of 'abuser of the world' for his rebellion against social convention ...

In many respects this is an admirable paragraph, providing a succinct and well synthesised overview of Othello's precarious social standing in the Venice of the play. And yet, there are statements here which need to be challenged and at least qualified if not corrected. It is not accurate to describe Othello as a mercenary, implying that he is a soldier of fortune who will fight for anyone who will pay him. Certainly he is a professional soldier, and (as the appointment of Cassio reminds us) it was the practice in Venice at the time Shakespeare was writing – it is another of the things he knew about Venice – for a non-Venetian to be in charge of the City's armed forces. This was enacted by decree to ensure that no one aristocratic family had access to the Venetian army or navy and the means thereby to overthrow the Republic. It was not an accident that at the time of his appointment Othello happened to be an outsider: it was a condition.

Shakespeare certainly knew enough about Venice to know that it was hospitable to foreigners and strangers, and that foreigners had equal rights of access to the courts and equal rights to justice once they had got there. By the end of the 16th century, the city's reputation as a model republic was one side of the 'myth of Venice', that cluster of ideas about the city that made it simultaneously admirable and exotic, dangerous and alluring, European and yet eastward facing. Certainly it is on this basis that Shylock is allowed to proceed with his claim for the Bond:

> A pound of that same merchant's flesh is thine,
> The court awards it, and the law doth give it. (IV.i.295–6)

At the same time, however, the law of Venice dealt severely with foreigners who threatened any Venetian citizen, stripping them not of their rights but of their possessions and proclaiming that:

> The offender's life lies in the mercy
> Of the Duke only, 'gainst all other voice. (IV.i.351–2)

By contrast with Shylock, Othello is not treated throughout the play as an alien. It is not true that he is a Muslim: Shakespeare is anxious to remind us that whatever his birth, Othello is now a Christian living and fighting alongside Christians. When he interrupts the brawl on the battlements of the citadel in Cyprus, after Cassio has been made drunk by Iago, Othello says:

> Are we turned Turks? And to ourselves do that
> Which heaven itself hath forbid the Ottomites?
> For Christian shame put by this barbarous brawl ...   (II.iii.166–8)

(These lines of course have a powerful proleptic irony, anticipating as they do the final words that Othello will speak before he kills himself at the end of the play.)

The word 'Moor' occurs twenty-four times in the play, used by eight different characters, either to or about Othello, and it is true that the more it is used the more it reminds us that Othello is not a native-born Venetian, that he is 'other' than both the Italians in the play and the Elizabethan audience in the playhouse. But it is significant that there are two quite different ways of using the word in the play: Roderigo, Emilia, Brabantio and Iago refer to Othello (not in his presence) plainly as 'The Moor' – Iago once referring to him as 'the lascivious Moor'; it is only Brabantio who uses the word directly to Othello's face 'Look to her, Moor, if thou hast eyes to see ...' (I.iii.293–4). By contrast the representatives of the state – Montano, Lodovico, the 3rd Gentleman and the 1st Senator – always refer to him as 'the valiant Othello', 'the war-like Othello' or (three times) as 'the noble Moor', the description Desdemona herself uses when she claims him as 'My noble Moor' (III.iv.26). When the Duke himself gives his blessing to Othello's marriage with Desdemona he addresses him as 'noble signor' and comments to Brabantio:

> If virtue no delighted beauty lack
> Your son-in-law is far more fair than black.   (I.ii.289–92)

It is surely significant that at this critical moment, the Duke himself, the presiding and most powerful figure in the Venetian republic, greets Othello not as 'Moor', but as 'signor', the same name given to any native-born Venetian nobleman, and goes on explicitly to describe him as 'fair' rather than coloured – 'one of us', in fact. It is, by contrast, precisely because the Duke of Morocco is not 'one of us' that Portia in *The Merchant of Venice* is only too pleased that he chose the golden casket:

> A gentle riddance! Draw the curtain, go.
> Let all of his complexion choose me so.   (II.viii.78–9)

Given, therefore, this endorsement by the Duke, proclaiming him both Venetian and white, Othello should not be described as 'stripped of the benefits of noble Venetian birth': it is precisely these benefits that are conferred upon him. And one of the prime benefits that would follow from this endorsement is that Othello's union with Desdemona would no longer be stigmatised as a mixed marriage, likely to produce unnatural monsters as children – a common xenophobic scare in England, which succeeded in keeping out economic and religious migrants for longer than most other European countries in the 16th century. This is the point behind Iago's bestial imagery when he warns Brabantio, 'You'll have your daughter covered with a Barbary horse; you'll have your nephews neigh to you' (I.i.110–1).

In this respect, Shylock's being specifically Jewish and Othello specifically a Moor are to Venetians such as Gratiano or Iago less significant than their being foreigners, outsiders. Indeed, Shakespeare sometimes deliberately links Jews and Moors: the villain of *Titus Andronicus*, Aaron the Moor, is given a Jewish name, and Jessica names one of her father's countrymen, Chus. In Genesis, Chus is the child of Ham, one of Noah's three sons who populate the earth after the Flood; but Ham, having seen his drunken father naked, is cursed by Noah and consequently, according to popular tradition, fathered the (black) children of the dark continent, Africa.

It might have seemed more appropriate to have given Shylock's friend the name of one of the children of Shem, from whom the Jewish, semitic, peoples traditionally claimed descent. Deliberately, however, to have allied the central Jewish character of the play with someone of supposed African ancestry shows how closely Shakespeare understood Venetian dislike of Ham and all that he stood for. And perhaps still stands for: on the corner of the Palazzo Ducale, within feet of the bridge where thousands of tourists each day take their photos of the Ponte dei Sospiri, stands a life-size carving of the Drunkenness of Noah, with the old man's two sons Shem and Japhet decorously covering their father's nakedness. It is one of the finest carvings in the city, in one of the most prominent positions, and from it Ham has been deliberately excluded – as if Venice were signalling that it wanted nothing to do with the Father of Africa. And this contempt is mirrored in *The Merchant of Venice*, when Lancelot Gobbo is criticised by Lorenzo for having made pregnant one of the maids attending the Prince of Morocco ('the getting up of the Negro's belly', III.v.31). To Lorenzo's indictment, 'The Moor is with child by you,' Lancelot cynically replies:

It is much that the Moor should be more than reason; but if she is less than an honest woman, she is indeed more than I took her for.   (III.v.33–5)

And there the matter rests, with the pregnant Negro girl shrugged off as not worth a second thought – by Lancelot or anyone else. Lorenzo simply comments on how easy it is to make puns on the name Moor: 'How every fool can play upon the word!'

Venice itself, then, can provide some illuminating contextual perspectives on Shakespeare's two Venetian plays, and it is apparent that his knowledge of the city, and of the traditions and rumours that attached to it, underpinned his approach to the shaping of *Othello* and of *The Merchant of Venice*. However, it is still a troubling context, complicated by recent history and changing attitudes. Few actors today (and probably even fewer producers) would risk casting a white actor to play Othello, even though audiences have no difficulty in accepting black actors in traditionally white roles – as the casting in the 2007–8 Royal Shakespeare Company's seasons of the History Plays demonstrated. At least one modern production of *Othello* has had a white Moor, standing out among a company of otherwise black actors. Perhaps the post-Holocaust shadow that falls on *The Merchant of Venice* is more troubling still, and equally surprising is the way in which English critics have continued, since the end of the Second World War, to sidestep the issue.

As early as 1946, John Palmer was writing, in an essay on Shylock:

> The debated question whether Shakespeare writing certain passages of *The Merchant of Venice* was pleading for toleration or indicting Christian hypocrisy, exalting equity above law or divine mercy above human justice, does not arise. He presents a situation in which all these issues are involved, characters in which their effects are displayed, arguments appropriate to the necessary incidents and persons of the comedy; and leaves it to his critics to draw the indictment or convey the apology. His purpose was to write a comedy ...[1]

The implicit assumption here is that a writer has no moral obligation other than to produce a text in whatever form he or she chooses and no subsequent responsibility for its interpretation, its moral evaluation – this being left entirely to the reader or the audience. This assumption has been tenaciously defended throughout the period since the end of the Second World War; but is hard to maintain with a play that, on some levels at least, creates its comedy by the remorseless employment of racial and religious stereotypes and achieves its happy ending by humiliating and hounding out the foreigner.

Other assumptions are at work too. In 1970, in the introduction to the *Twentieth Century Interpretations* series volume on *The Merchant of Venice*, the editor Sylvan Barnet set out to contextualise the play in terms of its first reception by an Elizabethan audience:

> We can never see the play exactly as the Elizabethans saw it, of course, but we
> can make at least some effort to approach their vision. We can try, that is, to
> guard against grossly simplifying it because of our modern prejudices. If we can
> see the play, even in only a small degree, as they may have seen it, we may find
> it a richer thing than the play we see only with our twentieth-century eyes.[2]

This sense of historical perspective is welcome, but there is something
discomforting about the phrase 'our modern prejudices' in the context of this play.
What modern prejudices? Against anti-semitism? Is post-Holocaust sympathy for
the Jews a 'modern prejudice'? Unease grows with the next sentences:

> The first thing we ought to try to do is to understand that although the word
> 'Jew' echoes throughout the play it is not in any important sense a play about
> Jews as we know them. Jews were banished from England in 1290, and the
> few that there were in Shakespeare's London practised their faith secretly.
> The play is not an Ibsenite or Shavian treatise on 'the Jewish problem'; for the
> Elizabethans there was no Jewish problem.[3]

It is as if, by this argument, the problem in 1970 had become the failure to realise
that the play, thirty-five years after the Holocaust, posed any problems at all about
attitudes to Jews. The audible relief expressed in the complacent assertion that this
is *'not in any important sense* a play about Jews as *we* know *them*' [italics added]
continues to represent the Jew as the foreigner, most definitely 'not one of us'.
What's more, because Shylock is to be regarded as a comic figure from a comedy
written when there was 'no Jewish problem', we are absolved from bringing our
Auschwitz *angst* to bear on the play. No significant link, it is clearly implied,
need be made between the treatment of Shylock in 16th-century Venice and the
treatment of Jews in 20th-century Europe. Which being so, the play remains a
comedy to be enjoyed, presenting no moral or intellectual ('Ibsenite or Shavian')
dilemma to be resolved. The audience can relax.

More recent, 21st-century research and criticism has rejected this view. Ania
Loomba, for instance, points out that 'In 1595, about a year before *The Merchant*
was staged, over a thousand artisans and apprentices in London had rioted
violently against foreigners', and she suggests that 'the play is shaped not just
by reports of Jewish life in Venice, but also by a specific English situation.'[4] This
situation was the trial and execution in 1594 of the Portuguese Jewish convert
Roderigo Lopez, convicted of attempting to poison the Queen, to whom he was
physician. Loomba admits that the 'part played by his Jewishness in the trial
remains open to debate,' but notes that Lopez' execution ensured the success

of a re-run of Christopher Marlowe's play *The Jew of Malta*, which had played to packed houses in the 1590s. She acknowledges

> ... that Jewish characters such as Shylock and Barabas [the Jew of Malta] embody negative traits shared by the society at large, such as the greed for money, and therefore they can be seen as a shorthand for a critique of such evil. But we still need to ask why Jews are used as shorthand, and why it is that the plays simultaneously question the difference between them and the Christians around them and focus relentlessly on their Jewishness.   (p.142)

This point, a much more complex reading of the underlying attitudes to Jews in Shakespeare's England and of the influence of these attitudes on the way Shakespeare wrote his play, is perfectly encapsulated in Portia's question when she takes over the running of the trial: by asking 'Which is the Merchant here and which the Jew?' (IV.i.170) simultaneously she defines them as indistinguishable to an outsider and seeks to separate them by profession and race.

Such an analysis of three pieces of post-war criticism is revealing in itself, and a good way to help students discover that critical opinion is never static. It serves also to illustrate how contextualising the play in terms of different historical perspectives, in terms of the anxieties unleashed by the facts of the Holocaust, and in terms of Venice itself, past and present, forces us back to the text of *The Merchant of Venice* for ever closer scrutiny. To do so is to enable students to realise that it is the play itself which demonstrates the inadequacy of saying Shakespeare only wanted to write a comedy, or of claiming that the play is not about the Jewish problem in the England of Elizabeth I (or of Elizabeth II) because there were / are no Jews in the play – at least not 'as we know them'.

The silent speaker in Shakespeare's sonnets

This discussion argues for the importance of placing any one of Shakespeare's sonnets in the context of the sequence as a whole. It also asks:

- Why was the sonnet so important a form for Shakespeare?
- How does the language of an individual sonnet become clearer when placed in the context of other sonnets – both those near to it in the sequence and those scattered throughout the 154 sonnets published together in 1509?
- What contextual points of reference emerge from a close reading of the sonnets themselves?
- Do students need to know a lot, a little or nothing about the biographical speculation surrounding the sonnets?

....

The first meeting between Shakespeare's 'star-cross'd lovers', Romeo and Juliet, is one of the most famous moments in drama. In the middle of Capulet's party this conversation takes place:

ROMEO: If I profane with my unworthiest hand
        This holy shrine, the gentle fine is this:
        My lips two blushing pilgrims ready stand
        To smooth that rough touch with a tender kiss.
JULIET: Good pilgrim, you do wrong your hand too much,
        Which mannerly devotion shows in this;
        For saints have hands that pilgrims' hands do touch,
        And palm to palm is holy palmers' kiss.
ROMEO: Have not saints lips, and holy palmers too?
JULIET: Ay, pilgrim, lips that they must use in prayer.
ROMEO: O, then, dear saint, let lips do what hands do.
        They pray; grant thou, lest faith turn to despair.
JULIET: Saints do not move, though grant for prayers' sake.
ROMEO: Then move not, while my prayer's effect I take.

[*Kisses her*]

A passage of fourteen lines in the middle of a long scene; but this is not prose, nor is it the blank verse Shakespeare most often uses. It is a sonnet – three cross-rhyming (ABAB) quatrains and a couplet – as if Shakespeare wants to enclose this moment and these lovers in a private space, separating them from the noise of the masked ball and the Capulet-Montague feud which will soon engulf them. In the first eight lines (the octave) Romeo speaks the first quatrain to argue why he should be allowed to kiss her; Juliet speaks the second, to explain why he should not. After the turn (the *volta*) between lines 8 and 9, their excitement rises and they swap speeches with increasing urgency until the climax of the passage / poem is reached and Romeo claims his kiss in the final line.

The sonnet form mattered to Shakespeare: he may have worked on the collection of poems finally published in 1609 as *Shakespeare's Sonnets* for up to twenty years. To read any one of them on their own, or to read them all as a sequence, is rather like listening to half of a private conversation – for (unlike the *Romeo and Juliet* sonnet) we only ever hear one voice: the speaker's. And if Shakespeare's plays are public performances requiring an audience, the sonnets read like speeches from a private drama. We are not so much audience as eavesdroppers; and, as with overhearing part of any conversation, it pays to know what has gone before. Each sonnet can make greater sense when read both in the context of the poems that come before and after it, and in the context of *Shakespeare's Sonnets* as a whole.

Be wise as thou art cruel, do not press
My tongue-tied patience with too much disdain,
Lest sorrow lend me words, and words express
The manner of my pity-wanting pain.
If I might teach thee wit, better it were,
Though not to love, yet love to tell me so,
As testy sick men, when their deaths be near,
No news but health from their physicians know:
For if I should despair, I should grow mad,
And in my madness might speak ill of thee;
Now this ill-wresting world is grown so bad,
Mad slanderers by mad ears believed be.
   That I might not be so, nor thou belied,
   Bear thine eyes straight, though thy proud heart go wide.   (Sonnet 140)

In this sonnet the speaker is appealing to a woman at least to pretend that she loves him, because the way she is treating him at the moment is driving him to despair. I have used the conventional word 'speaker' to avoid saying Shakespeare: we cannot know for sure whether all (or any) of the sonnets are directly autobiographical. True, Wordsworth said that in his sonnets 'Shakespeare unlocked his heart'; however, the idea that the sonnets are the key to understanding the 'real' Shakespeare only began with the Romantics.

To use the word 'speaker' implies a listener. But does the person to whom the speaker is speaking actually hear what is being said to her? After all, line two refers to the speaker's 'tongue-tied patience': only if the woman really drives him mad will he find the words to say what he really feels. Isn't he in this poem thinking, rather than speaking, aloud?

Can we be sure the poem is addressed to a woman? After all, we might have assumed that 'Shall I compare thee to a summer's day?' (Sonnet 18) was written to a woman if we had never read it before; but it is one of the poems addressed to the 'Fair Youth' – who may or may not have been the Earl of Southampton. Does this matter? Does appreciating this sonnet as a love poem depend on knowing whether it is addressed to a man or a woman? As it happens, 'Be wise as thou art cruel' is Sonnet 140 and so one of the 'Dark Lady' sonnets (Nos. 127–154). It also picks up the theme of Sonnet 138 which makes it quite clear that the man is speaking to a woman:

When my love swears that she is made of truth,
I do believe her though I know she lies ...

It does not matter who the Dark Lady was; what matters is that (if she existed as a real person) she gave Shakespeare (if he was writing from his own experience) a very hard time. How hard? Well, look at the first line: she is 'cruel' and the speaker begs her not to 'press' his

> tongue-tied patience with too much disdain ...

The general sense is clear: 'Don't drive me to despair with your obvious contempt.' Some editors suggest that 'press' implies 'torment' or 'oppress'; if so, it picks up the word 'o'er-press' used by Shakespeare in the previous sonnet, 139, to mean 'defeat' or 'overwhelm' – as when one army routs another. (See also T.S. Eliot's echoing of these lines in his poem 'Usk', Chapter 7, page 123.) But there is another, even more powerful meaning, linked to the idea of 'pressing' and being 'tongue-tied' and referring to a specific type of torture: in Shakespeare's day a person accused of committing a felony, who refused to plead at his or her trial, could be punished with *peine fort et dure*. This involved literally being pressed under heavy weights – to death, unless the victim broke silence and agreed to speak. It was a terrifying punishment imposed on women as well as men: in 1586, Margaret Clitherow was pressed to death in York for harbouring Roman Catholic priests. We now know that Shakespeare's family had been Catholic, and that he himself had possibly only abandoned the Catholic cause as a young man. Such tortures as Margaret Clitherow endured were uncomfortably close to home for him.

Shakespeare certainly used 'pressed' in this sense in his plays, and in *Troilus and Cressida*, he links the word to 'tongue-tied maidens' (3.ii.217–8). In Sonnet 140, though, he develops the image with an unexpected reversal: someone being tortured like this might have the words literally squeezed out of them by the pain of the weights, but here it is the words which will 'express' [that is, squeeze out, but also 'broadcast'] the true nature of the pain he is feeling. The woman is not merely torturing him, she is completely lacking [wanting] in pity. But in a further twist, the compound adjective 'pity-wanting' may reflect back on the speaker. He wants her to take pity on his pain. How? By at least pretending to love him, so that he can enjoy the illusion, if not the reality, of being loved:

> better it were
>> Though not to love, yet love to tell me so ...   (version A)

Look in any edition of *Shakespeare's Sonnets*. It will say (they all do) that the text is based upon, or 'follows closely' the original Quarto text of the 1609 edition. But how close is closely? Notice the way this line from Sonnet 140 (line 6) is punctuated in your edition. It probably looks like this:

> Though not to love, yet, love, to tell me so ...   (version B)

Punctuated like this, the meaning is subtly different, and it is revealing to see how different editors explain it. Katherine Duncan Jones (in the Arden edition, 1997, which follows the Quarto punctuation) gives this interpretation of version A: 'It would be better, though you are unwilling or unable to love me, at least to take pleasure (*to love*) in telling me that you do.' This would imply an almost sadistic delight on the part of the woman in deceiving the man who is infatuated by her.

Version B, in which 'love' is vocative – the speaker addressing the woman affectionately as 'love' – seems easier to explain. 'Yet' here could mean either 'but' or 'still', i.e. 'as you used to do'. This would suggest that the woman used to tell the speaker that she loved him, and he is begging her to go on doing so – calling her 'love' as a way of enticing her to do what he wants. But is it likely, in a poem which begins by calling her 'cruel' and ends by calling her 'proud', that the speaker would unexpectedly address the woman as 'love' without any apparent irony? Strangely, in a sequence of sonnets entirely dealing with love, Shakespeare very rarely calls either the Fair Youth or the Dark Lady 'love'. He does in Sonnets 13 and 22, when both times he speaks with clear fondness for the young man; and he does in Sonnets 148 and 149, but here there is a strong hint of irony and bitterness. In 148 he calls the woman 'O cunning love'; 'But, love, hate on', he says to her in 149.

I have mentioned these other poems in the sequence to try to throw light on the problem in Sonnet 140: which reading of line 6 ('love' as a verb or as a vocative) seems more convincing? It is of course quite possible to appreciate any of Shakespeare's sonnets just on its own: I originally discovered Sonnet 140 when I was eighteen and my girlfriend had dumped me for someone else. 'Be wise as thou art cruel' seemed to sum up not so much what I had been struggling to put into words myself, as what I had not even realised until I read the poem. In those days I knew nothing about the Dark Lady or the rest of the sonnets: this sonnet, on its own, spoke powerfully to me and for me. But coming back to it now, half a lifetime later, I can see it more clearly in the context of the other sonnets that surround it – and indeed in the context of Shakespeare's plays.

The sestet of the poem focuses on the damage done when despair drives a lover mad: in his madness, the speaker says, he might start to 'speak ill' of the woman, and he wants to protect her from the lies that he might spread. Ironically, then, she needs to lie to him (by pretending that she still loves him) to stop him from telling lies about her. Love, lies and slander are central to both Shakespeare's comedies and his tragedies. In *Much Ado About Nothing* Claudio slanders his fiancée, Hero, on their wedding day, denouncing her as a 'rotten orange' after being tricked into thinking she has been unfaithful. Othello, maddened by Iago's successful slandering of Desdemona, starts to slander her himself: 'Damn her, lewd minx!'.

Don John in *Much Ado* and Iago in *Othello* spread false rumour; the speaker in Sonnet 140 fears that, if driven to despair, he too could become a 'mad slanderer' of his mistress. She might be 'belied' (slandered) by what he says, and 'mad ears' will be only too keen to believe his lies. But if she has treated him so badly, will what he says really be slander?

Where then does the truth lie? To underline this question, Shakespeare carefully links 'believed' with the similar-sounding 'belied' in lines 13 and 14. And throughout the sonnet he exploits such echoes: 'Be wise' he begins; 'go wide' he ends, and these nearly identical words are linked by a chain of alliteration running through all fourteen lines (words, wanting, wit, wresting, etc.). Alliteration is a key device in the poem whose central simile – dying men being cheered up by the false assurance that they will soon be better – is reinforced by the echoing line 'No news but health from their physicians know'. It is a lie, but the old men will feel better for it – and so will the 'tongue-tied' speaker in Sonnet 140. After all, only two sonnets earlier he had decided that 'love's best habit is in seeming trust' (138), and with a nicely ambiguous ending he had admitted that he was as guilty as she:

> Therefore I lie with her, and she with me,
> And in our faults by lies we flatter'd be.

The publisher's blurb on the back of the Everyman edition of the Sonnets (1995) describes the sonnets as 'Poems that shaped our language of love'. Well, possibly. But what we discover from studying a single sonnet in the context of *Shakespeare's Sonnets* as a whole (not to mention his plays and his life and times) is that Shakespeare's language creates as many possibilities and complexities as love itself.

....

There are some excellent (and some poor) websites on Shakespeare's sonnets. A very good starting point is www.shakespeares-sonnets.com: this site prints all the sonnets, provides facsimile examples from the original Quarto edition of 1609, and gives a very thorough commentary on each poem. It is also very informative about how Shakespeare's sonnets link to (and differ from) earlier Elizabethan sonnet sequences, particularly Sir Philip Sidney's *Astrophil and Stella*. Additional contextual information and illustration helps to explain key images and references used by Shakespeare.

The identities of Mr W.H., of the Fair Youth and of the Dark Lady continue to fascinate readers and critics. An entertaining guide to all the controversies can be found in Jonathan Bate's *The Genius of Shakespeare* (1998). But as ever the question to get students to ask themselves is: does it make any difference to our response to the poems themselves to know who was the Fair Youth or the Dark Lady of the Sonnets?

A word and its contexts: 'watch' in *Twelfth Night, Henry V, Richard II*

The following discussion begins by revisiting the debate surrounding the increased emphasis on context at A level (see Chapter 1, pages 5–15). It does so to provide a context itself: for the arguments recently presented by critics such as George Steiner and the late Edward Said for a return to a focus on philology as an appropriate way to release literary studies from the sterile arguments between competing theoretical camps. To illustrate the potential of what Steiner and Said propose, the discussion focuses on a particular word in Shakespeare, 'watch', tracing it through a series of plays where it is used in different contexts and itself generates some surprising and revealing contextual possibilities. The discussion ends by reflecting on how this philological method can provide a model for teachers to use in stimulating students to understand the importance and rewards of contextual close reading. In doing so it offers a suggestion for a new approach to Shakespeare coursework.

· · · · · · · · · · · · · · · · · · · ·

'Meaning is context-bound, but context is boundless' (Jonathan Culler).
Discuss.[5]

Jonathan Culler's paradox challenges students, teachers, and examiners at A level as much as undergraduates and their tutors. A level English Literature, no less than a degree course in the subject, focuses these days on both how we read and what we read: literary studies as well as the study of literature. Much of the debate about the value of context in A level teaching needs to be understood in this light. The emphasis in the 2000 QCA *Subject Criteria for English Literature* on 'Evaluating the significance of cultural, historical and other contextual influences on literary texts and study' (Assessment Objective 5ii) did more than anything else in Curriculum 2000 to extend the scope of literary study beyond previous A level English syllabuses.

To some, this new emphasis was a long-overdue response to the changes that had dominated the academic study of Literature since the 1970s. Robert Eaglestone, for instance, had complained sweepingly in *Doing English* that:

> All the new ways of interpreting texts that are generally accepted in higher education have been marginalised or simply ignored at A level … in some cases, the subject is not very different from how it was in the 1930s and 1940s.[6]

Conversely, others saw the new emphasis on context as a betrayal of what English at A level should be: the formal study of individual texts and the opportunity for candidates to concentrate on their own personal responses rather than 'opinions and judgements informed by different interpretations by other readers' (AO4). As series editor of the *Cambridge Contexts in Literature* I am well aware that some teachers and reviewers have seen the series as part of this betrayal, while others have welcomed an approach which encourages students to place their study of individual texts within the wider cultural and critical contexts introduced in each book.

But now there are increasing signs of anxiety about context: Peter Barry, in a trenchant chapter, 'Is History the new English?' in *English in Practice* warns that:

> Context, then, has its claims; but if we allow its unlimited expansion, without ever formulating criteria which put *its* claims in context, then we may find that little is left which can properly be called literary studies.[7]

I fully share this concern to preserve the identity of English as a distinct discipline, but the greater emphasis on contextual close reading in the new specifications has, in my view, been valuable as a way of enabling candidates to show a more genuinely *informed* personal response to texts and language. On the other hand, I doubt whether future modifications to QCA's Subject Criteria for English Literature will take teachers any deeper into the increasingly contested domains of post-modernism or historicism. Influential voices are urging an ever-closer focus on texts and textual study: an article by Jonathan Bate, in the *Times Higher Educational Supplement,* has recently called for an end to the 'free for all of critical "isms"' and a return to the teaching of textual bibliography and literary biography as the basis for undergraduate English study.[8] Edward Said, in an essay published just before his death (a new Introduction to *Orientalism,* Penguin, 2003), argued for a humanist approach to literary study based on philology, defining philological understanding as 'sympathetically and subjectively enter[ing] into the life of a written text as seen from the perspective of its time and author'.

Philology may sound a dusty and unadventurous discipline, but it could actually offer English teachers the best way out of the increasingly sterile debate about the true nature of literary studies (intrinsic / extrinsic; formalist / historicist; humanist / materialist, etc.). It is significant that both Edward Said and George Steiner have continued to argue its importance so eloquently: Steiner (in an essay on Auerbach's *Mimesis*[9]) defined the job of the philologist as being 'to locate the written word within its etymological, historical and social contexts'; in the same essay he commented that Vico 'assigned to philology, to textual interpretation the privilege and task of interpreting man's especial humanity'. Said concluded his new Introduction to *Orientalism* by asserting that 'texts have to be read as texts that were produced and live on in all sorts of ... worldly ways'.[10] Helping students to understand what texts are and how they were created, and to explore the ways in which they live on, is an essential task of the teacher of Literature.

Are approaches such as these, centred on 'the life of a written text', compatible with the recent greater emphasis on context at A level? I think they are; indeed, I think they could give a valuable focus to contextual close reading and help to resolve the paradox posed by Jonathan Culler (the quotation used in the Oxford examination paper comes from his book, *Literary Theory: A Very Short Introduction*[11]). To illustrate this, I shall discuss an unexpected word from an unfamiliar speech in a familiar Shakespeare play; after which, I shall briefly suggest how some of the approaches I adopt could be deployed in A level teaching and assessment.

Twelfth Night and the problem of the Priest

The only Shakespearean role I ever played was the Priest in a school production of *Twelfth Night*. Not much of a part: he is brought on at the end of Act 4 to escort Olivia and Sebastian to his nearby chapel, and then in Act 5 he is brought back to tell a shocked Orsino, and an even more shocked Viola / Cesario, exactly what (as Olivia puts it) 'hath newly passed between this youth and me':

> A contract of eternal bond of love,
> Confirm'd by mutual joinder of your hands,
> Attested by the holy close of lips,
> Strength'ned by interchangement of your rings;
> And all the ceremony of this compact
> Seal'd in my function, by my testimony;
> Since when, my watch hath told me, towards
> My grave I have travell'd but two hours.   (V.i.150–157)[12]

It is the Priest's only speech.

On the face of it, there is little of interest here and few editors or critics bother to comment, other than to note the overlarding of legal language. But the 'holy father' is not without significance, and he helps to place at least two aspects of the play in a sharper context. First, since he is to be found at a nearby chantry chapel, he is presumably the (Catholic) priest employed to say mass for the repose of the soul of Olivia's dead brother. In the very English Illyria that is the play's setting, his presence thus sharpens the tension between the old religion to which the household remains faithful and the new puritanism represented by Malvolio and mocked through the persona of Sir Topas. Clearly, since Olivia employs a chantry priest but also regards Malvolio highly ('I would not have him miscarry for the half of my dowry', III.iv.60–2) she embodies the attempt to accommodate both old and new forms of worship – an accommodation with which Shakespeare himself was very familiar. So the presence of the Priest highlights the fact that *Twelfth Night* is not just anti-puritan: it points to a broader, more complex, context.

Second, in a play that is obsessed with the whirligig of time, the Priest is one more reminder of how quickly the times are changing. As he himself says, according to his watch it is only two hours since he heard Olivia and her lover promise to make an 'eternal' commitment. Shakespeare's audience would have enjoyed the irony of the priest, whose job was to help Olivia 'keep fresh' (for seven years of mourning) the memory of a brother's love, being the person summoned to marry this grieving sister to a man she has only just met.

There is something strange here, but it is hardly ever noticed: how come a superannuated Catholic priest should be carrying a watch? Watches at the end of the 16th century were the ultimate fashion accessory; Queen Elizabeth I liked to let ambassadors and favour-seeking courtiers know that a new watch would always be an acceptable gift. At the same time, they were hugely expensive, notoriously unreliable and deeply distrusted. John Aubrey has a story in *Brief Lives* about Thomas Allen (d.1632) who was one of the most notable mathematicians and astrologers at Elizabeth's Court:

> In those darke times, Astrologer, Mathematician, and Conjurer were accounted the same things; and the vulgar did verily believe him to be a Conjurer ... One time being at Hom Lacy in Herefordshire, at Mr John Scudamore's (grandfather to the Lord Scudamor) he happened to leave his Watch in the Chamber windowe. (Watches were then rarities.) The maydes came in to make the Bed, and hearing a thing in a case cry Tick, Tick, Tick, presently concluded that this was his Devill, and took it by the String with the tonges, and threw it out of the windowe into the Mote (to drown the Devill). It so happened that the string hung on a sprig of an elder that grew out of the Mote, and this confirmed them that 'twas the Devill.
> So the good old Gentleman gott his Watch again.[13]

Why should Shakespeare give a priest with a tiny part the honour of being the one character in any of his plays to possess ('*my* watch') a thing so desirable that Malvolio can only dream of owning one? The word 'watch' appears over ninety times in Shakespeare's plays and poems; the *Oxford English Dictionary* gives 1588 as the first recorded usage of the word to mean a portable timepiece; but only in *Twelfth Night* (1601) does anyone actually own one, or even mention one in a literal rather than a metaphorical sense. In *The Tempest* (1613) Sebastian says sneeringly of Gonzalo 'He's winding up the watch of his wit; anon 'twill strike' (II.i.12–13), but elsewhere the word is nearly always associated with the action of watching, of keeping watch – especially at night.

How Shakespeare uses the word, how he helps indeed to shape future usages of the word, is revealing. 'Watch' comes from an Anglo-Saxon verb *wæccan,* thought to be also the origin of the word 'wake'. Indeed, in the first full English translation of the Bible, Wyclif's, (c.1382) the question Jesus puts to his disciples in the garden of Gethsemene (Matthew 26:40) is translated as 'Could ye not wake with me one hour?' Only with Tyndale's translation (1534) does the more familiar 'watch with me' appear.

The act of watching, waking, staying alert, keeping watch by night ('watch' is also the collective noun for nightingales), failing to sleep, waiting for time to pass, having the means to count the hours as they go – these are all implied in different contexts in Shakespeare's plays. From being an apparently straightforward word, 'watch' becomes a complex trope: it carries an unexpected dramatic weight.

In *Love's Labours Lost* (1588), for instance, Berowne describes Rosaline as:

> A woman that is like a German clock,
> Still a-repairing, ever out of frame,
> And never going aright, being a watch,
> But being watched that it may still go right. (III.i.178ff)

Here Shakespeare takes the words 'clock' and 'watch' as interchangeable. The First Quarto of *Love's Labours Lost* referred to a 'German cloak' but this must be a compositor's error: Germany was the earliest centre for watchmaking, and watches were sometimes known as Nuremburg eggs when their mechanism was housed in an oval case. Shakespeare counts on his audience's knowing that watches are temperamental and unreliable, and thus enjoying Berowne's misogynistic comments about women and his apparent contempt for Rosaline. He also makes an obvious pun ('being a watch' / 'being watched') where, as a passive verb, the word implies 'having an eye kept on' or 'being checked from time to time' to ensure that the watch / the woman does what it / she is supposed to do, i.e. keep time / behave herself.

In the Prologue to Act 4 of *Henry V* the word 'watch' appears three times, on each occasion meaning 'guards sharing sentry duty':

> From camp to camp, through the foul womb of night,
> The hum of either army stilly sounds
> That the fix'd sentinels almost receive
> The secret whispers of each other's watch. (II.3–6)

'Watch' here requires more than a single sentry, as it always does in Shakespeare (Dogberry and Verges in *Much Ado*, Marcellus and Barnardo in *Hamlet*, etc.). The Chorus dwells much in this speech on the slowness with which time passes during the night: the impatient French chide

> ... the cripple tardy-gaited night
> Who like a foul and ugly witch doth limp
> So tediously away.   (II.20–22)

while Henry goes 'from watch to watch, from tent to tent' boosting morale among his troops:

> Nor doth he dedicate one jot of colour
> Unto the weary and all-watched night;
> But freshly looks ...   (II. 37–9)

'All-watched' here clearly implies that the night is almost ended: the slow watches of the night have passed and the waiting is over. The king is busily bidding his troops 'good morrow with a modest smile'. But it is of course not so much the night as the troops that are weary and 'all-watched' – in the sense that they have stayed awake all night long. This is the second time in the speech that the Chorus transfers an epithet – a few lines earlier he has described how:

> The poor condemned English
> Like sacrifices, by their watchful fires
> Sit patiently and inly ruminate
> The morning's danger ...   (II.22–5)

The watch fires take on the duties of the dispirited English soldiers. While the latter 'inly ruminate' on what horrors the 'foul womb of night' will engender, the 'paly flames' of the fires enable 'each battle' to see 'the other's umber'd face'.

In the context of these different plays, then, 'watch' and its variants take on a range of meanings and significances. Sometimes, however, the difficulty is to decide which one of two specific senses is intended. Some editors have wondered whether, when Richard III says 'Give me a watch' (V.iii.63) the night before the battle of Bosworth, he simply means a guard. More likely (because only seven lines earlier he has said to Norfolk 'Use careful watch; choose trusty sentinels') here he means a candle marked off to show the hours passing while it is too dark to tell the time by the sun. This is one of the ways in which the word 'watch' comes to denote a timepiece – the divisions of time during the night graphically represented on an instrument that fulfils the same role as a night watchman calling out the hour.

At least Richard sleeps, though he wakes to tell Ratcliff 'I have dream'd a fearful dream' (l.222); it is the usual fate of Shakespeare's kings to pass a sleepless night before a battle or some other moment of crisis. Henry IV, Henry V and Henry VI all contrast their lot unfavourably with that of a peasant: Henry V convinces himself that no one lying 'in bed majestical / Can sleep so soundly as the wretched slave' who

> little wots
> What watch the king keeps to maintain the peace,
> Whose hours the peasant best advantages.   (*Henry V*, IV.i.287–8; 302–4)

By contrast with this image of the king as the caring nightwatchman of the nation, Shakespeare presents Henry VI as a mere spectator, who sits apart while the battle rages and wishes he were either dead or someone quite different:

> O God! Methinks it were a happy life,
> To be no better than a homely swain;
> To sit upon a hill as I do now,
> To carve out dials quaintly, point by point,
> Thereby to see the minutes how they run,
> How many make the hour full complete;
> How many hours bring about the day;
> How many days will finish up the year;
> How many years a mortal man may live.   (*3 Henry VI*, II.v.21–9)

Thus Henry on the battlefield between Towton and Saxton: the dial evidently is a sundial, and the points which he imagines the contented peasant carving on the dial are what Shakespeare elsewhere refers to as 'watches' or subdivisions of the hours. These were usually marked on sundials, and on 16th and 17th century clock faces, to indicate the quarter, half and three quarter divisions of the hour – not the minutes in between. Like sundials, these clocks and watches only had a single hand. Thomas Hardy, in *Tess of the d'Urbervilles*, refers to an ancient street 'laid out before inches of land had value and when one-handed clocks sufficiently divided the day' (Part 1, Ch. 3).

It is Richard II, in his dungeon at Pomfret Castle, who provides the most extended and complex image of the watch:

> I wasted time, and now doth time waste me;
> For now hath time made me his numbering clock:
> My thoughts are minutes, and with sighs they jar
> Their watches on onto mine eyes, the outward watch,
> Whereto my finger, like a dial's point,
> Is pointing still, in cleansing them from tears.
> Now sir, the sound that tells what hour it is
> Are clamorous groans, that strike upon my heart
> Which is the bell: so sighs and tears and groans
> Show minutes, times and hours; but my time
> Runs posting on in Bolingbroke's proud joy,
> While I stand fooling here, his Jack o' the clock.   (*Richard II*, V.v.49–60)

Here, a numbering clock is one with a face (a watch) from which the time can be read. Though Richard's groans are like the tongue of a bell striking on his heart and announcing the time, his thoughts are like minutes because he sighs as regularly as a clock ticks ('jars'). Each sigh / jar / tick engraves another minute onto his face like the watches – divisions of time – painted on a dial (Richard's eyes, which both keep watch and represent the face – the outward watch – of the clock). Each thought brings another tear to his eye; and his finger, wiping the tears away, is likened, according to the editors of this play, to the clock hand.

Possibly, though, Shakespeare is thinking more of the fixed stylus on a sundial: after all, Richard's finger 'like a dial's point, / Is pointing still'. It is hard for Shakespeare (or any other poet) to resist the pun on 'still'; and poets such as Michael Drayton, Shakespeare's contemporary, memorably referred to 'the snayly motion of the moving hand' on a clock ('Of his Ladies Not Coming to London'). A clock hand may crawl but it isn't still.

The complexity of this passage doesn't just reflect Richard's state of mind. In making him struggle to explain the conceit – glossing the different meanings of 'watch' and 'watches' as he speaks – Shakespeare adds to the impression of a tortuous and tortured personality. But at the same time, having to spell out the different meanings like this shows that the word 'watch' was still in a state of flux: it had not yet settled down into usages which would be commonly understood.

A further illustration of how Shakespeare and / or his editors have intervened in the development of the word 'watch' occurs in *2 Henry IV*, where the king is – like his namesakes – unable to sleep and comparing his lot with that of the poor:

> O thou dull god! Why liest thou with the vile
> In loathsome beds, and leav'st the kingly couch
> A watch-case or a common 'larum bell? (III.i.15–17)

'Watch-case' here was originally glossed as 'sentry-box' (in Thomas Hanmer's 1743 edition of Shakespeare), though it is the only recorded example of this usage and editors these days tend to dismiss the interpretation as anachronistic. The latest Chambers Dictionary, however, still gives this meaning but adds: *(Shak)* – implying that this meaning is unique to Shakespeare. The idea of the king as nightwatchman is, as we have seen, not a new one; the linking reference to the 'common 'larum bell' – presumably a bell designed to rouse the whole castle / camp / neighbourhood – seems to add strength to this interpretation. But there is no evidence that such things as sentry boxes had even been invented in Shakespeare's day, nor that the word 'case' meant a structure large enough for one person to stand in – still less for more than one. With Shakespeare, as already seen, the word 'watch' implies more than one person: he usually calls a single person on watch a 'sentinel'.

There is anyway no difficulty in taking 'watch-case' here to mean the portable container in which a small timepiece is housed. The meaning of the word 'watch' is sufficiently fluid to encompass the idea of the king lying awake in bed through the watches of the night and in doing so counting the hours of darkness as they pass – hence likening himself to a timepiece. The *Oxford Shakespeare Henry IV, Part 2* (ed. Weiss, 1997) carries the following note on the passage:

> The king may here compare himself to the wound-up mechanism in a watchcase. Watchcases with alarms were already used in Shakespeare's time: cf. 'the watch rings alarum in his pocket!' (Middleton *A Mad World, My Masters* 5.2.240–1). The sense tentatively suggested by *OED* for 'watch-case', 'a place in which one must keep watch', would tend to support Hanmer's gloss: 'This alludes to the Watchman set in Garrison-towns upon some Eminence attending upon an Alarum-bell, which he was to ring out in case of fire or any approaching danger.'

So where does this leave the Priest in *Twelfth Night,* referring to his watch so casually? It is just possible that Shakespeare simply uses 'watch' here to mean clock for the sake of alliteration ('Since when my watch ...'). If so, it remains a puzzle that the Priest speaks of '*my*' watch; characters in Shakespeare usually refer to '*the*' clock when they hear it chime – as does Olivia herself: 'The clock upbraids me for the waste of time' (III.i.127). It might be a sundial to which the Priest is referring, especially since sundials scratched on the walls of churches were known as mass-dials; but the *OED* records no instance where Shakespeare or any other writer uses 'watch' as synonymous with 'sundial' (though, as we have seen, Richard II comes very close to doing so).

If neither of these is the answer, then the puzzle remains: why is the Priest unique in Shakespeare in actually possessing such an expensive (and unreliable) timepiece? In fact, of course, the very unreliability of watches may be the point: since Olivia and Viola / Cesario never did exchange vows, the Priest is quite wrong to say that it happened two hours ago. His evidence is as unreliable as a watch – and the audience would get the joke.

There are two other possibilities: the Priest's watch may prompt the audience to remember Malvolio's fantasies about being Olivia's lover: having come from his day-bed 'where I have left Olivia sleeping', he will:

Wind up my watch, or play with my – some rich jewel. (II.v.56–7)

The innuendo is obvious, and the idea of winding up a watch as a euphemism for sex possibly gets its first airing here.[14] The Catholic Priest, with his actual watch, scores over the puritan Steward, with his imaginary one, more tellingly than Feste's Sir Topas ever did.

Finally, though, the Priest's watch seems as much an anachronism as the Priest himself. *Twelfth Night* is set both in a fantasy world (Illyria) and in the real world of late Elizabethan England: the threat posed to the old way of life embodied in Olivia and caricatured in Sir Toby is a real one, and it is a truism that the comedy of the play is underscored by anxiety that the good times may soon be over ('no more cakes and ale?'). One of the first victims of this would have been the Priest himself. In the Chantries Act of 1547, in the first year of his reign, the protestant King Edward VI had abolished chantries and chantry priests. Olivia's Priest, more than any other character in *Twelfth Night*, was fifty years (never mind two hours) out of his time.

· · · · · · · · · · · · · · · · · · · ·

This discussion took as its starting point a single speech (and a single word from that speech) and explored some ways in which a philological and editorial approach to context could shed light both on the play and on Shakespeare's exploitation of language, finding evidence from a range of different plays and authors. Nothing has done more to increase the opportunities for relevant literary research than the Internet, and this type of exploration (appropriately taught and encouraged) is now well within the grasp of students: it takes only seconds to access a powerful, easy-to-use Shakespeare concordance, and the *Oxford English Dictionary* is available online. Even under the pressure of time that bedevils much AS level teaching, googling a word such as 'watch' (or any significant word from any Shakespeare play) can be done as a group exercise which introduces students to several other plays that they might not otherwise encounter (as with *Love's Labour's Lost* above). It can also lead outward to other texts and writers – here, John Aubrey and Thomas Hardy, among others: historical context can be valuably explored through intertextual links such as these. Students, discovering these connections, can gain great satisfaction from seeing how texts and writers talk to each other across time: reading backwards and forwards helps to sharpen, not to blunt, a sense of the importance of chronology. At the same time they learn how Shakespeare's language is itself the product of a society in a state of rapid evolution – political, technological and social.

Responding to the imbrication of meanings in Shakespeare is a sign of a student's growing confidence and maturity; when this leads to exploration of the etymology and historical development of words and language, it not only invites discussion of the complexity and elusiveness of meaning but also analysis and criticism of the way these complexities are discussed by editors and critics. Most students, for instance, only use one edition of a play they are studying; however, to contrast the ways in which different editions comment on a difficult speech (e.g. Henry IV's ambiguous conceit about the watchcase) will involve them in 'different interpretations by other readers' and help to show that neither critics, nor texts nor authors are infallible.

There is nothing radical about any of this, except to demonstrate that contextual close reading keeps all the time a sharp focus on the text while also opening up wider perspectives. As Rick Rylance and Judy Simons argue in *Literature in Context*:

> The function of contextual criticism at the present time is surely to spotlight the relationship between textual detail and the surrounding range of factors which bear upon the creation and understanding of its significance.[15]

Hence, Berowne's apparently cynical comparison of Rosaline to a watch that cannot keep time and the three King Henries contrasting their lot with that of their humblest subjects provide important perspectives on gender and class in Shakespeare. But in this context it is important to note Terry Eagleton's recent remark that 'There is surely more to *Twelfth Night* than class and gender.'[16] Reading these passages with the approach I have described is not to treat the texts in a purely instrumental way: contextual close reading helps to highlight questions of values, questions that students must ask of themselves as well as of Shakespeare. Eagleton's comment on *Twelfth Night* prefaces a radical reappraisal of the function of critical theory at the present time:

> It must strike out from the well-trodden paths of class, race and gender and look again at all those questions that it has shelved as embarrassingly large: questions of death, love, morality, nature, suffering, foundations, religion, biology and revolution.[17]

The approach to contextual study outlined above can be both valuable as a teaching method and worth assessing from the student's point of view. Since the aim of this approach is to encourage students to embark on their own open-ended investigations (open-ended in the sense that until they begin it they do not know what leads and cross-references they will discover) it is best assessed as part of coursework. Inviting students to use the resources of the Internet or of other reference tools in this way allows them to find their own points of departure in exploring a text, topic or author. It almost rules out the opportunities for plagiarism, since part of the task is to seek out and interrogate other interpretations as part of the investigation – not to pass them off as their own. Edward Said, in the essay from which I quoted above, is concerned that:

> Instead of reading in the real sense of the word, our students today are often distracted by the fragmented knowledge available on the Internet and in the mass media.[18]

Far from being fragmented, however, such knowledge can be focused and synthesised through contextual close reading in the sort of investigation I have sketched, tracing the evolution of a word such as 'watch' in Shakespeare. For A level students, a conventional essay may well not be the best way to report such an investigation: getting the candidate to act as editor and to produce critical notes and commentary on a passage from a play (or a poem or novel) could lead to coursework of a kind that is hardly ever set at present. Students would have to find the answers to questions they themselves want to ask of the text. In doing this they would explore the interrelationship between language and literature for themselves and gain insight into how texts work and what they can do. David Lodge has put this in terms that help to reconcile literary studies with the study of literature and offer a prospectus for all teachers of English:

> Criticism can be a useful, as well as a merely playful activity ... It can do for literature what literature does for the world – defamiliarising it, enabling us to see its beauty and value afresh.[19]

9 | Contexts and the novel

'There seems almost a general wish of decrying the novelist, and of slighting the performances which have only genius, wit and taste to recommend them.'
(Jane Austen Northanger Abbey, 1817)

All the sections in this chapter deal explicitly or implicitly with ways of seeing. Any introduction to the novel should involve students in thinking about narrative: narrative structure, narrative technique and – above all – narrative perspective. How we as readers 'see' the events of a novel depends both on ourselves and on the way the novel is presented to us. Terms such as 'unreliable narrator' and 'implied author', even focalisation, help students to investigate ways of writing and reading fiction that open up opportunities for the reader to expand the stock focus on plot, theme and character.

Continuing the emphasis on close scrutiny of single words (discussed in 'A word and its contexts: "watch" in *Twelfth Night, Henry V, Richard II*', Chapter 8, pages 158–169), the first section in this chapter, 'Meaning and context', spotlights the word 'handsome' in two novels by Jane Austen, *Emma* and *Persuasion*. It does so in the context of the way women in Austen perceive themselves and are seen by others, inviting a gendered perspective which may take some students by surprise, but for which all teachers need to make room in their teaching of Austen's novels. This discussion of 'handsome' ends with the phrase 'ways of seeing' (borrowed from the landmark 1970s TV series and book by John Berger); the phrase is then picked up in the second section, 'Ways of seeing – teaching a new novel', which deals with the problem of teaching a new and unfamiliar text for the first time. The two books discussed, Hilary Mantel's *A Change of Climate* (1994) and Joe Treasure's *The Male Gaze* (2007), can both be approached by asking who sees what, and from what perspective – an issue explicitly identified by the title of Treasure's first novel.

A central theme in much writing from the 20th century and through to the present day is concerned with cultural identity. This is the focus of the third section, 'Englishness in the contemporary novel', which first surveys the development of this theme from E.M. Forster through to Kingsley Amis, and then discusses in greater depth novels by David Lodge, Julian Barnes and Zadie Smith. Of course, as a theme it can be traced back further still – certainly through the Victorian novel – and the final section, 'Film and image as context', looks at two novels which also give powerful critiques of past concepts of Englishness, McEwan's *Atonement* and Dickens' *A Tale of Two Cities*. The focus of this discussion, however, is on the relationship between text and visual media, whether film (*Atonement*) or graphic image (*A Tale of Two Cities*). The aim here is to illustrate ways in which a focus on the transposition of a written text into a visual medium can once again encourage students to interrogate the different ways of seeing that fiction can offer.

Meaning and context: 'handsome' in Jane Austen

In this discussion, a digitally manipulated image of an actress on a magazine cover is used as the context for an examination of the ways in which women in Jane Austen's novels see themselves and are seen by others. Students can be invited to make similar connections themselves: for instance, how do the ways in which estate agents try to 'sell' country properties compare with Austen's descriptions of grand mansions (e.g. Pemberley in *Pride and Prejudice*) or modest houses (Barton Cottage in *Sense and Sensibility*)? The focus is on a key word – handsome – and the ways in which it carries meanings that Austen's original readers would have been alert to, but which students today need help to recover. Online concordances now make it possible for students to track words through a novelist's writing to work out their meaning for themselves, and this is a valuable way for them to learn how meaning always depends on context.

....

When Kate Winslet saw herself on the cover of *GQ* magazine in 2003 she wasn't pleased. She looked so lean and hungry that one newspaper described her as 'Belsen-skinny'. Had she *really* lost all that weight? The *Guardian* sent a reporter to find out what had happened to make Kate look like 'chopsticks in tights', and was shocked to be told by the editor, Dylan Jones, 'Almost no picture that appears in *GQ* … has not been digitally altered in some way.'[1] In other words, Kate Winslet was not nearly as thin, and certainly not as tall, as *GQ* had made her appear.

Something similar happens in *Emma*. Look at this first description of Harriet Smith:

> She was a very pretty girl, and her beauty happened to be of a sort which Emma particularly admired. She was short, plump and fair, with a fine bloom, blue eyes, light hair, and a look of great sweetness; and before the end of the evening, Emma was as much pleased with her manners as with her person, and quite determined to continue the acquaintance. (vol. I, ch.iii, p.19)[2]

'Plump' may be the exact opposite of how Kate Winslet looked in *GQ*; but it is a word Jane Austen might have applied to her, had she seen the 1995 film of *Sense and Sensibility*, in which Ms Winslet played Marianne and was, if not short, certainly 'plump and fair, with a fine bloom etc., etc.'. And she would have intended it as a compliment, because she only uses the word to mean 'having a full-formed pleasing figure', never to mean 'rather fat'. The clothes worn by women in the Regency period, when Jane Austen lived, were designed with this in mind: fashionable dresses in the early 19th century were gathered tight under the bust and then hung sheer to the ground. They accentuated the bosom and emphasised a woman's height.

What does this description of Harriet tell us about Emma's idea of beauty? That she would have liked to be short herself? It sounds unlikely. The first adjective used in the novel to describe Emma is 'handsome', a word Austen selects many times in her novels (208 times, to be precise: any Internet concordance of Jane Austen will quickly count them): it carries the sense of 'good-looking and tall' when applied to people. In *Mansfield Park*, when Fanny admits that she does not think Henry Crawford is handsome, Mr Rushworth retorts, 'Handsome! Nobody can call such an under-sized man handsome. He is not five foot nine.' (vol. I, ch. x, p.92). In the same novel, Maria and Julia Bertram are described as 'too handsome themselves to dislike any woman for being so too': they are happy enough to be seen with Mary Crawford. However, the narrator immediately adds, 'Had she been tall, full formed and fair, it might have been more of a trial' (vol. I, ch.v, pp.38-9). Evidently, Mary Crawford was short but not plump.

This cross-reference to another of Austen's novels helps explain why we are told Emma admired Harriet's particular type of beauty: it suited Emma to have a companion shorter than she – it accentuated her own height. Indeed, Austen later undermines that initial description of Harriet completely. When Emma draws Harriet's portrait, the narrator comments, 'She meant to throw in a little improvement to the figure, to give a little more height, and considerably more elegance' (vol I, ch. vi, p.41). Emma's 'improvement' – always a loaded word in Austen's vocabulary – of Harriet is like *GQ*'s digitally altering of its photographs to create a '50ft Winslet' with 'the stature of a tuning fork' (the *Guardian* again). Mr Woodhouse, Mrs Weston and Mr Elton all praise the portrait. Significantly, only one person cuts Harriet – and Emma – down to size:

> 'You have made her too tall, Emma,' said Mr Knightley.
> Emma knew that she had, but would not own [admit] it.   (p.42)

As Austen herself comments, later in *Emma*, 'Seldom can it happen that something is not a little disguised, or a little mistaken' (vol.III, ch.xiii, p.391).

So, appearances can be deceptive in novels as well as in real life and magazines. 'This means,' reflected the *Guardian's* Esther Addley when told there was nothing unusual about the pictures of Kate Winslet being digitally manipulated, 'that every image of every woman that *GQ* readers look at is, on some level, a lie'. In Austen's novels, the differences between 'false' and 'true' appearances are often hard for the characters (and therefore for the reader) to pick up. Look at this passage from *Persuasion*:

> When they came to the steps, leading up from the beach, a gentleman at the same moment preparing to come down, politely drew back, and stopped to give them way. They ascended and passed him; and as they passed, Anne's face caught his eye, and he looked at her with a degree of earnest admiration, which she could not be insensible of. She was looking remarkably well; her very regular, very pretty features, having the bloom and freshness of youth restored by the fine wind which had been blowing on her complexion, and by the animation of eye which it had also produced. It was evident that the gentleman (completely a gentleman in manner) admired her exceedingly. Captain Wentworth looked round at her instantly in a way which shewed his noticing of it. He gave her a momentary glance, – a glance of brightness, which seemed to say, 'That man is struck with you, – and even I, at this moment, see something like Anne Elliot again.'   (vol. I, ch. xii, pp.93–4)[3]

Though Anne does not know it, this stranger is her cousin William Elliot. Captain Wentworth is the man whom she still loves but whom she gave up eight years before, having been persuaded that he would not be a suitable husband for her. Now, William Elliot looks at Anne with 'admiration'; she registers his admiration ('which she could not be insensible of'); Wentworth notices Elliot looking at Anne, and looks at her himself – and in that 'momentary glance' he sees the woman he used to love, and now starts to love again. Anne has literally been 'restored' to her old self; she has regained 'the freshness of youth'. With Anne, the way she looks reveals the way she really is: 'something like Anne Elliot again'. It is a turning point in the novel, setting up the triangle (Anne, Wentworth and William Elliot) which will shape the rest of the story.

But what about William Elliot? Although he may be 'completely a gentleman in manner' (an example of what is sometimes called *free indirect style, narrative or discourse*: is this the narrator's opinion or Anne's? – we can't be sure) events will prove that he is not at all a gentleman. His behaviour to Anne's family and to her friends turns out to have been selfish and vicious. So at the same moment, the reader is presented with two people looking at each other and seen by a third. One of these people is not what he seems. Something has been 'a little disguised', the image has been manipulated, and both Anne and the reader are deceived. What she and we see is a lie.

And yet, there is a clue. It would have been perfectly possible for Austen to have left out the parenthesis '(completely a gentleman in manner)'. No apparent damage would have been done to the narrative. The fact is, though, that by pausing to make this comment about what his outward appearance and behaviour suggested, the narrator invites us to think twice. After all, William Elliot belongs to a type familiar in Austen's novels. Wickham in *Pride and Prejudice* at first seemed to Elizabeth Bennet much more a gentleman than Darcy. Henry Crawford (in *Mansfield*

Park) and Willoughby (in *Sense and Sensibility*) both had the manner, if not the manners, of a gentleman. A lot may hang on a single letter.

John Berger, in *Ways of Seeing* (1972), argues that 'Men look at women. Women watch themselves being looked at. This determines not only most relations between men and women but also the relation of women to themselves.'(p.47) What Berger says applies to all Austen's novels, and to *Persuasion* above all. *Persuasion* is about esteem and self-esteem, about the way people look at each other and at themselves. When, after they are reunited at the end of the story, Wentworth says to Anne, 'To my eye you could never alter' (vol. II, ch.xi, p.214) she knows he is lying: not so long before, he had said she was so changed he would not have recognised her (vol. I, ch.vii p.54). Nevertheless, she 'smiled and let it pass. It was too pleasing a blunder for a reproach.' Kate Winslet was less forgiving: seeing herself digitally altered on the cover of *GQ* she told reporters, 'The amount of retouching is excessive. I don't look like that. I don't desire to look like that.'

Jane Austen would have found the men's magazines of today surprising, but she was acutely aware of how women were perceived in a world controlled by men. The crucial conversation between Anne Elliot and Captain Harville (vol. II, ch. xi) makes this clear:

> 'I do not think I ever opened a book in my life which had not something to say upon women's inconstancy. Songs and proverbs, all talk of women's fickleness. But perhaps you will say, these were all written by men.'
> 'Perhaps I shall. – Yes, yes, if you please, no reference to examples in books. Men have had every advantage of us in telling their own story. Education has been theirs in so much higher a degree; the pen has been in their hands.'
>
> (p.206)

Anne's last remark here can be read in three contexts: the history of women's authorship, Austen's own experience as a writer, and the ironic fact that – moments earlier – Wentworth had actually dropped his pen in agitation as he overhead Anne's conversation.

Contexts for close reading

In looking closely at passages from *Emma* and *Persuasion*, I have tried to show how the author's choices of language and her narrative techniques have helped to shape meaning. But I hope I have also shown that meaning here – whether of a single word, or a sentence or a whole passage – must depend on the context. Words like 'plump' and 'handsome', when Jane Austen uses them, have meanings subtly different from today's. And with any passage from a novel, its relation to the book as a whole provides probably the most important context for close reading.

It is impossible, for instance, to spot the ambiguity of a phrase like 'completely a gentleman in manner' without reading it in the context of the whole story. Other books by the same writer may also help to show what is going on under the surface. The secret lives of so-called 'gentlemen' are exposed in all Austen's novels: a reading of *Persuasion* will be enhanced by a reading of *Emma*, and *vice versa*.

Contextual close reading of the kind I have described above is one of the central skills needed for literary study today, so an awareness of the contexts in which texts are written and understood should never be an add-on, or a bit of background to impress the examiner. Used as I have used them here, elements of context (within the texts and around the texts: events later in the story, Regency fashions, gender issues, etc.) can enrich the meaning of the texts and our enjoyment of them.

While contexts are often historical, helping to place a text in a particular period, texts themselves can have a resonance that echoes between the past and the present. *Emma* and *Persuasion* may have been written nearly two hundred years ago, but we are reading them today. A digitally altered picture of Kate Winslet is an unusual but revealing context for reading *Emma*: the parallel with Emma's altering of Harriet's appearance when she draws her portrait suggests that, then as now, things are all too often 'a little disguised or a little mistaken'. Similarly, John Berger's observation ('Men look at women. Women watch themselves being looked at.') challenges our response both to Kate Winslet and to Anne Elliot.

Come to think of it, 'Ways of Seeing' would be rather a good subtitle for *Persuasion*.

· · · · · · · · · · · · · · · · · · · ·

Students can explore Austen's vocabulary by using an online concordance such as victorian.lang.nagoya-u.ac.jp/concordance/austen. For a helpful introduction to using Internet resources for literary research see 'Online English' in Peter Barry's very accessible guide to English Studies today, *English in Practice* (Arnold, 2002).

The controversial Kate Winslet images and the accompanying cover story can be found at: www.guardian.co.uk/film/2003/jan/10/pressandpublishing.media

The surrounding news coverage is reviewed at: news.bbc.co.uk/1/hi/entertainment/showbiz/2751869.stm

Ways of seeing – teaching a new novel: Mantel and Treasure

Two novels are featured in the following discussion:
Hilary Mantel *A Change of Climate* (London: Penguin, 1994)
Joe Treasure *The Male Gaze* (London: Picador, 2007)

Neither of these books has yet featured on A level set text lists, but with increasing emphasis on literature post-1990, each of them could easily do so. Or they could be chosen for coursework: Ian McEwan's novel *Atonement* was chosen as a set text after it became clear this was a novel many teachers wanted to teach and were recommending it to students as a coursework text. The discussions focus throughout on strategies for preparing and teaching unfamiliar fiction texts, especially those for which there is no body of critical or contextual background material. Throughout, the emphasis is on the importance of being, as teachers, 'in full possession of the text' and of encouraging students in turn to discover how much more there is to be enjoyed in a novel once they have come to know a book really well.

·····················

Whether preparing to teach Jane Austen's *Persuasion* or the latest Man Booker Prize-winning novel for the first time, the starting principle is the same: teaching a novel means being in full possession of the text. Keeping barely a chapter ahead, or relying on published notes and chapter summaries, is hardly fair to the students we are teaching. By 'being in full possession of the text' I do not mean knowing everything about it: one of the main rewards of teaching literature is to be lucky enough to go on learning while we are teaching, and we may teach the same book several times during our career. Each time, with luck and good preparation we should feel our understanding (and admiration) of the book growing. When we don't, it's time to stop teaching it.

Of course, teaching *Persuasion* is made both easier and harder because of the amount of critical and supporting material (including TV adaptations) available. But none of this is useful until we are confident of knowing the text well enough, not merely to be able to recall the plot and the sequence of it accurately, but to have a clear sense of how the narrative works; in this instance of how Austen leads and misleads the reader as she introduces the characters, develops their relationships and indicates the main concerns of the novel. What are the tricks of vocabulary that a writer uses, and how do these help or unsettle the reader? What effect does Austen's frequent use of hendiadys (doubling) have? When Anne Elliot is said to 'smile *with pity and contempt*, either at herself or at Lady Russell', the reader who is familiar with Austen recognises a strategy that goes to the heart of her technique; however, a teacher who has never encountered Austen before needs first to discover the way this unsettling narrative device works in the novel as a whole, and then to introduce it to students early on in the teaching of the text, so that they know what to be looking out for. How can Anne be said to feel both pity and contempt at the same time? Is she feeling pity for Lady Russell and contempt for herself? Or *vice versa*? At this moment, she and her companion are walking down one of the main streets in Bath, and Captain Wentworth is walking towards them on the other side of the road. Anne is certain that Lady Russell must have seen Captain Wentworth and be judging how he has changed after eight years; in fact, though, Lady Russell tells Anne she has been looking at some expensive curtains in a house opposite. Is she telling the truth? If so, does this apparent concern for the trivial deserve Anne's contempt, or should Anne be directing the contempt at herself for assuming that Lady Russell must be as interested in Captain Wentworth as she is? If Lady Russell is dissimulating, how does this affect our response as readers to one of the central characters in the novel? 'Being in full possession of the text', on one level, certainly involves being this much aware of just how the writing works.

At least Jane Austen's techniques are well known. What are we supposed to do when we read a book for the first time and about which we know nothing? A new novel by an unfamiliar author, for instance? Here are two examples, first of a novel by an author who is well-respected but whose novels have not usually been studied as set texts – *A Change of Climate* (1994) by Hilary Mantel – and, second, of a first novel by an as yet completely unknown writer – *The Male Gaze* (2007) by Joe Treasure.

'Mirror, mirror': *A Change of Climate*

You have to read the book at least twice; no book can be taught that you have only read once. At first, following J. Hillis Miller's terminology in *On Literature* (see Resources, page 292) you read *allegro*, trying to finish the novel in as short a time as may be, aiming to be carried along by the story and the storytelling. Then you read it again, as soon as possible after the first reading, while details of events, characters, significant ideas and language are still in your mind. This is when you read *lente*, giving as much attention as you can to how the book is constructed and written. Inevitably, some features – especially of characterisation – will have struck you straightaway. *A Change of Climate*, for instance, begins

1970
SAD CASES, GOOD SOULS

One day when Kit was ten years old, a visitor cut her wrists in the kitchen. She was just beginning on this cold, difficult form of death when Kit came in to get a glass of milk.

This scene is presented in a remarkably matter-of-fact tone: Kit takes charge of the situation at once; we are told that 'at this stage in her life Kit was not much surprised by anything'. It is left to the reader to reflect on the background and upbringing of a child who can cope as calmly as Kit does with a situation which would challenge most adults. At the end of the episode, which only lasts one and a half pages, Kit overhears a conversation between her parents, Ralph and Anna, from which it becomes clear that the visitor had been introduced into the house by Ralph. Anna complains about the visitor's being a suicide risk, but Ralph does not apologise. Three days later, Kit finds her mother on the floor, obsessively scrubbing the flagstones. "'The blood's gone,'" Kit said, puzzled. "I wiped it up.'" Her mother does not reply.

After this, the narrator gives three paragraphs of background exposition: Ralph, a former missionary, works for a charitable trust, and the visitors to their home are people whom he brings from a hostel in London, or whom the Social Services asks him to look after:

> Sometimes they turned up of their own accord, crouching out of the wind in one of the outhouses until he came home. 'So-and-so's a sad case,' he would say; and over the years, this was what the family came to call them: the Sad Cases. Other people he called Good Souls. 'Your Aunt Emma is giving so-and-so a lift to her drugs clinic in Norwich – she's a good soul.'
> And this was how the world was divided, when Kit was growing up – into Good Souls and Sad Cases. There was no wickedness in it.   (p.3)

How should we react to such a prologue? At first reading, there is not much to be done except assimilate the information given. The house, for instance, is presumably old since the kitchen has flagstones on the floor; there are outhouses in the garden. In fact a visitor does emerge, dramatically, out of an outhouse at the very end of the story, and this detail alone should be enough to alert us, when we *re-read* the prologue for the first time, to the need to watch out for other examples of *prolepsis* (anticipation). The attempt by Anna to wash away blood that has already been wiped up will also come to have a clear significance later in the book – as will the very word 'visitor': much of the following story (set both in Norfolk and in Africa) involves visitors and violence. The prologue, therefore, anticipates key ideas and events in the book to come – and of course the reader cannot know this on first reading, but will immediately realise on coming back to the beginning and starting to read *lente*.

Already, the prologue will have suggested that Ralph is a man who classifies – people are not individuals, but Good Souls or Sad Cases – and it is no surprise to discover later on that he has been, since childhood, fascinated by geology and by the ideas of Charles Darwin. This not only becomes a central theme in the book, but also affects the language Hilary Mantel uses when describing how Ralph assesses other people: twice at least he comments to himself that people have 'evolved'. The first to be thus described is Daniel, who has become Kit's boyfriend (the main part of the story is set in 1980, by which time Kit has just graduated from university):

> He liked Daniel, he had decided, because he seemed to have evolved; in the present casual optimist, in his stiff new tweeds, you could seem to see his grandfather, the snappy dresser so slick on the dance floor and free with ginger-beer.
>
> (p. 268)

The second is himself. Caught having an affair with the mother of his son's girlfriend, Ralph is told by Anna to leave their home of twenty years, and is packing a suitcase in the bedroom:

> He hoped Anna would come in. She would not, of course. What would she see? Nothing to lift her spirits. You wreck your family once … years pass … you wreck it twice. He had evolved very nicely, he thought: along the only possible route.
>
> (p.336)

Ralph is fifty here (by this point in the novel Hilary Mantel has traced his whole life from boyhood onwards). Half a lifetime earlier, he had already come to 'realise you are no longer the person you were, and will never become the person you meant to be' (p.62). But in spite of such self-recognition, at that stage he was still an optimist:

> From a jelly speck to man the line improves, edging nearer all the time to the summit of God's design. As the species has evolved, the child in the womb grows, grows through its fur and becomes human. So society creeps forward, from savagery to benevolence: from cold and hunger and murder, to four walls and hearth stones and arts and parliaments and cures for diseases. At twenty-five Ralph believes this; he believes, too, in the complex perfectibility of the human heart.
>
> (p.63)

It is by the careful re-reading of the novel in this way that we come to be 'in full possession of the text'. It is thus that we read and remember a passage such as the one above and come to register its place and importance in the novel as a whole. It is best to try to devote as much time as possible to the re-reading: an intensive day's study will be more rewarding than a re-reading spread over a longish period when details cannot be remembered and links will be missed. Words like 'evolved' start to stand out because of their relationship to the main ideas of the novel, and by highlighting or underlining can be quite quickly retrieved. Looking at Ralph's first usage of the word in the context of the second emphasises the bitter sarcasm with which he, the Darwinian, applies the term to himself. As reader, you are left to judge whether or not Ralph at this point is being too hard on himself – or, perhaps, to ask whether the author herself is being too hard on her characters.

Other patterns or sequences unexpectedly emerge: that phrase 'the complex perfectibility of the human heart' comes at the very end of Chapter Three, which has described Ralph's childhood and his struggles as a young adult against the dour Christianity of his parents, whom he describes as 'East Anglian fossils'. Forced by his mother and father to abandon his plans to study geology at university (he is blackmailed by the threat that his sister Emma will not be allowed to study medicine if he insists on studying geology), he does not yet realise that his optimism about evolution is challenged by the narrative's insistent emphasis on hearts (including his own) that are fragile and damaged. Once you recognise how often Mantel talks about hearts, it is easy to pick out this important strand: identifying strands such as this for students to explore for themselves both gives focus to their own re-reading of the story and gives them confidence in handling textual detail and understanding something of the deeper structures of a novel. These deeper structures are also important in giving coherence to a narrative which otherwise moves backwards and forwards in time and across continents, contrasting the windy Norfolk landscape with the heat and dust of southern Africa. Thus a careful re-reading can alert you, for instance, to the fact that both the Red House in Norfolk and the Mosadinyana Mission House in Botswana contain hideous pieces of furniture that torment Anna. The Red House has a hall-stand, 'a vast and unnecessary article of furniture that Ralph had picked up in an antique shop in Great Yarmouth'. With a Jane Austen-like hendiadys, Mantel tells us that Anna

> looked with a fresh sense of wonder and dislike at its barley-sugar legs and its many little drawers and its many little dust-trapping ledges and its brass hooks for gentlemen's hats, and she saw her face in the dim spotted oval of mirror, and smoothed her hair back from her forehead, then took off her coat and threw it over the banisters. (pp.16–17)

This prompts the narrator to reflect that

> the Norfolk climate gave Anna a bloodless look, tinged her thin hands with violet. Every winter she would think of Africa; days when, leaving her warm bed in a hot early dawn, she had felt her limbs grow fluid, and the pores of her face open like petals, and her ribs, free from their accustomed tense gauge, move to allow her a full, voluptuary's breath. In England she never felt this confidence ... (p.17)

This passage, coming so near the opening of the book and introducing the reader to Anna's African life, implies that Africa had been an experience she longed to recapture. Yet (as we later learn) in South Africa she and her husband had been imprisoned for their defiance of apartheid, and were then exiled to the remote Bantu homelands in Botswana, where the central, decisive action of the whole novel occurs. Again it is only by re-reading that we can become aware of a narrative strategy like this one, designed to wrong-foot the reader and to make us subsequently question the reliability of the narrator. Teaching any novel at this level, it is important to find examples early on of narrative techniques that students can then look out for in their own re-reading of the book. Effectively, in teaching students how to read novels, we are teaching them how to re-read.

In the Mission House, Ralph and Anna find 'the sticks of furniture left behind by their predecessors ... Their bedroom was furnished with a bulky dressing table' (p.208). This dressing-table, like the Norfolk hall-stand, boasted 'a spotted mirror': in each one, Anna and Ralph are able to see only – and appropriately, since they are missionaries – as through a glass darkly. And they are not the only ones: back in England, and shocked almost out of his high Anglican faith by the news of the disaster that overwhelms Anna and Ralph in Africa, Ralph's uncle James

> caught sight of himself in a square of dusty mirror that hung on the opposite wall; saw a spare and desiccated old man, worn by humility, sucked dry by the constant effort of belief. He spoke aloud for a moment, as if Ralph and his wife were in the room with him. 'Anna, there is nothing, there is nothing worse, there is nothing so burdensome ... there is nothing so appallingly hard ... as the business of being human ...' His voiced died in his throat. I should take that mirror down, he thought, I have often meant to do it, glass is a danger in a place like this. (p.246)

It is no coincidence then that in dusty, spotted mirrors Anna and James see only the failure of their attempts to be good; nor is it a coincidence that eventually it is clear glass that enables Anna and Ralph to see their lives from a new perspective. Ralph's mistress, Amy, is called Mrs Glasse; and it is she who tells him:

> 'Look at any life – from the inside, I mean, from the point of view of the person who's living it. What is it but defeats? It's just knock-backs, one after the other, isn't it? Everybody remembers the things they did wrong. But what about the thousands and thousands and thousands of things they did right. You lost a child. And every day you think about it. But think of the children you didn't lose.' (p.332)

To which Ralph replies, 'Nobody has ever said that to me before.' And, as he leaves Amy for the last time, 'Her eyes had never been so pale and clear.' A similar enlightenment comes to Anna, when, after discovering Ralph's affair, she visits Ginny, a woman whose late, unfaithful husband Felix had helped her convert some old boathouses in Blakeney into a home whose 'most startling feature was a huge picture window of staring, blank plate glass':

> This window was one of the great acts of Ginny's life. Some women die and
> leave only their children as a memorial; but Ginny, like some anointed saint,
> would have a window. It represented a moral choice, an act of courage. Some
> would shudder at it, though secretly they would crave the vista. Questions of
> taste would cow them: questions of vulgarity, even. Ginny simply said, 'Why
> live at Blakeney, if you don't have the view?'   (p.315)

By the end of the novel, the reader is made aware that Ginny has survived the years of her unhappy marriage by looking outwards, not in. So, when Anna asks her 'What do you do, while you're sitting it out?' Mantel allows herself a wry variation on glass as she writes:

> Ginny reached for another cigarette, flipped it into her mouth. 'This,' she
> said. She flicked a nail at her glass. 'And this. Alternatively, you can count your
> blessings.'   (ibid.)

It is in essence the same advice that Amy Glasse has given Ralph. Anna decides to accept it, and when she returns to the Red House she finds that 'the vast hall-stand had a vast cobweb on it', stretching across the old spotted mirror: 'Just off-centre sat a small brown spider, its legs folded modestly.' (p.334)

....

Putting yourself in full possession of the text in such ways as these is one of the rewards of both studying and teaching the novel, and none of the process can be completed other than by developing the closest relationship between yourself and the book. Critics and cribs will not help. You discover and trace these patterns and listen to these echoes for yourself. But it is important always to remember that how you teach a particular novel will depend on the context within which it is to be taught (and probably assessed).

- Are you introducing students to analytical skills they won't have come across before, or do you want them to apply to a new text skills they have already begun to develop?
- Is the book to feature as a set text on an exam paper? If so, how does it fit into the particular paper? Is it to be discussed on its own, or in conjunction with other novels? What assessment objectives (if any) will be targeted on this paper? Is the emphasis to be on comparison with one other novel or with a group of texts to reflect a common theme?
- Is the text being studied for its own sake? Or to illustrate features of the style of the writer (e.g. *Persuasion*, to exemplify Jane Austen's use of irony), or perhaps the writer's attitude to wealth and class (*Persuasion* again)?

A novel such as *A Change of Climate* lends itself strongly to comparison with other texts for teaching purposes, whether studied whole or in extract form. The sections set in South Africa under apartheid bear comparison with scenes in Nadine Gordimer's *Burger's Daughter* (1978), or with passages from Rian Malan's memoir, *My Traitor's Heart* (1991). Equally, *A Change of Climate* is a novel with a strong East Anglian setting and could thus be read against Norfolk novels such as L.P. Hartley's *The Go-Between* (1953) or Graham Swift's *Waterland* (1983). The latter would be particularly appropriate since it deals, like *A Change of Climate*, with the loss of a child, with history and memory. Another novel that deals with a parent's attempts to come to terms with the loss of a child is Ian McEwan's *The Child in Time* (1987). Parts of Hilary Mantel's novel (those dealing with the young Ralph's conflict with his father over religion and evolution) should be read as a modern rewriting of Edmund Gosse's novel on the same theme, *Father and Son* (1907). The book can also be read in the context of other novels by Hilary Mantel, with Internet resources enabling students to research the range of her writing in her other novels to identify particular texts and parts of texts that would make for rewarding comparison or contrast. As a novel of the 1990s, its fragmented time sequence can be compared with that of, for example, Arundhati Roy's *The God of Small Things* (1997) – another book which has at its centre the loss of a child. It is always illuminating to discuss one book in terms of another, and this is a key literary skill that students need to develop, especially if they are intending to pursue Literary Studies at university. But it is always necessary to insist on the integrity of individual texts, each novel demanding to be read and evaluated on its own terms, not just in terms of other books and other writers. As the above list of novels for comparison with *A Change of Climate* suggests, Hilary Mantel's novel is a work which generates its own contexts, but these contexts only add value to the book once the reader (teacher or student) is in possession of the text.

The texts that fail to get set

Why do some books and some authors never seem to appear on reading lists? In many ways *A Change of Climate* is an ideal novel to study: its themes are adult and challenging; it is both witty and profoundly serious; it presents a world in which children are more often right than their parents; it offers a model of good writing and narrative subtlety – in fact it is highly readable, not a 'difficult' book at all. Unfortunately, at a time when the choice of texts is increasingly determined by the ready availability of support material and even by stocks in school English departments, a book may simply never make it onto teachers' radar, never mind examination set text lists. Hilary Mantel is not alone: writers such as John Banville and William Trevor notoriously fail to be introduced to pre-university readers. Occasionally a book such as Ian McEwan's *Atonement* (2001) will be adopted almost at once, but this is the exception, and anyway McEwan is a writer whose novels are widely reviewed / hugely hyped, attracting a great deal of attention. What hope is there for a completely unknown writer with a completely unknown novel?

One of the best hopes lies actually with the new requirement (in QCA's revised Subject Criteria for GCE English Literature, 2006) that texts post 1900 must now be studied as part of an AS or A level course. Another lies in the greater flexibility that the new criteria allow to coursework: where teachers and students can follow, within limits, their own inclinations in reading and comparing texts, there is less reason to stick to the old familiar faces. Thankfully, too, there will be more scope for teaching new novels for which no specially written study support material yet exists. If part of the purpose of teaching Literature is to train students to become readers, re-reading literary texts critically and with insight, this must embrace new writing as well as classics. Keeping aware of new writing is an activity that can be shared with students, but it does imply that teachers should continue to read new writing themselves whenever they can – the more so if now they will have to guide students in their choice of contemporary fiction. But, as ever, the principle of gaining full possession of the text will apply.

'What are you filming that for?' *The Male Gaze*

Joe Treasure's *The Male Gaze* (2007) is set in California though its central characters, David and Rebecca, are both British. She is an academic, an art historian; her husband is a writer of school textbooks. As with any novel, read for the first time, one is tempted to categorise: what kind of book is this? Is it going to be a campus novel or an 'Englishman-abroad novel' for instance? David, the first-person narrator, is good at very English self-deprecation: when Rebecca tries to get him to dress rather more smartly for their first meeting with members of her new Department, she pleads with her informally-dressed husband:

> 'Just try not to look so ...'
> 'So ... what?'
> 'So hopelessly English.'
> 'They like it that we're English.'
> 'But you don't have to wear it like a medal.'
> English is shorthand, of course, for a cluster of insecurities. Maybe it means not being up on Foucault.
> 'I'll change,' I say.
> 'That'll be the day.' The joke signals a truce. (p.3)

David's defensive jokiness tends to infuriate Rebecca, and the world of the English education system from which he comes puzzles the new Californian friends he makes. When he explains to one of them, a New Age groupie called Astrid, that the book he is trying to write is 'just a Key Stage Three thing', she responds in all seriousness, 'That's a stage of enlightenment, right?' (p.22)

There are enough clues here to make a search for Englishness in a Californian setting an appropriate starting point for investigating *The Male Gaze*. From the beginning, David's reluctance to get involved in the Los Angeles world his wife embraces with such enthusiasm is offset by his naive passivity which ensures that he is soon literally immersed in a world he does not understand. At the party hosted by Rebecca's new Head of Department, Frankie, and her TV producer husband, Max, a child falls into a swimming pool and almost drowns. 'There is a scream and one of the women leaps into the pool', but Astrid, not realising there has been an accident and thinking that this is how the party has been planned, rushes to the poolside shouting 'This is going to be so great!' David, trying to keep up with her, arrives to see Astrid jump into the pool, 'whooping with anticipation':

> I have time to see her blue dress billowing up around her waist. I have time
> to regret my Englishness, to regret that I must always stand at the edge and
> watch. But the water, sparkling with fragments of light, is tilting towards me.
> It throws itself at my face, washing over me with an intimate commotion.
> The old sounds of shouting and splashing are muted. Twisting in this low-
> gravity element, I see legs that might be Astrid's legs – green and distorted
> – and other women's legs, and legs in trousers. I see an arm waving frantically
> across my face and I see that it's my arm. (p.22)

At the very moment, then, that he stands back to reproach himself for his English reluctance to get involved, he also takes the plunge. And when he comes to the surface again, he sees that all eyes are on the child who has been dragged from the water and is being given artificial respiration. The only person looking at him is his wife.

In fact, how people see each other, and see themselves, is the central idea of this novel, and a prime reason why *The Male Gaze* is the type of book that students should be encouraged to explore for themselves to learn what fiction can do. The title is critical to this exploration. Taken from an influential essay on cinema by Laura Mulvey ('Visual Pleasure and Narrative Cinema' in *Screen*, 16, 3; Autumn 1975), 'the male gaze' describes how men perceive women and how women perceive themselves as objects of the male gaze. Even before the phrase had been invented, however, writers and critics were questioning the implications of the male gaze. John Berger, in *Ways of Seeing* (1972), suggested that a woman

> ... has to survey everything she is and everything she does because how
> she appears to others, and ultimately how she appears to men, is of crucial
> importance for what is normally thought of as the success of her life. Her

own sense of being in herself is supplanted by a sense of being appreciated as
herself by another.   (p.46)

In Treasure's novel, Astrid buys a burka on eBay to discover what it is like to
look out on the world as a woman who cannot be seen. Max makes a series of
TV programmes about women (women and Islam, women and the sex trade,
women and plastic surgery) which cause such controversy that he is subjected to
anonymous death threats. More sinister than this, David discovers that Max has
secretly filmed himself having sex with one of the women who features in his TV
film and with a young girl who has later committed suicide. Worse still, it seems
that Max has been having an affair with Rebecca and filming her too. The sequence
of events that leads David to discover how badly he has misinterpreted everything
he has seen lies at the heart of the novel, which has in its sights the devastating
potential of television itself to misinterpret the truth.

The climax of the plot comes when a young and thoroughly westernised
Iranian student, studying the male gaze in 17th-century Persian art, is suspected
of trying to murder Max. Pursued by the police and by TV crews, Amir Kadivar is
misrepresented at every turn: the media distort his name to Cadaver, and when he
reaches inside his suit for the asthma inhaler that he carries, police gunmen shoot
and kill him. When David, who has witnessed the shooting, explains that Amir
wasn't even a Muslim, never mind an extremist, and that he used an inhaler for
his asthma, the media at once interprets the word as a sinister term for a type of
weapon. David's narrative records the scene as the scene is being recorded for TV:

> The woman with hair like spun sugar is talking to the camera. 'Sources close
> to the police,' she says, 'are suggesting that the suspect was armed. This
> eyewitness has identified the gun as an inhaler. Whether this was the weapon
> used against TV producer Max Kleinman is not known at this time …' She
> seems to have more to say. But the screenwriter, who has rolled his face from
> the shop window and leant forward with his hand on my shoulder, chooses
> this moment to vomit on her shoes.
>
> 'Cut!' someone says. 'I said cut. Jesus, what are you filming that for?'
>
> (pp.258–9)

· · · · · · · · · · · · · · · · · · · ·

Re-reading *The Male Gaze*, it will become clear how important seeing and being
seen are in this novel. Indeed, it would be worth working with a group of students
to identify and classify every such reference in each chapter. Who looks at whom? In
what way do they look? Is it clear how this contributes to the themes of plot of the
novel? In what context is the gaze interpreted?

A key conversation occurs when Frankie explains her art history research to David:

'It's just that I'm curious about expressions ...'
  'It's what she's working on,' Rebecca explains.
  ' ... what's spontaneous, what's socialised, and what's merely contextually
determined, that sort of thing. I'm convinced that the influence of context
on our reading of expression is considerable ... Point a camera at a couple
of girls at a party,' Frankie says. 'They smile, lean towards each other to
compose a picture – their socialised conception of what a picture ought to be.
We value spontaneity, here, now, more than any time or place you can think
of. Everything's got to be spontaneous. So spontaneity itself becomes an
elaborate construct with its own iconography.'   (p.113)

David in the course of the novel has to observe his own expression and to observe
the expression on other people's faces as they observe him. Forcing himself to
watch the video that he thinks will show Rebecca and Max together, he identifies
in himself 'the desperate melancholy of the voyeur' (p.180) and is dismayed, after
a row with Rebecca, to see her give him a glare 'that makes me feel like a stalker'
(p.196).

The irony here is that David's devotion to Rebecca is total but that while he
loves to look at her, she hates it. The very first thing she says to him in the book
is, 'What are you looking at?' and she is cross when she catches him watching her
putting on her make-up:

'Please don't,' she says. 'You know I hate it.'
  She doesn't like to be looked at, and even with her eyes closed she knows
I'm still there. She's working on her wrinkles. She's been talking a lot about
wrinkles recently. It's nothing, I tell her. You can hardly see them. And anyway
they give your face more character. This doesn't seem to help.   (p.3)

David's gaucheness, even though he is seven years older than his wife, makes it
hard for him to cope with her almost unfounded suspicions that he is having an
affair with Astrid. When he tells her that Astrid had simply 'wanted to show me
her burka', Rebecca's predictable disbelief makes it impossible for him to see her
properly:

I'm staring at Rebecca as though the intensity of my expression will make
words unnecessary and my view of her is suddenly obscured. I look away. The
light from the window is a blur, and the tears are wet on my face, and the
catch in my breath has developed into a sobbing, a series of juddering spasms
that drag air into my lungs and push it back out again.   (p.60)

It's at a point like this in the novel, when we know the text intimately enough to be teaching it, that a phrase such as 'the intensity of my expression' registers as an echo from Frankie's later lecture on the influence of context on expression and on the constructedness of spontaneity. For just when the reader assumes that what David is describing is indeed spontaneous (the sequence of connecting 'and's' giving the sense of an experience which has achieved its own momentum and which David cannot control), David himself admits it is a performance: 'My body has taken control of itself, leaving my mind free to register discomfort at the fraudulence of this behaviour. I have a sense that I could stop at any time if I really wanted to.' Why is it fraudulent? Because, as David sees it, Rebecca is resentful of his having 'somehow usurped the role of victim by this uncharacteristic display of feeling'. Crying, of course (or more particularly being seen to cry), being a very un-English thing to do.

Taking possession of the text

It is depressing to hear teachers sometimes say they are reluctant to teach a text about which nothing has been written yet. The strategies described above for taking possession of the text are aimed at overcoming this reluctance. But even the most recent novels will have been reviewed, and these reviews can provide a good second point of departure. Getting students to find and compare reviews (most published reviews are downloadable from the Internet) will encourage them to weigh their own views against those of the critics. A reviewer in the *Guardian* said of *The Male Gaze* 'Its strength lies in the acutely realised and believable relationship between David and Rebecca.' The *Times Literary Supplement* agreed: 'The novel's greatest success is in its portrait of this relationship … Although the two spend little time alone together, the strain on their marriage is palpable, and their love – hers solid but exasperated, his adoring and unconditional – is moving … Joe Treasure takes an intelligent, nuanced and sympathetic look at the complex and rewarding process of crossing the boundary between looking on and taking part in a new life.'

It is revealing that both these reviews identify the relationship between David and Rebecca as the core of the novel, and it is true, too, that the resolution of *The Male Gaze* is a resolution of the tensions and misunderstandings that have almost destroyed their marriage. With any novel, we should ask what has been resolved, or remains unresolved, by the end of the book – this being a question both about structure and about theme. It would be worth comparing the end of *The Male Gaze* with the end of *A Change of Climate* to accentuate this question of resolution, and other endings could be compared as well.

'What sense is there in our life together unless we hold in common the stuff that presses on us?' asks David in the last chapter of *The Male Gaze*. It's a question also asked at the end of Zadie Smith's *On Beauty* (London: Penguin, 2005), in which another Englishman abroad, Howard, all but loses his wife, Kiki, through accident and emotional carelessness rather than design. Howard, like Rebecca, is an art history lecturer teaching in the States; like David he is unable to finish a book he has been trying to write. Whereas David's is a Religious Studies textbook for school children, Howard's is meant to be about Rembrandt for post-modern adults, but his iconoclastic approach to art history teaching has neither endeared itself to his students nor brought him academic success: nearing the end of his career, he still has to gain tenure. At the end of the novel, he is giving a public lecture (on which his future employment may depend) on Rembrandt's portraits. Unable to master the Powerpoint presentation he has been told to use, and distracted by the unexpected but welcome sight of Kiki in the audience (he thinks she has left him and their marriage is over), he can do nothing except enlarge the image of the painting that appears on the wall:

> '*Hendrickje Bathing*, 1564,' croaked Howard and said no more.
>
> On the wall, a pretty, blousy Dutch woman in a simple white smock paddled in water up to her calves. Howard's audience looked at her and then at Howard and then at the woman once more, awaiting elucidation. The woman, for her part, looked away, coyly, into the water. She seemed to be considering whether to wade deeper. The surface of the water was dark, reflective – a cautious bather could not be certain of what lurked beneath. Howard looked at Kiki. In her face, his life. Kiki looked up suddenly at Howard – not, he thought, unkindly. Howard said nothing. Another silent minute passed. The audience began to mutter perplexedly. Howard made the picture larger on the wall, as Smith had explained to him how to do. The woman's fleshiness filled the wall. He looked out into the audience once more and saw Kiki only. He smiled at her. She smiled. She looked away, but she smiled. Howard looked back at the woman on the wall, Rembrandt's love, Hendrickje. Though her hands were imprecise blurs, paint heaped on paint and roiled with the brush, the rest of her skin had been expertly rendered in all its variety – chalky whites and lively pinks, the underlying blue of her veins and the ever present human hint of yellow, intimation of what is to come.
>
> (*On Beauty*, pp.442–3)

Comparing this ending with the ending of *The Male Gaze*, or with any of the passages in which David describes his delight at gazing on Rebecca, illuminates both novels and gives students the chance to reflect how much studying, possessing and enjoying novels has to do with ways of seeing.

Englishness in the contemporary novel: Lodge, Barnes and Smith

Students are increasingly asked, whether in coursework or in written examinations, to compare texts or to discuss ways in which they are linked together, by genre, theme or topic, period or author.

One area of debate, which has persisted in English Literature certainly since Shakespeare and, arguably, since Chaucer centres on national identity. It is a debate that is just as important and every bit as contentious now as during the 19th century when novelists such as Disraeli and Dickens challenged their readers to contemplate 'the condition of England'. Since it is also a debate which involves the very concept of 'English Literature' – literature written by (mainly) English men; literature written in the English language; literature that reflects or rejects certain assumptions about what it is to be English rather than British, etc. – it is one that students studying English should engage with sooner rather than later. And a very good way to do this is to examine the approaches that different authors adopt in wrestling with the problem of nation and identity.

The following discussion explores ideas of 'England' and 'Englishness' in recent British fiction. It asks how far the very terms British and English are being redefined, by showing that the work of contemporary novelists reflects the tension between a conservative view of Englishness, rooted in continuity and tradition, and a more radical multicultural perspective on British identity. It begins with a brief survey of 'Englishness' exemplified in novels such as *Howards End* (1910) by E.M. Forster, *Brideshead Revisited* (1945) by Evelyn Waugh and *Lucky Jim* (1954) by Kingsley Amis. It then discusses *Nice Work* (1988) by David Lodge, *England, England* (1998) by Julian Barnes and *White Teeth* (2000) by Zadie Smith. The discussion here can be looped back to the discussion of Joe Treasure's *The Male Gaze*, in the previous section.

· · · · · · · · · · · · · · · · · · · ·

The terms 'English' and 'British' are becoming increasingly complex: they are certainly much harder to define at the start of the 21st century than they were one hundred years ago – or even ten years ago. Thirty years ago it would have seemed inconceivable that the question of independence for Scotland should be a live political issue, or that there should be a Scottish Parliament and a Welsh Assembly. Within schools and universities we now increasingly talk of British literature to distinguish it both from literature only written within the geographical area of England and from literature written in English anywhere in the world. Although the Nobel prize-winning poet Seamus Heaney is represented in many anthologies of English Verse, he insists that he is an Irish, not an English or British writer: 'My passport is green,' he has famously insisted. Can he be both? Is Salman Rushdie an English writer? And if he is, what kind of an English writer is he?

But to assume that the English, Irish, Scots and Welsh have all retreated behind their national boundaries – that Hadrian's Wall, Offa's Dyke and the Irish Sea have once again become real as well as symbolic dividing lines – is also to oversimplify. So much of urban England, like so much of Europe but not necessarily like so much of rural England or of Wales and Scotland, is now thoroughly multicultural. The second and by now almost third generation families originally from the former British Empire – West Indies, Pakistan, and Africa – have every right to regard Britain as their home and themselves as British, even if their representation in government is still disproportionately small. There is here perhaps, a sense of 'almost' belonging, hence the predicament of Haroon in Hanif Kureishi's novel *The Buddha of Suburbia*: he has spent most of his adult life as an immigrant in London 'trying to be more of an Englishman'.

The legacy of our colonial past continues to trouble us very much. This is a central issue in the last of the novels, *White Teeth*, to be discussed (see pages 201–204, below), but first here is an example of the unease with which the English (as opposed to the Welsh or Scots) confront the relationship between their past and present. Every summer the Promenade Concerts, the 'Proms' as they are affectionately known, are held in the Royal Albert Hall. The Last Night of the Proms, held in mid-September, is always an occasion for a boisterous but good-natured display of fancy-dress and patriotic song-singing, broadcast on TV and radio around the world. Songs such as 'Rule Britannia' and 'Land of Hope and Glory' are sung by the whole audience and a good time is had by nearly all.

At the start of the millennium, in 2001, the concert fell on Saturday 15th September, the end of the week which had begun with 9/11, the terrorist attacks on the World Trade Centre in New York. It was quickly decided that 'Rule Britannia' and 'Land of Hope and Glory' – both songs originally written to extol the power and influence of Britain – were inappropriate to the new mood of international solidarity. Instead, the programme was altered to include the *Adagio* by the American composer Samuel Barber and the last movement of Beethoven's Ninth Symphony. Only one of the traditional items from the Last Night of the Proms *was* retained, the musical setting of 'Jerusalem', that famous poem by William Blake. While 'Rule Britannia' and 'Land of Hope and Glory' celebrated Britain's imperial expansion of the last century – 'Wider still and wider shall thy bounds be set, / God who made thee mighty make thee mightier yet' – Blake's 'Jerusalem' offers a mystical, almost a millennarian, view of England as that 'green and pleasant land'.

Now 'Jerusalem' has nearly the status of an unofficial national anthem, a stirring song celebrating England's roots in the past ('in ancient time') and defining the country literally in terms of the southern English countryside, 'pleasant pastures' and 'clouded hills' rather than the 'dark Satanic Mills' of the north of England. That it should have been deemed suitable for a national occasion on which traditional songs like 'Rule Britannia' were rejected suggests both our unease about our former British triumphalism – 'Rule Britannia, Britannia rule the waves' – and our willingness (almost our eagerness) to see England as embodying the virtues of quiet, rural continuity: 'England's green and pleasant land'. It is no coincidence that a popular magazine called *This England* is advertised as appealing 'to all who love this green and pleasant land'. These tensions, between ideas of imperial Britain and ideas of insular England, between north and south, between the industrial and the rural, have been central to the debate about England and Englishness ever since Blake wrote 'Jerusalem'. They remain central today.

The English novel: history vs heritage
During the hundred years that followed the writing of 'Jerusalem', the English novel became perhaps the dominant literary mode of writing. Novelists as diverse as Benjamin Disraeli, Charlotte Brontë, Charles Dickens and Thomas Hardy all wrote novels that focused on what came to be known as 'the condition of England', a condition that was defined by the same tensions identified in William Blake's poem. Novels such as *Hard Times* by Dickens or *North and South* by Elizabeth Gaskell have come more recently to be labelled as industrial novels, and their analysis of society in terms of binary opposites – the dehumanised urban north against the civilised rural south, the cultivated man of letters against the philistine man of industry – has remained a recognisable caricature up to the present day.

Exploring this caricature, and its implications for an understanding of contemporary Britain, is at the heart of David Lodge's *Nice Work,* the first of the recent novels discussed below. But at the end of the 19th century a more subtle exploration of these tensions was to be found in the novels of Thomas Hardy, especially perhaps in *Tess of the d'Urbervilles.* In this story of a country girl from the south west of England, the area once known as Wessex, Hardy explores the pressures on an agricultural community of the arrival of industrialism and of changes to the ancient structure of English society. His heroine, Tess, is betrayed by the past, by her education and by a future already corrupted by money and arrogance. In Hardy's analysis, the traditional character of England is located quite explicitly in the rural communities and landscape of Wessex, and it is this way of life that is threatened.

It is significant that when Hardy was writing, Wessex (literally, the land of the West Saxons) still represented a real area of England with a distinctive character of its own. At the same time, the name Wessex harked back deliberately to a much earlier period of English history, the era of King Alfred. Now, whether the idea of England has more meaning as a real community of people or as a landscape of the imagination has always been a moot point. Today 'history' and 'heritage' seem to mean very different things: history (facts and their interpretation) seems to be less important (certainly less appealing) than heritage – the packaging of the past in ways which are more concerned to be commercial than educational. This is the issue explored in Julian Barnes' satirical novel, *England, England.*

Ideas of Englishness: *Howards End* and *Brideshead Revisited*

Before the First World War, one of the most interesting novels to deal with ideas of Englishness was E.M. Forster's *Howards End,* published in 1910. Forster contrasts in this novel the world of commerce and industry (the world of 'telegrams and anger' as he puts it) with the world of culture, sensibility and personal relations. On the one hand are the Wilcox family, wealthy, confident and making a fortune from exploiting the raw materials produced in the colonies; on the other are the Schlegel sisters, Helen and Margaret, socially concerned but living comfortable cultured lives in London. Their parents are both dead but their mother had been English and their father German. Their English aunt thinks of them as 'English to the backbone', and certainly not as 'German of the worst sort'; their German cousins regard them as 'not quite German to the backbone' but certainly not as 'English of the worst sort'. They admire Beethoven and dislike Elgar. Their aunt, Mrs Munt, lives in exactly the same part of Wessex from which Hardy's Tess of the d'Urbervilles came; and in a chapter set at Mrs Munt's home Forster writes this about England:

> If one wanted to show a foreigner England, perhaps the wisest course would be to take him to the final section of the Purbeck hills, and stand him on their summit, a few miles to the east of Corfe. Then system after system of our island would roll together under his feet ... Seen from the west, the [Isle of] Wight is beautiful beyond all laws of beauty. It is as if a fragment of England floated forward to greet the foreigner – chalk of our chalk, turf of our turf, epitome of what will follow. (p.170)

Forster's representation of the Isle of Wight ('beautiful beyond all laws of beauty') is as a miniature version of England 'chalk of our chalk, turf of our turf, epitome of what will follow'. His tongue may be almost in his cheek, but it isn't quite. In the book, just as the Schlegels' German background is offset by their having had an English mother, so the upwardly mobile Wilcoxes' commercial and industrial colouring is redeemed by the fact that Mrs Wilcox, the matriarch of the family, belonged to an old English family who had lived for generations in an old English farmhouse, the Howards End of the title. When the story ends, Margaret Schlegel has become the second Mrs Wilcox, living with her sister and Henry Wilcox in Howards End itself, having escaped from the growing commercialism of London and having rescued her husband from that same world of motor cars, of 'telegrams and anger' that was making the life of personal relations and quiet civilised values (as defined by Forster) impossible. It may sound from this that the novel adopts a backward-looking stance, seeing the future as wholly a bad thing; but much of the book has been concerned with what Forster called 'the flow and recoil' of human life and history. In its final pages, Margaret and her sister Helen discuss what Howards End means to them. Margaret says:

> Because a thing is going strong now, it need not go strong for ever. ... This craze for motion has only set in during the last hundred years. It may be followed by a civilisation that won't be a movement, because it will rest on the earth. All the signs are against it now, but I can't help hoping, and very early in the morning in the garden I feel that our house is the future as well as the past. (p.329)

There is of course a tradition in English fiction of embodying a certain view of the continuity and stability of Englishness in a place, and specifically in a country house. A classic example of this is Jane Austen's novel *Mansfield Park,* and perhaps the best example in 20th-century fiction (apart from *Howards End* itself), is Evelyn Waugh's *Brideshead Revisited,* written during the Second World War and published in 1945. It is worth mentioning that *Brideshead Revisited* was adapted for television in 1981 and was filmed at Castle Howard in Yorkshire, one of the grandest of English stately homes. So enduring has been the popularity of that TV serialisation, with its evocation of English life between the wars, that Castle Howard has become, nearly thirty years later, one of the most popular 'heritage' sites in England; and the reason visitors come is not because of its architecture or its history, but because it is where *Brideshead* has been filmed – now twice. The most popular rooms in the castle are those which display the costumes and props. As its own publicity leaflet proudly proclaims, 'Castle Howard, home of *Brideshead Revisited,* where history is still in the making.' What does this say about the ways in which our ideas of England and its history are constructed through fictions rather than through facts?

A post-war view: *Lucky Jim*

Part of the appeal of Evelyn Waugh's novel was its evocation of a lost world, specifically England between the wars. The first section of the novel, 'Et in Arcadio Ego', had described with tremendous nostalgia upper-class life at Oxford University in the 1920s – a world of status and wealth, where serious academic study had played very little part. Novels that attempt to examine ideas of Englishness in the contemporary world are often set in universities, and this has been particularly so since the second half of the 20th century. The first post-war novel to signal a complete break with the attitudes and values of pre-war England was *Lucky Jim,* by Kingsley Amis, published in 1954. The hero (actually an anti-hero) of this story is a young History lecturer, Jim Dixon who, far from being at home in the ivory towers of Oxford or Cambridge, is struggling to make a career at a remote provincial university.

Jim is a northerner, and the novelist is careful to tell his readers that Dixon speaks with 'a flat northern accent', as if this implies that his personality and social background are also lacking in colour. Dixon is an outsider, always in danger of making a fool of himself because he does not understand or will not accept the rules of the university's hierarchy. The university is a microcosm of an England with which the younger generation has lost patience. When Dixon is asked to give a public lecture on the subject of 'Merrie England' (spelt m-e-r-r-i-e to emphasise what an outdated concept this is) he is torn between making pious platitudes about traditional England (which will help to ensure that he is appointed to a permanent post in the university) and saying what he really thinks, which will certainly lose him his job.

Initially, he prepares a lecture speaking out against the modern world – 'What, finally is the practical application of all this? I'll tell you … To resist the application of manufactured standards, to protest against ugly articles of furniture and table-ware, to speak out against sham architecture.' The values he is proclaiming here are those Victorian values enshrined in the work of Ruskin, William Morris and Matthew Arnold. In this way he intends to conclude, '… we shall be saying a word … for our native tradition, for our common heritage, in short for what we once had and may, some day, have again – Merrie England'. (pp.204–5)[5]

That is the speech he intends to make. In the event, however, standing in front of an audience of university and civic dignitaries, he drunkenly delivers a very different lecture:

> What, finally, is the practical application of all this? Listen, and I'll tell you. The point about Merrie England is that it was about the most un-Merrie period in our history. It's only the home-made pottery crowd, the organic husbandry crowd, the recorder-playing crowd, the Esperanto … (p.227)

But he gets no further, for in his drunkenness and his anger at the hypocrisy of an England which seems to be forever going backwards he collapses on the stage – committing a very public form of academic suicide.

It is a curious fact that *Lucky Jim,* which was regarded when it first appeared as a rather radical and iconoclastic novel, actually reaches a thoroughly conservative conclusion. Jim Dixon's attacks make no impression on his audience, the university remains the enclosed and rather detached world it was when he joined it, and Dixon's fate (which the author, Kingsley Amis, implies is almost too awful to contemplate) is to leave higher education and become a school teacher.

Two nations? *Nice Work*

This same ironic tension between the radical and the conservative is to be found in another campus novel, *Nice Work* by David Lodge, one of the best known contemporary English novelists. Lodge began publishing fiction in the 1960s, and many of his books are satires of the academic world. This is not surprising for he was until his retirement Professor of English at the University of Birmingham and a distinguished literary critic: he specialised in writing about fiction often from the theoretical perspective of structuralism and Russian formalism. Hardly a conservative or a traditionalist, then, and neither is the central figure of *Nice Work*.

Dr Robyn Penrose is a lecturer in English Literature at the University of Rummidge, an affectionate portrait of Birmingham University itself. The usually masculine name Robyn (but spelt here with a 'y') is significant, for Dr Penrose is a staunch feminist who makes no concessions to the fact that her university is still largely dominated by male teachers and administrators. The novel is set in 1986, in the middle of what are now remembered as 'the Thatcher Years' – that period of considerable industrial unrest, when Mrs Thatcher as Prime Minister took on the unions, and government cuts meant widescale unemployment. This is the background to the novel, giving its title *Nice Work* ('Nice work – if you can get it') a distinctly ironic ring.

This irony is double-edged, for it was not only British industry that was contracting and restructuring at this time: the same process was going on in British higher education. To her dismay, Robyn Penrose finds that her lectureship is likely to be terminated when her three-year contract comes to an end. Her special subject is, appropriately, the Industrial Novel in 19th-century English Literature, and Lodge deliberately sets out to write a modern version of the industrial novel. Indeed, he prefaces *Nice Work* with a quotation from the novel *Sybil* (1849) by the Victorian Prime Minister, Benjamin Disraeli. Disraeli had coined the phrase 'two nations' to describe the condition of England as he found it:

> Two nations; between whom there is no intercourse and no sympathy; who are as ignorant of each other's habits, thoughts and feelings, as if they were dwellers in different zones, or inhabitants of different planets; who are formed by a different breeding, and fed by different food, and ordered by different manners. (p.9)[6]

Lodge sets out to show how the 'two nations' label still applied in 1980s Britain. The year 1986 (and this is a matter not of fiction but of historical fact) was designated by the government 'Industry Year', the idea being to stress the importance of industry – especially manufacturing and engineering – and to raise the status of industry in a country which traditionally has always tended to value the arts and the professions above the sciences. This is an idea that can be traced back to the Victorian critic and poet Matthew Arnold whose celebrated book, *Culture and Anarchy,* argued that the saving grace of the modern world should be Culture, especially an educational philosophy based on the liberal arts and focused ultimately on the values of the classical world. From this analysis really arose a view of education which has survived in Britain with great tenacity.

Birmingham / Rummidge is located in the Midlands, and Victorian Birmingham liked to promote itself not just as the heart of England but as the 'workshop of the Empire'. So it is a good setting for a modern industrial novel exploring both the clash of cultures in late 20th-century Britain and the continuing existence of the 'two nations', which Disraeli had defined one hundred and fifty years beforehand. For Robyn Penrose, though a specialist on the Industrial Novel, knows nothing about modern industry – indeed, she has never been inside a factory. Brought up on the south coast, close to the Isle of Wight, her life has been limited to school, university (Oxford), research at Cambridge and now her temporary lectureship at Rummidge. But she is in for a rude shock because, as the University's token contribution to Industry Year, she is assigned to shadow a local factory manager, learning about industry by following him for one day a week during his daily work of running a factory and trying to prevent its being taken over or closed down.

Nice Work is a comic as well as a cautionary tale. The manager whom she shadows is called Victor Wilcox (the name deliberately chosen by Lodge to recall the Wilcoxes of *Howards End)* and he is appalled to discover that a woman has been assigned to him; and not just any woman but a socialist and a feminist as well. This particular Industry Year experiment seems doomed to failure when Robyn causes a strike by warning one of the Pakistani workers in the foundry that he is about to be sacked because he is not efficient enough at operating a particular machine. For Birmingham is one of the most multi-cultural cities in Britain (another version of the two nations) and Robyn Penrose, for all her socialist principles, is uneasy in the presence of these second and third generation immigrants. On her way to the factory she has to drive through an area of the city she has never visited before:

> Caribbean faces now preponderate on the pavements. Youths in outsize hats, lounging in the doorways of shops and cafes, with hands thrust deep into their pockets, gossip and smoke ... How strange it is, strange and sad, to see all these tropical faces amid the slush and dirty snow, the grey gritty hopelessness of an English industrial city in the middle of winter. (p.99)

For Robyn (and perhaps for Lodge, too?) these people remain 'faces', strange and sometimes threatening. When her car stops, she finds herself looking at a young West Indian standing in front of a boarded-up shop. She smiles at him 'a friendly, sympathetic, anti-racist smile', but her friendly gesture turns to panic when the man comes towards her and leans into the car, offering to sell her some drugs.

Inevitably, perhaps, because *Nice Work* is a comic take on the conventions of the Victorian novel, the antagonism between Robyn Penrose and Vic Wilcox gradually breaks down: she learns something of the reality of modern industrial life and he starts to read *Culture and Anarchy*. More significantly, they fall in love, or at least Vic does: for when he tells Robyn (while on a business trip to Stuttgart) that he has been in love with her for weeks, she briskly replies, 'No you don't, Vic … There's no such thing. It's a rhetorical device. It's a bourgeois fallacy.'

But at least her relationship with Vic leads her to see factory workers in a new light – indeed, to see them at all. But her view of them is still a romantic, romanticising one. As she looks out of the window of her study in the English Department in the middle of the campus of Rummidge University, she sees the students enjoying the gardens and the tranquillity and decides that the university is

> the ideal type of a human community, where work and play, culture and nature, were in perfect harmony, where there was space and light, and fine buildings set in pleasant grounds, and people were free to pursue excellence and self-fulfilment, each according to her own rhythm and inclination. (p.346)

Such a vision is pure Matthew Arnold. But then Lodge makes Robyn think of the workers she has seen in Vic Wilcox's factory:

> And then she thought, with a sympathetic inward shudder, of how the same sun must be shining upon the corrugated roofs of the factory buildings … how the temperature must be rising rapidly inside the foundry; and she imagined the workers stumbling out into the sunshine at midday. (pp.346–7)

To Robyn the factory is a 'hell-hole' but she then imagines the entire workforce transported across the city to the university and welcomed onto the campus by the students and invited by them to 'exchange ideas on how the values of the university and the imperatives of commerce might be more equitably managed to the benefit of the whole of society'. (p.347)

This is pure Utopianism, of course, and the reality is quite different. Suddenly the factory is closed down and Vic loses his job. But Robyn, who (in the best tradition of the romantic novel) has unexpectedly been left a small fortune by an uncle, puts up the money for Vic to open up a new business on his own, one that will need far fewer workers to operate effectively. She herself, on the brink of moving to California where she has been offered an academic post, decides to stay in England after all.

At the end of the book, the two nations are still very much in place, and the appeal of a comfortable rural England (even if the rural here is only the university campus) proves stronger than her socialist instincts. The final image of *Nice Work* shows a young black workman mowing the grass in front of the English department, while the students lounge around in the summer sun. As Lodge puts it:

> There is no overt arrogance on the students' part, or evident resentment on the young gardener's, just a kind of mutual, instinctive avoidance of contact. Physically contiguous, they inhabit separate worlds. (p.384)

'It seems,' concludes David Lodge, 'a very British way of handling differences of class and race.'

Again, as in Kingsley Amis' *Lucky Jim,* nothing has changed. What Lodge has presented as the very English values of continuity and tradition, politely masking their implicit social exclusiveness, dominate the world of *Nice Work* as surely as they have done the other novels mentioned so far: *Tess*, *Brideshead* and *Lucky Jim*. By contrast, *England, England* by Julian Barnes offers an apparently rigorous challenge to the whole idea of 'Englishness'.

A challenge to the idea of Englishness: *England, England*

This novel, published in 1998, has as its central idea a scheme to market England for tourists so that everything anyone might want to see is all located on the Isle of Wight, which would become a giant theme park, a miniature England. In one glorious jumble of history and geography everything that represents Englishness is either relocated or recreated on that same island which E.M. Forster in *Howards End* had called the 'epitome' of England. The mastermind behind this scheme is Sir Jack Pitman, an uncouth but immensely wealthy businessman (who bears more than a passing resemblance in the book to the late 'real-life' Robert Maxwell). The person who actually runs theme park England as a profitable venture is Martha Cochrane, a forty-year-old woman who is the central character in the novel.

Julian Barnes, in writing *England, England,* has much to say about the ignorance most English people have about their own country and its history. When the venture is still at the planning stage Sir Jack Pitman gets his resident historian, Dr Max, to find out what people really know about English history. His research reveals that 'Most people remembered history in the same conceited yet evanescent fashion as they recalled their own childhood. It seemed to Dr Max positively unpatriotic to know so little about the origins and forging of your nation. And yet, therein lay the immediate paradox: that patriotism's most eager bedfellow was ignorance.' (p.82)[7]

It is precisely this ignorance which is at the heart of Barnes' satirical attack on a view of Englishness that is really a mixture of 'history', 'heritage', mythology and sheer nostalgia. The market research that Sir Jack has commissioned shows that the top ten things people associate with Englishness are as follows: '1 The Royal Family, 2 Big Ben and the Houses of Parliament, 3 Manchester United Football Club, 4 the class system, 5 pubs, 6 a robin in the snow, 7 Robin Hood and his Merrie Men, 8 cricket, 9 the white cliffs of Dover, and 10 Imperialism'. Given such a random list of icons of Englishness, Sir Jack has no difficulty in creating a miniature England in which any sense of historical chronology is completely lacking: Robin Hood and his Merrie Men, for instance, are twice daily seen having their hideout stormed by the SAS. The joke, or at least the irony, behind Barnes' view of England today is that people much prefer the replica to the real thing, and England on the Isle of Wight is a huge commercial success as a tourist attraction.

With its completely random mixture of all things English, it does indeed become the 'epitome' of England (though not in the sense that E.M. Forster had envisaged):

> They had a half-size Big Ben; they had Shakespeare's grave and Princess Di's; they had Robin Hood (and his band of Merrie Men), the White Cliffs of Dover, and beetle-black taxis shuffling through the London fog to Cotswold villages full of thatched cottages serving Devonshire cream teas; they had the Battle of Britain, cricket, pub skittles, Alice in Wonderland, the Times newspaper, and the One Hundred and One Dalmatians ... They had the Royal Shakespeare Company, Stonehenge, stiff upper lips, bowler hats, half timbering, jolly red buses, eighty brands of warm beer, Sherlock Holmes and a Nell Gwynn ...
>
> (p.142)

Eventually they even manage to persuade the King to move Buckingham Palace to the Isle of Wight, and from this point on it becomes increasingly hard to tell which is the real England and which is the replica. The actors playing the characters become more and more the people themselves, Robin Hood's merrie men choose to live permanently in the forest and repel the attacks by the SAS, smugglers begin to smuggle real contraband; history starts to go into reverse.

So far, so funny – and so absurd. But quite unexpectedly the mood of the final sections of *England, England* changes as the island goes from strength to strength, Old England (real England) becomes less and less relevant, losing its membership of the European Community and physically shrinking as both Scotland and Wales start to increase their territory. As Julian Barnes puts it: 'Old England had lost its history, and therefore – since memory is identity – had lost all sense of itself.' Eventually the mainland is all but abandoned and starts to revert (back) to its pre-industrial state, to be recolonised by those who wish to return to a simpler, more communal way of life. Martha Cochrane loses her job in charge of the island and discovers a new vocation for herself, as an old maid living contentedly alone in an English village which is rapidly recovering the sense of community and tradition that most such villages had lost during the 20th century. The final pages of the book seek to recreate a vision of England that all but disappeared with the appearance of what William Blake in 'Jerusalem' had called the 'dark Satanic Mills':

> Chemicals drained from the land, the colours grew gentler, and the light
> untainted; the moon, with less competition, now rose more dominantly. In
> the enlarged countryside, wildlife bred freely. Hares multiplied; deer and boar
> were released into the woods from game farms; the urban fox returned to a
> healthier diet of bloodied, pulsing flesh. Common land was re-established;
> fields and farms grew smaller; hedgerows were replanted ... migratory birds
> which for generations had passed swiftly over the toxic isle now stayed
> longer, and some decided to settle ... Meat-eating became popular again, as
> did poaching. Children were sent mushrooming in the woods ...   (p.255)

What has been recreated here by Barnes is a sense of England as once again
a 'green and pleasant land' and the book ends with the restoration of a village
fete, symbolising the return to a sense of community based on a shared sense of
tradition. But Barnes is careful not to offer just a sentimental vision and Martha's
last thoughts in the novel are to ask, 'Could you reinvent innocence? Or was it
always constructed, grafted onto the old disbelief? Were the children's faces proof of
this renewable innocence – or was that just sentimentality?'

As a novel, *England, England* is both funny as a savage satire on the way myths
of national identity are constructed and distorted, and serious in its analysis of
how central is history to the health of a community – whether an entire nation or
a small village. The final paragraph of the story describes the ending of the village
fete:

> The moon went in again; the air grew cold. The band played 'Land of Hope
> and Glory' for the last time, then fell silent ... It had been a day to remember.
> The Fete was established; already it seemed to have its history ...   (p.266)

England, England ends by strongly connecting a sense of Englishness not only to
the past but to the countryside and to the values of a rural, not an urban, culture.
This of course disregards both the very existence of any urban culture in Britain
and those for whom the English countryside is no part of their experience of living
in Britain. Indeed, one of the most striking features of this very conservative
expression of Englishness is that it is entirely monocultural. It is important, then,
to balance this pastoral 'England for the English' image by discussing a book
which approaches the idea of England and Englishness from an entirely different
perspective.

Issues of national identity: *White Teeth*
Zadie Smith's *White Teeth* has been much praised and much criticised (not least by
the author herself) since its publication in 2000, when the author was twenty-three.
Yet the book's two central characters are an Indian Muslim and an Englishman

who, having been thrown together as young men during the final weeks of the Second World War, remain friends all their lives. Samad the Bengali and his wife Alsana come to live in London to be close to Archibald Jones and his wife Clara, who is a West Indian. The novel moves backwards and forwards in time between 1945 and the eve of the millennium, but its setting is almost always London, and in particular that part of north west London which has the heaviest concentration of non-white communities. This is where Zadie Smith herself was born, and in a novel of over 500 pages the setting never once moves into the country. The story is concerned with Samad and Archie and their families, especially their children: it is through them that Zadie Smith explores relentlessly but with great humour issues of national identity and the difference between being British and being English.

Her central argument is that everyone carries the weight of their history with them and that this is just as true for immigrants as it is for those who have always lived in Britain. But, as she explains

> ... we often imagine that immigrants are constantly on the move, footloose, able to change course at any moment, able to employ their legendary resourcefulness at every turn. We have been told of the resourcefulness of Mr Schmutters, or the footloosity of Mr Banajii, who sail into Ellis Island or Dover or Calais and step into their foreign land as blank people, free of any kind of baggage, happy and willing to leave their difference at the docks and take their chances in this new place, merging with the oneness of this greenandpleasantlibertarianlandofthefree. (p.465)[8]

White Teeth convincingly shows that the opposite is true. Samad and Archie first become friends when they are stranded together in Bulgaria at the very end of the war and try to define their beliefs and identities to each other. Samad's proudest boast is that his grandfather had fired the first shot in the Indian Mutiny against the British, and this link with 'real' history greatly impresses Archie Jones:

> Well, well. That's something, isn't it? ... To have a bit of history in your blood like that. Motivates you, I'd imagine. I'm a Jones, you see. 'Slike a 'Smith'. We're nobody ... My father used to say: 'We're the chaff, boy, we're the chaff.' Not that I've ever much bothered, mind. Proud all the same, you know. Good honest English stock. But in your family, you had a hero. (p.99)

For Samad, his identity has been compromised by his fighting as a member of the British army. 'What am I going to do?' he asks Archie as the war ends. 'Go back to Bengal? Or Delhi? Who would have such an Englishman there? To England? Who would have such an Indian?' The problem becomes even more difficult when Archie underlines the differences between Samad and himself:

It's England's future we've been fighting for. For England. You know ...
democracy and Sunday dinners and ... and promenades and piers, and bangers
and mash – and the things that are *ours*. Not *yours*. (p.120)

Zadie Smith presents these cultural confusions and fault lines through the families
of the two friends. Samad has twin sons, Magid and Millat, and he sends the elder
(by ten minutes), more academic one, Magid, back to Bengal to be brought up in
the Muslim and Bangladeshi tradition while the younger, Millat, is to remain at
school in London where he is a charming but feckless teenager, never doing any
work and always on the edge of serious trouble. Ironically, when Magid returns to
London he has become more English than the English, while Millat has joined a
militant Muslim fundamentalist movement.

In fact there is only one character in the entire book who is English through
and through, and that is Archie Jones. Zadie Smith is careful to present him as
a man who appears to have no curiosity and no strong feelings about anything
– about politics, religion or people. Faced with any difficult decision, Archie's
instinct is to toss a coin, and his favourite expression is 'Can't say fairer than that.'
Yet his loyalty to Samad, his fidelity to his West Indian wife, Clara, and his affection
for his daughter Irie are shown in the book to be qualities which other characters
first mock, then take for granted and finally admire. In all his life he does only two
impulsive things: the first is to marry Clara, a woman thirty years younger than he
is; the second, at the very end of the story, is to prevent a tragedy by putting himself
in the firing line (literally) when Millat tries to create a terrorist outrage in the
centre of London. (The story has an uncanny prescience in view of later events.)

Zadie Smith puts herself into the novel in the character of Archie's daughter,
Irie. Both share the same date of birth, the same mixed parentage, the same
combination of a strange name (Zadie / Irie) with a very common one (Smith
/ Jones). Irie shares her mother's brown skin and white teeth (though Clara's
are in fact false), and the turning point in her life comes when, as a fifteen-year-
old schoolgirl, she meets the Chalfens, the most English family she has ever
encountered. Smith expresses her feelings in an important paragraph:

She wanted their Englishness. Their Chalfishness. The *purity* of it. It didn't
occur to her that the Chalfens were, after a fashion, immigrants too (third
generation, by way of Germany and Poland, nee Chalenovsky), or that they
might be as needy of her as she was of them. To Irie, the Chalfens were
more English than the English. When Irie stepped over the threshold of the
Chalfen house, she felt an illicit thrill, like a Jew munching a sausage or a
Hindu grabbing a Big Mac. She was crossing borders, sneaking into England;
it felt like some terribly mutinous act, wearing somebody else's uniform or
somebody else's skin.   (p. 328)

The importance of this revealing paragraph is that though Irie thinks of herself as British she does not see herself as English. To put it another way, she has a British passport, but she feels like an illegal immigrant into England: 'She was crossing borders, sneaking into England.' And because the Chalfen family are themselves third generation Jewish immigrants to England the reader is forced to confront the persistent question, 'What is Englishness?' It is a question that Samad's wife, Alsana, asks her husband in exasperation, 'Do you think anybody is English? Really English? It's a fairy tale!'

One of the strengths of *White Teeth* is that it refuses any of the easy answers. At the end of the novel, Archie ponders whether the past really was the way people claimed it was:

> Were they more honest, and did they leave their front doors open, did they leave their kids with the neighbours, pay social calls, run up tabs with the butcher? The funny thing about getting old in a country is people always want to hear that from you. They want to hear it really was once a green and pleasant land. They *need* it. (p.517)

William Blake's phrase from 'Jerusalem', England's green and pleasant land, has echoed through this discussion. But if Archie's comment, 'They *need* it', suggests that if this notion of England as an organic, unified community is an illusion, then it is a necessary one. But for whom? What all the novelists discussed above seem to agree is that the cultural and emotional concepts of England and Englishness are becoming more elusive – and possibly more exclusive. The plurality of Disraeli's 'Two Nations' still has a discomforting resonance, though now it is many more than two. And to students exploring the representation of this cultural diversity in the texts they are studying, the very notion of 'English Literature' should be held up for scrutiny.

. . . .

This discussion of Englishness and identity is not of course confined to contemporary fiction. It can be linked to the discussions of Rupert Brooke's *Letters from America* (Chapter 10, pages 236–244), essays by Virginia Woolf and Angela Carter (Chapter 10, pages 220–231), *A Change of Climate* and *The Male Gaze* (pages 175–189, above), and Wordsworth's sonnet 'Upon Westminster Bridge' (Chapter 6, pages 86–94). Questions that arise from this discussion include:

- Why is the picture of England presented in English writing so often a picture of southern England?
- What picture of England emerges from the canon of English Literature as reflected in, say, *The Oxford Book of English Verse* or a *Norton Anthology*?

- What alternative canons could students construct?
- Can there be a single 'English Literature'?
- Is a fair representation of national identity possible when writers choose to employ satire and caricature as the vehicle for their discussion?
- How deeply imbued in our descriptions of national identity are various assumptions about colours: 'the white cliffs of Dover', England's green and pleasant land', the 'dark Satanic mills', etc.?

Film and image as context: McEwan and Dickens

Film and image can provide two of the most valuable contexts for discussion of texts. What happens when we watch a film or television adaptation (and in the case of classic fiction by Jane Austen, Charles Dickens or E.M. Forster compare different adaptations) of a novel we have already read? How does the experience alter, enhance or diminish our response to the text?

From earliest childhood we read fiction and illustration side by side, and this has ever been so. It's hard to imagine *Alice in Wonderland* without the pictures, and Alice herself asks 'What is the use of a book without pictures or conversation?' Combining word and image is not only for children, however: illuminated manuscripts were designed to illuminate both the text itself and the reader's understanding of the text. Today, the graphic novel is enjoying a revival: *Tamara Drewe* (2007), by Posy Simmonds, who is no longer pigeonholed as a cartoonist but taken seriously as a novelist, was given a full-page review in the fiction section of the *Times Literary Supplement*.

The following discussion focuses on two novels: Ian McEwan's *Atonement* (2001) and Charles Dickens' *A Tale of Two Cities* (1859). In relation to the first, it compares the 2007 film with the novel, asking not just what is gained and lost when a work of fiction is converted from one medium into another but, how far does the transition enable students to see the inner workings of the original novel in a new light? *A Tale of Two Cities* is itself a book that has been famously adapted for both film and television. Here, a single illustration from the novel, by Dickens' original illustrator Phiz (the pseudonym of the artist Hablot K. Browne), is used to ask whether it is permissible for the alternative medium itself to provide new contexts for the reading of the novel.

Keira's costume: *Atonement*

January 1st 2008 dawned with the news that Keira Knightley's evening gown, worn in the film of *Atonement*, had come top of a poll to find 'the best film costume of all time' (www.sassybella.com/index.php/2008/01/02/keira-knightleys-green-atonement-dress-the-best-film-costume). Cecilia Tallis' dress, oriental green silk, backless and with a plunging V-neckline, had beaten even Marilyn Monroe's billowing white dress from *The Seven Year Itch*. This bizarre news headline not only beggars belief that such a poll ever took place – it was organised by Sky Movies and *In Style* magazine; more importantly, it sends us back to the book to see whether the dress is even mentioned by McEwan.

And it certainly is. When Robbie arrives for dinner on the night that will change his life forever, Cecilia answers the door:

> His only thought was that she was even more beautiful than his fantasies of her. The silk dress she wore seemed to worship every curve and dip of her lithe body. (p.131)[9]

We have met this dress before. Early in Chapter 9 Cecilia has been trying on dresses to wear for dinner. She dismisses the flapper dresses of her teenage years and other dresses in her wardrobe, including at first 'her latest and best piece, bought to celebrate the end of finals ... the figure-hugging dark green bias-cut backless evening gown with a halter neck' (p.98). But after trying on and taking off again a pink moiré silk dress, because it 'flared like an eight-year-old's party frock', she returns to her 'green backless post-finals gown'. It is this dress that signals she has left behind her childhood, her teenage years and her student life (the life to which, at this stage and to her irritation, Robbie is intending to return):

> As she pulled it on she approved of the firm caress of the bias-cut through the silk of her petticoat, and she felt sleekly impregnable, slippery and secure; it was a mermaid who rose to meet her in her own full-length mirror. (p.99)

....

There are three questions here to discuss with students: is it clever, or rather obvious, writing to use the onomatopoeic device of repeated /s/ sounds to emphasis the silkiness of the dress: 'caress ... silk ... sleekly ... slippery ... secure'? Does the image of Cecilia as a mermaid usefully remind the reader of her plunging into the fountain earlier in the day? Is it ironic that although her dress makes her feel 'impregnable ... and secure' actually, because it is backless and has a plunging neckline, it will very soon leave her explicitly vulnerable – open (as Briony sees the situation in the library) to attack?

....

As Cecilia leads Robbie into the dark library, 'towards the corner, into the deeper shadow' it is once again sound and touch that McEwan emphasises. Hearing 'a soft, wet sound,' Robbie realises that 'she might not be shrinking from him' before 'she slipped back'. In the next few lines of this paragraph, the repeated sounds of the words still drawing attention to the silk in which Cecilia ('Cee' as Robbie calls her) is sheathed and to the staccato progress of their love-making: 'stopped … stopped … speak … shrinking … steeple … enclose … pressed' (p.133). As they begin to make love, manoeuvring themselves against the bookshelves, he is able after 'some inexpert fumbling' to put his hand and then his lips on her breast; later he can reach down and feel for her buttocks, lifting 'the clinging, silky dress again'. It is certainly some costume, and the one worn by Keira Knightley is designed to enable Robbie to do in the film exactly what the novelist has described in the book. But perhaps we need the film to highlight the skill with which McEwan has imagined and described and used the dress in the book. Keira's poll-topping costume does, after all, illuminate the text.

In such unexpected ways film and book can illuminate each other. Novelists know that 'How faithful is the film to the book?' is the wrong question. 'How much new light does the film shine on the novel?' is a better one. For a student starting to think seriously about the nature of fiction and the uniqueness of the novel, there are few better novels than *Atonement*, which focuses specifically on the differences between fiction and drama, about the writing of fiction and about the responsibilities of the novelist. And there are few better films than the adaptation of *Atonement* (the screenplay not written by Ian McEwan himself, but by one of the most skilful of contemporary playwrights and screenwriters, Christopher Hampton) to illustrate the interrelationship between film and novel.

To take, first, a scene from Part 1 of the book and to compare its representation on the page and on screen: the key encounter between Cecilia and Robbie by the fountain, when Uncle Clem's Meissen vase is broken, is one of the key moments in the novel in terms of intertextuality, plot, symbolism and narrative control. The whole episode consciously echoes the encounter at the fountain between Julia Flyte and Charles Ryder in Evelyn Waugh's *Brideshead Revisited*, a novel which resonates loudly throughout the opening section of McEwan's. It is also the moment at which the relationship between Cecilia, the elder Tallis daughter just down from Cambridge, and Robbie, son of the family's cleaning lady and also just down from Cambridge, enters a new phase. In a struggle between them, which has much to do with Cecilia's irritation at the way Robbie is (in her eyes) deliberately mocking her, the fine vase breaks and two triangular pieces of porcelain fall into the fountain. When Cecilia strips off her clothes in front of Robbie and plunges into the icy water both to humiliate Robbie and to retrieve the broken pieces, the scene is witnessed from a window in the house by Briony, Cecilia's twelve-year-old sister, already an aspiring writer, who completely misconstrues what she sees. At first she assumes that Robbie is proposing to her sister, and this seems quite natural to her: after all, 'she herself had written a tale in which a humble woodcutter had saved a princess from drowning and ended by marrying her' (p.38). In the next instant, however, Briony revises her opinion and reinterprets Cecilia's gesture of defiance as evidence of some strange and evil power that Robbie has over her:

> Robbie imperiously raised his hand now, as though issuing a command that Cecilia dared not disobey. It was extraordinary that she was unable to resist him. At his insistence she was removing her clothes, and at such speed. (p.38)

After Cecilia has emerged from the fountain, dressed herself and gone back into the house leaving Robbie to gaze into the now empty pool, Briony has a sudden intuition of what a novelist should do:

> She sensed she could write a scene like the one by the fountain and she could include a hidden observer like herself ... She could write the scene three times over, from three points of view; her excitement was in the prospect of freedom, of being delivered from the cumbrous struggle between good and bad, heroes and villains. None of these three was bad, nor were they particularly good. She need not judge. There did not have to be a moral. She need only show separate minds, as alive as her own, struggling with the idea that other minds were equally alive ... only in a story could you enter these different minds and show how they had equal value. That was the only moral a story need have. (p.40)

It is only later that the reader becomes aware that the author of this passage is not an omniscient narrator but the older Briony herself, and that the episode by the fountain is one that she does indeed write and rewrite – first of all as an eighteen-year old, when she sends it as a short story to Cyril Connolly's *Horizon* magazine during the war, and finally in the ultimate draft of the novel that will never be published in her lifetime. The statement that immediately follows this epiphany introduces a new narrative voice:

> Six decades later she would describe how she had written her way through a whole history of literature, beginning with stories derived from the European tradition of folk tales, through drama with a simple moral intent, to arrive at an impartial psychological realism which she had discovered for herself one special morning during a heat-wave in 1935. She would be well aware of the extent of her self-mythologising, and she gave her account a self-mocking, self-mythologising tone ... (p.41)

This meta-fictional device (not only a story, a fiction, but simultaneously a story about the writing of fiction and a critique of the limits and possibilities of fiction) is prominent in the novel but less apparent in the film, which does nevertheless frequently show episodes from two points of view. The audience is thus given the clear impression that there are two perspectives: what Briony as a child sees and what 'actually' (?) happened. This is straightaway a key issue of interpretation, where the camera inevitably simplifies the narrative complexity of the novel. What the film does finally and effectively achieve, however, is to present the author Briony, in old age, looking back over her career in a televised interview and reflecting on the importance of this episode as the impetus for both her first and her last novel. It is an intelligent compromise, but a compromise nevertheless, for what the film cannot replicate is the novel's capacity to 'show separate minds struggling with the idea that other minds were equally alive'.

Can cinema, in fact, ever do what the novelist and critic David Lodge has claimed is the novel's unique achievement? In *Consciousness and the Novel* (2002), he argues that:

> The novel is arguably man's most successful effort to describe the experience of individual human beings moving through space and time ... Works of literature describe in the guise of fiction the dense specificity of personal experience, which is always unique, because each of us has a slightly or very different personal history, modifying every new experience we have.
>
> (pp.10–11)

It is revealing, for instance, that McEwan devotes a whole chapter (Part 1, Chapter 6) to what goes on in the mind of Emily Tallis (Briony's mother) as she lies in bed trying to keep a migraine at bay and listening to the sounds coming from different parts of the house. By contrast, in the film the single shot of Emily in bed occupies no more than a few seconds, and allows no sense of 'the dense specificity of personal experience'.

Neither the camera nor the acting is able to tell the audience what Emily is thinking; in the novel, on the other hand, the narrator carefully ensures the reader can follow these thoughts. Briony may frequently be described, both by her mother and by the narrator (herself when old?) as 'away in her thoughts'; Emily is never 'away' – she is always focused, directing her consciousness into one area of need or another. While dealing with her headache, she listens to the sound of the hot water pipes which tells her that her errant sister's boys, the twins from the north, must be having their bath. At this she ponders for a moment why she is not more interested in them or their feelings, and concludes:

> They were not her own. It was as simple as that. And they were little boys, therefore fundamentally uncommunicative, with no gift for intimacy, and worse, they had diluted their identities, for she had never found this missing triangle of flesh.   (p.69)

The 'missing triangle' is an inevitable reminder of the missing triangles of porcelain from the vase broken at the fountain – a connection that Emily cannot make (she does not know the vase is damaged) but one which the reader is expected to make instead. So often in this novel things, people and situations occur in threes.

Just because a novelist can show a character's consciousness of being conscious, however, this does not mean of course that the character is always aware of things as they really are. The 'dense specificity of human experience' – Lodge's telling description of what the novel provides – is always conditional, and subject to revision. It is precisely this disjunction that fiction explores and exploits. When Emily next hears 'a little squeal of laughter abruptly smothered', she interprets the noise as 'Lola, then, in the nursery with Marshall'. Correct as far as this goes; however, her extrapolation from this evidence is wide of the mark. She concludes that Marshall (the young chocolate millionaire) might 'not be such a bad sort, if he was prepared to pass the time of day entertaining children'. This is a classic fictional device: the reader is lulled into trusting the way one of the characters interprets events and only discovers later, by revisiting this and further evidence, that actually Marshall has been attempting to seduce the fifteen-year-old Lola while the twins are not in the nursery.

The film adaptation of *Atonement* omits this, and much else. But film can make different connections in ways that a novel cannot. In Part 1 of the book, McEwan gives two accounts of Cecilia's leaping into the fountain:

> He stood with his hands on his hips and stared as she climbed into the water in her underwear. Denying his help, any possibility of making amends, was his punishment. The unexpectedly freezing water that caused her to gasp was his punishment. She held her breath, and sank, leaving her hair fanned out across the surface. (p.30)

> Cecilia, mercifully still in her underwear, was climbing into the pond, was standing waist deep in the water, was pinching her nose – and then she was gone. (p.39)

There is of course a third description of this seminal moment, later in the novel. Alert students will recall that CC – presumably Cyril Connolly – who writes to the eighteen-year-old Briony (now a student nurse in London) summarises the account she has given of the incident in the novella she has sent to *Horizon*. In this version the girl goes into the fountain 'fully dressed', and CC asks, 'Wouldn't it help you if the watching girl did not actually realise that the vase had broken? It would be all the more of a mystery to her that the woman submerges herself.' (p.313) Does CC unwittingly evoke the echo of Cecilia as a mermaid here?

The second of the above descriptions is seen from Briony's point of view – 'mercifully' being her surprisingly adult articulation of relief that Cecilia had not stripped off altogether. But who sees the first? In the first sentence of the passage from page 30 the gaze of the observer is fixed on Robbie staring at Cecilia, but are the next two sentences still Robbie's interpretation of her behaviour towards him or (more likely) has the point of view shifted so that the reader is now told what Cecilia is thinking as she enters the water? And the third sentence: is this the narrator telling us what remains visible after she has gone beneath the surface? The angle of vision at this moment is directly above the water since we can see the hair fanned out across the surface. In the passage from page 39 the statement 'and then she was gone' implies that Cecilia (as far as Briony could see) had disappeared completely under the water, hair and all. Indeed, a moment later 'her sister's head broke the surface – thank God! –'. In other words, the reader cannot follow her under the water.

In the film, however, the camera does follow Cecilia under the water or, more accurately, is already waiting for her there. We watch her groping for and then finding the broken handle (not the triangles) of the vase. We see everything but understand nothing of what Cecilia is thinking and it is hard, at the time, to see why we need to be shown this sub-aqua sequence, unless this is the film picking up Cecilia's own image of herself (from the novel) as a mermaid. But it has a function, though we only realise this at the very end of the film when Cecilia is drowned by the flooding of the underground station after the bomb has exploded in Balham High Street. For the second time, we follow her underwater and so it is as if the fountain episode at the start of the story has been an ironic foreshadowing, both of the nine-year-old Briony's jumping into the weir for Robbie to save her (an event later recalled by Robbie, and one that also merits an underwater sequence in the film) and of Cecilia's death at the end. Is this a significant or merely a contingent triangulation? The film hints at the former, but a reader coming to the film might be unconvinced – especially since there is no reference in the book to the fact that Cecilia is drowned at all. What the dying Briony writes in her coda to the final version of the story that she will have to leave unpublished is simply this:

> I can no longer think what purpose would be served if, say, I tried to persuade my reader, by direct or indirect means, that Robbie Turner died of septicaemia at Bray Dunes on 1 June 1940, or that Cecilia was killed in September of the same year by the bomb that destroyed Balham Underground Station. (p.370)

This is quite different from the film and contains a further complication if read in the context of the actual events of 1940. There was indeed a bomb which destroyed Balham Underground Station, and the loss of life was so great that the event was officially hushed up lest it should be too damaging to civilian morale in London during the Blitz. Now it appears that Briony has imposed her own censorship on the event. What is more, the bomb actually fell in October, not September, 1940.

Is this a mere careless slip on Briony's part (or McEwan's?) or yet another hint that the reality of any event is always in a certain sense provisional, subject to revision and correction – just as Briony eventually promises to correct the evidence she gave against Robbie, which sent him to prison? The film is less willing to deal in the provisional: Briony tells the interviewer the precise date of the Balham Bomb, 15th October. Again, these are reflections prompted by the book; and the novelist himself / herself is categorical:

> When I am dead, and the Marshals are dead, and the novel is finally published, we will exist only as my inventions. Briony will be as much of a fantasy as the lovers who shared a bed in Balham and enraged their landlady. No one will care what events and which individuals were misrepresented to make a novel. I know there's always a certain kind of reader who will be compelled to ask, But what really happened? The answer is simple: the lovers survive and flourish. (p.371)

It is easier for the reader, closing the book, than for the audience, leaving the cinema, to believe this. A final scene in the film, showing the lovers miraculously revived and enjoying an ecstatic holiday by the sea, is an echo from the novel of the holiday in Wiltshire that Cecilia and Robbie had hoped to have in the two weeks' leave he was due when his army training ended. But hasn't the film already persuaded us that Robbie has died of septicaemia in France and that Cecilia is actually drowned – the sheer explosive power of the water rushing through the underground station platform being visually one of the most arresting images of the whole film?

Students need the chance to debate and argue the case for and against these different endings. Does the Christopher Hampton, as opposed to the original Ian McEwan, version of *Atonement* make it clear that the happy ending is a 'what might have been', not an alternative reality? Does it matter that the film abandons the novel's (too neat?) final episode? This is the return to Briony's childhood home, now a country house hotel, where *The Trials of Arabella* is at last performed in the same library where Briony had interrupted Cecilia and Robbie making love. How effectively does, or can, or should, film simulate the meta-narrative and meta-fictional strategies of the novel? These strategies in *Atonement* are worth comparing with those in *The French Lieutenant's Woman* – and again there are opportunities for comparing screenplay (Harold Pinter's) with the original novel (John Fowles').

For the film *can* enhance, as well as illuminate, the book. There is one key episode in *Atonement* where it certainly does so. In Part 2 of the novel Robbie and his companions, Nettles and Mace, finally reach the coast where they expect to join an orderly evacuation across the Channel already under way. Instead, they find a scene that is almost impossible to comprehend, let alone to describe. What Robbie takes at first to be a long jetty stretching into the water turns out to be a column of men waiting in line for the boats that show no sign of coming. And this is the only evidence of army discipline he can see. There are horses galloping across the sand, a few men playing football, others using their helmets to dig fox holes in the beach, for protection from the attacks of the Stuka dive-bombers. From somewhere comes 'the feeble sound of a hymn being sung in unison, then fading' (p.248). Off to his left he sees the sea-front of Bray: cafés, a park, a bandstand, a merry-go-round. Some soldiers are opening up the cafés, others are larking about on bikes; one man is sunbathing in his underpants. McEwan's description is detailed and comprehensive; it takes two pages. But somehow the feeling one has in reading it is of anti-climax, a distant panorama which Robbie sees but to which he hardly reacts.

McEwan concludes the description with the single sentence: 'It was not difficult to choose between these circles of suffering – the sea, the beach, the front'. However, the Dantesque echo here seems merely rhetorical; the first-time reader, anxious to find out what is going to happen next, is relieved when Robbie leaves the scene and goes to join Nettles and Mace who have already dived into the first bar along the front.

Re-reading this passage (pp. 247–9), one may be surprised to find how much detail it contains and how little one remembers of it. Ask students how many details they can recall of what Robbie actually sees as he climbs over the sand dunes onto the beach. By contrast, on screen this scene is one of the most vivid and dramatic moments of the film.

In a single sustained tracking shot, four minutes long, the camera takes in everything Robbie sees and moves with him, watching him taking in the whole appalling spectacle while he walks across the beach and towards the front. Some of the details McEwan sketched in lightly are given fuller prominence: for instance the choir singing the hymn ('Dear Lord and Father of Mankind') are positioned in the bandstand and sing with a kind of hysterical urgency. Meanwhile the merry-go-round becomes just one feature of a macabre funfair in which human bodies cling to the framework of a Ferris Wheel, like scarecrows going endlessly up and down and round and round on a grotesque wheel of fortune. The image, to which the camera keeps returning, invites a range of comparisons: one of the infernal scenes from a painting by Hieronymus Bosch, for instance, or the surreal end-of-the-pier funfair from the film of *Oh What a Lovely War!* In the novel, when Robbie and his colleagues first see the beach, 'they stood in silence for many minutes …

> the actual beach, the one he and the corporals gazed on now, was no more
> than a variation on all that had gone before: there was a rout, and this was its
> terminus. It was obvious now they saw it – this was what happened when a
> chaotic retreat could go no further.   (p.247)

Here the novelist has to tell; the film, by contrast, is able to show. McEwan has to tell the reader that Robbie 'saw thousands of men, ten, twenty thousand, perhaps more, spread across the vastness of the beach' and add the rather inadequate simile 'In the distance they were like grains of black sand' – how could distant grains of black sand stand out distinctly on a beach? The camera, though, can encompass and encapsulate the whole scene. A re-visiting of this account of the evacuation beach in the novel is thus given greater resonance when read again in the context of the film's account of the same scene. Like Keira Knightly's costume, it brings the text into clearer focus.

'The Sea Rises': *A Tale of Two Cities*

Is it appropriate to read back from image to text in this way? With a film adaptation of a novel the word precedes the image, but this has not always been the case: in the Victorian novel, illustrations usually accompanied the original text and it comes as a shock to find that Thackeray, for instance, provided his own rather cartoon-like illustrations for *Vanity Fair*. Other novelists employed popular artists to do their illustrations. John Everett Millais, at the height of his fame, provided (and took great pains over) the engravings for Anthony Trollope's *Orley Farm*. The celebrated cartoonist Cruikshank illustrated some of Dickens' novels. No artist, however, is more closely associated with Dickens than Hablot K. Browne, who published his work under the pseudonym Phiz. Their working relationship came to an end after the publication of *A Tale of Two Cities* in 1859, and it is usually assumed that this was because Dickens felt the style of illustration Phiz produced was no longer in keeping with the times or with modern taste. Dickens wanted to create an effect that he described in the Preface to the novel as 'popular and picturesque' by which he implied 'theatrical' and 'sentimental'. An analysis of just one illustration from the novel will suggest how far he had underestimated his artist, and how this picture, 'The Sea Rises' (see page 215) can provide an illuminating context for re-assessing the novel as a whole.

The title, 'The Sea Rises', comes from the novel's central chapter, which depicts the storming of the Bastille and the capturing of the Governor. What Browne does in this picture is to incorporate elements from all over *A Tale of Two Cities* to create a dramatic tableau, emblematic of the novel as a whole. At first glance the scene is little more than a noisy street procession: a character on the left seems to be dancing (so energetically indeed that his clog has just flown off his foot) while on the right a cheerful, buxom woman is banging a drum and beckoning on those behind her. Only when we notice that both the dancing man and the drumming woman are brandishing weapons (an axe and a cleaver, each looking already blood-stained) do we realise that this is no mere carnival.

The Sea Rises.

Figure 2: Hablot K. Browne (Phiz): 'The Sea Rises'. An engraving to illustrate the novel *A Tale of Two Cities* (1859) by Charles Dickens.

Ambivalence, of course, underlies Dickens' attitude to the French Revolution from the opening words of the novel onwards: 'It was the best of times, it was the worst of times.' Browne's picture proves his point, illustrating as it does how Dickens is on the side of the poor, but terrified at the same time of the mob. In the very centre of the picture a screaming woman surges forward, so emaciated that her neck is as thin as her arm. She is an object both of pity and of terror. In an earlier chapter Dickens had described how in the peasants one could see 'the slow sure filing down of misery-worn face and figure, that was to make the meagreness of Frenchmen an English superstition which should survive the truth through the best part of a hundred years'. (p.115)[10]

Behind her, by contrast, looms a menacing creature who looks like a case-study from one of Lavater's treatises on phrenology. Browne is anticipating here Dickens' later description of the 'shaggy-haired man, of almost barbarian aspect, tall ... grim, rough, swart', who meets the mender of roads shortly before the Chateau of the Marquis is burnt to the ground. In this one figure (by no means the most important in the picture) Browne has incorporated all the features of the original Jacques, including 'the bronze face, the shaggy black hair and beard, the coarse woollen red cap, the rough medley dress of homespun stuff and hairy skins of beasts'. (p.230)

And what of the dancing man and the drumming woman? They are performing the *carmagnole*, the revolutionaries' dance which terrifies Lucy Manette while she stands in the street trying to catch a glimpse of her imprisoned husband. The woman is The Vengeance, Mme Defarge's blood-curdling friend, who is described in a later chapter as 'uttering terrific shrieks and flinging her arms about her head like all the forty Furies at once'. It is her drum which enables the dancing mob to keep 'a ferocious time that was like a gnashing of teeth in unison'. Observing the dancers 'with their heads low down and their hands high up', Dickens comments that their dancing was 'emphatically a fallen sport – a something, once innocent, delivered over to all devilry'.

Amid this frenetic activity two figures stand out: an elderly, uniformed, bareheaded man is jostled forward by the crowd whose swords, knives and staves all seem poised to strike him. He is the Governor of the Bastille, and it is M Defarge who has him by the sleeve; but the Governor's eyes stare beyond his captor to a woman who 'stood immovable close to the grim old officer'. Looking almost prim (until one notices that she hides a knife behind her neat skirts), Mme Defarge stands like an offended bride waiting for a reluctant husband.

Here it is as if Hablot Browne has enlarged Dickens' own vision and turned the scene into a *charivari*, the traditional raucous French street procession accompanying an unsuitable marriage. (Phiz would have known all about *charivari*: he was a contributor to the recently founded magazine *Punch*, whose subtitle 'The London Charivari' acknowledged its debt to the satirical Paris magazine *Charivari,* founded in 1836.) But this marriage will have a sudden and violent consummation. As Dickens describes it, Mme Defarge

> remained immovable close to him when the long-gathering rain of stabs and blows fell heavy, was so close to him when he dropped dead under it, that, suddenly animated, she put her foot upon his neck and with her cruel knife – long ready – hewed off his head. (p.222)

The shocking power of Browne's picture lies in the way we only gradually realise the full horror of what is about to happen.

In writing *A Tale of Two Cities,* Dickens drew on Thomas Carlylye's *French Revolution* and on the play by Wilkie Collins, *The Frozen Deep.* In the same way, Hablot Browne looks back a century to Hogarth's celebrated picture 'The Roast Beef of Old England', with its depiction of emaciated and ragged French soldiers and citizens and back only thirty years to one of the most important French paintings from the early 19th century, Delacroix's 'Liberty Leading the People' (1830). In terms of its composition, Browne's engraving seems to echo, almost to parody, Delacroix's painting. In each picture the revolutionaries surge forward while Paris burns behind them. Precisely where Delacroix placed Notre Dame in his picture, Browne puts the Bastille. The arms and weapons of the ordinary citizens are so posed in each picture as to create a central triangular area of focus. Only the figure of Liberty herself is missing from Browne's engraving.

Or is she? We have seen how Phiz referred so closely to Dickens' text in creating his engraving of 'The Sea Rises' that even the minor figures in the crowd can be identified. Strangely, however, one major figure in the picture seems to defy identification altogether. Closest to the reader, with her back turned, stands a young woman. She is drawn full length; brandishing a sword, she urges on the crowd, but like Mme Defarge (whom she balances in the composition) she stands slightly apart from it. Unlike the other people in the picture, this girl is no caricature; indeed, her stance and her streaming hair suggest an active romantic heroine (very different from the passive Lucy Manette or the demonic Mme Defarge), someone for whom there is apparently no model in the novel at all.

It is true that Dickens elsewhere describes the Paris women in general as 'a sight to chill the boldest ... they ran out with streaming hair, urging one another, and themselves, to madness with the wildest cries and actions', but this particular young woman, as drawn by Phiz, is neither Amazon nor Harpy.

Delacroix's Liberty is famously bare-breasted; Dickens, writing again about the *carmagnole,* has a significant sentence: 'The maidenly bosom bared to this, the pretty almost-child's head thus distracted, the delicate foot mincing in this slough of blood and dirt, were types of the disjointed time.' If this was to be the source of Browne's inspiration for this girl, he could not of course (in mid-Victorian England) draw a bare-breasted woman for a 'popular and picturesque' novel, but he could avoid this by drawing the young woman from the back.

Imagine Delacroix's Liberty turned through 180 degrees, and compare her with Browne' s drawing. Uniquely among the forty or so characters in the engraving, Browne's girl is bare-footed (as is Liberty) and her back foot is clearly shown to have stepped into the mire; the forward knees of both women are bent, suggesting that they are at once posed and poised to move forward. The streaming hair of the girl echoes closely the streaming sash of Liberty; the position of her two arms (one raised, one stretched out behind) is also close to Liberty's.

It must be said that if the girl in Browne's picture does reflect Delacroix's Liberty she does so very ambiguously. Though she shares a similar heroic posture, her back is turned; though romantically drawn, her hands and forearms are blood-stained; she waves a sword, while Liberty carries the flag; though she inspires the mob, her outraised arm and flowing hair point in the opposite direction from that in which the people are rushing. In giving her such prominence as this, Browne has again gone further than Dickens himself: he has not only created a girl who is a 'type of the disjointed time' but has thrown into sharp relief the whole double-edged relationship between the principle of freedom and the reality of mob-violence.

Hablot Browne's picture is thus a distillation of all Dickens' descriptions of the Revolution, but 'The Sea Rises' stands in its own right as a rich and disturbing composition. In it Browne's creative imagination has managed to enlarge even the imagination of Dickens himself – and this may be one, unacknowledged, reason why Dickens never used Phiz as an illustrator again: their great collaboration, which had begun with *The Pickwick Papers* (1837) ended abruptly with *A Tale of Two Cities* in 1859.

Allan Grant, in *A Preface to Dickens*, has argued that 'as Dickens' art gains in dramatic power so the obviousness of the theatrical surface diminishes, thus making redundant illustration of the kind in which Browne excelled'.[11] But, as 'The Sea Rises' shows, there is nothing obvious or superficial about the way Browne interprets Dickens' vision of 'the remorseless sea of turbulently swaying shapes, voices of vengeance, and faces hardened in the furnaces of suffering'. 'The Sea Rises' deserves to be better known as one of the most telling images of the French Revolution to come out of England. And by relating Dickens' novel back to one of the most disturbing paintings of the 19th century, Phiz succeeds in placing *A Tale of Two Cities* in an altogether broader and more challenging context. It is a context for which the epithets 'popular and picturesque' seem frankly inadequate.

Non-fiction prose in context

'Only connect the prose and the passion, and both will be exalted, and
human love will be seen at its height. Live in fragments no longer.'

*(E.M. Forster **Howards End**, 1910)*

The QCA Subject Criteria for English Literature are careful to identify 'prose' rather
than exclusively 'fiction' as one of the three key genres that must be studied for AS
and A level. This helpfully opens the way for discussion of various forms of non-
fiction prose, and it is perhaps a missed opportunity that most of the specifications
on offer choose to concentrate here on critical writing – though, to be fair, QCA
gives a strong steer that this is what it expects. If the opportunity to study, either
as a major set text or for wider reading, other forms of writing is offered, surely it
is valuable for students of Literature (and of course of integrated Language and
Literature courses) to test their definitions of 'the literary' by exploring journalism,
reportage, biography and autobiography as well as criticism and theory. Why
not study Dorothy Wordsworth's *Grasmere Journals* or Susan Sontag's *On
Photography*? The one will afford valuable insights into the Romantic imagination,
the other into ways of seeing.

The first section in this chapter, 'Essays and blogs', deals with the essay in
the hands of three writers who happen to be women. Students can decide for
themselves how important it is for contextualising and understanding each of the
texts under discussion that the writer is a woman. The final text, a blog, is used to
demonstrate the kinship that blogs can have with the tradition of the essay – and,
at the same time, the distance that blogs put between themselves and their print-
bound predecessors.

The second section, 'Travel writing – a literary context?', revisits a largely
undervalued book by Rupert Brooke, *Letters from America*. Here the discussion
focuses first on the circumstances of the book's production, asking in what sense
it can be described as a book by Rupert Brooke at all. Then it explores the way in
which, by trying to explain the emptiness of Canada, Brooke moves towards a
definition of what he means by Englishness.

But why spend time on non-fiction at all? Perhaps because one of the most
effective ways for students to learn how to define the character of fiction is to get
them to begin with a set of tentative definitions and then to test them against other
forms of prose writing – biography, history or, as here, essays and travel writing.

Essays and blogs: Woolf, Carter and Beard

The following discussions of essays by Virginia Woolf and Angela Carter, and of a blog by Mary Beard, attempt to highlight some of the ways in which it is possible to respond to one form of non-fiction prose. Is it inevitable that Literature students should assume that extended-fiction prose (the novel first, and then the short story) comes top of the hierarchy of prose writing? Certainly it is important that they should have the opportunity to challenge this assumption or at least to assess prose fiction in the context of other types of prose production.

Even the term 'non-fictional' implies negative value – writing which is defined as not being something else – and the essay as a literary form has been severely downgraded since the Second World War. Not that the essay has disappeared, of course: it has survived under different guises, mostly as journalism or media production of one kind or another. Its most recent manifestation is in the blog, and it may be, especially with younger students, that the blog is the right place to begin. The following discussions, however, are sequential: the analysis of a blog takes place in the context of the two essays previously reviewed.

The discussion of Virginia Woolf's essay, 'Thoughts on Peace in an Air Raid', suggests one way of approaching such texts. It focuses on the following questions as prompts for analysis and exploration by students:

- What insights into the text can be gained from a close reading and analysis of its language and structure?
- How can these insights be extended by discussing the text in the context of other related work by Virginia Woolf?
- How far is the text, and the reader's response to it, illuminated by knowing the circumstances in which it was written and published?
- How much does the biographical context contribute to an appreciation of the text?

Virginia Woolf: 'Thoughts on Peace in an Air Raid'

This essay was written in the last summer of Virginia Woolf's life, in August 1940. She was living in Sussex, in a village near the south coast, having been driven out of London by the Blitz; in fact, her Bloomsbury home was to be severely damaged by a bomb during an air raid. Air raids, aeroplanes and bombs all feature in this essay, which was commissioned as a contribution to a women's symposium in America. It was not published in her lifetime, but appeared as the concluding piece in the posthumous collection of her essays, *The Death of the Moth* (1942), edited by her husband Leonard Woolf. It is as if he intended this essay to stand as her last word; indeed, it can hardly be an accident that the final sentence of the essay is so apt:

And now, in the shadowed half of the world, to sleep.

It is a short essay, fewer than 1800 words, and is rarely republished today, though it is easily accessed on the Internet. However, it quickly appeared in an anthology, *Modern Essays 1941–1943* (1944), for use in schools: here it was again the last essay, and the only one by a woman writer. It is not usually discussed by Woolf critics, perhaps because they find little in it that is not said more extensively in *Three Guineas* (1938), her polemic against the unthinking oppression of women by men, or more allusively in *Between the Acts* (1941), her last novel, also published posthumously. *Between The Acts* is a novel about England on the brink of possible annihilation by war: a chaotic village pageant is interrupted by a succession of technical hitches, by acting failures and actors' tantrums, by an unexpected shower of rain and, finally, by a flight of low-flying aeroplanes that interrupt the Rector in mid-sentence while he is proposing a rather bumbling vote of thanks and making an embarrassed appeal on behalf of the church funds. The aeroplanes are flying in V-formation, which reminds Woolf of a skein of wild ducks; and in 'Thoughts on Peace', too, Woolf finds a metaphor from the natural world to describe aircraft. The essay begins:

> The Germans were over this house last night and the night before that. Here they are again. It is a queer experience, lying in the dark and listening to the zoom of a hornet which may at any moment sting you to death. It is a sound that interrupts cool and consecutive thinking about peace. Yet it is a sound – far more than prayers and anthems – that should compel one to think about peace. Unless we can think peace into existence we – not this one body in this one bed but millions of bodies yet to be born – will lie in the same darkness and hear the same death rattle overhead. Let us think what we can do to create the only efficient air raid shelter while the guns on the hill go pop-pop-pop and the searchlights finger the clouds and now and then, sometimes close at hand, sometimes far away, a bomb drops.

It's an object lesson in how to start an essay, not a formal academic essay (the only type most students ever consciously encounter these days, either to read or to try to write) but the kind of literary essay that used to be admired both for what it had to say and – as much or even more – for the way it said it. Condemned after the war as *'belles-lettristic'*, the literary essay hung on for a time, most often appearing in the guise of radio broadcasts, reviews or other forms of journalism. Critics of the essay condemned its tendency to whimsy and charm, its apparently self-conscious solipsistic way of viewing the world – a world that belonged to the leisured classes who had time for keeping diaries and writing long letters but who would not engage seriously with literature that was more demanding than – well, than the essay. Francis Bacon, the father of the English essay, had himself declared, 'To write just treatises [i.e. full-length scholarly books that do justice to their subject] requireth leisure in the reader and leisure in the writer … which is the cause which hath made me choose to write certain brief notes … which I have called essays.' Bacon's 16th-century essay style is often that of a lecturer or preacher of a secular sermon: a Polonius anxious to pass on his accumulated wisdom to a patient Laertes. By contrast, the tone of the literary essay in the earlier 20th century is often private rather than public – someone thinking aloud or speaking to a friend, rather than addressing a large audience – and this first paragraph from 'Thoughts on Peace', therefore, seems to exhibit both what is good and what is bad about essays.

It's personal: the speaker is writing about her own experience in her own home, 'this house', and is unable to sleep or to think because of the 'zoom of a hornet which at any moment may sting you to death'. It's immediate: 'Here they are again.' But it isn't just personal: the voice that speaks, almost to herself, as if she is really lying awake in her bed thinking rather than sitting at her desk writing, appeals to her readers / audience at the same time: 'we' need to start thinking collectively in order to 'think peace into existence'. By the end of the paragraph it is clear that 'we' embraces both 'this one [female] body in this one bed' and all the other women to whom she is speaking – not least the audience in America for whom the essay was intended. It is, the final sentence implies, only women who can build 'the only efficient air raid shelter', and this must be done by creating a world in which men will no longer want to play soldiers: 'the guns on the hill go pop-pop-pop'. Although she would probably not have used it herself, Virginia Woolf might have appreciated the phrase 'toys for the boys'.

In 1940 she was, not surprisingly, preoccupied by air raids. Her rural home in the village of Rodmell, near Lewes, lay directly under the enemy flightpath to London. In her diary for Friday 16th August 1940, as the Battle of Britain was fought over her head, she recorded: 'Many air raids. One as I walked. A haystack was handy. But walked on. And so home.' The tone and style are here are Pepysian, but all the time she is investigating, as well as recording, her thoughts and feelings, her consciousness of being conscious:

> The sound was like someone sawing in the air just above us. We lay flat on our faces, hands behind head. Don't close your teeth, said L [Leonard, her husband]. They seemed to be sawing at something stationary. Bombs shook the windows of my lodge. Will it drop? I asked. If so, we shall be broken together. I thought, I think, of nothingness – flatness, my mood being flat … Hum and saw and buzz all around us.

In her essay, war is an entirely masculine activity: 'young Englishmen and young German men are fighting each other. The defenders are men, the attackers are men.' So too are the weapons and equipment they use: searchlights 'finger' the clouds; later, 'all the searchlights are erect'. But, though the Englishwoman 'must lie weaponless tonight' she also, Woolf argues, can fight – with 'ideas that will help the young Englishman who is fighting up in the sky to defeat the enemy'. She remembers 'a woman's voice in *The Times* this morning saying, "Women have not a word to say in politics"', and complains that only the ideas of men get heard or turned into action, a situation that simply encourages women to give up thinking for themselves at all.

The voice is actually that of Lady Astor, the first woman MP, speaking in Parliament on Thursday 21st August and reported in *The Times* the following day:

> 'Lady Astor said they wanted a woman in the Government with the power to co-ordinate; women had not a word to say in policy. Women of ability were held down because of a sub-conscious Hitlerism in the hearts of men. She felt very strongly that this was a struggle for freedom.'

In her essay, Woolf develops this concept of Hitlerism:

> Certainly we are held down. We are equally prisoners tonight – the Englishmen in their planes, the Englishwomen in their beds. But if he stops to think he may be killed; and we too. So let us think for him. Let us try to drag up into consciousness the subconscious Hitlerism that holds us down. It is the desire for aggression: the desire to dominate and enslave. Even in the darkness we can see that made visible. We can see shop windows blazing; and women gazing; painted women; dressed up women; women with crimson lips and crimson finger-nails. They are slaves who are trying to enslave.

Virginia Woolf's argument that, by their willingness to be enslaved, women simply reinforce men's aggressive instincts and their desire to enslave is one that she was pursuing in both her non-fiction and her fiction at this time: it is a key theme in *Three Guineas* and it surfaces in passing in *Between the Acts*, where Mrs Manresa is said to have 'given up dealing with her figure and had thus gained freedom' (p.28). Gaining freedom in this way, Woolf argues in the essay, also frees men: 'If we could free ourselves from slavery we should free men from tyranny. Hitlers are bred by slaves.' And if men can be freed from being tyrants, they can, she suggests, also be freed from being instinctual fighters. Picking up the implications of 'Disarmament' as one of the promises of a post-war settlement, Woolf asks how men are to cope in a world where their warlike instincts will have no outlet: 'Othello's occupation will be gone, but he will remain Othello.' In *Three Guineas*, she had specifically attacked the way in which education had trained men to love medals, uniforms and decorations; here she argues that it is up to women to wean them away from such dependency:

> We must help the young Englishmen to root out from themselves the love of medals and decorations. We must create more honourable activities for those who try to conquer in themselves their fighting instinct, their sub-conscious Hitlerism. We must compensate the man for the loss of his gun.

The tone here is becoming not so much polemical as rhetorical. The anaphora ('We must help ... We must create ... We must compensate') is the sort of resounding male rhetoric that Churchill was employing to such effect just then ('We shall fight them on the beaches ..., etc.'). And as if in recognition of going too far, Woolf abruptly breaks off. Retrieving the metaphor she had used in her diary entry the previous week, she writes 'The sound of sawing has increased overhead ... at any moment a bomb may fall on this very room': her attention is refocused on the air raid. She counts the seconds – it's a false alarm – but 'during those seconds of suspense all thinking stopped. All feeling, save one dull dread, ceased. A nail fixed the whole being to one hard board.'

As the Battle of Britain intensified, Virginia Woolf more than once tried to put into words what it might be like to be killed by a bomb, and expressed her frustration as a writer that she would not be able to describe the event after it had happened (did she envy George Orwell's ability to write, in *Homage to Catalonia*, 'The whole experience of being hit by a bullet is very interesting and I think it is worth describing in detail'?). In October she wrote:

> It – I mean death; no, the scrunching and scrambling, the crushing of my bone shade in on my very active eye and brain: the process of putting out the light – painful? Yes. Terrifying. I suppose so. Then a swoon; a drain; two or three gulps attempting consciousness – and then dot dot dot.

She sounds here almost offended that her 'very active eye and brain' should be destroyed in such a way; in 'Thoughts on Peace in an Air Raid' she is offended that the air raid stops one from being able to think: 'The emotion of fear and of hate is therefore sterile, unfertile.' But as soon as the immediate danger is past, 'the mind reaches out and instinctively revives itself by trying to create'. In the first moments of being able to think again, since the room is dark and she can see nothing, she can create 'only from memory'. She remembers other Augusts, visits to the opera at Beyreuth, holidays in Rome (both places she can now no longer visit and may never be able to visit again); walks in London – one of her favourite activities, and again something that she may have done for the last time:

Friends' voices come back. Scraps of poetry return. Each of those thoughts, even in memory, was far more positive, reviving, healing and creative than the dull dread made of fear and hate. Therefore if we are to compensate the young man for the loss of his glory and his gun, we must give him access to the creative feelings. We must make happiness. We must free him from the machine. We must bring him out of his prison into the open air.

One of the key structural elements of this essay is the way it moves backwards and forwards between the immediacy of private lived experience, described with almost a child's sense of astonishment ('the guns go pop-pop-pop'), or matter-of-factness ('the raider was brought down behind the hill') and the repeated (repetitive? – the same anaphoric trope used twice) rhetorical effects. The essay has been a demonstration by a woman writer of what she demands from and on behalf of women: that they should build a better world by exercising the positive power of thought. There is no sentimental longing for a return to a pre-war, pre-lapsarian England, though there is a keen sense of the continuing presence of the natural world. In the final paragraph Virginia Woolf describes this through a sequence of unspoken contrasts: after the searchlights have been switched off, 'the natural darkness of a summer's night returns'. Now that the guns are silent, 'the innocent sounds of the country are heard again'. Instead of a bomb being dropped, 'an apple thuds to the ground'. After the hornet-buzz of the aeroplanes, 'an owl hoots, winging its way from tree to tree'. Then in a neat ending Woolf invokes one of her favourite writers, Sir Thomas Browne, to unite the intended American readers of her essay with the Englishwomen on whose behalf, and to whom, she has been speaking within the essay itself.

Browne, the 17th-century English philosopher and author of books such as *Religio Medici* and *Urn Burial*, was a prose writer whose style sometimes anticipated Woolf's own. Here, as if allowing her ideas to range by free association (but notice even here the careful repetition and progression of sounds: 'An apple … an owl … And some …'), she brings to her mind a half-sentence from one of Browne's most obscure books, *The Garden of Cyrus* (1658): 'The huntsmen are up in America …':

> Let us send these fragmentary notes to the huntsmen who are up in America, to the men and women whose sleep has not yet been broken by machine-gun fire, in the belief that they will re-think them generously and charitably, perhaps shape them into something serviceable.

There is in this final sentence something engagingly disingenuous. Timewise, it's not that the American hunstmen are up early: they haven't yet gone to bed. But in as much as the whole essay is meant to read as if she has been capturing on paper (by the illumination of the searchlights?) the random thoughts that have sustained her through the night of the air raid, the phrase 'these fragmentary notes' is appropriate. After all, 'consecutive thinking' has hardly been possible. It echoes too the 'certain brief notes … which I have called essays' of Francis Bacon. In fact, of course, they are not random at all; or, if they were, Woolf has carefully reconstructed them ('shaping them into something serviceable') to give the illusion of spontaneity. Her recycling of words and images from her diary is evidence of this, and in the Introduction to *The Death of the Moth* Leonard Woolf records that even her most trivial pieces of journalism went through as many as eight typed drafts. The idea that the sleep of the Americans has 'not yet' been disturbed by the first-hand experience of war is perhaps a glancing dart at America's reluctance to enter the War and a recognition that it would have to do so sooner or later.

There is, therefore, something very inclusive about the way this essay is aimed, but it is important to see how the pronouns Woolf uses can be deceptive. In the opening paragraph, she appears to define 'we' – she never once uses 'I' to refer to herself – as 'not this one body in this one bed but millions of bodies yet to be born', but then immediately says, 'Let us think what we can do', referring primarily or solely to herself. In the second paragraph she elides singular and plural, third person and first:

> Arms are not given to Englishwomen either to fight the enemy or to defend herself … How can she fight for freedom without firearms? … But there is another way of fighting for freedom without arms; we can fight with the mind.

Later, Woolf appears to appeal to all women when she asks, 'Could we switch off the maternal instinct at the command of a table full of politicians?' and in one of the most revealing passages of the whole essay she claims that:

> If it were necessary, for the sake of humanity, for the peace of the world, that child-bearing should be restricted, the maternal instinct subdued, women would attempt it. Men would help them. They would honour them for their refusal to bear children. They would give them other openings for their creative power. That too must be part of our fight for freedom.

What these 'other openings' could be Virginia Woolf doesn't say, but her own complicated sexuality and her ambivalence about not having had children herself underpin this passage. Hermione Lee, in her biography of Woolf, has shown how contradictory is the evidence as to whether Virginia and Leonard had ever wanted children and whether she was or was not relieved, on balance, to have been childless. Here, it is almost as though she is *willing* other women to endorse her own subduing of the maternal instinct, and turning what was an unresolved private self-denial into a laudable public renunciation.

In this way, then, the essay encompasses both the public and the private anxieties of its author, what is open and what is 'shadowed'. The peace about which she is thinking while the air raid is in progress outside is a peace that will depend on new ways of thinking, ways that in the end she has to leave to others to 're-think generously and charitably' so that they can 'perhaps shape them into something serviceable'. After all the rhetoric of tyranny and enslavement, liberation and freedom, in this final essay's final sentence she retreats, exhausted as it were, from the public forum of debate into the Pepysian privacy of her room: 'And now ... to sleep'. Earlier in the essay she had quoted Blake: 'I will not cease from mental fight,' and had added, 'Mental fight means thinking against the current, not with it'. As an essay, 'Thoughts on Peace in an Air Raid' demonstrates how Virginia Woolf thought against the current and, in its last words, it anticipates the price she was to pay for doing so.

Angela Carter: 'Bath, Heritage City'

Angela Carter (1940–1992) made a name for herself as a novelist while still in her twenties, but throughout her career she also wrote for magazines and newspapers. Her essays and reviews were collected in an anthology, *Nothing Sacred*, published by the feminist press Virago in 1982 and reprinted four times before her death at the age of fifty-one in 1992. Many of her essays were first printed in *New Society*, a magazine with a sociological perspective and a left-of-centre political stance. The following discussion of an essay about one of the most celebrated cities in England invites the following questions:

- How far does the style of writing in this essay reflect the writer's contradictory attitude(s) to her subject?
- Is this an essay primarily about the city of Bath or about a certain kind of Englishness?
- Are there any similarities between this essay and Virginia Woolf's 'Thoughts on Peace in an Air Raid'?
- Does this essay, taken in parallel with Virginia Woolf's, make it easier to define some of the distinctive characteristics of the essay as a literary form?

It takes as its starting point Carter's own description, seven years after the essay's original publication, of how she came to write 'Bath, Heritage City' in a particular way.

• •

> Between 1973 and 1976, I lived in the city of Bath Spa, one of the most
> beautiful cities in England, nay, in Europe, a different kettle of fish to
> Bradford, or Doncaster: or Sheffield, where I spent two years after I moved
> out of Bath. (Oh, I do like a change ...) I always find beautiful places obscurely
> troubling, especially beautiful English places, and I wrote the following piece,
> a formal reverie about the City of Bath, on purpose in a style that matched
> it, Fine Writing, the evocative voice, the dying fall. Bath was a lovely place in
> which to live. Yet it is England at its most foreign to me ...
>
> *(Nothing Sacred, p.70)*

The way this essay – and even Angela Carter's introduction to the essay – is written
reflects the ambivalence of the author's feelings towards Bath. She loved living
there, but felt she was a foreigner. This ambivalence is reflected in the style of the
opening sentences of the first three paragraphs:

> Getting a buzz off the stones of Bath, occupying a conspicuous site not fifty
> yards from the mysterious, chthonic aperture from which the hot springs
> bubble out of the inner earth, there is usually a local alcoholic or two on the
> wooden benches outside the Abbey.

> I once saw a man puking exhaustively inside the Abbey, surrounded by
> memorial plaques of soldiers and sailors who seem to have come here to die
> in large numbers.

> On the Abbey facade, angels climb up the ladder towards God, sort of nutty
> Disney. The Palladians who turned Bath into what it is today pulled down
> almost everything else, they must have left the Abbey facade because it was
> so charming. Charm, the English disease; charm, mask of dementia?

'Getting a buzz', 'puking', 'sort of nutty': this informal register clashes straight
away with the register of words such as 'conspicuous', 'chthonic', 'exhaustively',
'Palladian'. 'Palladian' is an architectural term most serious readers about Bath
can be expected to know, though how many readers would feel competent to place
the term accurately in the following list: Classical, Baroque, Georgian? As for
'chthonic', this is highly specialised lexis: you'd need to be familiar with classical
mythology and the idea of spirits living under the earth, or with the early novels
and short stories of E.M. Forster, to see what Angela Carter is getting at. It is as if
these contrasting registers reflect Carter's own contrasting feelings towards the city
of Bath.

In fact Carter's opening paragraph, so different from the opening of 'Thoughts on Peace in an Air Raid', economically introduces all the key ideas that are to dominate the rest of the essay. She comments on the 'great numbers' of alcoholics who appear in summer 'as if to inform the tourists this city is a trove of other national treasures besides architectural ones'. She recalls seeing one 'demented youth' singing a tuneless song, 'I am an angel' and being ignored by 'clean' French and Scandinavian tourists. Which leads her to comment in passing, 'we only get upper market tourism'. What kind(s) of heritage ('national treasures'), therefore, does Bath offer the tourist? Carter's argument is evidently going to be that what really distinguishes Bath is not so much its architecture, but the crazy mixture of styles and people and modes of thinking: the classical and the gothic, Christianity and paganism, the well-heeled and the down-and-out, the demented (stoned out of their heads) young and the demented (senile) old people who have been coming to Bath for two hundred years, like the soldiers and sailors, to die in large numbers. The young alcoholic who sings 'I am an angel' is as much a feature of Bath, Carter implies, as the gothic angels who climb up and down the west wall of the Abbey.

Not all her arguments necessarily carry conviction – least of all the suggestion that the Palladians left the Abbey facade standing 'because it was so charming'. For Bath, as it was refashioned by the architects John Wood the elder and the younger, was built at the same time as the fashion for gothic was beginning to catch on (and which by the time of *Northanger Abbey* had become a full-blown craze). In the Georgian rebuilding of Bath, the Abbey, with the Pump Room and the Baths beside it, is a focal point occupying an absolutely central position – a rational planning decision which has nothing to do with charm. For Carter, nevertheless, charm and madness remain essential components of the scene:

> There's a lot of fine-boned, blue-eyed English madness in Bath, part of its charm, a population with rather more than its fair share of occultists, neo-Platonists, yogis, theosophists, little old ladies who have spirit conversations with Red Indian squaws, religious maniacs, senile dements, natural lifers, macrobiotics, people who make perfumed candles, kite-flyers, do you believe in fairies?

Carter's technique is thus to introduce these words and phrases which then recur like *leitmotifs* through the essay. After describing a pair of evangelists and a West Indian grocer who, 'Crying "Hallelujah!", disappear into the heart of heritage Bath', she comments:

> Too much fine-boned, blue-eyed English dementia around here already to raise an eyebrow.

As with Virginia Woolf, she combines in her essay carefully constructed formal paragraphs with the immediacy of aphoristic sentences and short-hand phrases ('sort of nutty Disney') designed to sound as if they have been transferred straight from her notebook, first thoughts and first impressions mediating her considered opinions. Contrast these two sentences:

> Marvellous, hallucinatory Bath has almost the quality of concretised memory; its beauty has a curiously second-order quality, most beautiful when remembered, the wistfulness of all professional beauties, such as that of the unfortunate Marilyn Monroe whom nobody wanted for herself but everybody wanted to have slept with ...

> Bath was built to be happy in, which accounts for its innocence and its ineradicable melancholy.

Or these:

> The lucid and serene architecture of this city confronts me with an Englishness I attempt to deny by claiming Scottish extraction. I always give Jock a shilling when he pan-handles me.

Although from the start Angela Carter has made it clear that her account of Bath is based on personal observation ('I once saw a man puking exhaustively inside the Abbey ...') and her status as a resident of the city, this short paragraph is the only one in the essay where she actively, if defensively, engages with the city itself. This is where she makes good her claim in the introduction to the essay that Bath is 'England at its most foreign to me'. When the architecture confronts her with its Englishness, it's with the Scottish beggar she claims kin: 'I always give Jock a shilling'. And at this moment she enlists her own nostalgia to make the point: by the time she wrote this essay, English currency had been decimal for five years already and the shilling had been consigned to history – though a few surviving coins were still in circulation, re-branded as five new pence.

What starts out, then, as an essay trying to define the essential character of a city in which she lives but in which she does not quite feel at home becomes for Carter an argument about Englishness. The 'evocative voice, the dying fall' she employs to define the 'Fine Writing' appropriate for this 'formal reverie' becomes the instrument with which she analyses what she calls the English sensibility:

> The softly crumbling stone; those tumultuous skies across which, now and then, the wild swans fly; that light with the elegiac quality that brings a lump in the throat ... Bath, a city so English that it feels like being abroad, has become so distorted by what Pevsner called the Englishness of English art

that the city itself has become an icon of sensibility ... It is an art that does not bear the marks of having been jostled in the market-place, and such a jostling would have brushed away a good deal of its melancholy boom. It is not so much bourgeois art – that would be vulgar – as a truly middle-class art, and, since the English middle class is unique, then perhaps this class origin is what gives the sensibility itself its characteristically English charm. It is reflective, the product of reverie and introspection.

That final phrase betrays the fact that Carter herself has chosen to write a characteristically English essay, a formal reverie, (cf. Charles Lamb's celebrated essay, 'Dream Children: a Reverie') about Englishness by the end of which she has severed her claim to be a part of Bath at all. No longer one of its residents – 'we only get upper market tourism', she had said at the start of the essay – she takes leave of Bath, and heads for Sheffield, with a final single-sentence paragraph – again reading as though lifted straight from her journalist's notebook – that simultaneously sums up and demolishes her quintessentially English city:

On the hill beyond the river, they illuminate at night, a folly called 'Sham Castle'.

As with her own sinister subverting of fairy tales, here Angela Carter subverts the image of Bath she has previously created. 'We' have become 'they'. The 'Fine Writing' essay style that she had adopted to match the 'hallucinatory' quality of the city she was writing about is abandoned. If it is true, as she has earlier said, that 'the Georgian city has the theatrical splendour, the ethereal two-dimensionality of a town of dream', 'Bath, Heritage City' ends by suggesting that the dream is not a sweet one. The contradictions that have been threaded through the whole essay are finally resolved. No longer 'ethereal', let alone 'marvellous', 'lucid' or 'serene', the city's charm and its middle-class sensibility are presented as a fake, a fantasy world for 'fine-boned blue-eyed English madness'. Sham Castle? Sort of nutty Disney, after all.

Mary Beard: 'Self-promotion?'

The blog is a phenomenon already shifting our perception of how ideas, opinions and prejudices can be shared and expressed in print – even if in cyberprint. Curiously, it has led to a revival in the art of the conversational essay: everyone who writes a blog tries, consciously or otherwise, to shape their prose in such a way as to get across effectively what they want to say, and in doing so, to give an impression of themselves as someone participating in a conversation. The blog positively encourages this: it allows cyberlinks, so that the discussion can take off in different directions, as face-to-face conversations are always prone to do; its register is usually casual rather than formal, and it invites readers to react to what they are reading so that frequently a writer gets almost instant feedback in a way that rarely happens in print.

Mary Beard is a classicist, an academic and a writer and broadcaster. As Classics Editor for the *Times Literary Supplement* she reviews and commissions others to review books on all aspects of the ancient world; she also writes a blog for the *TLS*. She has been described as 'the best-known classicist in Britain'[1]. The following blog was written to describe her experiences in publicising her book on *The Roman Triumph* [2].

Self-promotion? (posted 16.11.07)

Confession. I have spent a lot of last week in book promotion. Yes, I want it to sell – and yes I want people to like it too, which may not be quite as closely connected to sales as one would like to think. There are, sadly, loads of wonderful books, brilliantly reviewed which actually sell in trivial numbers, and others which sell in their thousands but no one ever reads. How many people actually finished even the first chapter of *A Brief History of Time*?

So I started the week with *Start the Week*. It gets 2 million listeners so is probably the biggest audience who'll ever get to hear about the book. For that reason, it's also pretty terrifying – and seems more so when you've left Cambridge at 6.00 in the morning to make absolutely sure you can get there for 8.30. I thought we were a motley crew of guests honestly, talking on some not entirely sexy subjects. Climate change in China and the role of the Commonwealth can usually be guaranteed to make even a worthy Radio 4 audience glaze over, I fear. *The Roman Triumph* I suppose seemed quite jolly in comparison. But what is more, everyone had a ghastly cold ... so it felt a bit as if it was being broadcast from a sanatorium.

Did it sell the book? To judge from Amazon's rating – yes, a bit.

Then there were the launch parties: one in a really great location in Greek St (perfect place to have a Triumph party ... geddit?) and the other in our friendly neighbourhood bookshop in Cambridge. Memory of these is predictably a bit fuzzy. It felt rather like being the birthday girl at a kid's party: hostess behaviour started off pretty well ... but after an hour or so decorum lapsed and the rest is history. The best bit in Cambridge was that some undergraduates had got to hear of it and just turned up. I don't think they realised how flattering that felt.

Then of course there were the reviews ...

More than anyone, I should be pretty calm about this. After all, I spend a big part of my life commissioning, editing and publishing reviews, and I know that they are simultaneously very important and of little significance in the great order of books' success.

That said, I can't read a new review of my own stuff without the prop of a stiff drink (so this has been a very bad week for 'units' as we now call them). And even then, I can't read them straight through. I take a look at the start, then at the end – and on that basis I try to work out what has gone on in between. If the last paragraph starts 'despite' (as in 'despite all these faults, not a bad book'), my heart goes to my boots.

So far, I've done pretty well, and pretty luckily. There was a great piece in the *Sunday Times*. I was particularly taken by Allan Massie's review in the *Literary Review* (sorry not on the Internet). I am a great admirer of Massie's prose, but I honestly don't much like his novels about the Roman Empire, and indeed said so pretty publicly on one occasion. So I was especially taken when he said he liked what I'd written. It's a generous man who gives the thumbs up to someone who has given him the thumbs down.

But, don't worry, it hasn't gone to my head! Partly because of the little torrent of bile poured over me by Freddy Raphael in the *Spectator*. If you are heartily fed up of this blog, and Beard's obsession with her book, then I am confident you will enjoy this one. Quite what I did to deserve it, I'm not sure.

(timesonline.typepad.com/dons_life/2007/11/self-promotion.html, reprinted by permission of *Times Online*)

You post a blog. And this suggests two things: not only sending it by mail as if it were a letter that someone will open and read at the other end, but also pasting it on a wall like a poster so that any casual passer-by can read it. Letters are personal: they are directed to an individual who is addressed in the letter as 'you'; they expect or invite a response. Posters are general, aimed at a wide audience who may or may not take any notice.

A good blog will have characteristics of both the letter and the poster. Mary Beard's blog talks directly to the reader ('Don't worry … If you are heartily fed up', etc.); it also addresses a general audience, more in the tone of a speech or lecture: 'How many people actually finished even the first chapter of *A Brief History of Time*?'

These characteristics are not unique to the blog. Read the essays of Addison and Steele in *The Spectator* from 1711–1712, or some of Charles Lamb's nearly a hundred years later and you'll find them frequently written in the form of letters, combining informality with a subtle rhetoric. And even a blog as apparently informal as Mary Beard's pays careful attention to the need to catch the attention

of the audience: 'Confession' is not a bad opening statement. Repetition, too, is
used casually, but carefully and wittily:

I started the week with Start the Week.

It's a generous man who gives the thumbs up to someone who has given him
the thumbs down.

The style, midway between aphorism and sound-bite, engages or enrages – which
is as it should be, because blogs (like essays) cannot afford to be bland. So, how far
should informality in a blog go? It used to be common to reprove schoolchildren
for using the word 'pretty' to mean 'very' or 'to a great extent' (though Jane Austen
wasn't bothered: 'Lady Russell had nothing to do but admit she had been pretty
completely wrong' [*Persuasion*]). Still, is the use of 'pretty' as in 'So far, I've done
pretty well, and pretty luckily', followed four lines later by 'pretty publicly' too
much of a good thing, or just good blogging rhetoric?

One of the features of a blog is that it often draws attention to its own unlikely
circumstances of writing – quite different from the scholar or novelist labouring
over every word in a book-lined study or the hushed atmosphere of an academic
library. Immediacy is a key element to a blog: it can be written, posted and therefore
published worldwide within half an hour. No other form of publishing is so quick.
There may be little time for revision or careful crafting: to put it another way, the
style of writing should almost suggest spontaneity. A Christmas Day blog from
Mary Beard begins:

I am posting this between putting the turkey in the oven and getting the
pudding on the boil. (25 December 2007)

And another goes to an even greater extreme:

Blogging again from 37,000 feet, I have come to the conclusion that air
stewards/esses fall into two types, much like nannies. (10 December 2007)

How different is this, though, from Virginia Woolf's opening line in 'Thoughts on
Peace in an Air Raid'?

The Germans were over this house last night and the night before that. Here
they are again.

Clearly, the sense of immediacy in an essay is not an invention of the blog. Indeed,
in many respects the blog has simply revived some of the characteristics of the
literary essay and enabled them to flourish again. Essays used often to be written

– not least as a means of ensuring some additional income and publicity between books – by people generically described as 'Bookmen', those whose professional lives were bound up with writing about books to and for literary-minded readers. Literary gossip, literary in-jokes, often found their way into such people's essays and find their way today into literary blogs. And just as serious-minded critics from Leavis onwards dismissed the essay as *belles-lettristic*, literary chatter, so some critics today – for instance John Sutherland – are beginning to complain that the rise of the blog is hastening the demise of serious reviewing (i.e. by serious, professional literary critics). When Mary Beard writes that Greek Street is the 'perfect place to have a Triumph party ... geddit?' she is expecting her readers to recognise the catchphrase of the *Private Eye* gossip columnist, Glenda Slag, who always tagged her corny puns and innuendos with 'Geddit?' And referring to 'Freddie Raphael', she implies an acquaintance with the novelist Frederic Raphael which justifies her in feeling even more aggrieved at receiving a bad review from him. But she turns the joke neatly against herself, first by telling her readers that if they are fed up with 'Beard's obsession with her book' they will enjoy the Raphael review – and then by providing a hyperlink to it. This also allows her to round off the blog, in the best tradition of the essay, with an ending that neatly echoes the opening word, 'Confession', for if confession implies admitting something for which punishment may be deserved, the 'little torrent of bile' heaped on her by Frederic Raphael seems (she complains more-in-sorrow-than-in-anger) like excessive retribution: 'Quite what I did to deserve it, I don't know.'

A good essay, and a good blog, should leave the reader feeling that the writer has said what needed saying: there should be a sense of progression – and a sense of completeness. Compare Mary Beard's beginning and ending (Confession ... punishment) with Virginia Woolf's essay: this began with her lying awake in the middle of an air raid, and ended with her finally being able to get to sleep. Or Angela Carter's essay which began with the illusion of history and mystery – the stones of Bath, the 'chtonic aperture' from which the hot springs bubbled, and the Abbey – but ended with the disillusionment of the folly called Sham Castle.

Of course, the analysis of any blog should pay attention to the context in which that blog appears. Mary Beard writes a weekly – often more than weekly – blog, commissioned by the journal for which she is an editor. The regularity of her blogs gives them something of the flavour of a journal, as their heading, 'A Don's Life', implies. It also means that she gathers a cluster of readers who regularly respond to her posts and carry on a conversation in which she herself may decide to take part. This in turn gives the writer of the blog a better sense of who her audience is than a traditional essayist, publishing only in hard copy, is likely to gain.

The majority of blogs are, of course, completely independent and take their chance in cyberspace along with every other blog. Some may never be read by anyone at all apart from the author. This does not mean they are devoid of literary interest: some of the most admired journals and diaries were never written for publication. Nor are all blogs as consciously literary either in form or content as the one discussed here, though again this does not mean that the medium itself is not as important as the message. Blogs such as 'Metro Cities' are open to everyone and can combine a range of reportage, reflection and commentary that no single newspaper can supply. Indeed, it is becoming a characteristic of modern journalism that when a big story breaks on the far side of the world, for instance the assassination in Pakistan of Benazir Bhutto, journalists can get instant *vox pop* reactions to the event by reading the metblogs.com postings as they appear. All of them have the vividness of immediacy; some have flashes or sustained passages of writing that communicate the more powerfully because of the quality of that writing. Thus, in any discussion of non-literary prose it is worth asking students whether, in the end, what the American critic Helen Vendler has said of poetry isn't equally true of blogs posted in the Punjab:

> Both we as readers, and poets as writers, participate in the necessary belief that it is the urgent theme that drives the writer. So it does – but it is the writing that gives the theme life. *(Coming of Age as a Poet*, p.9)[3]

....

Your students will know more about blogs than you do, so they should have plenty to say in response to the following questions:

- Can a blog really claim to be taken seriously as a literary text?
- How does the blog, as a new literary form, relate to the older form of the essay?
- Do blogs have their own distinctive forms of rhetoric?
- Do we read blogs on-screen differently from the way we read essays on a page?

Travel writing in a literary context: Brooke's *Letters from America*

Travel writing occupies a twilight literary zone. Many novelists and poets have also been travel writers. It is more rare for professional travel writers also to be novelists or poets. Most students will equate travel writing with the *Rough Guides* or *Lonely Planet* publications, and few will have started to read or even consider travel writing as a literary genre. Books of travel writing are beginning to spawn books on travel writing, however; a small but growing number of university departments now offer modules on travel writing. At A level, it has been almost invisible, though as long ago as 1993 Cambridge offered a 'topic paper' module with travel writing as an option.

It is still a snobbish critical commonplace to dismiss travel writing as simply a form of journalism, and it is true that many books of travel writing do consist of pieces compiled from various previously published sources. Rupert Brooke's *Letters from America* (1915) falls into this category, with the added complication that the book was compiled after his death, for reasons that had little to do with a desire to promote Brooke as a travel writer. The following discussion investigates the background to the book, and invites students to consider whether the descriptions of America and Canada, visited by Brooke in 1913, actually helped him to clarify what he meant by England. It thus provides a context both for a re-examination of poems such as 'The Soldier' and of the ideas of Englishness explored in the work of English novelists discussed in Chapter 9 (pages 190–205).

· ·

> I suppose an Englishman in another country, is continually and alternately struck by two thoughts: 'How like England this is!' and 'How unlike England this is!'
> *(Letters from America*, p.50)[4]

If it is a truism that most travel writing is a form of autobiography, then it is certainly true that the journey undertaken by Brooke in 1913–1914 was also a journey of self-discovery. *Letters from America*, published after his death, is not the book for which Brooke is remembered, but I want to argue that it is important for what it reveals about the way Brooke's thinking developed in the crucial year leading to the outbreak of the First World War. What he actually discovered, in the United States, in Canada and in the Pacific Islands, was not so much what England meant to him, as what he meant by England.

However, *Letters from America* is a textbook example of the dangers of taking a book at face value, of judging it by its cover.

To take the title first: *Letters from America* is not really a collection of letters at all. It consists mostly of travel articles written for publication in a newspaper, the *Westminster Gazette*. These were articles that Rupert Brooke was commissioned to write (for four guineas per article, plus travel expenses) and which were the ostensible reason for his leaving England in May 1913. As is well documented, however, Brooke had personal and emotional reasons for wanting to put a considerable distance between himself and England at this time.

Admittedly, some of the material which found its way into the articles had originally been tried out in personal letters sent by Brooke to his mother and to friends. But as they appeared in the *Gazette*, and as they appear in the book, they are not even letters in the loose sense in which Alastair Cooke's weekly 'Letter from America' was understood: a well-known voice – almost a member of the family – explaining the oddities of life abroad for the benefit of those back home. In *Letters from America*, Brooke's real audience is himself.

Second, the word 'America' in the title is seriously misleading. Of the first thirteen chapters, the travel writing, only four deal with the United States – so America here must be understood to embrace Canada too – though some of the most interesting discussion of the book centres on the ways in which Canada is very definitely not America. Of his fellow-passengers on a steamer travelling up the St Lawrence, for instance, he writes, 'We were a cosmopolitan, middle-class bunch' and then notes 'the distinction between the Canadian and American languages [is] that Canadians tend to say "bunch" but Americans "crowd"' (p.76). The last two chapters do not deal with the American continent at all: a chapter provocatively (and with heavy irony directed against American tourists visiting the Pacific Islands) called 'Some Niggers' discusses Samoa, but is in no sense a dispatch from that country; it is written by someone who is very firmly back in England. So, too, is the last chapter of the book, 'An Unusual Young Man', which contains his own reflections on the outbreak of the War.

Henry James, who wrote the Preface to the *Letters from America*, gets it both right and wrong when he says that 'the pages from Canada, where as an impressionist, he increasingly finds his feet … are better than those from the States, while those from the Pacific Islands rapidly brighten and enlarge their inspiration.'(p.xxxiv) James goes on to spend two pages extolling the virtues of Brooke's accounts of life in the Pacific Islands, none of which is related to the single essay which actually appears in *Letters from America*. It is as if James, who did not live to see the publication of the book, had been led to believe that it would contain more South Pacific material. Which begs the question, who decided what should and should not be included?

The answer, not surprisingly, is Edward Marsh, Brooke's friend and unofficial literary agent, later his literary executor. But what is surprising is that Marsh is completely disingenuous about the material and about his hand in editing it. It is worth quoting in full his Note which prefaces the book:

> The author started in May 1913 on a journey to the United States, Canada, and the South Seas, from which he returned next year at the beginning of June. The first thirteen chapters of this book were written as letters to the *Westminster Gazette*. He would probably not have republished them in their present form, as he intended to write a longer book on his travels; but they are now printed with only the correction of a few evident slips. The two remaining chapters appeared in the *New Statesman*, soon after the outbreak of war.

Although Marsh clearly wanted to give the impression that he was exercising only the lightest of editorial touches, the book was very carefully organised by him to serve a number of crucial purposes. The tone of that editorial Note (though Marsh never describes himself as the book's editor, and his name is not on the title page) implies that *Letters from America* is simply a collection of pieces of occasional journalism and unrevised travel writing. Marsh rather disingenuously gives the impression that it is the sort of material Brooke himself would almost certainly not have published in such a format had he lived, but which a public eager to read anything by the late author of 'The Soldier' would snap up eagerly. As indeed it did: the book reprinted immediately, and three times within six months – both in the UK and in the United States.

Brooke certainly made no great claims for the quality of the pieces he sent back to the Editor of the *Westminster Gazette*. When his friend Noel Oliver wrote asking for a 'real account' of his travels, he replied mockingly from Arizona:

> You know, the Westminster articles weren't meant for you intellectuals – they were just for ordinary people who like that sort of thing, – people who read the Westminster –, people, in short, like myself … I'm quite commonplace & I *cannot* write prose, & Canada's a bloody dull place.
>
> (Letter to Noel Oliver, 25 April 1914)[5]

1914 and Other Poems apart, *Letters from America* was actually the first book of 'new' Rupert Brooke material to be published after his death, and it preceded the *Collected Poems*, with the celebrated Edward Marsh memoir. From Marsh's point of view, as executor and editor as well as friend and literary impresario, it was important to keep Brooke well in the public view, and to whet the appetite of readers for the forthcoming *Collected Poems*, which Marsh intended should be his true memorial. *Letters from America* had to serve three purposes, to which the actual letters themselves were almost incidental.

First, it had to act as a trailer for the memoir, which had been written by 1916 but which was still awaiting final approval from Brooke's mother. The public wanted to know about Brooke the man, but they would have to wait a little longer. Marsh's memoir is twice mentioned by Henry James in his extraordinary (and very long – nearly 10,000 word) Preface to *Letters from America*. After the preliminary section, James writes:

> I owe to his intimate and devoted friend Mr Edward Marsh the communication of many of his letters, these already gathered into an admirable brief memoir which is yet to appear and which will give ample help in the illustrative way to the pages to which the present remarks form a preface. (p.xxi)

And as if that is not a sufficient trailer, Henry James returns to this theme at the start of his next section:

> No detail of Mr Marsh's admirable memoir may I allow myself to anticipate. I
> can only announce it as a picture, with all the elements in iridescent fusion, of
> the felicity that fairly dogged Rupert's steps, as we may say, and that never
> allowed him to fall below its measure. (p.xxix)

Surely Marsh had not quite bargained for the Preface that Henry James actually
wrote? If the main aims of *Letters from America* had been to fill the gap before the
Collected Poems with the Memoir could appear and to prepare the public for this
major publishing event (which indeed it was), a further purpose was to present
an image of Brooke not as soldier poet but as the amiable and admirable young
Englishman of peacetime, in a sense to refocus the legend of the 'most beautiful
young man in England'. The frontispiece of the book is another portrait by the
photographer Sherril Schell; but, unlike the ethereal bare-shouldered profile
by Schell which prefaced *1914 and Other Poems,* here Brooke appears almost
informally, leaning into the photograph, hair tousled not combed, and wearing a
very un-Edwardian soft-collared shirt with a loosely knotted tie. This is a portrait
of the artist as an unusual young man – which is the title of the last chapter of the
book. The oddness of this photograph can be measured by contrasting it with any
of the thousands of stiffly posed portrait photographs that were taken of young men
in and out of uniform as they went off to war.

But Henry James, when he got to work, presented an image of Brooke that
must have been embarrassing even to Marsh:

> Rupert Brooke, young, happy, radiant, extraordinarily endowed and irresistibly
> attaching, virtually met a soldier's death, met it in the stress of action and the
> all but immediate presence of the enemy; but he is before us now as a new, a
> confounding and superseding example altogether, an unprecedented image,
> formed to resist erosion by time or vulgarisation by reference, of quickened
> possibilities, finer ones than ever before, in the stuff poets may be noted as
> made of. (p.xii)

The whole Preface is written in this vein, and some of it is hilarious. Describing
Brooke's tendency to go nude swimming at every opportunity, James describes his
'abundance of amphibious felicity' and comments that 'he was as incessant and
insatiable a swimmer as if he had been a triton framed for a picture.' (p.xxxvi)

On the other hand, James did focus on one theme of which Marsh would have
approved, and which in a sense became the dominant idea of the book, Brooke's
Englishness. This was Marsh's third and overriding aim of *Letters from America*:
to show, through the disparate material that he had gathered, how travelling to the
far side of the world only served to sharpen and define Brooke's sense of England
and Englishness. In fact, though, the book as it was published (and it is important
to stress again that this is not in a sense Brooke's own book at all) presents a more

complex picture of Brooke's identification with England than either Brooke or Marsh themselves can have recognised.

But first let it be said that, as travel writing, Brooke's letters to the *Westminster Gazette* are both readable and illuminating about the United States and, especially, about Canada. There are moments that retain a strong immediacy –for instance when, sunbathing on the edge of the St Lawrence Seaway, he sees some white logs of driftwood, and wonders whether they can have come from the wreck of the Titanic. There are moments, too, which are a poignant foreshadowing: watching a march-past of former Harvard University alumni representing each class of the previous half century he observes:

> The orderly procession of the years was unbroken, except at one point. There was one gap, large and arresting. Though all the years were represented, there seemed to be nobody in the procession between fifty and sixty. I asked a Harvard friend the reason. 'The War,' he said [that is, the American Civil War]. He told me there had always been that gap. Those who were old enough to be conscious of the war had lost a big piece of their lives. (p.44)

Brooke was one of the first English commentators to understand and protest strongly against the treatment of native American Indians: he was appalled both by the way 'Civilisation, disease, alcohol and vice' had almost dehumanised those who lived on the edges of the new cities and by the policy of isolating the Indians in reservations:

> Shall we preserve these few bands of them, untouched, to succeed us, ultimately, when the grasp of our 'civilisation' weakens, and our transient anarchy in these wilder lands recedes once more before the older anarchy of Nature? (p.143)

He was scathing too about the damage modern capitalism would do to an emerging country like Canada: as he put it, 'Nationalities seem to teach one another only their worst.' When he came to Winnipeg, which he noted had grown from being a place of a few shacks in 1870 to a city of 100,000 at the time of his visit in the fall of 1913, he described the future as envisaged by

> the true Winnipeg man, who, gazing on his city, is fired with the proud and secret ambition that it will soon be twice as big, and after that four times, and then ten times ...
>
>   'Wider still and wider
>   Shall thy bounds be set,'
> says that hymn which is the noblest expression of modern ambition. (p.104)

He added, '*That* hope is sure to be fulfilled.'

Brooke's sarcastic comment about 'Land of Hope and Glory' is typical of his mockery of British imperial expansion. And when he comes to contemplate the future destruction of the peace and open spaces of the Canadian prairie his writing has a bitterness not matched in English prose perhaps until the novels of Richard Aldington fifteen years later. To his surprise he finds that he loves the emptiness and what he calls the 'fresh loneliness' of the wild, where 'there is no one else within reach, there never has been anyone; no one else is *thinking* of the lakes and hills you see before you.' (p.117) 'Such', he says

> ... is the wild of Canada. It awaits the sun, the end for which Heaven made it, the blessing of civilisation. Some day it will be sold in large portions, and the timber given to a friend of –'s, and cut down and made into paper, on which shall be printed the praise of prosperity; and the land itself shall be sub-divided into town-lots and sold, and sub-divided and sold again, and boomed and resold, and boosted and distributed to fishy young men who will vend it in distant parts of the country; and then such portions as can never be built upon shall be given in exchange for great sums of money to old ladies in the quieter parts of England, but the central parts of towns shall remain in the hands of the wise. And on these shall churches, hotels, and a great many ugly skyscrapers be built, and hovels for the poor, and houses for the rich, none beautiful, and there shall ugly objects be manufactured, rather hurriedly, and sold to the people at more than they are worth, because similar and cheaper objects made in other countries are kept out by a tariff ...   (p.119)

But if these satirical sideswipes at the England he had left behind – Elgar and old ladies in the quieter parts of England – suggest Brooke was simply expressing a disenchantment with aspects of English life he found irksome, his experience of the wide open spaces of Canada also forced him to articulate feelings of a very different kind. His first impressions of Ontario, for instance, provoked what he described as 'a faint grey-pink mist of *Heimweh* [homesickness]'. Men, he wrote,

> ... have lived contentedly on this land and died where they were born, and so given it a certain sanctity. Away north the wild begins, and is only now being brought into civilisation, inhabited, made productive, explored and exploited. But this country has seen the generations pass, and won something of that repose and security which countries acquire from the sight.   (p.76)

So he found, when he reached what he calls 'the wild', an empty landscape both compelling and repelling: 'To love the country here', he wrote, 'is like embracing a wraith. A European can find nothing to satisfy the hunger of his heart. The air is too thin to breathe. He requires haunted woods, and the friendly presence of ghosts. The immaterial soil of England is heavy and fertile with the decaying stuff of past seasons and generations.' (p.154)

There then follows a remarkable passage, one which belongs clearly to that particular late Edwardian English aesthetic – expressed in the essays of G.K. Chesterton and Edward Thomas, for instance, or E.V. Lucas's best-selling anthology *The Open Road*. E.M. Forster's Leonard Bast in *Howards End*, too, would have recognised this writing:

> A Canadian would feel our woods and fields heavy with the past and the invisible, and suffer claustrophobia in an English countryside beneath the dreadful pressure of immortals. For his own forests and wild places are windswept and empty. That is their charm, and their terror. You may lie awake all night and never feel the passing of evil presences, nor hear printless feet neither do you lapse into slumber with the comfortable consciousness of those friendly watchers who sit invisibly by a lonely sleeper under an English sky. Here one is perpetually a first-comer. The land is virginal, the wind cleaner than elsewhere, and every lake new-born, and each day is the first day. The flowers are less conscious than English flowers, and breezes have nothing to remember, and everything to promise. There walk, as yet, no ghosts of lovers in Canadian lanes. This is the essence of the grey freshness and brisk melancholy of this land. And for all the charm of those qualities, it is also the secret of a European's discontent. For it is possible, at a pinch, to do without gods. But one misses the dead. (pp.154–5)

It would be a mistake to dismiss writing like this simply as sentimental neo-pagan whimsy or the condescension of a visitor from the old world trying to redress what he sees as the imbalance of the new. In this passage Brooke begins to define, perhaps for the first time, that imagined English landscape of his last poems. It is not so much that the printless feet recall the 'lissom, clerical printless toe' from 'The Old Vicarage, Grantchester', as that the 'lonely sleeper under an English sky' anticipates the 'hearts at peace, under an English heaven'. Even more specifically, the 'immaterial soil of England ... heavy with the decaying stuff of past generations' is precisely where, as 'the 'richer dust concealed', he will later locate himself in 'The Soldier'.

It is important to emphasise, then, that the England of which he writes is an England of the imagination. The whole appeal to the listener in 'The Soldier' is an appeal to that person to use her imagination, to conceive of an England that cannot literally exist. And the imagined 'rich earth' of the poem is also anticipated in *Letters from America*, in the last chapter – 'An Unusual Young Man' – where the speaker, thinly disguised as Brooke himself, hearing of the outbreak of war, imagines that there might be a raid on the English coast:

> He didn't imagine any possibility of it succeeding, but only of enemies and
> warfare on English soil. The idea sickened him. He was immensely surprised
> to perceive that the actual earth of England held for him a quality ... which,
> if he'd been sentimental enough to use the word, he'd have called 'holiness'.
> He felt the triumphant helplessness of a lover. Grey, uneven little fields, and
> small, ancient hedges rushed before him, wild flowers, elms and beeches,
> gentleness, sedate houses of red brick, proudly unassuming, a countryside of
> rambling hills and friendly copses.   (p.178)

It makes sense to identify the listener in 'The Soldier' as 'her', to imagine the speaker in that poem addressing a mother, a wife or a girlfriend. But when, as in this vision of the English countryside, Brooke conceives of himself as a lover, then his mistress here must be England itself. Significantly the vision of England that he describes is one from which living human beings are excluded entirely, and in this respect it is the logical completion of the vision of England he had imaged for himself in the *Letters from America*, where Englishness ceases to be defined as the character of the living English people (for whom Brooke clearly signals his impatience and contempt); instead it is defined as the character of the English landscape peopled only by the English dead.

In this sense, therefore, his travel writing of 1913, produced at a time when he had no idea of the imminence of war or of his own death, offers an important and unexpected anticipation of his best known poem. No wonder Eddie Marsh, the only begetter of Brooke's *Letters from America,* ensured that it ended with the following words:

> 'Well, if Armageddon's on, I suppose one should be there.' ... He thought
> often and heavily of Germany. Of England, all the time. He didn't know
> whether he was glad or sad. It was a new feeling.   (p.180)

·····················

Brooke's *Letters from America* are available online. They provide a valuable insight into Brooke's life and attitudes before the start of the Great War. Students could explore the different contexts they afford, for instance:

- Brooke's writing as an early example of eco-criticism
- travel writing as a context for discussing Brooke's poetry written abroad
- a context for discussion of his war poetry
- Anglo-American attitudes.

The two last chapters also offer important insights into Brooke's very ambivalent attitudes towards Germany, where he had a number of good friends. In this context they offer students an illuminating contrast with 'The Old Vicarage, Grantchester'.

1 Conflict and calamity as contexts in literature

'It is the essential characteristic of literature that it concerns values. And values are not amenable to scientific method.'

(David Lodge *Language of Fiction*, 1966)

Whereas Chapters 7 to 10 have focused on different genres and on Shakespearean contexts, this final chapter deals first with a major A level topic, the literature of the Great War, and then explores ways in which contemporary calamities or current events can provide unusual but significant contexts for literary and textual study.

The first section of this chapter, 'War poetry, close reading and context', centres on a poem by Edmund Blunden which is read in the context both of Blunden's own prose memoir, *Undertones of War* (1928), and of Sebastian Faulks' *Birdsong* (1994). It is then contrasted with a little known poem by Siegfried Sassoon to pose for students the question, how does this pair of poems reinforce or alter their preconceptions of what constitutes war poetry? The second section, 'Memorialising the Great War', takes as its starting point two contrasting war memorials to ask how far an analysis of visual commemoration can inform an analysis of poems written by survivors of the Great War, Edmund Blunden again and Richard Aldington. Both Blunden and Aldington wrote poems in the 1930s that were addressed to Wilfred Owen and those who had died with him. This comparative analysis is further contextualised by discussion of responses in literature to the New Menin Gate and the Thiepval Memorial, focusing on another poem by Sassoon, on further passages from *Birdsong* and on a short story by Christopher Arthur.

The final section of the chapter, 'Unusual contexts – tsunamis, hangings and the Holocaust', is divided into two parts, the first using the Asian tsunami of 2004 as a context for discussing Julian Barnes' novel *A History of the World in 10½ Chapters* (1989), which has as its central point of reference the story of Noah's Ark. Finally, the execution of Saddam Hussein by hanging, an event shown shockingly and graphically on television and on the Internet worldwide, prompts a discussion of hanging in literature as a symbolic response to traumatic and tragic events. This discussion ranges from the essays and letters of Charles Lamb, via the poetry of Great War survivor Richard Aldington to the Holocaust narratives of the Italian writer Primo Levi. Its purpose is both to show how current events can be used to introduce students to fundamental moral issues placed in both historical and literary contexts and (as in the previous sections on the Great War) to demonstrate how literary exploration can move between genres and periods. Students should always be given opportunities to discover and articulate new connections between literary texts for themselves.

War poetry, close reading and context: Blunden, Sassoon and Faulks

War poetry, and specifically the poetry of the Great War (1914–1918), has become the poetry students are most likely to have studied by the time they leave school. It continues to feature prominently on syllabuses and Wilfred Owen is almost certainly more widely read today in schools than John Keats. But to say this is at once misleading, for the number of poems by Owen, or by Sassoon or Robert Graves actually studied is usually tiny. The experience of Great War poetry for some students stretches little further than 'Dulce et Decorum Est', 'Anthem for Doomed Youth' and 'The General'.

The following discussion looks for ways to extend this range and, in doing so, to get students to start asking themselves questions:

- What is meant by 'war poetry'?
- Is 'writing about the Great War' the same as 'writing produced during the Great War' or 'writing produced by those who fought in the Great War'?
- Why should we read war poetry differently from the way we read memoirs or novels about the Great War?
- Why do some poems get endlessly quoted and discussed, while others are overlooked?
- What effect does the writing of the Great War have on the way we, in the 21st century, think about the Great War itself?

The discussion begins with a detailed analysis of one of Edmund Blunden's best known poems, 'Concert Party: Busseboom', placing the poem in various contexts – topographical, literary and military. It is then contrasted with a little known poem by Siegfried Sassoon, 'Concert Party (Egyptian Base Camp)', before the discussion then widens out to suggest other material that could be used to compare and contrast with these poems: extracts from Blunden's memoir *Undertones of War* and Sebastian Faulks' *Birdsong*.

. . . .

Concert Party: Busseboom
The stage was set, the house was packed,
   The famous troop began;
Our laughter thundered, act by act;
   Time light as sunbeams ran.

Dance sprang and spun and neared and fled,
  Jest chirped at gayest pitch,
Rhythm dazzled, action sped
  Most comically rich.

With generals and lame privates both
  Such charms worked wonders, till
The show was over – lagging loth
  We faced the sunset chill;

And standing on the sandy way,
  With the cracked church peering past,
We heard another matinée,
  We heard the maniac blast

Of barrage south by Saint Eloi,
  And the red lights flaming there
Called madness: Come, my bonny boy,
  And dance to the latest air.

To this new concert, white we stood;
  Cold certainty held our breath;
While men in tunnels below Larch Wood
  Were kicking men to death.[1]

Busseboom today is hard to find. It isn't on most maps, and when you get there all you see is a crossroads, a few cottages (a face peers at you suspiciously from behind net curtains) and a small ugly farmhouse with a big barn behind it. It's in Belgium, in the middle of open fields on the back road between Ypres and Poperinghe. There's no sign to tell you you've reached the right place, but once upon a time every British soldier fighting near Ypres knew Busseboom. Today a small plaque hidden by the roadside explains that in the First World War these fields housed a huge encampment where troops either came for training before going to the Front or for a few days' rest and recuperation away behind the lines.

Perhaps the old barn was the setting for the concert party Edmund Blunden writes about. In the second line, the military term 'troop' rather than the theatrical 'troupe' indicates that this poem is about the sort of entertainment soldiers often had to provide for themselves when it was too dangerous for professional actors or singers to come and entertain them. But everything in the first two and a half stanzas suggests this improvised concert was a great success: 'laughter thundered', time passed quickly, the performance was 'comically rich'.

The cheerful mood of the audience is emphasised by the jaunty rhythm of the poem, which is written in the form of a ballad: four-line stanzas (quatrains) with lines of alternating eight and six syllables and an insistent rhyme scheme. Blunden's first line parallels the first line of the story told by Coleridge's Ancient Mariner:

> The ship was cheered, the harbour cleared,
>> Merrily did we drop
> Below the kirk, below the hill,
>> Below the light house top.

Just as in Coleridge's ballad the cheerful departure of the ship is only a prelude to horrific events in store, so in Blunden's poem the frenetic gaiety of the concert party is merely a brief distraction from the reality of the war going on outside. The entertainment only lasts for two and a half stanzas, and the abrupt change of mood is emphasised by the way the third stanza is written:

> With generals and lame privates both
>> Such charms worked wonders, till
> The show was over: lagging loth
>> We faced the sunset chill ...

The momentum at the start of this stanza is still so strong (no pause at the end of the first line, alliteration of the first word 'With' linking to 'worked wonders'), it's easy to miss the point that whereas the generals are all fit, the private soldiers are the ones who have been wounded. Blunden pauses after the word 'wonders', holding back the inoffensive little 'till' to the end of line two so that it tips the poem and the soldiers into a different mood altogether. After the excitement of the concert ('sprang ... spun ... chirped ... dazzled') not surprisingly the soldiers are reluctant to leave ('lagging loth'). The other matinée they can see and hear as they come out is all too close: just over the horizon, south east of Busseboom, St Eloi is being shelled to destruction.

The whole effect of the poem depends on contrasts. The gaiety of the concert when 'Time light as sunbeams ran' is replaced by 'the sunset chill'; the 'latest air' (tune) the soldiers hear from over the horizon is a 'maniac blast' which accompanies a very different kind of dance from the one they had enjoyed in the barn. And while describing these contrasts, Blunden manages to establish a new momentum, again using the ballad form effectively, but this time ironically. Ballads traditionally make full use of repetition and alliteration – for example:

> There was a wife of Usher's well
>> And a wealthy wife was she –

– and Blunden exploits these conventions to the full: 'matinee ... maniac ... madness' link stanzas four and five, while the phrase 'blast ... Of barrage' ensures that the reader is tugged from one stanza straight on to the next. Then, 'Called madness: Come' introduces the conventional ballad and folk-song phrase 'my bonny boy' which adds another layer of irony. Search for the phrase 'My bonny boy' on the Internet and you'll quickly find that it is the title of a traditional Irish ballad telling the story (for nearly all ballads are storytelling poems) of a young man who does not live long enough to see his own son born – a possibility all too real for soldiers. Finally, the three strings of alliteration on the sounds *m, b* and *c* all come together in the last stanza. The 'new concert' is terrifying the soldiers above ground who know what they are about to receive: 'Cold certainty held our breath'. But this is nothing compared with what is happening under the ground where

> men in tunnels below Larch Wood
> Were kicking men to death.

The shock effect of these last two lines is one of the most powerful in Great War poetry: although the previous stanzas have prepared us for the horror of the bombardment the soldiers are about to face, nothing prepares us for the final image of men trapped underground, fighting one another desperately like animals.

So much has been written about the fighting in the trenches and across No Man's Land, that the idea of 'going over the top' has become a clichéd expression. Everyone has seen photographs and grainy film of the battlefields, of Flanders mud and the stumps of shattered trees. By contrast, no one has seen photographs of the underground warfare that went on beneath the battlefields: there are none. This is one reason for the impact of Sebastian Faulks' novel *Birdsong*, which made many readers aware for the first time of what life underground in the First World War might have been like. But Faulks was not the first person to describe it: Blunden had done so in *Undertones of War*, his memoir published in 1928. Recalling life in the trenches near Cambrin, for instance, he writes:

> The tunnellers who were so busy under the German line were men of stubborn determination, yet, by force of the unaccustomed, they hurried nervously along the trenches above ground to spend their long hours listening or mining. At one shaft they pumped air down with Brobdignagian bellows. The squeaking noise may have given them away, or it may have been mere bad luck, when one morning a minenwerfer [a short-range mortar] smashed this entrance and the men working there. One was carried out past me, spouting blood at twenty paces. (p.67)[2]

Here, as in the poem, the shock comes at the end of the passage: twenty paces is almost the length of a cricket pitch. For blood to spout that far, the human heart would have to be pumping like 'Brobdignagian bellows'. Blunden borrows this adjective from the giants in Swift's *Gulliver's Travels*. A few lines later, he passes a corporal in a trench casually making a cup of tea and then discovers on his return that the corporal has been blown to pieces by a shell. The appalling details of what he sees are wrapped inside a complex sentence which poses an unanswerable question: 'For him,' asks the writer, how could 'the earth wall sotted with blood, with flesh, the eye under the duckboard, the pulpy bone be the only answer?' Here again, as with 'Concert Party: Busseboom', the apparently objective descriptions ('while men … were kicking men to death' or 'the eye under the duckboard') deliver a powerful subjective impact – the more so because they hit us with a delayed reaction. Like the poet, we have to go over the ground again, to register their full significance and horror. At the time, though, Blunden had other things to do: he had to hold the sack into which a sergeant shovelled the corporal's remains.

An author's other writings often provide a valuable context for exploring a particular text. Here, *Undertones of War* helps illuminate Blunden's technique in a poem about two very different kinds of concert, but the process is not all one-way. Thus, in *Undertones*, he briefly describes a new training depot ('M Camp') to which he is sent:

> Our quarters were a set of huts and tents surrounding a small ugly farmhouse, a mile or less from the road to Poperinghe, with field paths leading past the biscuit-tin and sugar-box dwellings of refugees around.   (p.144)

This single sentence opens up a new landscape, for our mental images of British encampments in the Great War do not include grim little shanties erected by Belgian refugees from now-uninhabitable towns like Ypres. Again therefore, as in the poem, apparently childish, fanciful description ('biscuit-tin and sugar-box dwellings') masks the human tragedy Blunden points to behind the picture.

And you have to read Blunden's poem to realise that the small ugly farmhouse with the huts and tents surrounding it is the setting for the concert party, and that M Camp is Busseboom.

· · · · · · · · · · · · · · · · · · · ·

Blunden's poem 'Concert Party: Busseboom' is worth contrasting with 'Concert Party' by Siegfried Sassoon. There is an evocative description of an impromptu concert party in Sebastian Faulks' *Birdsong* (Part 2, pp.253–254).

Blunden frequently wrote about Larch Wood. Two such poems worth comparing with 'Concert Party: Busseboom' are 'Can You Remember?' and 'On a Picture by Dürer'. Information about Larch Wood in the Great War can be found on this website: www.firstworldwar.com/today/larchwoodcemetery.htm

Edmund Blunden and Siegfried Sassoon

It is always important to remind students studying war poetry that they are dealing with literary texts as well as with historical evidence of war. A poem may document an event, but it always does so from memory and with imagination, and it frames the event in a particular way. In 'Concert Party: Busseboom' Blunden does this by writing the poem in the style of a ballad, and distances it by writing in the past tense. The devices he uses to create the contrasting atmospheres inside and outside the concert are all literary, and again they depend upon memory: Blunden did not know at the precise moment he was attending the concert that German soldiers had penetrated the English tunnels under Larch Wood and that hand-to-hand fighting was going on there. He was only able to put the two events together afterwards, recording them as facts but coupling them imaginatively in the poem. To emphasise the 'constructedness' of such a poem it is worth contrasting Blunden's concert party with one described by Sassoon:

Concert Party
(EGYPTIAN BASE CAMP)
They are gathering round ...
Out of the twilight; over the grey-blue sand,
Shoals of low-jargoning men drift inward to the sound –
The jangle and throb of a piano ... tum-ti-tum ...
Drawn by a lamp, they come
Out of the glimmering lines of their tents, over the shuffling sand.

O sing us the songs, the songs of our own land,
You warbling ladies in white.
Dimness conceals the hunger in our faces,
This wall of faces risen out of the night,
These eyes that keep their memories of the places
So long beyond their sight.

Jaded and gay, the ladies sing; and the chap in brown
Tilts his grey hat; jaunty and lean and pale,
He rattles the keys ... some actor-bloke from town ...
God send you home; and then A long, long trail;
I hear you calling me; and Dixieland ...
Sing slowly ... now the chorus ... one by one

We hear them, drink them; till the concert's done.
Silent, I watch the shadowy mass of soldiers stand.
Silent, they drift away, over the glimmering sand.

Kantara, April 1918[3]

The contrasts between this poem and Blunden's are so marked that students should need little prompting to identify them: the different settings, of course, the contrasting endings and the entirely different forms in which the two poems are written – how do Sassoon's irregular stanzas and rhyme scheme help to create a distinctive mood, different from Blunden's strict ballad form? It is particularly important for students to spot the different perspectives of the two speakers: Blunden's identifies himself throughout as one of the soldiers who have made up the audience ('We heard another matinée', etc.) while Sassoon's keeps aloof from the soldiers nearly throughout the poem ('Silent, I watch the shadowy mass of soldiers stand'). Even when he becomes one of the audience in stanza two ('the hunger in our faces') he immediately becomes the observer again: 'this wall of faces risen out of the night ... their eyes'. The reference to 'memories of the places / So far beyond their sight' suggests a powerful nostalgia, even a homesickness. This becomes the dominant emotion for the soldiers as they watch the performers, since this time, unlike the 'famous troop' (of soldiers) in Blunden's poem, the entertainers giving Sassoon's concert party are probably professionals: the ladies in white are probably real women, not soldiers in drag; it is likely that the man in brown really is 'some actor-bloke from town' who has come out to entertain the troops, and it is a shock to find that in the middle of the Egyptian desert London is still referred to simply as 'town', as if the speaker were a commuter from Surbiton rather than a soldier stationed near Alexandria. The music too is designed to reinforce this longing for homeland felt by those in exile. There is no word quite to describe this in English; the Welsh *hiraeth* has no English equivalent. 'The songs of our own land' such as 'I hear you calling me' are not the 'comically rich' entertainments that temporarily block out the reality of war in 'Concert Party: Busseboom'. And when the concert is over, the stage, the audience and the speaker himself are all reduced to silence:

> Silent, I watch the shadowy mass of soldiers stand.
> Silent, they drift away, over the glimmering sand.

....

These two poems in fact offer a powerful illustration of how two texts on the same subject can be so utterly different in theme, tone and technique: getting students to identify, to analyse and to articulate these differences is a valuable exercise in itself. It also reinforces the important message that war poetry is not confined to trench poetry.

Blunden and Sassoon both focus on the contrast between soldiers relaxing away from the fighting and the same soldiers facing the reality of war. They emphasise the fragility of such moments of relaxation and how it is this fragility which gives the moments their intensity. Exploring the ways in which writers, in prose as well as in poetry, convey this intensity can provide an important context for a discussion on the function of literature of the Great War today:

- Is this literature primarily of literary or historical significance in the 21st century?
- Has it over-emphasised the suffering of soldiers and the 'futility' of war?
- Does the continued fascination with the Great War in literature sentimentalise the experience of warfare by foregrounding its emotional and psychological impact on individual soldiers?

These questions need to be brought to the attention of students, and can be articulated by discussion of passages such as the following. The first, from *Undertones of War*, describes Blunden's experience on first reaching Busseboom (M Camp); the second, from Sebastian Faulks' *Birdsong*, enacts a scene in which Jack Firebrace (one of the central characters in the novel) leads the entertainment in an impromptu concert party:

> So we have come North. We did not expect this, ten days ago. It is midnight, with intense stars and darkness, and one has rarely felt the frost strike sharper (the ponderous journey scarcely having aided those bodies so long in the mud and gunning to repel the climate); but we have come North, and the ground is solid and clean. The battalion detrains at an unknown siding and its forerunners guide it in to unknown M Camp. I am warmed by the sight of my old confederate Sergeant Worley, in the exit of the siding; he gives his usual candid views on the situation, but is on the whole favourable to it; and we go along the cobbled road between level fields. Suddenly turning aside we find the Quartermaster and the Transport Officer, Swain and Maycock, who, stamping their feet, rejoice with me, and Maycock seizes my shoulders with gloved hand and pretends to dance. These invincible officers have a pleasant surprise for us, and, although it is midnight, there is soon a sound of revelry. In a large wooden tavern a cheerful Belgian girl, under the argus-eyed direction of a masculine mother, is soon running hither and thither among the veterans, from colonel to subaltern, with some of the best victuals ever known. Rave on, you savage east, and gloom, you small hours: we will take our ease in our inn, by the red-hot stoves. We have come through.
>
> (from *Undertones of War*, p.144)

The men loved the jokes, though they had heard each one before. Jack's manner was persuasive; few of them had seen the old stories so well delivered. Jack himself laughed little, but he was able to see the effect his performance had on his audience. The noise of their laughter roared like the sea in his ears. He wanted it louder and louder; he wanted them to drown out the war with their laughter. If they could shout loud enough, they might bring the world back to its senses; they might laugh loud enough to raise the dead. ...

Jack always ended with a song. It was odd how the cheapest, simplest things were the best; these were the ones that enabled the men to think of home, each in his own mind. He began to sing, 'If you were the only girl in the world'. His voice rose, and he waved his arms in invitation to the men to join with him. Relieved that his stories were finished, many added their voices to his.

Seeing their faces, once more friendly and approving, Jack was moved and encouraged. The features of his dead friend came back. Shaw had been, in this strange alternate life, the only person in the world to him: his handsome head with its level eyes, his muscular back and huge, broken-nailed fingers. Jack could almost feel the supple shape of Shaw's body as it had curved to accommodate him in the narrow, stinking dugouts where they had slept. The words of the foolish song began to choke him. He felt the eyes of the growing audience, friendly once more, boring into him. He looked out over their red, roaring faces as he had once before looked out when singing this same song. At that time he had told himself that he had no wish to love any of these men more than any other, knowing what lay in store for them. (from *Birdsong*, p.276)[4]

· · · · · · · · · · · · · · · · · · · ·

'Knowing what lay in store for them' is the theme that underpins both the poems and the prose passages: no matter how intense the temporary relief offered by the concert parties, the mood can only be temporary: for every soldier in the audience or in the tavern, it will soon be time to return to the trenches.

· · · · · · · · · · · · · · · · · · · ·

Having taken the discussion this far, and with these texts (two poems, two prose) in view, it is worthwhile to get students to start thinking about the questions they themselves would ask about what they have been reading: if good English teaching is about knowing what questions to ask, so often is good learning. Again, comparing and contrasting helps to get the process moving:

- In what ways does the passage from *Undertones of War* differ from the passage from *Birdsong*?
- What difference does it make that *Birdsong* was written by a novelist born after the Second World War, rather than by a poet who served as a frontline soldier during the First?
- Do the Blunden poem and prose passage illuminate each other in any way?
- Does the *Birdsong* passage strike you as an authentic reconstruction, or not?
- What is the effect of seeing the passage from the viewpoint of Jack Firebrace rather than that of a neutral observer (as in the Sassoon poem)?
- How far do these poems and passages alter your understanding of what is meant by 'the literature of the Great War'?

Memorialising the Great War: war memorials and war poetry

War memorials still arouse strong feelings. In August 2007, almost ninety years after the end of the Great War, a sign advertising the annual garden fete was propped against the modest war memorial of Ogbourne St Andrew, a tiny village in Wiltshire. It was a good spot to choose: the memorial stands at the junction where the lane into the village turns off from the main road. Lots of people would see it. But within an hour the sign had been ripped down and an outraged neighbour had scrawled across it, 'DISGRACEFUL. HAVE YOU NO RESPECT FOR THE DEAD?'

A miniature drama like this is a reminder of how war memorials these days, though mainly taken for granted, are yet invested with strong symbolic significance. They are part of the furniture of every town and village, only to be briefly the centre of attention once a year for those to whom Remembrance Sunday still means church parade and the laying of wreaths. For most people, much of the time, war memorials are not much more than objects of passing curiosity – if that. But tamper with them at your peril.

This itself is curious at a time when the Great War is probably more intensively studied at school, and the battlefields and cemeteries of the Western Front are more extensively visited than ever. The poetry of the First World War (or at least a very small amount of it) is religiously taught in schools and universities, where studying war poetry has come to be as much a rite of literary passage as studying Keats and Shelley used to be a century before.

It's possible to read (and to misread) war memorials in the same way as one can read the literature of war. And just as war poetry is now more frequently read than it used to be, so the memorials in France and Belgium – and, from the Second World War, in the Far East and Africa – are also more visited, more reflected upon, than in the past. On almost any day of the year now several coachloads of visitors from across Europe will come to attend the daily Last Post ceremony at the Menin Gate in Ypres or to inspect the Thiepval Memorial to the Missing of the Somme. At the latter, a new, enlarged car park has been provided and carefully landscaped to avoid impeding the view of the Memorial itself, and there is now a state-of-the-art Visitor Centre (2004) with exhibition space, shop and toilets all discreetly provided for the heritage tourist. But it wasn't always like this. In 1978, at the time of the 60th anniversary of the Armistice, such facilities were not merely not there, they were not even imagined.

In Sebastian Faulks' novel, *Birdsong*, a thirty-eight-year-old woman, Elizabeth Benson, who has been struck by an article commemorating that 60th anniversary, sets out in November 1978 to visit the battlefields of the Somme for the first time. Born in 1940, educated during the 1950s when the aftermath of the Second World

War had seemed so much more immediate, she is almost completely ignorant about the First World War, but finds she has developed what she calls 'a mild curiosity' about a past that, she suddenly realises, was for some still a living memory: 'Something about the war article had unsettled her: it seemed to touch an area of disquiet and curiosity that was connected to her own life and its choices.' (p.200) As she drives towards the town of Albert,

> Through the fields to her right Elizabeth saw a peculiar, ugly arch that sat among the crops and woods. She took it for a beet refinery at first, but then saw it was too big: it was made of brick or stone on a monumental scale. It was as though the Pantheon or the Arc de Triomphe had been dumped in a meadow ... From near to, the scale of the arch became apparent: it was supported on four vast columns; it overpowered the open landscape. The size of it was compounded by its brutal modern design; although clearly a memorial, it reminded her of Albert Speer's buildings for the Third Reich.
> (p.210)

This is the Thiepval Memorial, though Elizabeth does not recognise it (she has never heard of it) and Faulks does not identify it. Both the novelist and his protagonist have difficulty in describing the structure. The building looks nothing like the Pantheon and Elizabeth is wrong to describe the great central arch as supported on columns (later she calls them pillars); in fact it is supported on a set of smaller arches, but she is right when she talks about the 73,357 names of the Missing of the Somme inscribed on its walls

> from the level of her ankles to the height of the great arch itself; on every surface of every column as far as her eyes could see there were names teeming, reeling, over surfaces of yards, of hundreds of yards, over furlongs of stone ... She looked at the vault above her head and then around in panic at the endless writing, as though the surface of the sky had been papered in endless footnotes. (p.211)

This description ends with a self-consciously literary image, but at least the Thiepval Memorial had been an attempt to memorialise the footnotes of war, those soldiers who had simply disappeared off or under the face of the earth and who had no known grave. It was the last such memorial, completed in 1932, and controversial because of its design, its size and its cost. Questions of scale raised issues of sincerity: for the survivors, these memorials were hard to take.

When the Menin Gate, recording the names of the unburied dead who had fought around Ypres, Passchendaele and the Messines Ridge had been unveiled in 1927, Siegfried Sassoon was appalled:

> Who will remember, passing through this Gate,
> The unheroic Dead who fed the guns?
> Who shall absolve the foulness of their fate, –
> Those doomed, conscripted unvictorious ones?

('On Passing the New Menin Gate')

The two emphatic negatives here ('unheroic … unvictorious') challenge everything the Menin Gate as a memorial stands for. But Sassoon is unrelenting. In the sestet (the poem is a sonnet) he writes:

> Here was the world's worst wound. And here with pride
> 'Their name liveth for ever,' the Gateway claims.
> Was ever an immolation so belied
> As these intolerably nameless names?
> Well might the Dead who struggled in this slime
> Rise and deride this sepulchre of crime.

The biblical utterance, 'Their name liveth for evermore', prominent on the Menin Gate (as on thousands of other memorials) had been selected for the Commonwealth War Graves Commission by no less a person than Rudyard Kipling, and here Sassoon explicitly rejects what 'the Gateway claims'. Condemning the fighting around the 'sullen swamp' of the Ypres Salient as an 'immolation' – the word implies sacrifice as well as death by fire – Sassoon describes as 'intolerably nameless' the names of the Dead inscribed on the walls of the Gate, which in any case (monumental as it was) wasn't large enough for all the names to be included. In the war itself Sassoon had published his famous 'Soldier's Protest' on behalf of the ordinary, nameless soldiers still alive and fighting in the trenches. Here, though, with his further double negative ('intolerably nameless', the second word almost rhyming back to echo the previous double negative 'unheroic … unvictorious'), Sassoon now enters a protest on behalf of the Dead, invoking their resurrection to 'rise and deride this sepulchre of crime'. This is hardly the language of understatement; but, seen in the context of his earlier poems and protests, 'On Passing the New Menin Gate' justifies Sassoon's heightened rhetoric. The word 'Passing' from the title anticipates the alliteration that underscores the sonnet's second quatrain –

> Paid are its dim defenders by this pomp;
> Paid with a pile of peace-complacent stone …

– and the undertones in the sestet of Christ's death and burial ('the world's worst wound' … 'sepulchre') suggest that if the Menin Gate represents the payment of a debt then, Judas-like, it is a debt of dishonour paid by those who themselves had betrayed the Dead.

Right from the start of the Great War the problem, how best to memorialise the Dead, had preoccupied writers and artists no less than politicians and pundits: within months of the outbreak of hostilities, Laurence Binyon had written the lines that were to become part of the National Act of Remembrance ('They shall grow not old as we that are left grow old') and Rupert Brooke's 'The Soldier' was clearly a poem about how others should remember a soon-to-be-killed son or lover, the consolation the poem proposes being intended for those who will have to grieve for him, not for the soldier himself. Later on, Sassoon's poem 'The Hero' and Wilfred Owen's 'Anthem for Doomed Youth' would offer a very different slant on memorialising, and this tension between honouring heroic self-sacrifice and condemning the slaughter of the 'unheroic Dead' continued in the aftermath of the War. As early as 1919, the poet Charlotte Mew had published 'The Cenotaph' – a cenotaph is an empty tomb or monument erected in honour of someone buried elsewhere – which begins with all the sentimentalising imagery associated with the former (honouring) –

> Not yet will these measureless fields be green again
> Where only yesterday the wild sweet blood of wonderful youth was shed ...

– but soon develops quite a different tone, clearly identifying the poet's feelings with the latter (condemning):

> Only, when all is done and said,
> God is not mocked and neither are the dead.

Mew looks to the future and imagines war memorials standing ignored in market places all round the country as the daily commerce of life, of buying and selling, returns after the War to normal; and the poem ends starkly:

> Who'll sell, who'll buy
> (Will you or I
> Lie to each other with a better grace)?
> While looking into every busy whore's and huckster's face
> As they drive their bargains, is the Face
> Of God: and some young, piteous, murdered face.

Mew's anger, as summed up in that final phrase, anticipates Sassoon's. And Sassoon too found the Cenotaph ceremonies hard to take:

To-day we have remembered sacrifice and glory
And the Cenotaph with flowers is overstocked:
A single gun to soundlessness has clocked
And unified King, Communist, and Tory ...   ('To One in Prison')

Is such scepticism about the political posturing associated with Remembrance still appropriate (or *more* appropriate) today? Some of the questions that war memorials pose now, in a different century, may be different from those asked in the immediate aftermath of the Great War, but they still need answering. It is possible, indeed, to read a war memorial with the same scrutiny and to ask the same questions that need to be asked of a war poem.

The War Memorial in Cambridge (see page 260) stands awkwardly on a traffic island at a busy junction, where the road from the station meets one of the main roads into the city centre. The first question one wants to ask is, what is it doing there? Why isn't it in a more accessible, more appropriate spot? But its location is part of its point: literally and metaphorically it provides the context in which to read (*sc.* to interpret) the memorial. For this memorial is not primarily to the fallen at all, it is designed to celebrate the safe return of the living. The inscription on the plinth reads:

TO THE MEN OF CAMBRIDGESHIRE,
THE ISLE OF ELY, THE BOROUGH
AND UNIVERSITY OF CAMBRIDGE
WHO SERVED IN THE GREAT WAR
1914–1919

(As with so many Great War memorials, a further reference, to the Second World War, was added in 1946.)

On top of the plinth a victorious young soldier marches away from the station, heading towards the centre of the city. His stride is athletic, and this is not surprising since the artist who designed the statue, the Canadian R. Tait MacKenzie, was best known for his sculptures of athletes. (MacKenzie has signed his name in a prominent cartouche at the foot of the sculpture.) As the soldier heads purposefully towards his college (for he looks like a young undergraduate eager to resume his studies), he casts a final glance over his shoulder. His gaze is back towards the station, as if his thoughts are still with those friends and comrades who had set out from there with him for France, but had not returned. That is why the memorial is sited in this precise location: take it out of context, move it somewhere else, or look at it without knowing where it stands, and you cannot read it properly.

Figure 3: The return of the soldier (i): the Cambridge War Memorial, by the Canadian sculptor R. Tait MacKenzie

Figure 4: The return of the soldier (ii): the Trumpington War Memorial, by the English sculptor Eric Gill

The whole statue is a remarkable exercise in realism and symbolism: every detail of the soldier's uniform and kit is accurate and lifelike, down to the sharp creases on the sides (not the fronts) of his battledress trousers, and the slightly curling leather strap on his pack; but it is the imagery that counts: over his left shoulder his rifle is weighed down, not so much by the wreath of victory slung over its barrel as by the German helmet he carries home as spoils of war. The path he treads is strewn with roses, but his rear heel carefully avoids crushing them. He holds one in his right hand, given to him, one is to suppose, by a cheering girl lining the street from the station. In the same hand he holds his own helmet – and this is an interesting detail: in full marching order he should have been wearing his cap, but his helmet suggests he has come straight from the battlefield where he has left his fallen comrades; and it is to them that he gives a smart eyes-right, doffing his helmet as he does so. Finally, and all but invisible to the naked eye, etched onto the back of the helmet is a butterfly representing – what? the fragility of peace? the paradoxes of war? One of the most famous and powerful post-1918 images of the Great War is of a soldier's hand stretching out over the parapet of a trench, into No Man's Land, trying to catch a butterfly. It's the closing shot of the 1930 film of Erich Maria Remarque's novel, *All Quiet on the Western Front*. And it is an irony the original sculptor, Tait MacKenzie, cannot have intended, that whereas the German soldier is shot in the act of stretching to catch the butterfly, a butterfly is carried on the helmet of the victorious English soldier, returning from the trenches home to Cambridge.

It would be hard to imagine a greater contrast in style and image than between the Cambridge War Memorial and the Memorial in Trumpington, barely two miles away. This is the village of Chaucer's devious miller in *The Reeve's Tale*, and its War Memorial stands on the junction of the main road into Cambridge and the village street leading down to the mill. Unlike the Cambridge memorial, Trumpington's is explicitly Christian, in the form of a cross; explicitly it is for the fallen, whose names are engraved on the sides of the upright shaft, and explicitly it rejects any idea of celebrating a victorious return. Indeed, the soldier's return depicted in a panel beneath the names of the dead villagers (see page 261) is the precise antithesis of everything the Cambridge memorial celebrates. For Eric Gill, the distinguished sculptor of this memorial (though you will look in vain for his signature) has shown a soldier leaving the battlefield dejected and exhausted. Behind him a signpost marked W and E shows him heading homewards, while the battle continues all around: a shell explodes, trees are shattered. As on the Cambridge memorial, he carries his rifle over his shoulder, he has a helmet and a pack; but unlike MacKenzie's striding scholar-soldier, Gill's exhausted everyman – his shoulders slumped, eyes closed, face reduced to a blank mask – is so burdened by the weight of what he has endured that his elongated arm trails, like his trench coat, down towards the ground. Gill's soldier, represented in a strikingly modernist idiom, has in fact nothing in common with MacKenzie's realist hero. They might almost come from two different wars. At the very least, they articulate two entirely contrasting responses to the same war. And yet they are both pigeon-holed by the single generic term, 'war memorial'.

Comparing two such images of the returning soldier in this way highlights graphically the difference in meaning between these two neighbouring war memorials. A similar result can be achieved by contrasting two war poems, each (to judge from their titles) on the same subject:

In Memory of Wilfred Owen

I had half-forgotten among the soft blue waters
And the gay-fruited arbutus of the hill
Where never the nightingales are silent,
And the sunny hours are warm with honey and dew;

I had half-forgotten as the stars slid westward
Year after year in grave majestic order,
In the strivings and in the triumphs of manhood,
The world's voice, and the touch of beloved hands.

But I have never quite forgotten, never forgotten
All you who lie there so lonely, and never stir
When the hired buglers call unheeded to you,
Whom the sun shall never warm nor the frost chill.

Do you remember ... but why should you remember?
Have you not given all you had, to forget?
Oh, blessed, blessed be Death! They can no more vex you,
You for whom memory and forgetfulness are one.[5]

To W.O. and His Kind

If even you, so able and so keen,
And master of the business you reported
Seem now almost as though you had never been,
And in your simple purpose nearly thwarted,
What hope is there? What harvest from those hours
Deliberately, and in the name of truth,
Endured by you? Your witness moves no Powers,
And younger youth resents your sentient youth.

You would have stayed me with some parable,
The grain of mustard seed, the boy that thrust
His arm into the leaking dike to quell
The North Sea's onrush. Would you were not dust.
With you I might invent, and make men try,
Some genuine shelter from this frantic sky. [6]

Both poems name Wilfred Owen (W.O.) in their titles, both are written by poets who fought in, but survived, the Great War. The first is by Richard Aldington, originally one of the Imagist poets, who in 1931 (the year in which 'In Memory of Wilfred Owen' was published) was enjoying a strongly revived literary reputation because of two recent publications: his powerful anti-war novel, *Death of a Hero*, and a long romantic poem, *A Dream in the Luxembourg*. The second is by Edmund Blunden, the author of *Undertones of War*, whose reputation by 1939 (when 'To W.O. and his Kind' was published) had been considerably eclipsed: he was stigmatised as one of the now deeply unfashionable Georgian poets, he had been teaching abroad (in Japan) and so had been less in evidence in London literary circles; worst of all, his strongly pacifist leanings in the approach to the Second World War had led to his being labelled a pro-German appeaser.

These details are not simply background colour: they contextualise the two poems in important ways: the difference in date of publication is clearly significant: by 1939 Blunden's 'frantic sky' lowers over a very different world from Aldington's, where, in 1931, 'the stars slid westward / In grave majestic order'. Aldington's poem still looks back to the nightmare horrors of the First World War which the Dead have earned the right to forget, while Blunden's looks forward bleakly to the Second, dismayed that the warnings issued by Owen and others like him ('His Kind') about those horrors have been ignored. Aldington's speaker longs to be dead like those who were killed; Blunden's speaker wishes that Owen were still alive: 'Would you were not dust'.

Structurally the two poems are different: Aldington's consists of four quatrains, Blunden's appears to be a Shakespearean sonnet. The former seems to be unrhymed, the latter adopts the conventional rhyme scheme. But to make these bland statements is to underestimate both poems. Aldington's has internal rhymes barely hidden – 'sunny' / 'honey' in line 4 and, more significantly, 'blue' (the penultimate word of line 1) picked up by 'dew' at the end of the quatrain. The importance of this rhyme is that it anticipates the word 'you' which does not appear at all in stanzas 1 and 2 but occurs insistently no fewer than eight times in the last two stanzas: 'All you' indeed are those to whom the poem is addressed – the Fallen of the Great War. In fact, although the poem is sixteen lines in length it almost functions like a sonnet, with the first two stanzas (as it were, the octave) describing the post-war retreat into a self-indulgent, 'normal' life and the second half of the poem (like an extended sestet), introducing the counter view with the emphatic 'But' (line 9) as it turns its, and the reader's, attention to 'All you who lie there so lonely' – those left behind on the battlefields of France. This shift in perspective is further highlighted by the movement from the repeated 'half-forgotten' in stanzas 1 and 2 to the increasingly insistent 'never quite forgotten, never forgotten' of stanza 3 – a movement finally resolved in the last line of the poem when the question 'Do you remember?', quickly abandoned as inappropriate and absurd ('But why should you remember?'), is replaced by the concluding phrase, 'You for whom memory and forgetfulness are one.'

In Blunden's sonnet, the rhyme scheme is secure but the expected metrical form of iambic pentameter lines is constantly disrupted in the octave. This is most evident in lines 2 and 4, with its feminine rhymes (significantly, the words 'reported' / 'thwarted') but even the lines which appear to scan normally (3, 6, 7 and 8) actually have eleven syllables: what is outwardly normal is inwardly disturbed. This disruption is continued in the sestet, both the first and last lines having the additional syllable. Equally significant, in both parts of the sonnet, is the way Blunden varies the syntax to dramatic effect: in the octave, the main clause, 'What hope is there?' is deferred until the start of the second stanza, giving it a despairing tenor. This despair is accentuated by the speaker's acknowledging that the 'harvest', the apparently successful outcome of the Great War that might have made the war worth fighting and dying for, is now being squandered – in fact, the implication is, there turns out not to have been any harvest at all. The resentment of 'younger youth' towards the 'sentient youth' of Owen and 'his kind' (i.e. the poets of the Great War) only accentuates the speaker's feeling of isolation, of having no one left who speaks or thinks in the same way as he does. After all, it was Owen who had written in what was intended as the Preface to his collected war poems, 'All poets can do today is warn. That is why the true poets must be truthful.' It is significant that the word which disrupts the pentameter flow of the poem's final line (again, by inserting an eleventh syllable) is 'genuine'.

These two poems both single out Owen as the representative figure of the Great War, but it is important to note that Aldington's title does not claim that the poem is actually addressed to Owen himself, as Blunden's is. Aldington's poem is a meditation on the aftermath and implications of the War, memorialising Owen but nowhere addressing him: the addressees are 'All you', not just one man. On the other hand, Owen's poetry is clearly invoked. First, the 'hired buglers' ironically recall the line from 'Anthem for Doomed Youth' –

And bugles calling for them from sad shires.

Second, 'whom the sun shall never warm' recalls perhaps the most telling of all Owen's works, 'Futility', which begins by hoping that the 'kind old sun' might be able to revive a just-killed soldier ('Move him into the sun') but ends:

> O what made fatuous sunbeams toil
> To wake earth's sleep at all?

By contrast, Blunden's title appears to address multiple listeners ('His Kind') but actually speaks to Owen directly. Neither Aldington nor Blunden ever met Owen, but it is clear that, in their titles explicitly and in their poems indirectly or directly, each claims a kind of kinship with him.

Comparing these two poems in this way highlights their significant differences no less clearly than to compare the two war memorials of Cambridge and Trumpington, discussed above. Both memorials had as their central idea the return of the soldier, but treated the idea in diametrically opposite ways. So here, Aldington's speaker wishes that he could share the oblivion that Owen and all the fallen had earned by their deaths ('Have you not given all you had, to forget?'); Blunden wishes Owen were still alive so that his voice could still be listened to. In their different ways, therefore, these two poems acknowledge that what Owen wrote and what he had come to represent give his name a metonymic significance at the opposite extreme from Sassoon's 'intolerably nameless names' inscribed on the walls of the Menin Gate at Ypres.

The importance of retrieving and memorialising individual names to represent all the dead from the Great War is still stressed in the unvarying ritual at the Menin Gate. The nightly 'Last Post', accompanied by the reading-out of names from the Roll of Honour, has become for many essentially a tourist attraction ('Been there, done that'); however, the sight of great grandchildren, and now even great-great grandchildren or pupils from the former schools of those whose names are read out coming forward to lay wreaths is a telling way to insist that the names are not just names.

Writers, too, continue to wrestle with the problem of retrieving the individuals behind these names. Sebastian Faulks, in *Birdsong*, retrieves the dead *and* the living (including an ex-soldier who has lost his memory and been 'buried' for sixty years in a Star and Garter Home for old servicemen) and the short-story writer Christopher Arthur has dealt with this theme in 'The Menin Gate' (2006).[7] In this story a young man, Martyn Sharpe, gazes at his reflection in a window and sees staring back at him a face that is like but not like his own: it belongs to Jack Cade, a First World War soldier whose name he had recently seen on the walls of the Memorial in Ypres. In a series of meetings like this, Martyn and Jack each begin to share the experiences that the other has missed: Martyn, an aspiring historian, is anxious to discover what it was like to live, and more specifically to die, in the mud of Passchendaele; Jack is eager to know who won the War, what it is like to make love, and indeed where his body lies now:

> 'My body. What happened to it? You wouldn't have any idea, would you?
>> 'As I said, they never found it. That's why your name is on the Menin Gate.'
>> 'So it's still out there ... under all that mud?' Jack laughed.
>> 'Very likely, but it's not a swamp any more, Jack. A field with cows grazing in it, I expect.'
>> 'I rather like that,' mused Jack. 'Not that it really matters, of course. It's just a nice idea.'
>> They smiled at each other and, for a moment, did not speak.
>> 'Thanks, Mart,' said Jack, 'for putting me in the picture, about making love, I mean.'
>> 'I'm afraid nothing I can say is a patch on the real thing.'
>> 'It's better than dying,' replied the other.

The writing here, with its careful use of cliché ('putting me in the picture ... not a patch on the real thing', etc.) to emphasise that these experiences are only second-hand, effectively expresses the tentative, embarrassed friendship developing between these two young men meeting across time. Gradually, as the conversations continue, Martyn realises that it is himself he is talking to, that Jack Cade and Martyn Sharpe are the same person:

> Martyn found himself looking at the other face – the one he was more familiar with – but really it made no difference which one it was.

Memorials memorialise names, and it is part of their power that memorials like Thiepval and the Menin Gate contains more names than the eye or the mind can encompass. They are indeed the 'endless footnotes' papering the sky in Sebastian Faulks' *Birdsong*. In Arthur's story, the name Jack Cade had jumped out at Martyn because he recognised it as a name from history – Jack Cade, one of the rebel leaders in the Peasants' Revolt – but it has come to have a resonance that transcends a particular historical moment: it names a certain type of typical English Everyman, specifically a type of the indomitable English soldier, the 'poor bloody infantry' who are the cannon-fodder in every war. The poet Edward Thomas realised this, and in his poem 'Lob' (written during the First World War) explained:

> The man you saw – Lob-lie-by-the-fire, Jack Cade,
> Jack Smith, Jack Moon, poor Jack of every trade,
> Young Jack, or old Jack, or Jack what d'ye call,
> Jack-in-the-hedge, or Robin-run-by-the-wall,

Robin Hood, Ragged Robin, lazy Bob,
One of the lords of No Man's Land, good Lob,
Although he was seen dying at Waterloo,
Hastings, Agincourt, and Sedgemoor, too –
Lives yet.[8]

Christopher Arthur's story emphasises how the ongoing negotiation between past and present, dead and living, characterises the way the 20th century's defining ('Great') war continues to be a persistent object of curiosity. That the two most immediate points of focus for this curiosity – war memorials and war poetry – remain so ubiquitous and so contested is reason enough, it seems to me, for greater attention to be paid in teaching the Great War (its history, its literature, its art; above all, its persistence in memory) to the relationship between them.

....

- Charlotte Mew's poem 'The Cenotaph' can most easily be found in Catherine Reilly's defining anthology of women's writing from the Great War *Scars Upon My Heart* (Virago, 1981).
- Siegfried Sassoon's poem 'On Passing the New Menin Gate' was first published in *The Heart's Journey* (Heinemann, 1928), a collection of his post-war poetry.
- Edmund Blunden's poem 'To W.O. and his Kind' appears in *Overtones of War* (Duckworth 1996), a complete and annotated edition of Blunden's poetry edited by Martin Taylor.
- Richard Aldington's poem 'In Memory of Wilfred Owen' was published in his *Complete Poems* (Wingate, 1948), long out of print.

All these poems can be found in Adrian Barlow *The Great War in British Literature* (Cambridge University Press, 2000). Those by Mew, Sassoon and Blunden can also be readily accessed on the Internet.

- Sebastian Faulks' novel *Birdsong*, first published by Hutchinson in 1993, is published in paperback by Vintage.
- Christopher Arthur's 'The Menin Gate', appears in his collection of short stories, *Cappadocian Moon* (Melrose, 2006).
- For discussion of war memorials, see the following:
  Geoff Dyer *The Missing of the Somme* (Weidenfeld and Nicolson, new ed. 2001)
  Gavin Stamp *The Memorial to the Missing of the Somme* (Profile, 2007)
  Jay Winter *Sites of Memory, Sites of Mourning* (Cambridge University Press, 1998).

Unusual contexts – tsunamis, hangings and the Holocaust: Barnes, Lamb, Aldington and Levi

Current events sometimes offer themselves as prompts for teaching literature: the unexpected fall of an over-ambitious politician provides illustrations of *hubris* and *nemesis*. Sometimes literature itself becomes a current event, as when Monica Ali's novel *Brick Lane* is hailed by the critics, becomes a bestseller, but is then condemned by members of the Bangladeshi community of Brick Lane itself for what they claim is an insulting portrait of their community. Or when Turkey's leading novelist, Orhan Pamuk, writes a novel, *Snow*, deeply critical of the social, religious and political situation in his own country; is controversially awarded the Nobel Prize for Literature, and eventually – after death threats and the assassination of one of his close friends – is forced into exile in America.

Discussing with students literature in the news is always worthwhile. In fact it is important, putting into context the very question of why literature matters in the modern world: the hype surrounding book prizes; the debate over whether this or that author (Graham Swift with *Last Orders* or Ian McEwan with *Atonement*) was or was not guilty of plagiarism; non-stories such as whether Martin Amis is or is not 'England's greatest living author' – all of these raise important questions which expand students' awareness of what literature is and what value society places upon it.

Sometimes, too, a news item not apparently related to literature will provoke discussion which may best be answered by finding literary parallels or examples. English teachers become experts in handling difficult subjects. Here are two contrasting illustrations, the first provoked by the devastating tsunami which struck on Boxing Day 2004 and the second by the grim films (both official and unofficial) of the hanging of Saddam Hussein on 30th December 2006.

The tsunami and its aftermath are used here as prompts for *A History of the World in 10½ Chapters* (1989) by Julian Barnes, including:

- a detailed re-reading of the novel
- an examination of how a single defining image, Noah's Ark, can resonate throughout a book
- a discussion, based on an analysis of the register and tone of different passages, of how what is apparently comic can have unsettling and ultimately horrific undertones and how, as readers, we have to be alert to listen for these undertones
- a debate about how far it is appropriate to use modern events as contexts for revisiting earlier texts.

Worm's eye view: *A History of the World in 10½ Chapters*

A family is enjoying a seaside holiday. The mother goes along the beach to buy ice cream for her children and is swept away by a giant wave. Thousands of miles across the Indian Ocean, the same wave carries out to sea a man who clings for eight days to the branches of a tree which becomes his floating home. He survives by catching coconuts that float past him, along with the corpses and flotsam that accompany his voyage. Another couple of days, and fishermen returning to their village discover that their fishing boats have been beached hundreds of yards inland, beyond hope of ever putting out to sea again. Two weeks later, an elderly man flies back to London's Heathrow Airport after a Christmas holiday and is disgruntled that none of his family is there to meet him. They had all assumed he'd been killed by the tsunami.

Sometimes events in history change forever the way we read literary texts. I think it will be difficult in future to pick up Julian Barnes' *A History of the World in 10½ Chapters* without reading it in the context of the Asian tsunami that caused such devastation on Boxing Day 2004. The Internet is still full of survivors' accounts. It is striking how many said that they expected to see Noah's Ark floating by at any moment. It is as if the survivors needed that myth of the flood to enable them to make sense of what had happened. As Barnes himself comments, 'The point is this …'

> not that myth refers us back to some original event which has been fancifully transcribed as it passed through the collective memory; but that it refers us forward to something that will happen; that must happen. Myth will become reality, however sceptical we might be. (p.181)[9]

One purpose of the Noah's Ark chapter that launches *A History of the World* is to challenge the established Bible history of the Flood by giving a (wood)worm's eye view of events and to show how partial and inadequate is official History's presentation of the facts. 'History isn't what happened. History is just what historians tell us' (p.242). Even the title of the book makes this point: it is *A* History, not *The* History. And Barnes shows, through all the different subjective narratives that go to make up his novel, that how you see events depends on where you are standing. Far from being the hero of the woodworm's story, Noah, the man chosen (according to Genesis) by God to save the human race and the animal kingdom, was an incompetent fool with a dysfunctional family. Incidentally he was also responsible for the loss of several species that have passed into myth – the behemoth, for instance, and the unicorn ('the Noahs had him casseroled one Embarkation Sunday'). Noah simply wasn't up to the job.

That at least is the way the worm tells it.

So far, so amusing: for many critics, when *A History of the World* was first published in 1989, the first chapter was the best. It followed in a long tradition of literary debunking of Noah, going back to the medieval mystery plays in which he was presented as a drunken henpecked husband. But underneath its cheerful iconoclasm the woodworm's narrative sounds a more sinister note. At first you don't notice it:

> As far as we were concerned the whole business of the Voyage began when
> we were invited to report to a certain place by a certain time. This was
> the first we heard of the scheme. We didn't know anything of the political
> background. (p.6)

But only a page later, you start to feel uneasily that the description of the selection and transporting of the animals prefigures something only too familiar:

> There were families which refused to be separated from their offspring and
> chose to die together; there were medical inspections, often of a brutally
> intrusive nature; and all night long the air outside Noah's stockade was heavy
> with the wailing of the rejected. (p.7)

The literary technique that Barnes uses here is *prolepsis*, a rhetorical device for treating an event in the future as if it has already happened. His description of the behaviour of the animals and the way in which they are abused anticipates all the forced migrations that will feature in later history. In particular, of course, it anticipates the treatment of the Jews in the Shoah (the Hebrew name for the Holocaust). Familiar as we now are with the forced transport during the Second World War of Jews across Europe to Auschwitz and the other death camps, it's hard to miss the connection between the way the woodworm describes the panic among the animals and the feelings of the Jews being herded *like animals* onto the cattle trucks that would transport them to their deaths. When the worm comments that 'At times we suspected a kind of system behind the killing that went on ... [we] began to suspect that Noah and his tribe had it in for certain animals simply for being what they were' (p.14), we know that he is speaking in the same terms that politicians inside and outside Germany afterwards used to explain away their failure to stand out against the persecution of the Jews. 'I can see,' he says, 'there might be a positive side to this wilful averting of the eye: ignoring the bad things makes it easier for you to carry on' (p.29).

But for whom is the worm speaking? For himself, as one of the prospective victims of this persecution? As one of those who found it convenient to turn a blind eye to what was going on? Or on behalf of the dead, as a witness to the systematic killing that took place? Besides, can we trust the worm any more than the author of Genesis? After all, though he talks proudly of 'those of us who made the Voyage on the Ark', he claims there was actually a small flotilla of arks and admits that some of what he describes happened on the other boats. He wasn't there himself. Then again, he is clearly addressing us as modern readers: 'I gather that one of your early Hebrew legends asserts that Noah discovered the principle of intoxication by watching a goat get drunk on fermented grapes' (p.29). As a narrator, the woodworm is just as elusive as he was when a stowaway. He needs watching.

These links with Holocaust history are made explicit when in the third of the 'Three Simple Stories' in *A History of the World* (Chapter 7), Barnes describes the abortive voyage of the liner *St Louis*, a 20th-century ark with its cargo of Jewish refugees whom the free countries on either side of the Atlantic hypocritically disdain to accept.

Alone of all the narratives in *A History of the World*, this one is written as if by an impartial anonymous historian, an objective narrator marshalling his facts and drawing inevitable conclusions. It is the most shocking and most powerful story in the whole book. Its anger comes from the manner of its telling and from its inescapable Biblical echoes:

> In Antwerp [NB in Belgium, not yet occupied by Germany – this is before the outbreak of war] a pro-Nazi youth organisation had distributed handbills bearing the slogan: 'We too want to help the Jews. If they call at our offices each will receive gratis a length of rope and a long nail.' The passengers were disembarked. Those admitted to Belgium were put on a train whose doors were locked and windows nailed shut; they were told that such measures were necessary for their own protection ... On Wednesday 21st June the British contingent from *St Louis* docked at Southampton. They were able to reflect that their wanderings at sea had lasted precisely forty days and forty nights. (p.188)

Two echoes are worth picking up here. First, 'Forty days and forty nights' recalls the length of time Jesus spent in the wilderness; the additional word 'wanderings' echoes the Old Testament wanderings of the Jews in the wilderness searching for the promised land. Second, the contemptuous offer to give the Jews 'gratis a length of rope' reminds us of Gratiano's outburst at Shylock's trial in *The Merchant of Venice*. When Portia is about to pronounce judgement against Shylock, she asks the Merchant, Antonio, 'What mercy can you render him?' Before Antonio can answer, Gratiano (who has already called out from the gallery, 'Beg that thou mayest have leave to hang thyself') butts in again:

> A halter gratis – nothing else for God's sake. (IV.i.374)

Like the young Nazis of pre-war Antwerp, Gratiano believes that the best thing a Jew can do is literally 'go hang'.

So Noah's Ark, in Julian Barnes' novel, resonates through history. It continues to do so. After Prince Harry, while training to become an army officer, caused offence by dressing up in Nazi uniform at a fancy dress party, his father apparently made him watch the Stephen Spielberg film *Schindler's List* (1993). This film, about Jews being rescued from the Holocaust by a modern-day Noah called Oscar Schindler, was based on a novel by the Australian writer Thomas Keneally. The novel's title? *Schindler's Ark*.

And in the wake of the 2004 disaster, a Jewish Charity, Nechama, set up a project to build fishing boats for families in India, Sri Lanka and Africa whose boats had been destroyed by the tsunami floods. The project's name? *Operation Noah's Ark*.

Many a good hanging?

One way in which the Internet has radically changed the way that teachers can teach and students can learn is by making available news events, and increasingly film and video evidence of news events, long after they have disappeared from the front – or even the back – pages of the papers. This can have good and less good consequences: it will continue to be possible for students to access information about the tsunami, as if it had happened only last week; it will also be possible for children to watch the appalling unofficial film of the hanging of Saddam Hussein. It is as if the age of public execution has returned with a vengeance.

The following discussion begins with Shakespeare and ends, like the discussion of the tsunami above, with the Holocaust:

* tracing the way that imagery of hanging appears in the writing of three very different writers: Charles Lamb, Richard Aldington and Primo Levi
* placing this recurring image in both a psychological as well as a literary context
* illustrating links between texts and writers, offering opportunities for discussion with students and research into the difference between intertextuality and allusion
* identifying and highlighting the importance of intertextuality as a literary strategy.

....

'Many a good hanging prevents a bad marriage,' jokes Feste the Jester in Shakespeare's *Twelfth Night*. But hanging is no joking matter, nor does Shakespeare use it as such: in *Henry V*, the discovery that the King has hanged his old drinking companion Bardolph 'for stealing of a pyx' – looting from a church – shocks his friends, and perhaps the audience. The discovery by a distraught Lear at the end of *King Lear* that his daughter Cordelia has been executed ('My poor fool is hanged') breaks his heart; and the sight of the dying king carrying the corpse of his daughter, whom he has just cut down from the gallows, is perhaps the most shattering climax of any Shakespeare play.

Images of the noose, and of the hanged man or woman, resonate powerfully through literature. The execution of Tess is the climax of *Tess of the d'Urbervilles*; Coleridge's Ancient Mariner is condemned to live with the dead albatross hanging around his neck like a grotesque noose; Herman Melville's Billy Budd, the innocent ship's boy, is hanged from the yard arm, and (Thomas Hardy again) Jude's children hang themselves on the back of a door, leaving behind the most pathetic suicide note in literature: 'Done because we are too menny [*sic*].'

The Ancient Mariner is eventually reprieved, the removing of the albatross from his neck like being cut down from the gallows in the nick of time. But he is condemned to go through the rest of his life feeling guilt for his crime and forced continually to tell his story to anyone who will listen.

Whether or not the Mariner is actually 'guilty', he finds himself an outcast, rejected and cursed. This sense of being utterly abandoned, this concept of the soul in agony, exactly matches the experience and the vocabulary of writers who themselves have been survivors of traumatic events and have lived to become victims of what is now understood as traumatic stress (PTSD – post traumatic stress disorder); the ambiguous attitude of survivors towards their very survival becomes a crucial factor both in their lives and in their writing: the idea that that they should not have survived; the sense that, in terms of psychological damage and loss of personality, they did die, and that their survival is no more than a passport to a form of living death – these archetypal responses have a prominent place in the literary treatment of post-traumatic stress.

Eventually, in Coleridge's poem, the Ancient Mariner's ship is blown back to his home port, only to sink at the harbour entrance. The Ancient Mariner is rescued by a boat containing a pilot and a hermit, to whom the wretched man is able to confess – the first time he has been able to speak to anyone about the horrors he has experienced:

> Forthwith this frame of mine was wrenched
> With a woful agony,
> Which forced me to begin my tale;
> And then it left me free.
>
> Since then, at an uncertain hour,
> That agony returns:
> And till my ghastly tale is told,
> This heart within me burns.

These are stanzas we shall meet again later: Coleridge makes his victim speak twice of his 'agony' – a word used to denote extreme pain, and one which the poet would not have used lightly. It is this pain which forces the Mariner to seek relief by telling his story, and until he finds the right listener his heart 'burns' within him. The imagery here – agony, burning – surely suggests nothing less than a soul in torment, and when we bear in mind that Coleridge describes the Mariner's tale as 'ghastly' (that is, not only horrific but literally ghost-like), we see how carefully he locates the sufferer's experience in an ambiguous world, one hovering between guilt and innocence, life and death, belief and incredulity, reality and nightmare. And this is precisely the world inhabited by the victims of traumatic stress.

An early critic of *The Ancient Mariner* perceptively commented that the Mariner 'undergoes such trials, as overwhelm and bury all individuality or memory of what he was. – Like the state of a man in a bad dream, one terrible peculiarity of which is that all consciousness of personality is gone.' This critic was Charles Lamb, writing to Wordsworth on 30 January 1801, and he is the first of the three writers I want to consider in some detail.

Lamb was an important figure in the early Romantic movement in England: a close friend of Wordsworth as well as Coleridge, he was an influential critic and essayist, as well as being a poet and playwright. To many people he is remembered for his *Essays of Elia,* but more will have heard of *Lamb's Tales from Shakespeare,* which he wrote with his sister, Mary. It is through Mary, in fact, that Lamb features in our discussion, for on 22 September 1796, he witnessed his sister murder their mother in a fit of insanity. He was twenty-one at the time. Five days after this tragedy, Lamb was able to give a brief outline of the events in a letter to Coleridge:

> My dearest friend – ... some of my friends, or the public papers, by this time may have informed you of the terrible calamities that have fallen on our family. I will give you only the outlines: My poor, dear, dearest sister, in a fit of insanity, has been the death of her own mother. I was at hand only time enough to snatch the knife out of her grasp. She is at present in a madhouse, from whence I fear she must be moved to an hospital ... My poor father was slightly wounded, and I am left to take care of him and my aunt ... but, thank God, I am very calm and composed, and able to do the best that remains to do. Write as religious a letter as possible, but no mention of what is gone and done with. With me, 'the former things are passed away,' and I have something more to do than to feel ... Mention nothing of poetry. I have destroyed every vestige of past vanities of that kind.

As this letter indicates, Lamb reacted with remarkable calmness to the catastrophe that overwhelmed his family. Indeed, he so impressed the Coroner and Magistrates with his maturity that he was entrusted with the future care and supervision of

Mary, thereby saving her from a lifetime in Bedlam. His subsequent life, both as a writer with an impressive reputation for wit and critical insight, and as a generous friend, might suggest that he had not suffered any long-term after-effects from the family tragedy of which his sister's presence was a daily reminder. And yet he expresses in his writing many of the classic symptoms of post-traumatic stress. These, for him, included a sense of shame, an awareness of the severance that had occurred between his past and present life, a feeling above all of being separated, cut off from his friends and rejected by society at large: 'we are in a manner marked', he wrote to Coleridge in 1800, referring to himself and Mary, and this sense of being 'marked' by events for which he was not responsible but for which he had to bear the burden is strongly present in his writing over the next twenty years.

It is significant that in the letter to Coleridge quoted above, Lamb is already showing an awareness that he has been rudely divorced from his former self, by telling his friend that he has destroyed everything he had written before the traumatic event. Equally significant is a famous poem, 'The Old Familiar Faces', written two years later in which he articulates most movingly his sense of having been abandoned by the world and by his friends.

This poem begins with the line, 'Where are they gone, the old familiar faces?' which provides the refrain for each successive stanza, and implies at once the anguish that the speaker feels, left alone in a world emptied of friends and companions. The first stanza confronts at once the central traumatic event: 'I had a mother, but she died and left me … in a day of horrors.' From this initial separation (and one notices, too, the sense of rejection: 'she died and left me') follow all the subsequent rejections. Friends from childhood and adulthood – 'all, all are gone'. The fourth stanza recalls his rejection by the woman he had hoped to marry, and the inference is clear that his family tragedy is the cause: 'closed are her doors to me, I must not see her'.

Significantly, the only stanza in the poem to contain simile and metaphor is the sixth, which attempts to dramatise his sense of rejection and severance:

> Ghost-like, I paced round the haunts of my childhood.
> Earth seem'd a desert I was bound to traverse,
> Seeking to find the old familiar faces.

Here, by likening himself to a ghost, Lamb introduces the same image of Life-in-Death, which we saw in *The Rime of the Ancient Mariner,* and in the second line there is also the image of the wanderer, the outcast forced like Orestes into exile, 'bound to traverse' the desert that his life has become.

'The Old Familiar Faces' was written only fifteen months after the death of his mother, but for the rest of his creative life Lamb was to betray the same or additional symptoms in his writing, notably by returning often to the themes of rejection and shame arising from unfair disgrace. In a play, for example, written as late as 1825, *The Pawnbroker's Daughter,* Lamb creates a hero who is unfairly convicted of a felony, and who is only reprieved at the last moment – indeed, he has actually to be cut down from the gallows, and so is permanently marked by the rope that nearly killed him.

It is hard to imagine a more potent image of undeserved shame than that of the hanged man who lives to bear the mark of the rope. Critics have noted that this image recurs frequently in Lamb's work; but the hanged man also features in the writings of other victims of traumatic stress. In Lamb's case, there was a clear trigger for this image. Dr Jane Aaron, discussing 'Images of Damnation in Charles Lamb's Writings' has commented:

> Protracted existence after the repeal of a death sentence is a theme which had a strong morbid fascination for Lamb. One reason for his obsession lies, perhaps, in the fact that no atonement of a life for a life was made at his mother's death. He and Mary are both 'marked' as with the hangman's rope, in that both were spared the crudest consequence of Mary's act, but both must continue to live on bearing its social and psychological stigma.[10]

At the end of this play, *The Pawnbroker's Daughter,* the hero finally achieves happiness when the heroine accepts him, and he is, as it were, socially redeemed. No such redemption had been evident, however, in Lamb's famous essay of 1810, 'On the Inconveniences Arising from Being Hanged'. The title suggests a certain irony or humour will underlie this work, as indeed it does; but the essay describes all the familiar features of the landscape of suffering experienced by a man who, like the hero of the play, has been cut down from the gallows when his reprieve comes through at the very last moment: the victim complains that, even though cleared of all guilt:

> In a short time, I found myself deserted by most of those who had been my intimate friends, cut off from all respectable connections, rejected by the fairer half of the community ... punished because I was once punished unjustly; suffering for no other reason than because I once had the misfortune to suffer without any cause at all.

For Lamb, the very image of hanging is sufficient to remind him that it is the most degrading form of death, reducing the hanged man to a figure of contempt 'condemned to dance ... upon nothing ... whisking and wavering in the air ... like a weathercock, serving to show from which point the wind blows'. With a bitterness one rarely encounters in his work, Lamb concludes, 'We string up dogs, foxes, bats, moles, weasels. Man surely deserves a steadier death.'

Lamb's original traumatic experience occupied no more than a moment or two, but its effects stayed with him for the rest of his life. It is more common, perhaps, to consider traumatic stress when it follows exposure to a prolonged nightmare such as war. The poet Richard Aldington, for instance, fought in France during the First World War and his poetry, short stories and novels illustrate in an almost classic form the stages of post-traumatic stress experienced by many war veterans. Aldington, who was twenty-two when the war began, had already established a reputation as an innovative poet and critic, a protégé of Ezra Pound and a rising figure in the literary movement known as Imagism. He enlisted in 1916 and served in France, writing a number of war poems that are still widely anthologised, but his reputation today mainly rests on his novels, especially *Death of a Hero* (one of the first and most important works of fiction to deal with the Great War), and on his biographies, notably of D.H. Lawrence and of Lawrence of Arabia.

Aldington survived the war without being seriously wounded physically but he was (in the convenient phrase of the time) shell-shocked. His marriage did not survive the war, and after demobilisation he withdrew from literary life in London to live in seclusion, first in the country and ultimately abroad. His outward symptoms of traumatic stress were predictable enough: he suffered acutely from nightmares and sleeplessness, and for several years reacted instinctively whenever any sight or sound reminded him of the trenches. He dreaded, for example, travelling in a train as it entered a tunnel, for the sound reminded him of the firing of shells. He found it very hard to come to terms with having survived the war, and once wrote to a friend, 'Somehow, I have never recovered from those war years – it was too long, and I still think it would have been better to have stopped a bullet in 1916 than to struggle on with a shattered life.'

More vividly than any other English writer who had actually survived the war, Richard Aldington exposed the inner turmoil of traumatic stress in his post-war writing, first in poetry and then, from 1929 onwards, in his short stories and novels. Two examples will illustrate how, in the words of Anthony Burgess, Aldington 'dared to transform his suffering into art'.

A 1930 short story, 'The Case of Lieutenant Hall', presents a young survivor in the spring of 1919, unable to come to terms with peace at all. He is haunted by the image of a German soldier whom he had killed with a bayonet. In his diary he writes:

I should be happy if it were not that the murdered German – the bayoneted one – seems never to leave me now. I caught him gazing at me over the dinner table last night. The others were amazed because I jumped out of my chair, and yelled: 'Go away! Go away! Don't torture me!'[11]

The parallel with Macbeth, disturbed at his feast by the murdered Banquo's ghost and crying out 'Never shake thy gory locks at me!' is inescapable. Like the guilty Macbeth, the young man is unable to sleep, and the last entry in his diary reads:

> I've had no sleep for three nights now. Every time I fall into a doze the German comes and presses his decaying face against mine. God in hell, it's horrible! I can't stand it.

Pursued to the end of his tether by this ghastly image, Lieutenant Hall finally commits suicide, rejoining at last those he describes as 'the lucky ones', the men who had actually died on the battlefield. What made the image of the dead German so unendurable for Hall was not only the physical revulsion, but the acute sense of shame and horror he felt at having killed a man in order that he himself should survive. The irony of being commended for his bravery and awarded the Military Cross for this deed, only makes his sense of guilt worse.

One of Aldington's most powerful and moving poems was published in 1923 in a collection significantly entitled *Exile*. It is a very personal poem: a confession of his failure to come to terms with life after the war, and an analysis of precisely how his life has been shattered. Borrowing the title from Aeschylus, he calls the poem 'Eumenides' and begins with sleeplessness:

> I do not need the ticking of my watch
> To tell me I am mortal;
> I have lived with, fed upon death
> As happier generations feed on life;
> My very mind seems gangrened.[12]

He asks, 'Have I not striven and striven for health?' and goes over all the steps he has taken to recover his former equilibrium, but he admits that his efforts have failed:

> I lie awake staring with sleepless eyes,
> And what is my mind's sickness,
> What the agony I struggle with,
> I can hardly tell.

Immediately, images from the war flood his mind ('the thousand images I see / And struggle with and cannot kill') and he describes these images as resembling the Eumenides, the avenging Furies that had pursued Orestes and who now haunt him as they haunt millions of others who fought in the war. Aldington is quite clear that this is a form of life-in-death experience; and contrasting his own mental agony with the peace of mind achieved by those who actually died, he asks:

What is it I agonise for?
The dead? They are quiet;
They can have no complaint.
No, it is my own murdered self –
A self which had its passion for beauty,
Some moment's touch with immortality –
Violently slain, which rises up like a ghost
To torment my nights,
To pain me.
It is myself that is the Eumenides,
That will not be appeased, about my bed;
It is the wrong that has been done me
Which none has atoned for, none repented of,
Which rises before me, demanding atonement.

This idea of the murdered self, the outraged victim who in a sense died even as he survived, is a crucial one. Like Charles Lamb's innocent victim marked by the rope of the noose from which he had just escaped, Aldington's murdered self demands atonement for the 'wrong' that has been done him. His real personality has, he maintains, been destroyed by the trauma of the war; and I think it can be fairly said that all of Aldington's writing in the decade following the war was an attempt to come to terms with this need for atonement, to try to supply an answer to the question that ends 'Eumenides':

Tell me, what answer shall I give my murdered self?

The search for that answer is complicated by Aldington's sense of guilt at having survived at all while others died. In a second poem from the *Exile* volume, 'In the Palace Garden' he describes how his mood changes from relief and optimism ('I was happy. / It was enough not to be dead') to guilt and shame:

And I was whispering:
'This happiness is not yours;
It is stolen from other men.
Coward! You have shirked your fate.'[13]

The tortured consciousness of having survived because others died is an obsession in Aldington's prose work as well as in his poetry. In *Death of a Hero*, he quotes against himself an imagined accusation, 'You have a vendetta of the dead against the living', and he answers, 'Yes, it is true, I have a vendetta … When I meet an unmaimed man of my generation, I want to shout at him: How did you escape?

How did you dodge it? What dirty trick did you play? It is dreadful to have outlived your life, to have shirked your fate, to have overspent your welcome.'

These were the stresses that Aldington the man, the traumatised soldier, had to confront. As a poet and novelist he resolved them by enacting the atonement he felt his 'murdered self' demanded. First, in *Death of a Hero*, the central character, clearly modelled on Aldington himself, deliberately gets himself killed while fighting in one of the final engagements of the war. It is not, however, a premeditated suicide: 'Something seemed to break in Winterbourne's head. He felt he was going mad and sprang to his feet. The line of bullets smashed across his chest ...'. Second, in what is perhaps the key poem of the *Exile* volume, 'Epitaph in Ballade Form', Aldington adopts the persona of the celebrated French brigand, Francois Villon, about to die on the gallows for his crimes. The words of the condemned man, in Aldington's mouth, become a moving testament uttered on behalf of all those who feel themselves guilty for having survived the war:

> As to our flesh, which we fed wantonly,
> Rotten, devoured, it hangeth mournfully;
> And we, the bones, to dust and ash are riven,
> Let none make scorn of our infirmity,
> But pray to God that all we be forgiven.[14]

The image of the hanged man is here once again used to evoke the sense of shame and guilt. Charles Lamb had complained at the excessive humiliation of hanging; for Aldington, the body swinging in the wind is to be pitied because right up to the moment of death it is allowed no peace:

> Never rest comes to us in any wise;
> Now here, now there, as the wind sways, sway we;
> Swung at the wind's high pleasure ceaselessly.

Both Lamb and Aldington had begun to write before their traumatic experiences overwhelmed their lives: by contrast, Primo Levi, the distinguished Italian writer, took up his pen as a direct result of what had happened to him. Levi was by profession a chemist, but is now recognised as one of the most important writers about the Holocaust. His writing has its root in his experience of imprisonment in Auschwitz, from 1944 until the end of the Second World War. His own explanation of why he turned to writing is startling enough:

> The things I had seen and suffered were burning inside me: I felt closer to
> the dead than the living, and felt guilty at being a man because men had
> built Auschwitz and Auschwitz had gulped down millions of human beings

> ... It seemed to me that I would be purified if I told its story, and I felt like Coleridge's Ancient Mariner, who waylays on the street the wedding guests going to the feast, inflicting on them the story of his misfortune ... by writing I found peace for a while and felt myself become a man again, a person like everyone else, neither a martyr nor debased nor a saint: one of those people who form a family and look to the future rather than the past.[15]

Telling the story was to be an act of purification, as well as a form of therapy. It is important to understand this idea that the victim of a traumatic experience may believe he can actually cleanse himself by telling his story, for like Lady Macbeth frantically rubbing her hands in her sleepwalking, he may continually be asking himself 'will these hands ne'er be clean?' In this respect, therefore, telling the story is more than simple therapy. Richard Aldington said in his memoirs, 'By writing *Death of a Hero* I purged my bosom of perilous stuff that had been poisoning me for a decade', and this need to be purged and purified is an urgent one. Primo Levi identifies himself with the Ancient Mariner, and we recall that it was only after the Mariner had confessed and been shriven by the hermit that he felt his 'dreadful agony' subside.

Levi's first book, *If This is a Man,* was an account of his experiences in Auschwitz but it should not be read as an historical record. To begin with, it is written in the present tense; secondly, Levi deliberately isolates ('foregrounds' in today's literary jargon) certain representative or specially significant events and characters. He does not apologise for this; on the contrary, he insists that 'the tendency to round out the facts or heighten the colours ... is an integral part of writing, without it one does not write stories, but rather accounts'.

Early in the book he describes a frequently recurring dream in which he is back at home among his friends and family telling them the story of his experiences in the camp. 'It is,' he says, 'an intense pleasure, physically inexpressible, to be at home, among friendly people, and to have so many things to recount: but I cannot help noticing that my listeners do not follow me. In fact, they are completely indifferent: they speak confusedly of other things among themselves, as if I was not there. My sister looks at me, gets up and goes away without a word.' When he wakes from this dream, he remembers that it is a dream he has often had before, and when he tells a friend in the camp about it, he is surprised to find that not only has this friend had an identical dream, but that it is shared by many of the other prisoners.

Here we see two by now very familiar features: first, the compulsive need to tell his story, and the relief – described here as an 'intense pleasure' – at doing so; second, the shock followed by what he calls 'a desolating grief' at finding no one is interested in his story, and, indeed, that those closest to him (the 'old familiar faces' of Charles Lamb) turn their backs on him. Remarkably, after his liberation, when he was making his way back to Italy, Levi experienced in reality precisely the situation he had dreamed about: 'I had dreamed,' he was to write in *The Truce,* 'something like this, in the nights at Auschwitz: of speaking and not being listened to, of finding liberty and remaining alone.'

The other obsessive dream that preoccupies Levi is one that only starts to haunt him after his liberation. It is perhaps best summed up in his poem 'The Survivor' which begins with the verse from Coleridge's Ancient Mariner – 'until the ghastly tale is told / This heart within me burns'. The speaker in the poem, the survivor, is haunted by the ghosts of his dead companions whose faces he sees 'tinged with death in their uneasy sleep'. Like the Eumenides, these ghosts *(i somersi,* the submerged) seem to pursue and accuse the survivor. Defensively he tries to justify himself –

> I haven't dispossessed anyone,
> Haven't usurped anyone's bread.
> No one died in my place. No one.

– but it is clear from the tone of the final lines, that he is not convinced by his own self-justification. Almost apologetically he ends:

> It's not my fault if I live and breathe,
> Eat, drink, sleep and put on clothes.

The sense of guilt at having survived when others did not is only too evident.

The most haunting and harrowing episode in *If This is a Man* occurs when the prisoners have to watch the public hanging of a man accused of taking part in a prison revolt. As the condemned man is brought into the blaze of the searchlight, he cries out *'Kamaraden, ich bin der Letz!'* ('Comrades, I am the last one!') The prisoners are then forced to witness his death: 'the trapdoor opened, the body wriggled horribly; the band began playing again and we were once more lined up and filed past the quivering body of the dying man.'

In view of the hanging imagery adopted by the other writers discussed above, it is interesting that Levi should focus also on this most potent symbol of guilt and shame. For him, the episode of the hanging is the key to understanding the survivor's sense of shame: in his last book *The Drowned and the Saved,* he explains that the cry of the doomed man, 'Comrades, I am the last one!' is a reproach to all the other prisoners who have been too frightened or too exhausted or too apathetic to try to fight back. 'When all was over,' Levi writes, 'the awareness emerged that we had not done anything, or not enough, against the system into which we had been absorbed.' It is a classic instance of the survivor's guilt at having survived, and for Levi it was to provide one of the most powerful compulsions for writing: 'We, the survivors, are not the true witnesses … we speak in their stead, by proxy.' Speaking thus, on behalf of the millions of 'true witnesses' – those who died in the concentration camps – forces Levi to articulate the question that has to be put perhaps to every survivor of a traumatic event in which others have died: 'Are you ashamed because you are alive in the place of another?' It is notable that the book in which Primo Levi asks himself that question was written more than forty years after he had left Auschwitz.

In examining the work of three writers who have themselves been victims and survivors, and comparing their insights with those of other authors who have dealt with the phenomenon of traumatic stress, it has been possible to demonstrate that there is a shared vocabulary and imagery of suffering on which all these writers draw, and to which students can respond, recognising (perhaps unconsciously) the deeper significance of images of exile and pursuit, of life-in-death, of guilt and shame and of the need to make atonement. This recognition can be a powerful turning point for students: a moment when they realise the power of literature, discovering that it can fulfil for them, what Philip Larkin called 'a hunger to be more serious'. Reading unfamiliar (as opposed to well-known) authors like Lamb, Aldington and Levi may make it easier for them to grasp how the writer, as poet or storyteller, is able to reconcile these discordant elements of grief and shock so that out of psychological disorder may come creative order. That this process of creative ordering is an essentially cathartic one for the writer is attested by the use of words such as 'purging' and 'purifying' chosen by Aldington and Levi; in this way, perhaps, wounds can begin to be healed as the survivor starts to reconcile himself to his survival. After all, writing is a creative act, and creative activity is life-affirming rather than denying. Aldington was later to call his memoirs *Life for Life's Sake,* and Levi argued passionately in his books that 'the aims of life are the best defence against death: and not only in the *Lager*'.

But while suffering can be transformed by art and into art, the implications for both writer and reader are important; this is not to imply that 'the memory of the offence' (Levi's words) or 'the wrong that has been done' (Aldington's) is ultimately erased. Charles Lamb's hanged man could not disguise the scar on his neck and Primo Levi never lost the prison number tattooed on his arm. In his last book, *The Drowned and the Saved*, Levi invoked the Eumenides when he wrote these words:

> Once again it must be observed, mournfully, that the injury cannot be healed: it extends through time, and the Furies, in whose existence we are compelled to believe, not only wrack the tormentor … but they perpetuate the tormentor's work by denying peace to the tormented.

In 1987, forty-two years after leaving Auschwitz and within months of completing the book from which these words have been quoted, Primo Levi committed suicide. At first, it was assumed that his death (he fell down the stairwell of the apartment block where he lived) must have been an accident: that Levi, of all people, should in the end not have been able to find peace through his writing seemed unthinkable. Today, however, people understand the force of what Levi had been saying; they accept that he took his own life; they acknowledge, too, that psychologists sometime call the drop down a stairwell 'hanging without the rope'. Above all, they hear in the words of Levi, and of Aldington and of Charles Lamb what D.H. Lawrence called, in a telling sentence from his novel *Aaron's Rod*, 'the hot, blind, anguished voice of a man who has seen too much, experienced too much, and doesn't know where to turn'.

Conclusion: understanding the insights of others

'Teaching is essentially a rhetorical activity, seeking to persuade students to change the way they experience the world through an understanding of the insights of others.'

*(Diane Laurillard **Rethinking University Teaching**, 2002)*

In the Introduction to this book I described teaching literature as the central part of the job of an English teacher. It seems important to restate this, particularly at a time when even the concept of an 'English teacher' is being replaced by that of a 'Literacy teacher' and where children can leave primary school unaware that there is such a subject as English because on their timetable for the previous six years English lessons have been labelled 'Literacy'. There has been for over a decade now a 'Literacy Strategy' (originally a 'National Literacy Strategy') a kind of Five-Year Plan designed to improve the literacy of the nation's children. This emphasis on literacy has overshadowed any emphasis on the literary, and it has forced those who believe in the value of teaching literature to articulate these beliefs – sometimes in the form of an almost public confession.

Here, for instance, is Rick Rylance, Professor of English at Exeter:

> I hold a cluster of beliefs about which I am prepared to argue ... I think, for instance, that great literary writing is important (though I don't believe in a canon of 'great works' or authors), because aesthetic pleasure is an important resource in human culture and for human achievement. I think that the style of intensely dialectical, often unresolved exploration that characterises the intellectual achievement of major literary texts is a style of thinking appropriate to our times and the human situation in which, as far as I can see, values are mainly provisional and consensual. I believe that the mode of knowledge with which we engage when we discuss literature – open, discursive, provisional, revisable, intersubjective – is emblematic of the way values should operate in a society such as our own. I also believe in the value of clear, successful communication and, in a rather Orwellian way, that it is a political and ethical imperative to spread this as widely as possible.[1]

Rylance's defence of English as a subject involves the student as much as the teacher: discovering why great literary writing is important is a shared enterprise. And in another polemical defence of English ('Literacy is not Enough') Richard Hoggart, whose seminal book *The Uses of Literacy* (1957) helped to establish the whole subject of Cultural Studies, has warned:

Here we have to defend the uses and meanings of several unfashionable words. To talk about the value of reading in and for itself is to talk of fine poetry, great drama, remarkable novels. It is to speak of words that show a respectful, gifted and, as may seem needed, wanton regard for language; a wish to make some sort of shape in life, even if it is no more than a mad shape; it is in most but not all instances fed by the wish to pass on all this to anyone who will make the effort to listen.[2]

Hoggart here seems to be giving the cue to Hector, the English teacher in Alan Bennett's play *The History Boys*:

HECTOR: Pass the parcel.
 That's sometimes all you can do.
 Take it, feel it and pass it on.
 Not for me, not for you, but for someone, somewhere, one day.
 Pass it on, boys.
 That's the game I wanted you to learn.
 Pass it on.[3]

Helping students to understand the insights of others, to see how writers try to make 'some sort of shape in life, even if it is no more than a mad shape' is what English teachers do. They help students to become readers, and occasionally writers, themselves. And writers celebrate the 'mad shape' of life, no one more effectively than Louis MacNeice in his poem 'Snow':

The room was suddenly rich and the great bay-window was
Spawning snow and pink roses against it
Soundlessly collateral and incompatible:
World is suddener than we fancy it.

World is crazier and more of it than we think,
Incorrigibly plural. I peel and portion
A tangerine and spit the pips and feel
The drunkenness of things being various.

And the fire flames with a bubbling sound for world
Is more spiteful and gay than one supposes –
On the tongue on the eyes on the ears in the palms of one's hands –
There is more than glass between the snow and the huge roses.[4]

I know of no poem that better expresses what happens when we suddenly see something in a new way because we see it in an unexpected context. The winter snow outside the window enriches the warm room, bringing its summery rose-patterned curtains or wallpaper to life with the same intensity that the mundane action of eating a tangerine sharply awakens all one's senses and makes one experience life with a greater sense of its excitement and potential: 'World is suddener than we fancy it.'

'Snow' celebrates just such an epiphany. I read this poem once with an A level class that included a boy who had cancer. I could tell then how the poem meant a lot to him; and he said to me afterwards that now he could really see, for the first time, the point of doing English. Undefeated by chemotherapy, he went on to direct a sixth-form production of Pirandello's appropriate play, *The Bald Prima Donna*, and later to win a place at Cambridge. He died after one term of his English degree, and I read 'Snow' at his funeral. Everyone understood why.

Resources

The following list of resources does not claim to be comprehensive, but it highlights some places where teachers of English Literature will find useful information and thought-provoking ideas. No attempt is made to list websites devoted to particular authors or literary topics or to university English departments and faculties: some of these have already been identified during the discussions earlier in Part 2. In any case, investigation and evaluation of such sites is a constructive way for students to do their own web-based research.

Professional associations, websites, journals

There are two professional associations for secondary teachers of English in the UK, the English Association (EA) and the National Association for the Teaching of English (NATE). With the advent of the Government's plans for Chartered Teacher Status, designed to boost the professional standing of teachers and to recognise their subject expertise, it is likely that membership of a professional association will be a pre-condition of becoming a Chartered Teacher of English – or of any subject.

The English Association

www.le.ac.uk/engassoc

The EA was granted a Royal Charter in its centenary year (2007) in recognition of its contribution to English teaching as a profession. Its scope ranges from university to primary teaching, and its regular publications reflect this: it publishes *The Year's Work in English Studies* and *English* for those working in HE, *The Use of English* for those teaching in secondary education and *English 4–11* (published in collaboration with the UKLA (United Kingdom Literacy Association). The Secondary Education Committee acts as the editorial board for *The Use of English*, which publishes articles on the teaching of English Literature and Language, as well as reviewing a wide range of books, often with a strong emphasis on poetry. The Committee also organises an annual conference for teachers, with a running concern for issues of transition from school to university. In addition the EA runs conferences for sixth-formers in London, Leicester and elsewhere in the country. It also runs courses on Shakespeare in association with the Shakespeare Institute.

Its website is particularly useful: the EA has a secondary web portal and a site devoted to teaching poetry. In addition, it has put its long-running series of *Bookmarks* (pamphlet-sized discussions of individual set texts or authors aimed at A level students and specifically intended to encourage wider reading) onto its website, so that all *Bookmarks* are freely downloadable by students or teachers.

The National Association for the Teaching of English
www.nate.org.uk

With over 3000 members, NATE is a major voice in all debates about the present state and future direction of English teaching. It operates through a series of committees (Primary, Secondary, Post-16 and HE) and working parties to cover the full range of members' interests and concerns. Its 2004 report, *text: message – The Future of A level English*, made an important contribution to the arguments surrounding English after Curriculum 2000.

NATE's publications cover a wide range. Its main journal, published three times a year, is *English in Education*. This is an important point of reference and update, providing challenging, research-based articles on the theory and practice of teaching English. *English Drama Media*, also published three times a year, is described on the NATE website as 'the Association's platform for discussion and thought on any issues which are relevant to the teaching of English in the four countries of the UK'.

The website is the main source of information about the courses and conferences run by the Association, and NATE's national Conference is the largest annual gathering of English teachers in Britain. In addition, its regional and local branches also organise events and workshops. One of the most useful resources on its website is the NATE REVIEWS section, where members contribute reviews of books and articles of interest to teachers of English in whatever sector of the subject or level of education they are working.

The English and Media Centre
www.englishandmedia.co.uk

The English and Media Centre (EMC) is not a professional association as such (it does not have a membership), but it is an invaluable resource for teachers. Its flagship publication, *e-magazine*, is written for A level students of both Literature and Language and is accessible and stimulating. It provides subscribers with access to the *e-magazine website*, including:

- *emagclips*, a library of video clips on texts and topics for A Level English
- *emagplus*, extra articles each issue, plus downloadable interactive 'tutorials'
- *emagpast*, the *emag* archive, with over 700 articles

The English and Media Centre runs a full programme of practical courses for teachers. These are targeted at particular A level specifications and set texts. They also focus on English Language, Media and Film Studies. Their magazine *MediaMag* is an important resource for students and teachers of Media Studies. Other publications include poetry posters, plus *emcextra* and *emcallsorts* – online resources and archives for teachers to use.

English Subject Centre
www.english.heacademy.ac.uk

The English Subject Centre (ESC) is the network for university teachers of English Studies. Its website is often full of insights into the state of English and English teaching in Higher Education. It runs conferences, publishes an online Newsletter (free) and commissions and publishes reports that deal specifically with issues of transition in English from school to university. All these reports can be downloaded free, and you do not have to be an HE lecturer to be able to access them. Of particular interest to A level teachers are three reports:

Four Perspectives on Transition – English literature from sixth-form to university Report 10 (2005)

Teaching Shakespeare – A Survey of the Undergraduate Level in Higher Education Report 13 (2006)

As Simple as ABC? Issues of transition for students of English Language A level Report No. 14 (2007)

A further report, *Survey of the English Curriculum and Teaching in UK Higher Education* (Report 3; 2003) offers an overview of the state and range of English studies in Higher Education. Despite its rather dry title, this report is invaluable for any teacher advising students on what to expect if they go on to read English at university. The ESC also publishes the leaflet *Why (You Should) Study English?* For sixth-formers thinking of making English their degree choice; it also runs a website www.whystudyenglish.ac.uk with which every secondary teacher should be familiar.

ITE English
www.ite.org.uk/ite_home/index.php

Initial Teacher Education (ITE) is a project aimed primarily at those with the responsibility of training future English teachers. It is co-ordinated by Canterbury Christchurch University, NATE and the UK Literacy Association (UKLA). The part of the site devoted to teaching Literature post-16 is authored by Richard Jacobs of Brighton University and should be much more widely known than it is. Jacobs argues that teaching English post-16 is quite different from teaching English at GCSE or at university, that the subject at this transitional stage occupies a 'sacred space' where the engagement with individual texts and authors is more intense than it may ever be again, and that the responsibility of the teachers at this stage is also greater than at any other. The site is particularly strong on contextual approaches, comparative study and critical reading. Richard Jacobs is also the author of a book valuable to A level Literature students and teachers alike, *A Beginner's Guide to Critical Reading* (London: Routledge, 2001).

Converse – the Literature Website
aspirations.english.cam.ac.uk/converse/alevel/alevel.acds

This website has a section aimed directly at A level students and teachers, and is designed to supplement (not replace) the teaching that they receive in their English lessons at school. It is administered by the Faculty of English at Cambridge University. Some parts of the site target students directly – for instance the 'Degrees/Careers' section giving advice to anyone thinking about applying to read English at university (not just at Cambridge). Others provide teaching resources for teachers: there is an excellent area of the website devoted to Chaucer, for instance, and another which provides a startlingly wide range of teaching materials for a complete course on the literature of the First World War. The Converse Teachers' Handbook is worth bookmarking:

aspirations.english.cam.ac.uk/converse/teachers/handbook.asp

The English Review

The English Review is a magazine written by teachers and academics specifically for A level English Literature students. According to the publisher (Philip Allan Updates: www.philipallan.co.uk), 'the magazine's aims are simple: to increase your students' enthusiasm for English Literature and help them achieve higher grades'. It is published quarterly and has an editorial board, based at the English Faculty of Oxford University, chaired by John Carey. The articles usually focus on books chosen from A level set text lists, and are complemented by regular features, including 'Close Reading' and 'Literature in Context'.

Books

The following titles in no sense amount to a bibliography. They highlight a few of the books that have been useful in the preparation of *World and Time*, but more importantly they suggest titles that all teachers of English and English Literature at A Level will find worth reading.

Peter Widdowson *Literature*
(London: Routledge, *New Critical Idiom* series, 1999)
J. Hillis Miller *On Literature*
(London: Routledge, 2002)

These two books, published just when Curriculum 2000 was being introduced and examined for the first time, neatly contextualised the arguments surrounding the concept of literature in the post-modern period. Widdowson's book is structured as a series of questions: What is 'Literature'? What has 'Literature' been? What has happened to 'Literature'? What is 'the literary'? The first three of these questions (each a chapter heading) allow him to sketch the history of 'Literature' as a cultural construct and as a subject of academic study; the fourth provides him with an opportunity to 'establish a coherent working term ['the literary'] for a kind of written discourse I believe has some irreplaceable uses in our society, and without which our cultural lives would be impoverished and diminished'. (p.93) Having thus signalled his conviction that Literature is a cultural good thing – he is able to argue that his notion of 'the literary'

> is intended to identify a category of writing which is distinguished, first, from 'writing' in general – both in its own self-consciousness of being 'literary' and in its reader's apprehension of that property; and second, from other conventionally related art-forms such as music, painting and film. These distinctions will be based principally on an assessment of the social and cultural effects of 'the literary' rather than on any attempt to locate intrinsic aesthetic or linguistic characteristics of 'literariness'.   (p.94)

J. Hillis Miller agrees with Widdowson – but only up to a point. For where Widdowson is concerned with the social and cultural contexts of a text's reception, Miller is keen to focus on how a text works as a way to identify what gives it the right to be termed 'literature':

> Literary study hides the peculiarity of literary language by accounting for it, naturalising it, neutralising it, turning it into the familiar. This usually means seeing it as in one way or another a representation of the real world. Whether this accounting takes the form of relating the work to its author, or of trying to demonstrate that is typical of its historical time and place, or characteristic of the class, gender, and race of its author, or of seeing it as a mirroring of the material and social world ... the unspoken goal is to appease the unconscious or conscious fear people have of literature's true strangeness.   (p.33)

In developing this argument against context, Miller nevertheless goes on to suggest that literary works 'have always had a powerful critical function. They challenge hegemonic ideologies, as well as reinforcing them.' Literature in the modern Western sense, Miller reminds his readers, 'has taken full advantage of the right to free speech'. (p.123)

The value of these two books, Widdowson's and Miller's, is to challenge anyone teaching literature in context to be clear in their own mind what they are dealing with, and how they are dealing with it. It is a measure of how far Curriculum 2000 and its successors have brought A level English that close textual study can no longer be divorced from the cultural and social contexts in which the text is located. And yet Miller acknowledges this with a certain wistfulness: he longs for the time when innocent reading was still possible and when the 'magic' of the text was sufficient reason to go on turning the page. Now, he concludes, 'critical reading means being suspicious at every turn, interrogating every detail of the work, trying to figure out by just what means the magic is wrought' (p.122). It is perhaps uniquely the job of the A level English teacher, occupying what Richard Jacobs calls 'the sacred space' (see page 291, above) to teach students how to do the one while preserving, if possible, the other.

Jon Davison & John Moss, eds. *Issues in English Teaching*
(London: Routledge, 2000)
Ellie Chambers & Marshall Gregory *Teaching and Learning English Literature*
(London: Sage, 2006)

Both of these books are polemical, arguing strongly against what they see as the inertia and authoritarianism of much National Curriculum-dominated English teaching: 'Today, given the challenges the discipline faces, there is even more reason to jump outside the authoritarian frame that teachers and students may sometimes still inhabit.' (Chambers and Gregory, p.11) Although *Teaching and Learning English Literature* calls for a rigorously theoretical critique of English teaching, it makes clear its own stance: the authors have little time for post-modernism. Their position is more nearly located in discourse analysis and reader-response:

> The text's meanings and significance stand in need of analysis, interpretation and evaluation. This entails the *making* of *meaning*. Meaning does not reside 'in' the text, as it were ready to jump out at us, but is made in the active process of encounter between object and inquirer, text and reader. The reader questions the text and the text 'questions' the reader. Processes of analysis-interpretation-interpretation-evaluation are central to the study of Literature, then; they are the means through which we produce knowledge in our discipline. (p.35)

Chambers and Gregory are concerned with arguing for change in Higher Education; Davison and Moss, in *Issues in English Teaching*, question the lack of theoretical underpinning they find in English teaching at every stage from primary up to A level. John Moss asks whether there is a place for the explicit use of critical theory in English teaching, and surveys the different theoretical perspectives of the past forty years from reader-response, *via* stylistics to post-structuralism; he suggests that 'we have to learn to teach pupils about the different ways in which the power of the writer and the power of the reader can be balanced (or unbalanced) as part of teaching literacy in school' (Davison and Moss, p.203). In saying this he is clearly talking about critical literacy, and by the end of the chapter he is arguing that teachers need to empower students to discuss literature in a variety of theoretical contexts:

> The function of the selection of a text or a pedagogical strategy, and the selection of a reading practice derived from a particular critical theory, should be to stimulate the extension of the semiotic, generic, cultural and ideological repertoire of pupils. (p.210)

The implications of what Moss is arguing here need to be taken seriously, even if the language used sounds already curiously dated. Can one really have 'an ideological repertoire'? And if one can, is expanding it really what A level students need, or universities want? One cannot help recalling the comment by the novelist Michèle Roberts in *Food, Sex & God* (London: Virago, 1998):

> The language of theory and of literary criticism ages far more quickly than the language of poetry and novels, perhaps because the theories themselves go out of fashion so fast and are replaced by something new. (p.111)

The danger for the teacher of becoming too much a dedicated follower of theoretical fashion is something highlighted in the next and final book to be mentioned.

Elaine Showalter *Teaching Literature*
(Oxford: Blackwell, 2003)

This book, by one of the dominant figures of English Studies in the past thirty years, draws on the experience and testimony of Literature teachers from universities both in the UK and in the United States. It is less a guide to how to teach than a description of the ways in which people actually manage to do the job and the reasons they do it. Much of what Showalter discusses in terms of Literature teaching in HE is also directly applicable to teaching at A level. She notes, for example, that 'not very long ago everyone assumed that teaching poetry was at the centre of teaching the mysteries of literature' but adds that

> these days poetry has been dislodged from the centre of the literary curriculum by fiction, drama, cultural studies, and even literary theory. Teachers lament that students find it difficult and intimidating. (p.62)

She cites Stephen Regan, Professor of English at Durham, who told her that debates in the UK over English and the National Curriculum had ignored poetry as a distinct genre, 'so that "while the poetry festivals flourish, some undergraduate students are likely to arrive at university with little or no interest in poetry, confessing that they don't know how to read it and therefore can't be expected to understand or appreciate it"' (pp.62–3). That this is so should give everyone who teaches Literature, whether at A level or in HE, serious pause.

But it is her closing reflections that make Elaine Showalter's book one every English teacher should read. She observes that 'teaching offers the illusion of a fountain of youth: it brings us into contact with young people and their enthusiasm and freshness, and allows us to have an impact on their lives. But the teaching persona we adopt when we are young fits less well as we age.' She quotes a colleague who says, 'Authentic teaching requires reflective practice. Teaching personalities that fit at twenty-five are not those that are authentic at fifty.' (p.142). There is something sobering about her final comment that as teachers grow older they have to 're-examine the compromises and accommodations that they have made with their real beliefs for the sake of professional status and theoretical fashion.' (*ibid.*) As teachers ourselves we have to be sure of our real beliefs about the value of teaching literature. We should check these beliefs each term by asking, as we begin teaching Jane Austen for the first or the thirty-first time, 'What are we doing here?'

Notes

Introduction
1   Stefan Collini *Times Literary Supplement*, 30.11.07, p.8

Chapter 1
1   Italo Calvino *Why Read the Classics?* (London: Jonathan Cape, 1999) p.5
2   Quality Assurance Agency for Higher Education *Benchmark Statement for English*, 2007 (www.qaa.ac.uk/academicinfrastructure/benchmark/statements/english07.asp)
3   Philip Larkin *Required Writing* (London: Faber and Faber, 1983) pp.81–2
4   Pat Barker 'Double Vision' in *Guardian Review*, 30.06.07, p.11
5   Susan Sontag *At The Same Time* (London: Hamish Hamilton, 2007) p.213
6   Nick Peim 'The Cultural Politics of English Teaching', in J. Davison and J. Moss (eds.) *Issues in English Teaching* (London: Routledge, 2000) p.172
7   Sontag, p.213
8   Hilary Mantel 'On the one hand …' in *Guardian Review*, 22.12.07, p.3
9   Sontag, p.213
10 *New York Times*, 07.08.71
11 Alan Bennett *The History Boys* (London: Faber and Faber, 2004) p.37
12 *The History Boys*, p.55
13 Thomas Hardy 'The Dorsetshire Labourer' in *Longman's Magazine*, July 1883
14 Umberto Eco *On Literature* (London: Vintage, 2005) pp.4–5

Chapter 2
1   Malcolm Bradbury (ed.) *E.M. Forster: A Passage to India* (London: Macmillan, 1970) p.23
2   Jeremy Tambling (ed.) *E.M. Forster* (London: Macmillan, 1995) pp.10–11
3   Peter Barry *English in Practice* (London: Arnold, 2003) p.86
4   *ibid.*
5   John Hodgson *et al* (eds.) *text : message* (Report on the Future of A level English, Sheffield: NATE, 2004) p.7
6   *ibid.*, p.10
7   *ibid.*, p.28
8   Peter Barry 'Editorial Commentary' in *English* (Leicester: the English Association, vol. 56, no. 216, Autumn 2007) p.369
9   Helen Gardner *In Defence of the Imagination* (Oxford: The Clarendon Press, 1982) p.47
10 Elaine Showalter *Teaching Literature* (Oxford: Blackwell, 2003) p.136

Chapter 3
1   *Times Higher Education Supplement (THES)*, 16.02.07, p.4
2   image.guardian.co.uk/sys-files/Guardian/documents/2006/08/17/alevels.pdf
3   Gary Day 'The logic resembles George Orwell's doublethink' in *THES*, 16.02.07, p.13

4   Terry Eagleton *How to Read a Poem* (Oxford: Blackwell, 2007) p.1
5   data quoted by William Stewart 'No degree? No problem' in *Times Educational Supplement (TES)*, 16.02.07, p.18
6   John Hodgson *et al* (eds.) *text : message* (Report on the Future of A level English, Sheffield: NATE, 2004) p.10
7   It will be seen that, in this change of nomenclature from SCAA to QCA, 'qualifications' (i.e. 'assessment') came to take precedence over 'curriculum'.
8   A. Hodgson and Ken Spours *Beyond A Levels* (London: Kogan Page, 2003) p.34
9   *ibid.*, p.144
10   *ibid.*, p.89
11   *How to Read a Poem*, p.1
12   *ibid.*, p.2
13   Andrew Green *Four Perspectives on Transition: English Teaching from Sixth Form to University* (London: English Subject Centre, 2004) para. 5.4.6
14   Neill Thew *Teaching Shakespeare: A Survey of the Undergraduate Level in Higher Education* (London: English Subject Centre, 2006) paras. 3.2, 3.3
15   *ibid.*, 3.3
16   J. Hillis Miller *On Literature* (London: Routledge, 2002) p.122
17   *ibid.*, p.123
18   Elaine Showalter *Teaching Literature* (Oxford: Blackwell, 2003) p.56
     Showalter is citing Eagleton's *Literary Theory: An Introduction,* 2nd Edition (Oxford: Blackwell, 1996) p.37
19   Showalter, *op.cit.,* p.56
20   www.english.cam.ac.uk/vclass/pracrit.htm

Chapter 4
1   Zadie Smith *White Teeth* (London: Penguin Books, 2000) pp.270–1
2   *ibid.*
3   www.shakespearesglobe.org/buildingyourlibrary/volumesthatiprize/tonyhoward/
4   Virginia Mason Vaughan *Othello, a Contextual History* (Cambridge, Cambridge University Press, 1994), p.3
5   *ibid.*, p.8
6   Janet Todd *Jane Austen in Context* (Cambridge: Cambridge University Press, 2005) p.22
7   Niall Ferguson *The Pity of War* (London: Allen Lane the Penguin Press, 1998) p.xxvi
8   *ibid.*, xxxiv
9   Alan Bennett *The History Boys* (London: Penguin Books, 2004) p.73
10   *ibid.*, p.74
11   Peter Barry *English in Practice* (London: Arnold, 2003) p.78
12   *ibid.*, p.76
13   Richard Jacobs *A Beginner's Guide to Critical Reading* (London: Routledge, 2001) p.4
14   *ibid.*, p.5
15   *The History Boys*, p.69
16   *ibid.*, p.55

17   R. Rylance and J. Simons (eds.) *Literature in Context* (London: Palgrave, 2001) p.xvii

18   *ibid.*, p.xxiii

Chapter 5

1   QCA GCE AS and A level subject criteria for English Literature (September, 2006) 3.1

2   QAA Benchmark Statement (revised 2007): www.qaa.ac.uk/academicinfrastructure/ benchmark/statements/english07.asp

3   Oxford University English Faculty website (2008): www.english.ox.ac.uk/ undergraduate/structure.htm

4   Manchester University English and American Studies website (2008): www.arts. manchester.ac.uk/subjectareas/englishamericanstudies/ undergraduatestudy/ course/?code=00060

5   Exeter University Department of English (2008): www.sall.ex.ac.uk/english

6   University of Auckland, Faculty of Arts (2008 details): www.arts.auckland.ac.nz/ online/index.cfm?S=OL_ENGLISH111

7   York University Department of English, Undergraduate Prospectus 2007, p.22

8   *Stanford Bulletin 2007–08*: Stanford University Department of English, p.7: http://english.stanford.edu

9   Durham University Department of English, Undergraduate Programmes 2007–08: www.dur.ac.uk/programme.specifications/progspec/?prog=Q300

10   York: p.46

11   York: p.48

12   University of Cambridge *Guide to Undergraduate Study: English* (2007)

13   'Bann Valley Eclogue' was first published in its eleven-stanza version in *Times Literary Supplement*, 4 October 1999. In its shortened and revised version it appeared in Seamus Heaney *Electric Light* (London: Faber and Faber, 2001) p.11

14   T.S. Eliot *Selected Essays* (London: Faber and Faber, 1932; 1999) p.16

15   Seamus Heaney *District and Circle* (London: Faber and Faber, 2006) pp.20–21

16   Roderick Beaton *George Seferis – Waiting for the Angel* (Yale, 2003) p.403

17   George Seferis 'Aspalathoi', translated by Edmund Keeley; in E. Keeley and P. Sherrard (trans.) *George Seferis Complete Poems* (London: Anvil Press; new ed. 1993)

18   George Seferis 'On Gorse', translated by Peter Levi; in Peter Levi *The Hill of Kronos* (London: Collins, 1980) p.175

19   Brian Friel *Translations* (London: Faber and Faber, 1981) pp.40–41

20   *ibid.*, p.43

21   W.B. Yeats *Quarante-cinq poèmes*, translated by Yves Bonnefoy (Paris: Gallimard, 1993) p.35

22   W.G. Sebald *Austerlitz* (paperback ed., Frankfurt: Fischer Taschenbuch Verlag, 2003) p.90

23   W.G. Sebald *Austerlitz*, translated by Anthea Bell (London: Penguin, 2003) p.83

24   Seamus Heaney *Beowulf* (London: Faber and Faber, 2001) Introduction, p.xxix

25   *ibid.* pp.xxix–xx

26 Janet Maybin 'The Canon: historical construction and contemporary challenges' in J. Davidson and J. Moss (eds.) *Issues in English Teaching* (London: Routledge, 2000) p.186

27 AEA English Specification (QCA 2002): www.qca.org.uk/qca_5613.aspx. See also a description of the AEA published by OCR, the awarding body which runs AEA English on behalf of all the UK examination boards: www.ocr.org.uk/qualifications/ aea/english/

28 John Hodgson *et al* (eds.) *text : message* (Report on the Future of A level English, Sheffield: NATE, 2004) pp.25–6

29 In 2008 QCA finally announced the demise of the AEA from 2010 onwards, arguing that the now fully synoptic A2 components of A level would provide sufficient 'stretch and challenge' and that the advent of the A* grade would give admissions tutors as much additional information about students' performance as they would need.

30 The ELAT website provides a full description of the examination together with sample and past papers: www.elat.org.uk

Chapter 6

1 Peter Burra *Wordsworth* (London: Duckworth, 1936) p.93

2 G.D. Leslie *Our River* (London: Bradbury, Agnew and Co, 1881) pp.134–5

3 Quoted in Timothy Hyman and Patrick White (eds.) *Stanley Spencer* (London: Tate Publications, 2001) p.18

4 Adrian Glew (ed.) *Stanley Spencer: Letters and Writings* (London: Tate Publications, 2001) p.103

5 *ibid.*

6 *ibid.*

7 *ibid.*

8 Ivor Winters *Forms of Discovery* (Chicago: Swallow Press, 1967) pp.167–8

9 Robert Eaglestone *Doing English* (London: Routledge, 2000) p.41

10 Roger Knight 'Doing English In' in *Use of English* (2000)

11 All references are to the first Oxford World's Classics edition of *The Golden Treasury* (1907), the school textbook used for well over fifty years.

12 *op.cit.* p.498

13 *ibid.*, Preface, p.xiii

Chapter 7

1 *Paradise Lost, IX*, ll.445–6

2 'Landscapes III, Usk' in T.S. Eliot *Collected Poems 1909–1962* (London: Faber and Faber, 1963) p.154

3 John Ezard 'T.S. Eliot scholar finds answer to pub poet's riddle' in the *Guardian*, 6.08.03

4 Eliot to John Hayward, quoted in Helen Gardner *The Composition of Four Quartets* (London: Faber and Faber, 1978) p.67

5 T.S. Eliot *Selected Essays* (London: Faber and Faber, 1932; 1999) p.15

6 William Plomer (ed.) *Kilvert's Diary* (Pimlico, 1999) pp.187, 190

7 Quoted in *Guardian Review* 24.11.07, p.6

Chapter 8

1 From *Comic Characters of Shakespeare*, 1946; reprinted in Laurence Lerner (ed.) *Shakespeare's Comedies: an Anthology of Modern Criticism* (Harmondsworth: Penguin, 1967) p.135

2 Sylvan Barnet *Twentieth Century Interpretations of The Merchant of Venice* (New Jersey: Prentice Hall Inc., 1970) p.1

3 *ibid.*

4 Ania Loomba *Shakespeare, Race and Colonialism* (Oxford: Oxford University Press, 2002)

5 Question in a June 2003 Oxford University English paper: 'Text, Context, Intertext: an Introduction to Literary Studies'

6 Robert Eaglestone *Doing English* (Routledge, 2000) p.37

7 Peter Barry *English in Practice* (Arnold, 2003) p.78

8 Jonathan Bate 'Navigate the circus of fancy with fact', *THES*, 01.08.03, p.23

9 George Steiner 'Grave Jubilation', *TLS*, 19.09.03, p.3

10 Edward Said Introduction to *Orientalism* (rev. ed., 2003) reprinted as 'A window on the world', *Guardian Review*, 02.08.03, p.6

11 Jonathan Culler *Literary Theory: A Very Short Introduction* (OUP, 2000) p.64

12 All Shakespeare references are to the *Alexander* edition (Collins, 1953)

13 John Aubrey (1626–1697) *Brief Lives* (1818)

14 The *locus classicus* for this euphemism is *Tristam Shandy*, chapter 1. Sterne's novel provoked the publication of a famous pamphlet, *The Clockmaker's Outcry* (1760), which complained that 'No gentleman could wind his watch without a woman thinking he had designs on her, and the market for clocks was suffering.' (Carol Watts 'Re-readings: *Tristram Shandy*' in *Guardian Review*, 23.8.03)

15 R. Rylance and J. Simons (eds.) *Literature in Context* (London: Palgrave, 2001) p.xxiii

16 Terry Eagleton 'Bin Laden sure didn't read any beer mats', *THES*, 03.10.03, p.22

17 *ibid.*

18 Said, *loc.cit.*

19 David Lodge *Consciousness and the Novel* (Secker and Warburg, 2002) p.106

Chapter 9

1 Esther Addley 'Faking It', *Guardian*, 10.01.03

2 Extracts from *Emma* and *Mansfield Park* from Oxford World's Classics editions of 1990 and 1980 respectively

3 Extracts from *Persuasion* (Penguin Classics, 1998)

4 Extracts from *Howards End* (Penguin Classics, 1985)

5 Extracts from *Lucky Jim* (Penguin Twentieth Century Classics, 1992)

6 Extracts from *Nice Work* (Penguin, 1989)

7 Extracts from *England, England* (Picador, 1998)

8 Extracts from *White Teeth* (Penguin, 2001)

9 Extracts from *Atonement* (Vintage, 2002)

10 Extracts from *A Tale of Two Cities* (Everyman edition, 1994)

11 Alan Grant *A Preface to Dickens* (London: Longman, 1984) p.161

Chapter 10

1   The *Guardian* (10.11.07)
2   Mary Beard *The Roman Triumph* (Boston, Mass.: Harvard University Press, 2007)
3   Helen Vendler *Coming of Age as a Poet* (Boston, Mass: Harvard University Press, 2003)
4   All quotations are from Rupert Brooke *Letters from America* (London: Sidgwick and Jackson, 1916). The book can be freely accessed from various Internet sites.
5   Letter to Noel Oliver, 25 April 1914; quoted in Pippa Harris (ed.) *Song of Love: the Letters of Rupert Brooke and Noel Oliver* (London: Bloomsbury, 1991) pp.267–8

Chapter 11

1   'Concert Party' in Edmund Blunden *Overtones of War* (London: Duckworth, 1996) p.105
2   Quotations are from Edmund Blunden *Undertones of War* (London: Penguin Classics, 2000)
3   Sassoon's poems quoted in this section were first published in *The Heart's Journey* (London: Heinemann, 1928)
4   Quotations from Sebastian Faulks *Birdsong* (London: Vintage 1994)
5   Richard Aldington *The Complete Poems of Richard Aldington* (London: Allan Wingate, 1948) p.302
6   'To W.O. and His Kind' in Edmund Blundon *Overtones of War* (London: Duckworth, 1996) p.187
7   'The Menin Gate' is one of the stories in Christopher Arthur *Cappadocian Moon* (Ely: Melrose Press, 2006)
8   'Lob' in Edward Thomas *Collected Poems* (London: Faber and Faber, 2004) pp.61–2
9   Quotations are from Julian Barnes *A History of the World in 10½ Chapters* (London: Picador, 1990 ed.)
10 Jane Aaron 'We Are In a Manner Marked: Images of Damnation in Charles Lamb's Writings' in *Charles Lamb Bulletin* (NS33) 1981, pp.1–10
11 Quotations from 'The Case of Lieutenant Hall' in Richard Aldington *Roads to Glory* (London: Heinemann, 1930)
12 'Eumenides' in *The Complete Poems of Richard Aldington*, pp.152–4
13 'In the Palace Garden', p.160
14 'Epitaph in Ballade Form', p.161
15 Quotations are from Primo Levi *The Drowned and the Saved* (London: Abacus, 1988) and *If This is a Man* and *The Truce* (London: Abacus, 1987)

Conclusion

1   Rick Rylance *But ... Why Study English?* (English Subject Centre, 2007) www.whystudyenglish.ac.uk/you-are/but-why-study-english-literature.htm
2   Richard Hoggart *Between Two Worlds* (London: Aurum Press, 2001)
3   Alan Bennett *The History Boys* (London: Faber and Faber, 2004) p.109
4   Louis MacNeice *Collected Poems* (London: Faber and Faber, 1966; 1979) p.30

Index

Kott, Jan, *Shakespeare Our Contemporary* 37

Kureishi, Hanif *The Buddha of Suburbia* 191

Lamb, Charles Romantic writer 245; Coleridge's poem to 118–23; *Essays of Elia* 233, 275; hanging imagery 273, 277–8; 'The Old Familiar Faces' 276–7; 'On the Inconveniences Arising from Being Hanged' 277; *The Pawnbroker's Daughter* 277

Lamb, Mary murder of mother 275–6

Lamb's Tales from Shakespeare 275

'Land of Hope and Glory' 191

Larkin, Philip 6; *High Windows*, comparison of exam questions 67; 'hunger to be more serious' 284

Laurillard, Diane *Rethinking University Teaching* 286

Lawrence, D.H. 19; *Aaron's Rod* 285

Leavis, F.R. *Scrutiny* 20

Lee, Hermione biography of Virgina Woolf 226

Leslie, George Dunlop *Our River*, swan upping 81–2

Levi, Peter translation of 'Epi Aspalathoi' 61–2

Levi, Primo in Auschwitz 281–84; *The Drowned and the Saved* 283–4; hanging imagery 273; Holocaust narratives 245; *If This is a Man* 282–3; suicide of 285; 'The Survivor' 283; *The Truce* 283; writer on Holocaust 281

liberal humanism of Malcolm Bradbury 21

Literacy Strategy 286

literary biography 159

literary canon, lack of knowledge of 22–3

literary criticism 28, 32; a dying art 29–30

literary technique, *prolepsis* 271

literature in context 15, 16–28; definition 40, 45; disappearance from schools 29; in the news 269

Lodge, David 190; on criticism as useful activity 169; *Language of Fiction* 245; *Nice Work* 192, 196–9

London Eye, view from 93–4

London University Institute of Education 31

love and madness in Shakespeare's sonnets 152–7

MacNeice, Louis 'Snow' 287–8

Mantel, Hilary *A Change of Climate* 170, 175, 177–83, 204; on texture of texts 9

Marlowe, Christopher 5; *Dr Faustus* 5; *The Jew of Malta* 152

Marxist rhetoric of Tambling 21

Maybin, Janet on 'Leavisite' close reading 68–9

McEwan, Ian *Atonement* 25, 176; Englishness 170; film of 205–14; on reading lists 183–4

Melville, Herman *Billy Budd* 274

memorising Shakespeare 139, 140

Menin Gate, Ypres 255–7, 268

metaphysical poets 52

metonymy 126

Mew, Charlotte ' The Cenotaph' 258

Miller, J. Hillis *On Literature* 34, 177

Milton, John *Paradise Lost* 10, 52; quatercentenary (2008) 52; sonnets 130

Modern Essays 1941–1943 221

moral dilemmas in texts 7, 8

moral obligations of writer 150, 151

Motion, Andrew, Poet Laureate 56

multicultural urban England 191

Muslim fundamentalism 203

myth, and history 270

Napoleonic Wars 99

National Act of Remembrance 258

National Association of Teachers of English (NATE) *text : message* 22, 30

national identity 190, 201–5

National Poetry Day (October 1st) 1999 56

Native American Indians, Brooke's sympathy with 241

nemesis 269

New Historicism 37

No Man's Land 39

Noah's Ark 245, 270–3

Nobel Prize for Literature 269

non-fiction prose 219–44

novel and contexts 170–218

novel writing of human experience 208–10

Olivier, Laurence film version, *Henry V* 36–7

Operation Noah's Ark 273

Option Internationale, French Baccalauréat 34

Acknowledgements

The authors and publishers acknowledge the following sources of copyright material and are grateful for the permissions granted. While every effort has been made, it has not always been possible to identify the sources of all the material used, or to trace all copyright holders. If any omissions are brought to our notice, we will be happy to include the appropriate acknowledgements on reprinting.

University of Auckland for an extract from the Faculty of Arts website by permission of Professor Brian Boyd; University of Cambridge for extracts from the Faculty of English website and *Guide to Undergraduate Study: English* (2007) by permission of Dr Colin Burrow; Cengage Learning Ltd for extracts from Robert Eaglestone *Doing English: A Guide for Students*, Routledge (1999) pp.37, 41–2; David Higham Associates on behalf of the Estate of the author for Louis MacNeice 'Snow' in *Collected Poems* by Louis MacNeice, Faber and Faber (1966; 1979) p.30; Gary Day for an extract from his article 'The logic resembles George Orwell's doublethink', *Times Higher Education Supplement*, 16.2.07 p.13; University of Durham for an extract from the Department of English Studies website; Terry Eagleton for extracts from his article 'Bin Laden sure didn't read any beer mats', *Times Higher Education Supplement*, 3.10.03 p. 22; Eland Publishing Ltd for George Seferis 'On Gorse', from Peter Levi, *The Hills of Kronos*, translated by Peter Levi, Collins (1980) p. 175; The English Association for extracts from Peter Barry 'Editorial Commentary' in *English* vol. 56, 216 (Autumn 2007) p.369; and Roger Knight 'Doing English In', *Use of English* (2000); University of Exeter for an extract from the Department of English website; Faber and Faber Ltd with Farrar, Straus and Giroux LLC for Seamus Heaney, 'Bann Valley Eclogue', and 'Sonnets into Hellas' in *Electric Light* by Seamus Heaney (2001) pp.11, 38. Copyright © 2001 Seamus Heaney; and 'To George Seferis in the Underworld' in *District and Circle* by Seamus Heaney (2006) pp.20–21. Copyright © 2006 Seamus Heaney; with W W Norton & Company, Inc for extracts from 'Introduction' to *Beowulf* translated by Seamus Heaney (2001) pp.xxix–xx. Copyright © 2000 Seamus Heaney; Guardian News and Media Ltd for extracts from Esther Addley 'Faking it: Hasn't that Kate Winslet got terribly thin? Or has she', the *Guardian*, 10.1.03. Copyright © Guardian News & Media Ltd 2003; John Ezard 'New hart T.S. Eliot scholar finds answer to pub poet's riddle', the *Guardian*, 6.8.03. Copyright © Guardian News & Media Ltd 2003; Susanna Rustin 'Double vision: Pat Barker returns to the setting of her Regeneration trilogy for her 11th novel. Her daughter, Anna, has just published her first – but isn't worried about comparisons', the *Guardian*, 30.6.07. Copyright © Guardian News & Media Ltd 2007; and Hilary Mantel 'On the one hand ... Journalism is as fast as the turnover in Topshop, but fiction should be couture, argues Hilary Mantel', the *Guardian*, 22.12.07. Copyright © Guardian News & Media Ltd 2007; Hermann Editeur for W.B. Yeats, 'Au Bas des Jardins de Saules' translated by Yves Bonnefoy in *Quarante-cinq poèmes* by W.B. Yeats, Gallimard (1993) p.35; Barbara Levy Literary Agency on behalf of the Estate of the author with Viking Penguin, a division of Penguin Group (USA) Inc for Siegfried Sassoon 'Concert Party' and 'On Passing the New Menin Gate' from *Collected Poems of Siegfried Sassoon*. Copyright © 1918, 1920 E P Dutton. Copyright © 1936, 1946, 1947, 1948 Siegfried Sassoon; University of Manchester for an extract from the English and American Studies website; National Association for the Teaching of English for extracts from John Hodgson et al (eds.) *text : message, The Future of A level English*, NATE (2004); News International Syndication Ltd for Mary Beard 'A don's life', *Times online*, 16.11.07; University of Oxford for an extract from the English Faculty website; Oxford University Press for an extract from *Shakespeare: Henry IV, Part 2*, edited by Rene Weis (1998); Peters Fraser & Dunlop on behalf of the Estate of the author for Edmund Blunden 'Concert Party: Busseboom' and 'To W.O. and his Kind' from *Overtones of War by Edmund Blunden*, Gerald Duckworth & Co Ltd (1996). Copyright © 1996 Edmund Blunden; Princeton University Press for George Seferis 'On Aspalathoi' in *George Seferis: Collected Poems* translated by Edmund Keeley, revised edition (1995). Copyright © 1967 Princeton University Press, renewed Copyright © 1995 Princeton University Press; Palgrave Macmillan for extracts from Malcolm Bradbury *E.M. Forster: A Passage to India* ed. Malcolm Bradbury, Macmillan Casebook (1970) p.23; and Jeremy Tambling, *E.M. Forster* ed. Jeremy Tambling, Macmillan Casebook (1995) pp.10–11; Qualifications and Curriculum Authority for extracts from *GCE AS and A level subject criteria for English Literature* (Sept 2006); and *AEA English Specification* (2002); Quality Assurance Agency for Higher Education for extracts from its *Subject Benchmark Statement for English* (2007); The Random House Group Ltd with Doubleday, a division of Random House, Inc and with Alfred A Knopf Canada for extracts from Ian McEwan *Atonement*, Jonathan Cape. Copyright © 2001, 2002 Ian McEwan; The Random House Group Ltd with Houghton Mifflin Harcourt Publishing Company for extracts from Virginia Woolf 'August 16, 1940' and 'October 2, 1940' in *The Diary of Virginia Woolf Volume V: 1936–1941*, The Hogarth Press. Copyright © 1984 Quentin Bell and Angelica Garnett; Rosica Colin Ltd on behalf of the Estate of the author for extracts from Richard Aldington 'In Memory of Wilfred Owen', 'Eumenides' and 'Epitaph in Ballade Form' in *The Complete Poems of Richard Aldington*, Allan Wingate (1948) pp. 302, 152–4, 161; Royal Holloway University of London for an extract from Rick Rylance 'But ... Why Study English?' *HEA: English Subject Centre* (2007) by permission of Rick Rylance; The Shakespeare Globe Trust for an extract from the Claire Daniel interview with Tony Howard on its website; Tate Publishing for extracts from *Stanley Spencer: Letters and Writings* edited by Adrian Glew, (2001) p.103; the *Times Literary Supplement* for an extract from Nora Mahoney 'Review of the Male Gaze by Joe Treasure', *TLS*; A.P. Watt Ltd on behalf of Gráinne Yeats for an extract from W.B. Yeats 'Down by the Salley Gardens' in *Selected Poems* by W.B. Yeats, ed. Norman Jeffares, Macmillan (1962) p.5; University of York for extracts from *Undergraduate Prospectus* (2007)

Thanks are also due to the following for permission to reproduce photographs and illustrations: photographs of Cambridge War Memorial and Trumpington War Memorial courtesy of Adrian Barlow; Swan Upping by Stanley Spencer © The Estate of Stanley Spencer 2008. All rights reserved DACs, 2008; © Tate, London 2008; 'The Sea Rises' by Hablot K. Browne (Phiz). Reproduced by courtesy of the Charles Dickens Museum, London

Printed in the United States
By Bookmasters